POETRY
An Introduction
& Anthology

POETRY
An Introduction
& Anthology

Edward Proffitt
Manhattan College

Houghton Mifflin Company   Boston

Dallas   Geneva, Illinois   Hopewell, New Jersey   Palo Alto   London

for Nan

"To me, so arch-especial a spirit . . ."

G. M. Hopkins

Printed in the U.S.A.

Library of Congress Catalog Card Number: 80-80842

ISBN: 0-395-29486–X

Text acknowledgments appear following the Glossary.

To the Teacher

Although adaptable to the teaching of poetics on any but the most advanced level, this book is, as its title states, an introduction to poetry. Therefore, its format is standard: a progression of chapters treating the essential elements of poetry in ascending order of difficulty.

The salient features of the book, however, are unique. For instance, the typical initial reaction of beginning students to the study of poetry is assessed realistically in Chapter 1 and tackled head on. And at no point do I forget the resistance to poetry (even among English majors) that every teacher of the subject faces. Thus, although the text necessarily analyzes the formal attributes of poetry, its focus throughout is on function. Nor do I assume an audience that brings to the subject much by way of conceptual background. Accordingly, the emphasis of the book is on conceptual development and reinforcement. The exercises and poem assignments that thread through the text are intended to promote these ends, as well as to demystify poetry and return it to the sphere of human discourse. Equally important, the exercises—and especially the poem assignments—encourage activity on the part of the student and thereby foster personal engagement.

Keats tells us that "nothing ever becomes real till it is experienced." The poem assignments lead toward the realization that experience brings. More generally, the view of the reading process that characterizes *Poetry: An Introduction*—a view neither subjectivist (anything goes) nor objectivist (the poem itself)—intends to compel the student's engaged response. This view—that reading is a dynamic activity, an experience that takes shape in the *dialectic* of reader and text—is stressed and demonstrated by the readings offered of various poems. It is a view, of course, that necessitates a certain degree of nondirectiveness. As much as possible, therefore, I leave open matters of general interpretation. The questions asked about the study poems at the end of each chapter, for example, are usually restricted to the topics covered in the given chapter. The Anthology, which is extensive and wide-ranging, is deliberately eclectic and free of questions and comments. Indeed, one of my goals overall has been to combine the advantages afforded by a textbook and those of a straight anthology.

Another of my goals has been to convey the significance of poetry to the living of a life. Our mutual endeavor is to teach the language—its mechanics and rich heritage—and also to communicate to our students that the discipline we profess bears a meaningful relationship to the lives that both we and they lead. For if that relationship is not conveyed, we can hardly teach the language with effect. This text is aimed at meeting both tasks: such is the rationale for its specific features and its existence alike.

Acknowledgments

This book is the product of half a lifetime of absorption. To list all the people to whom I am indebted, therefore, would be impossible. But a few to whom I immediately owe thanks: Marilyn Gigliuto, unfailing scribe; Arnold Penenberg, consultant on all matters of the mind and heart; my wife Nancy, most lovingly demanding of critics; and John Fandel, poet and friend.

I am grateful to the following individuals for reading the manuscript at various stages in its development and for their helpful suggestions: Chuck Whitchurch, Golden West College; Victoria Jacoby, Southern Methodist University; John Gill, College of San Mateo; O. Howard Winn, Dutchess County Community College; Jane Mooney, Tallahassee Community College; George R. Levine, State University of New York at Buffalo; and M. Beverly Swan, University of Rhode Island.

Most of all, I am in the debt of a generation of students who have instructed me all along the way. I look forward to another such generation, now with book in hand.

E.P.

To the Student

Any teacher of English who has taught for very long is aware that the majority of beginning students come to "Poetry" with some degree of fear, if not outright dread, in their hearts.

I begin on this negative note in order to suggest what is different about this book: my approach to poetry springs from my recognition that most beginning students know little about the subject and wonder, at the start, why they should study it at all. Does it matter? Yes, it matters a great deal. But I don't expect you to take that on faith. I expect only that you will be open to reason. This book will describe *what* happens in poems and will give reasons for *why* it happens. My object is to make poetry make sense to readers not used to reading it. To do so, I will focus on basic concepts and principles, always with the "Why" uppermost in mind.

Learning is by nature an active process—we learn primarily from doing. This is why I'll be asking you to write poems yourself as we proceed. My approach is based on the work of Kenneth Koch, a teacher and poet whose books—especially *Wishes, Lies, and Dreams,* but also *Rose, Where Did You Get that Red?* and *I Never Told Anybody*—demonstrate that we all have a wealth of poetry in us. I believe that if you do the poem assignments in this text, you will experience some of the pleasures of poetry. And if you put yourself into these assignments, you might also find in poetry a way to self-exploration and understanding. Many of my own students, some of whose poems appear in this book, discovered this to be true.

It is my hope that this book will reach you on a personal level and will show you that poetry is a form of knowledge. It seems to me that if you are given good reasons for the whys of poetry, you can allow yourself to begin to understand and even to like it.

Contents

Chapter Five
Rhythm & Meter 102

Chapter Six
Rhythm & Other Constituents of Voice 132

Chapter Seven
Rhyme Schemes & Formal Designs 166

Chapter Eight
Approaching Definition 202

Anthology 217

Contents

Contents

Contents

Contents

Introduction
Chapter One

THE TROUBLE WITH POETRY

Poetry gives us trouble. That's why, no doubt, relatively few of us read it of our own accord and for our own pleasure. At the very outset of our study, I would like you to answer honestly two questions:

1. What is your response to poetry?
2. What do you think poetry is?

Many of you probably answer these questions as most of my students always do:

1. I do not like poetry.
2. Poetry as I see it is a very difficult, complicated way of communicating.

1. I don't like poetry. I never took a course in it, but I know that it's hard.
2. Something that has an abstract meaning and is in meter.

1. Well, I really don't care for it too much. I think it's hard to interpret. I'm just taking the course because it's a requirement.
2. It is writing that for some reason always rhymes.

1. I have never really liked poetry.
2. I believe that poetry is a way to express ideas in a flowery way.

1. I have no opinion about poetry because I have never read any.
2. Therefore, I don't have any definition of it either.

The last answer is refreshingly unbiased. Few of us, however, are so open in the face of the unknown. What we don't know somehow threatens us and we don't like it. Yet poetry has never harmed anyone—at any rate, not its readers. In fact, it has often done a great deal of good. For instance, William Wordsworth's poetry helped the nineteenth-century social philosopher John Stuart Mill to recover from a mental breakdown. In the fifth chapter of his *Autobiography,* Mill states what he learned from Wordsworth: that the emotions need to be cultivated as much as the intellect, and that poetry can be a healing bridge between the two. But to come to feel its healing power, we need to rid our minds of prejudices and preconceptions. So consider your attitudes about poetry. Question them each in turn. Is your immediate response negative? If so, perhaps one reason is that your conception of poetry is faulty.

Certainly, the attempted definitions listed above are flawed. Poems do not have to have a rhyme scheme or a meter. And successful poems are as concrete (sensuous) as language can be and the very opposite of "flowery." Misconceptions aside, however, a more pervasive problem still remains. I understand the responses of my students because I, too, disliked poetry when I was young; I, too, thought it difficult. Now I see that the problem lay in me—in my difficulty not with words or ideas but more with feeling. If poetry is difficult, it is because it asks us to turn in and to examine what we feel as we progress through life toward death. It is the feeling that gives us trouble.

Consider a poem by William Blake:

Infant Sorrow

My mother groand! my father wept.
Into the dangerous world I leapt:
Helpless, naked, piping loud;
Like a fiend hid in a cloud.

Struggling in my father's hands,   5
Striving against my swadling bands,
Bound and weary I thought best
To sulk upon my mother's breast.

(1794)[1]

What's hard here? The words? No. The ideas? No. The feeling? Yes. With his images and rhythms, Blake asks us to experience in the imagination the moment of birth and all its attendant anxieties, the moment when each of us took that leap "Into the dangerous world" to discover our dependency and to begin the long struggle toward independence. But we resist delving into these primitive areas of feeling. Therein lies our difficulty.

Our trouble with poetry stems primarily from our problems with feeling and secondarily from our lack of training in a language based in feeling (both physical and emotional). Three cultural factors may cause our trouble.

1. First, we in the West are trained to look out rather than in, to deal with things more than ourselves, to deal with fact more than with feeling. Charles Dickens isolated this training as a central cause of adult grief. At the beginning of his novel *Hard Times,* a businessman named Gradgrind says to a teacher named M'Choakumchild:

> Now, what I want is Facts. Teach those boys and girls nothing but Facts. Facts alone are wanted in life. Plant nothing else, and root out everything else. You can only form the minds of reasoning animals upon Facts: nothing else will ever be of any service to them. This is the principle on which I bring up my own children, and this is the principle on which I bring up these children. Stick to the Facts, sir!

As the novel progresses, we witness the results of this emphasis on bare facts: both of Gradgrind's own children end in emotional ruin.

[1] I have dated most previously published poems by date of publication. In a few cases, however, the dates of composition and publication are so removed from each other that the latter gives no sense of the historical moment of the poem in question. In these cases I have indicated the approximate date of composition with the abbreviation "c.," for "circa."

To be sure, we need to be trained in fact; fact without feeling, however, is only a husk. Feelings also need to be cultivated. And when they are not, we are left bewildered. To the extent that we're trained more in things external than internal, we are trained neither in the ways to identity nor in the ways of poetry, which always asks us to take a hard look in.

2. A second reason for our uneasiness with poetry is that as we grow in our world, our minds get filled with superficialities: getting a car, getting a degree, getting a job, getting a promotion. Getting, getting, getting. We lose sight of the fundamental matters of existence—birth, growth, death. The getting obscures the being. Becoming ever more preoccupied with the surface of living, we lose contact with the wonder of life. Wordsworth said as much in 1807, at the inception of the industrial world:

> The world is too much with us; late and soon,
> Getting and spending, we lay waste our powers;
> Little we see in Nature that is ours;
> We have given our hearts away, a sordid boon!
> This Sea that bares her bosom to the moon,   5
> The winds that will be howling at all hours,
> And are up-gathered now like sleeping flowers,
> For this, for everything, we are out of tune;
> It moves us not.

"We are out of tune" with the great forces of life in ourselves as well as in nature; and so poetry becomes alien ground.

3. Finally, by being trained to look out rather than in, which perhaps causes our preoccupation with the surfaces of living, we are brought up to be passive observers—watchers instead of doers. But poetry demands activity. As Robert Penn Warren puts it, "the basic fact about poetry is that it demands participation, from the secret physical echo in muscle and nerve that identifies us with the medium, to the imaginative enactment that stirs the deepest recesses where life-will and values reside." [2] To come to enjoy poetry, we must learn to read actively, which means that we must open ourselves to feeling and learn its language.

THE LANGUAGE OF FEELING

Dreams and the Structure of the Brain

Dreams can help us. For we already know a good deal about the language of feeling from our dreams. What the function of sleep is is still some-

[2] Robert Penn Warren, *Democracy and Poetry* (Cambridge, Mass.: Harvard University Press, 1975), p. 89.

thing of a mystery. All we know definitely is that we do not sleep simply to restore cells. Could it be that we sleep to dream? Whatever the reason, during sleep the logic that guides our waking lives dissolves, and we drift into a realm wholly internal. Operating under laws of their own, dreams embody our deepest feelings in a language of their own.

Probably because of its structure, the brain seems to have two languages: the verbal language of consciousness and the essentially nonverbal language of dreams. In fact, recent work in brain physiology has demonstrated that the two hemispheres of the brain—left and right—are each distinct in function. In right-handed people, the left hemisphere controls all verbal processes and the right hemisphere governs the perception of such phenomena as music and spatial depth. (The opposite is true of left-handed people.) [3] During waking life, the two hemispheres operate more or less in accord, although, since our awareness is tied to our ability to verbalize, we are mainly conscious of the operations of the left hemisphere. In sleep, the right hemisphere speaks as it knows how: in colors, images, and rhythms significant to the dreamer. When we ponder about a dream's significance, we are translating one language into another, a language of dense particulars into one of verbal abstractions. We never quite succeed, of course; the coloration and radiance of dreams always seem to elude rational discourse.

To explore this language of dense particulars, let's look at two dreams written down by students in answer to the following assignment:

> Write down a dream that you had recently, a dream that seems significant to you. Don't interpret; just present the details as vividly as possible so as to capture the mood and flow of the dream. Write as though you are having the dream rather than talking about it. In this regard, you would probably do best to use the present tense and first-person point of view.

NO, I WON'T

William Vahey

It is very late at night. The darkness is all around. I can hear the dogs scampering and growling around me. I dare not move. They want to make me one of them. Yet I won't be one of them, those hungry dogs who have no feelings. They'd consume anything without a thought. The trees hover above, keeping out the moonlight, making what's below as black as the dogs' eyes. Hiding in the bush,

[3] See Julian Jaynes, *The Origin of Consciousness in the Breakdown of the Bicameral Mind* (Boston: Houghton Mifflin, 1977). Chapter 5, entitled "The Double Brain" (pp. 100–125), is especially relevant here. But all that Jaynes says in this fascinating book bears on my argument.

I can see them, yet I am hidden. Thinking to myself, I say that I had better get out of here. As soon as there's a chance, I'll make a run for it. They can't be heard now, but they are there—they are always there. I make my dash, not turning back. I don't hear them. "Where are the dogs?" I wonder. "Have I really escaped them? Am I free?"

THE ABYSS

Stephen Maher

I hear the sound of water lapping against pilings. I must be on a wharf somewhere. It is very dark, and the air is sticky and oppressive. There is no sound except for the sea.

As I stand on this structure, I keep asking myself why it is so dark, so quiet. I stumble forward with uncertainty in an effort to feel out this place. I have no sense of direction. After a few minutes of probing, I can gather no inkling of this platform's boundaries. It seems devoid of edges.

Suddenly, the surface under me gives way. I stretch out my arms in desperation, but it's no use. My fall is rapid and terrifying. I scream out in protest, but my cries are swallowed up by the darkness.

As my descent continues, I realize that I am approaching the point where I will no longer hear the sound of the sea.

These are not dreams, but verbal recollections. Nevertheless, both provide access into the way dreams speak. Like dreams, both descriptions mean whatever they mean through their concretions (words that spark mental sensations)—dogs yelping and threatening, water lapping and engulfing. Like dreams, too, both seem to call for interpretation. Each gives expression to some underlying fear, but fear of what? Think first of "No, I Won't," with its darkness and omnipresent dogs. However much we may love man's best friend, we often associate dogs with negative feelings ("dog days," "in the dog house," "you dirty dog," "a dog's life," "S.O.B.," "I wouldn't feed that to a dog," "sick as a dog"). A dream in which a pack of hungry dogs tries to make the fleeing dreamer one of them seems to express a fear of one's own primitive impulses. In "The Abyss," we are confronted with water and falling. Water is often a symbol of life and sexuality; and falling commonly signifies loss of control. We speak of "the waters of life" and of "falling asleep" and "falling in love." We might interpret "The Abyss," then, as expressing a human ambivalence: we desire sexual attachment, yet fear the loss of autonomy that such attachment entails.

But interpretation alone will never take us to full understanding. We interpret to clarify to our conscious selves; interpretation is only rationalization, however, if unaccompanied by feeling. We must not forget that dreams speak in a language of their own—a language of sensations that must be felt to be truly understood.

Dreams and Poetry

Like dreams, poems present us with dense particulars—scenes, rhythms, shapes, images—that call for interpretation. Like dreams, too, successful poems touch what is of fundamental importance to us. They give expression to the deepest reaches of self, its profound concerns and responses, and ask us to feel.

My three-year-old daughter said with great seriousness: "Some days tigers bite. Some days, they don't." What did she mean? I interpreted her to mean that reality can be terribly threatening, though we can't always know for certain when it will be so. But the point is that hers is the poet's way of speaking. She knows nothing of the abstraction *reality*. Tigers, however, she does know about, and they're as vivid in her imagination as the most vivid image in a dream. So she speaks in tigers and thereby gives shape to the depth of her feeling.

The poet speaks in much the same way. For example, take one version of a poem we all know:

> Ring around the rosie
> Pockets full of posies;
> Ashes, ashes,
> We all fall down.

Much is being said in the dreamlike language of this poem. It begins with a child's game, which involves a springtime dance. We might imagine a group of young people dancing round a rosebush in bloom, with spring flowers (*posies* are flowers) dangling from their pockets. That's a splendidly evocative image, full of vitality and budding sexuality. Then the converse: "Ashes, ashes, / We all fall down." Imagine the dancers literally falling down, imitating the final fall of death. (In "Ashes, ashes" I hear "ashes to ashes.") The poem, then, ranges from youth to age, and speaks of generation and growth balanced by a poignant awareness of death. With its sharp, dreamlike juxtapositions ("posies" and "ashes") as well as its rhythmic contrasts (notice the shortening of the second two lines), it gives vivid expression to our uniquely human awareness of the paradox of life—growth that always leads to death. But it does not speak through statement. Its language is one of sensuous particulars, which is the language of feeling. It asks us to think as we do in dreams: in unexplained concrete images of a dance and of flowers, of ashes and of falling down.

Poems, of course, are not dreams. Though poets have sometimes been called dreamers and often call themselves singers, when they write they are usually awake and aware of what they're doing. And what they write is, after all, made out of words, not musical tones or dream pictures. Nor are poems private in the way that dreams are. We can interpret dreams because they are composed of symbols that have generalized cultural characteristics; nevertheless, dreaming itself is a private act, whereas writing a poem is communal insofar as the poet expects others to read it. Still, there is an analogy. Like dreams, poems engage us as sensory creatures; like dreams, poems ask us to give free play to the deeper mind; and like dreams, poems can be a bridge to our buried selves.

It is such a bridge, I think, that William Carlos Williams had in mind when he wrote of poetry: "men die miserably every day / from lack / of what is found there." We "die miserably" from losing touch, one part of the self with another. Poetry can help us toward what William Butler Yeats called "unity of being." Poems are not dreams, but, because they tap the same sources of psychic energy, they can move us toward a greater realization of ourselves and so toward wholeness.

APPROACHING POETRY

To be so moved, we must be willing to engage ourselves actively and to develop new habits of mind. Three habits in particular are necessary to active engagement: starting with particulars, bringing experience to bear, and staying with the poem.

Starting with Particulars
Many beginning students, overtrained in problem solving, approach poems looking for a "key," a "message," a "hidden meaning," something said "between the lines"—for some *solution* to what a poem means, as though it were in code. This approach only substitutes thought for feeling. Poems don't have keys. They are not riddles to be solved, but experiences to be lived through line by line. Living through also means living with. That is, really to experience a poem one must stay with it and test one's feelings line by line. Many readers, however, let things go with "Well, that's what it means to me." To rest with this type of response is to avoid engagement and merely to project a passing mood onto the text at hand.

Where, then, does the poem exist—in the reader or on the page? Certainly, it doesn't exist only on the page; all that literally exists there is printer's ink. Yet it doesn't exist solely in the reader either, for the written text is clearly external to the reader. The poem exists in neither and in both. It exists in the two-way commerce between the page and the reader.

To read a poem as a problem to be solved is to avoid what poetry would touch—the "I" of the reader. To settle for "that's what it means to me" is to avoid the probing into this "I" that poetry would initiate. Holding that poetry is "concerned with two questions about which [we] all . . . seek clarification," W. H. Auden clarifies what poetry would have us ask:

1. *Who am I?* What is the difference between man and all other creatures? What relations are possible between them? What is man's status in the universe? What are the conditions of his existence which he must accept as his fate which no wishing can alter?

2. *Whom ought I to become?* What are the characteristics of the hero, the authentic man whom everybody should admire and try to become? Vice versa, what are the characteristics of the churl, the unauthentic man whom everybody should try to avoid becoming? [4]

To engage ourselves through our reading of poetry in this double task of understanding and growing, we must cultivate the habit of responding to poems in their specificity. Like dreams, poems speak primarily by what they are. To work into them, we need to start with what they are: with their images and sounds and shapes. Begin to read poetry by sensing in your imagination and by letting sensation give rise to emotion.

Consider "Ring Around the Rosie" again. In interpreting it, we began with particulars. We envisioned a group of young people dancing in spring and then falling down; felt out the implications of "Ashes, ashes"; and responded to certain of its formal qualities, such as its sharp juxtapositions of images and rhythms. In reading it this way, we came to feel joy and sorrow, and to see that the poem presents human life in miniature. This little poem, or the way in which it speaks, is a model of the way all poems speak. The way we approached it is a model of the way poems should be approached.

Bringing Experience to Bear

Poetry is experience in that it both stimulates and evokes sensation. For a poem to work, however, we must respond to its sensory qualities (its rhythms and its sounds) and bring to it our experience of the world. When John Keats speaks of bursting "Joy's grape," for example, he means to evoke the taste of a grape—neither sweet nor bitter, but an inextricable mixture of the two. To grasp the meaning of his image, we must remember that taste. Poems ask us to bring to them our understanding, gained through experience, of people and things. If poems mystify, they do so because we expect them to be high flown and difficult and so fail to relate them to our experience.

[4] W. H. Auden, *The Dyer's Hand* (New York: Random House, 1962), pp. 344–345.

In approaching poetry, bring your senses into play and bring your experience to bear. Is "Ring Around the Rosie" difficult? Surely not, if we let its images and rhythms work on us; if we remember what spring feels like, and dancing, and falling down; and if we allow ourselves to feel our deeper concerns. The poem puts us in contact with those concerns through its images, rhythms, and the shared experience it draws on. That experience is central. If we tap it, then the poem opens up; then it is ours at first hand.

Staying with the Poem

By now, I have said a good deal about this "nursery" rhyme, and I hear objections. How do I know what the poem means or what the anonymous author(s) meant? Am I not "reading in" a meaning and being purely subjective? These are important questions. As to intention, we can never really know a poet's intentions. All we have to go on is the text before us. So we deal with the text and with *its* intention, or the implied intention that we come to understand by working through a text.

This does not mean that anything said about a text is merely subjective or that every reading is equally valid. For an interpretation to be credible, it must be consistent and it must be borne out by the text. Meaning is limited by context. Granted, most poems allow for more than one interpretation. Indeed, it is because they do that one can come to perceive oneself: I see *my* relationship to a text (and myself in that relationship) by seeing that other relationships are possible. Still, all readings are not equally apt. The number of legitimate interpretations (interpretations verified by the text) is finite.

Dreams, once more, offer a good analogy. What does a dream mean? To answer this, we have to take into account every detail of the dream; test our reading of it against what we know about the unconscious and its use of symbols; consider the historical circumstance of the dreamer; and weigh the dreamer's biographical background. We interpret a literary text in pretty much the same way. Because a text is under the conscious control of its author, however, these elements are not always of equal importance. For example, biographical background is not always relevant to a given text, and often we don't even know that background. When we do know it, though, and when it seems relevant, we bring it to bear in testing our response. As to historical matters, if we read a poem by Shakespeare, for instance, and know that a specific word or phrase meant something quite different in the Renaissance from what it means today, we apply our knowledge and read the poem accordingly. But access into a poem is gained primarily through an active consideration of its details in light of a knowledge of how poems work. To move toward such an understanding is the purpose of our study.

POEMS TO LIVE THROUGH

Put out of your mind any previous thoughts you have had about poetry. Start to feel, both emotionally and physically (through your imagination hear, see, taste, smell, touch, and let sensation give rise to emotion). By living through a few poems with our senses in play, we will see the questions that poems ask us to ask.

[It Was Not Death]

Emily Dickinson

It was not Death, for I stood up,
And all the Dead, lie down–
It was not Night, for all the Bells
Put out their Tongues, for Noon.

It was not Frost, for on my Flesh   5
I felt Siroccos–crawl–
Nor Fire–for just my Marble feet
Could keep a Chancel, cool–

And yet, it tasted, like them all,
The Figures I have seen   10
Set orderly, for Burial,
Reminded me, of mine–

As if my life were shaven,
And fitted to a frame,
And could not breathe without a key,   15
And 'twas like Midnight, some–

When everything that ticked–has stopped–
And Space stares all around–
Or Grisly frosts–first Autumn morns,
Repeal the Beating Ground–   20

But, most, like Chaos–Stopless–cool–
Without a Chance, or Spar–
Or even a Report of Land–
To justify–Despair.

(c. 1862)

With the power and immediacy of a nightmare, this poem gives voice to desperation. The speaker remembers being whirled into a moment of emotional chaos by "It" (some unnameable experience), so thoroughly identified with the feeling it elicited as to be transformed into that feeling immediately. Because feelings are never quite nameable, however, the speaker speaks in metaphors of what "It" (the feeling) was like. As usual in human experience, causes for feelings fade from memory, whereas the feelings remain, at least such a feeling as this—a flood of pure "Despair," and upswelling of irrational terror (cf. "[There's a Certain Slant of Light]," page 233). The speaker doesn't think about the feeling and say, "I felt in a state of emotional collapse because . . .". Rather, the feeling is rendered in all its palpable horror. An experience itself, the poem does not intervene with comment or explanation. We feel the depth of despair directly.

Now live through it yourself. Read the poem aloud. How does your voice move—in long, easy breaths or haltingly, gaspingly? How does the figure of bells sticking out their tongues strike you? Can you not feel frost and fire on your flesh, the hot desert winds ("Siroccos") simultaneously with the cold marble of the inner sanctuary ("Chancel") of a church? Taste the taste of gall; then imagine yourself locked in a coffin (lines 13–14) and waking to "some" midnight, your sense of time lost in the heavy blackness of space. Everything around has death written on it, and you, overwhelmed by vertigo, seem to be adrift in Chaos, falling helplessly. It is the end of human order, the end of land. Now we understand the poem, for now we know it at our nerve ends—its sense of entrapment, suffocation, isolation. We all have such moments, to which Dickinson gives shape and, by giving shape, expression.

The Jewel Stairs' Grievance

[Translated from the Chinese by]
Ezra Pound

> The jewelled steps are already quite white with dew,
> It is so late that the dew soaks my gauze stockings,
> And I let down the crystal curtain
> And watch the moon through clear autumn.

(1915)

After his translation, Pound appended the following note:

> Jewel stairs, therefore a palace. Grievance, therefore there is something to complain of. Gauze stockings, therefore a court lady, not a servant who complains. [Here's another example of bringing histori-

cal background to bear.] Clear autumn, therefore he has no excuse on account of the weather.... The poem is especially prized [by readers of Chinese] because she utters no direct reproach.

We must bring our senses into play as we read a poem; we must also reason from the text (as Pound does) and remember our experience of life generally. The speaker of this miniature is a female (implied by "gauze stockings"), who has been waiting, surely, for her lover, who has stood her up. The full pathos of this almost painted scene is given expression at the end of the poem. In the very quietness of its last line—typical of Chinese restraint—is to be felt the intensity of the hurt, so intense that it numbs. Emily Dickinson knew this hurt: "After great pain, a formal feeling comes," she wrote, and called it "the Hour of Lead." We find the speaker of "The Jewel Stairs'" at that hour. She can do no more than gaze at the moon, which lends an autumnal, regretful feeling to the scene.

The poem communicates what it does without statement. We are not told what the speaker is feeling or what to feel; we feel it directly to the extent that we can participate in the poem's design. Does this mean that we are "reading in"? No. We are responding in an active manner, responding by remembering what we know about the areas of human life relevant to the poem. We should respond also to the poem's formal qualities. Observe, for example, the long lines in which Pound cast his translation, lines marked by many pauses but also by a certain evenness of flow. Compare the movement here with the quite different movement of "[It Was Not Death]." The Pound translation has the sound of simple sadness, and the immediate sensory effect of that sound helps to shape the feeling and to impart it. Observe as well, especially at the end, the long low vowels ($\overline{oo}$, *aw*), the nasals (*m*, *n*), and the way the poem trails off with its last unaccented nasal syllable (au-tummmmm). The long vowels slow us up and carry a sense of moaning; the nasals are soft and help capture a sense of subdued feeling, or of feeling subdued. It is the poet's job to forge language into a vehicle of expression, which means to use words in all their attributes—not only their dictionary meanings but also their sounds, the way they move, their colorations. So Pound does here.

Marin-An

Gary Snyder

sun breaks over the eucalyptus
grove below the wet pasture,
water's about hot,
I sit in the open window
& roll a smoke.

5

distant dogs bark, a pair of
cawing crows; the twang
of a pygmy nuthatch high in a pine—
from behind the cypress windrow
the mare moves up, grazing.   10

a soft continuous roar
comes out of the far valley
of the six-lane highway—thousands
and thousands of cars
driving men to work.   15

(1968)

One critic has described Wordsworth's poetry as evolving from "the accretion in his mind of specific and concrete observations coalescing almost of themselves to establish a general significance." [5] This description seems equally applicable to Snyder's poem, which asks us to start with its specific and concrete observations. To focus in on its concretions and their significance, consider the following questions:

1. In what state of the United States is the speaker? (Where are "eucalyptus/grove[s]" juxtaposed with "six-lane highway[s]"?)
2. Pinpointed also by the title, this state seems particularly relevant to the poem, given the implied social comment on contemporary American life at the end. How so? (With its massive automobile population, this state was once called by one of its better-known politicians "the harbinger of the future of the U.S.A.")
3. What is the significance of the reversal at the end of the poem ("cars/ driving men to work" rather than "men driving cars")? What contrast is implied between these "men" and the speaker of the poem?
4. What other contrasts are established in the poem? What do these contrasts say about the feeling of the speaker toward this age of transience and perpetual motion?

The Emperor of Ice-Cream

Wallace Stevens

Call the roller of big cigars,
The muscular one, and bid him whip
In kitchen cups concupiscent° curds.   *ardently desired*

---

[5] Karl Kroeber, *The Artifice of Reality* (Madison, Wisc.: University of Wisconsin Press, 1964), p. 35.

Let the wenches dawdle in such dress
As they are used to wear, and let the boys   5
Bring flowers in last month's newspapers.
Let be be finale of seem.
The only emperor is the emperor of ice-cream.

Take from the dresser of deal,
Lacking the three glass knobs, that sheet   10
On which she embroidered fantails once
And spread it so as to cover her face.
If her horny feet protrude, they come
To show how cold she is, and dumb.
Let the lamp affix its beam.   15
The only emperor is the emperor of ice-cream.

(1923)

The poems we've looked at so far concern states of being, though "Marin-An" has social implications as well. Stevens's poem also touches a state of being or awareness—a state involving an emotional affirmation of life leading ever to death—but "the Emperor of Ice-Cream" is more philosophical than "[It Was Not Death]" or "The Jewel Stairs' Grievance." Still, it is a poem and not a philosophical treatise. However philosophical, it speaks through particulars rather than logical proposition and analysis. In a dreamlike language of things rather than the abstract language of philosophical discourse (which Stevens is perhaps poking fun at), the first stanza speaks of ordinary life, the second of ordinary death. With its many intimations of pleasure even in the face of death, the poem moves us to accept life and thus death.

1. What intimations of pleasure are there in the first stanza? Are there any in the second stanza? What of the opening image of the big muscular roller whipping "curds" in "kitchen cups"? What of the sound of "concupiscent curds"?
2. Life means sexuality, perhaps our greatest pleasure. What in the poem intimates sexual pleasure specifically?
3. Yet life is always circumscribed by limitations, the final one being death. What in the poem suggests limitation? (Consider the "newspapers" and the condition of the "dresser of deal." *Deal* is cheap pine, so the locale of stanza two is just as ordinary as that of stanza one.)
4. Finally, why ice cream, festive but frozen? How do ice cream and its emperor (who takes the place here of any traditional god) sensuously sum up the attitude toward life that underlies the poem?

Reuben Bright

E. A. Robinson

Because he was a butcher and thereby
Did earn an honest living (and did right),
I would not have you think that Reuben Bright
Was any more a brute than you or I;
For when they told him that his wife must die,   5
He stared at them, and shook with grief and fright,
And cried like a great baby half that night,
And made the women cry to see him cry.

And after she was dead, and he had paid
The singers and the sexton and the rest,   10
He packed a lot of things that she had made
Most mournfully away in an old chest
Of hers, and put some chopped-up cedar boughs
In with them, and tore down the slaughter-house.

(1897)

Communicating a depth of human tenderness, perplexity, and suffering, this is a sad poem. Yet it can give much pleasure. There's a paradox here: however sad its subject, the poem heightens our sense of existence in moving us to feel intensely. But to feel the poem fully, we must see it for what it is.

1. Occasionally, a student says that "Reuben has murdered his wife." What in the poem goes against such a conclusion?
2. How, possibly, has the wife died? How do people normally die?
3. We're not told exactly how, nor do we need to know. Our focus is on Reuben and the transformation of this large, strong man into a "great baby." What emotional weight does the word *baby* carry?
4. A student once wrote: "Reuben takes down the slaughter-house to prevent other wrong doing." What in the poem invalidates this interpretation?
5. Reuben did not "take down" but "tore down" the slaughter-house. What's the difference? What does the word *tore* (as opposed to *take* or *dismantle*) communicate. What does the act signify?
6. The poem is a **Petrarchan sonnet,** a form marked by a division between the first eight lines and the last six. How does Robinson make use of this division?
7. The movement of the poem is particularly meaningful. Observe that

many lines, especially toward the end of the poem, do not come to a pause, but slop over rather awkwardly to the next line. What feeling does this movement impart?

8. The last six lines end with a contrast full of pathos. What is the contrast?

POEMS FOR FURTHER STUDY

from **Out of Our Blue**

John Fandel

The medium white onion
in the wooden bowl
(shaped by a craftsman)
on the kitchen counter
has sprouted three slender shoots   5
primevally green as April.

What do you think you're doing,
I say to it,
making an oasis
while waiting to be pared.   10

And I say to my soul,
Observe it, look at it.

I say,
Observe.

(1977)

Questions

1. What feelings does April usually arouse in people? To what end does the poet evoke these feelings?
2. What implications does the word *oasis* carry?
3. The onion is like the craftsman. How so?
4. As the poem moves from description to observation about observing, its lines are pared down. Why?
5. What would the speaker learn from his onion about life as it faces death?

Fowles in the Frith

Anonymous

Fowles° in the frith,°	*birds / woods*
The fisshes in the flood,	
And I mon waxe wood;°	*I must go mad*
Much sowre° I walke with	*sorrow*
For beste° of boon° and blood.	*best / bone*
	(13th cen.)

FOWLES IN THE FRITH. Though we can never know the intentions of an author directly, we sometimes know for sure what was *not* intended. For example, the language of "Fowles in the Frith" was not intended to be quaint. Its language is the language of the day.

Questions
1. To what or whom does "beste of boon and blood" refer?
2. The poem turns on a contrast that gives expression to something central to human awareness. What is this contrast? Of what is the speaker aware?
3. What is it, then, that fills him with sorrow?
4. The last three lines seem rather abstract compared to the first two, which are entirely concrete. How does this difference help dramatize the contrast referred to in question 2?

Melody

Edward Proffitt

Pods split their seams
for laughter
rollicking warmly
with the wind

this seedy   5
September morning

but spruced up
like an Old Indian
waiting for Pilgrims
with his corn   10

    smelling of corn
    and of laughter:

    it is a moment
    now to h-u-m
    a mellow moment   15
    ripe with song

    a little hymn
    a tiny season.

(1976)

Questions

1. In "The Jewel Stairs' Grievance," the reference to autumn evokes a sense of sadness. How is autumn used in this poem? What particular aspects and qualities of the season does this poem stress?
2. At the center of this poem (literally) is an image. What is this image? What associations does it carry?
3. How does "Melody" differ from "The Jewel Stairs' " in its line length, line division, and general movement?
4. What vowel sounds does the poet use and to what effect?
5. Like "The Jewel Stairs'," "Melody" contains many nasal sounds. But their effect is quite different. What is their effect?

A Slumber Did My Spirit Seal

William Wordsworth

A slumber did my spirit seal;
    I had no human fears:
She seemed a thing that could not feel
    The touch of earthly years.

No motion has she now, no force;   5
    She neither hears nor sees;
Rolled round in earth's diurnal course,
    With rocks, and stones, and trees.

(1800)

Questions

1. Taking "she" as a dead female (no hidden meanings here), pay careful attention to the difference in tense between the two stanzas and the period of time to which each stanza refers. Both stanzas are spoken

after the death. But with what period of time is the first stanza concerned?

2. What are "human fears"?
3. Intellectually, the speaker knew that "she" would eventually die. In what sense, then, did he not know? (Does intellectual awareness always coincide with emotional?)
4. What effect does the pile of negatives in the second stanza and its many long "o" sounds have?
5. What effect does the word *diurnal* have?
6. In the closing line, Wordsworth arouses certain feelings in the reader with the compound image of "rocks, and stones, and trees." What associations does this type of landscape carry for you?

Abstraction, Concretion, Imagery
Chapter Two

THE RULES OF THE GAME

Think of football for a moment. Do you feel that knowing something about the game takes away from the pleasure of watching it? I doubt that you do. Knowledge of the possible plays and the ground rules is necessary to see what's going on. In contrast with the uninformed spectator, who sees nothing more than a bunch of men piling on top of each other, the informed spectator sees a trap play up the middle. The former is bewildered; the latter, delighted.

Yet it is not unusual for students to complain that to study poetry is to "rip poems apart," as though knowledge and pleasure were mutually exclusive. But what is true of football is just as true of poetry: it asks us to know certain things (about language and about poetics) and to bring that knowledge to bear.

In this book, you'll be studying the rules of the game through poems by recognized poets as well as through poems written by former students of mine and by you. The object of my asking you to write poems is not to turn you into a poet—when one plays touch football, one isn't aiming to play in the Super Bowl—but to help you relate to the poems you will be reading and to see that your own experience has as much potential for poetry as anyone's. By trying your hand at writing poems, you will extend your knowledge of and, consequently, your pleasure in poetry.

WORDS AND THINGS

We need to understand first the relationship between words and things. No words, obviously, are things as things are things; but some words, both in reference and in effect, are closer to things than others. Words can be divided into two broad categories: **abstractions** (from the Latin meaning "removed") and **concretions** (from the Latin meaning "solid"). Any word that denotes some general quality or concept or feeling without stimulating in the mind a particular sensation is an abstraction: *democracy, economics, love, refraction, being.* Such words remove us from sensed experience into the realm of idea. In contrast, a concretion is a word that denotes an object, an action, or a quality perceptible to the senses and that to some extent stimulates in the mind the sensation(s) associated with whatever it is the word denotes: *stretch, tangy, blast, red apple.* Concretions, thus, have a kind of sensuous solidity that abstractions do not have. Abstractions are abstract; concretions, concrete.

Exercise

Make a list of five abstract words and five concrete words. Though adjectives, adverbs, and verbs all fall into one or the other category, restrict yourself to nouns for this exercise. What is the difference in effect between your two lists?

Here is one such list:

Verbal Abstractions	Verbal Concretions
detail	sky
communication	sun
endeavor	banana
philosophy	grass
time	snake

The words in the first list do not call up sensations; those in the second do. There is the difference.

Verbal concretions are not necessarily preferable to abstractions, nor do poets never use abstractions. But the language of poetry does tend to be concrete. Whatever the verbal abstractions allowed into a poem and whatever the general significance a poem might have, the poet always strives to create an immediate perceptual experience.

Consider the following poem by William Blake:

Ah Sun-flower

Ah Sun-flower! weary of time,
Who countest the steps of the Sun,
Seeking after that sweet golden clime
Where the traveller's journey is done;

Where the Youth pined away with desire,   5
And the pale Virgin shrouded in snow,
Arise from their graves and aspire,
Where my Sun-flower wishes to go.

(1794)

"Weary of time" is a verbal abstraction, conceptual rather than perceptual in that it cannot be perceived by the senses. But it gains the force of perceptual experience in the context of the concretion "Sun-flower." Have you ever seen sunflowers in September? Fully grown and at the end of their natural cycle, they droop under the heavy weight of seed and enormous blooms; barely able if at all to fulfill their heliotropic nature, they look unbearably weary, like a host of exhausted soldiers limping off a battlefield. Wallace Stevens called poetry "an abstraction blooded"; Blake's "Ah Sun-flower! weary of time" is an example of what Stevens had in mind. Blake would have us see, and by seeing feel this weariness as a physical presence, carrying a sense of frustration and unfulfillment in the face of life's end. Then we can feel keenly, as a heavy weight, the unfulfillment of the youth's desire and the snowbound virgin's frigidity. In context, Blake's words evoke sensation; though they are not exactly things, they have the effect of things on the mind.

FEELING INTO WORDS

How can we speak feeling? It is not enough just to name a feeling. "I feel tired," "I am in love," "I am happy"—these abstractions communicate on the level of idea, not of felt experience. In contrast, verbal concretions can communicate feeling as *experience,* and thereby make language a true means of expression. Concretions can make us feel (emotionally) by making us feel (physically).

Concretion and Imagery

At its simplest, an **image** is a verbal concretion: the two terms are interchangeable. However, the words *image* and *imagery* are usually used in a more extended sense, according to which images are verbal concretions —words that call up sensations: visual, olfactory (smell), auditory, gustatory (taste), tactile(touch), and kinesthetic (muscular movement)—used to convey intangible states of mind or feeling through sense impressions. The list *sky, sun, banana, grass, snake,* thus, is composed of restricted images— sometimes called "tied" or "literal" images, for these images mean only what they refer to. Should the title "Eden in the Tropics" be provided, then the words would become extended images—sometimes called "free" or "figurative" images. Then they would carry directed associations and implications along with their literal meanings.

The end of Wordsworth's "A Slumber Did My Spirit Seal" should help to clarify what extended images do.

> No motion has she now, no force;
>   She neither hears nor sees;
> Rolled round in earth's diurnal course,
>   With rocks, and stones, and trees.

"With rocks, and stones, and trees" refers to a glacial landscape, one of the oldest landscape types. But Wordsworth doesn't mean simply to describe a landscape; he means to arouse feeling through evoking the specific landscape referred to. His imagery, that is, is not tied to descriptive reference, but is figurative because it has associational value. Close your eyes and imagine a glacial landscape. What emotions does it arouse? To me, this still landscape imparts a feel of stability, endurance, and permanence in the middle of life's flux. In realizing that the place has been as it is for 200 million years, I feel a sense of calm that somehow eases the pain of existence. For me, Wordsworth's concluding imagery thus intimates acceptance. One could, however, feel much the reverse: that the scene evoked is a gravescape and that the last lines of the poem reinforce the shocked awareness of the inertness of the dead girl, who has become only a thing. Or better yet, because divergent feelings are seldom mutually exclusive in us, one might feel both consolation and grief simultaneously. In any case, Wordsworth's compound image of "rocks, and stones, and trees" is a verbal concretion and more. The scene literally depicted carries emotional resonance; it calls up feeling by way of association.

The same is true of my daughter's "Some days tigers bite. Some days,

they don't" (see page 7). Her verbal concretion "tigers" has literal refer-
ence to tigers, but its meaning does not stop there. Because her "tigers"
has associational value as well, it is an extended image. Poetic imagery is
most often extended: through their images, poets aim at evoking the feel-
ings associated with whatever it is those images refer to. So the way into
a poem is through its concretions and their associations.

To be sure, imagery is not limited to poetry. Prose fiction, for instance,
feeds on imagery; and we use imagery (both tied and free) constantly in
speech. That we do suggests that what can be learned about language
from studying poetry applies to everything composed of words. The poet
concentrates and heightens what is concrete in language; still, the poet's
treatment of language is not divorced from the ways of language gener-
ally. Therefore, the study of poetry has bearing on the many other uses of
words. Our immediate interest, of course, is in poems. So let's look at an-
other poem to see how poets use imagery.

Sonnet 73

William Shakespeare

That time of year thou mayst in me behold
When yellow leaves, or none, or few, do hang
Upon those boughs which shake against the cold,
Bare ruined choirs, where late the sweet birds sang.
In me thou see'st the twilight of such day   5
As after sunset fadeth in the west;
Which by and by black night doth take away,
Death's second self that seals up all in rest.
In me thou see'st the glowing of such fire,
That on the ashes of his youth doth lie,   10
As the deathbed whereon it must expire,
Consumed with that which it was nourished by.
This thou perceiv'st, which makes thy love more strong,
To love that well which thou must leave ere long.

(1609)

SONNET 73. All Shakespeare's sonnets are from a sequence of sonnets
(1–154).

Shakespeare is saying "I am aging." But "aging" is an abstraction that
simply names a process; it imparts none of the feel of what it names, and
so stands outside our immediate experience. In contrast, the images of the

poem convey the feel of growing old. Itself an experience for the reader, the poem vividly imparts a sense of the chill and depletion of autumn, the grayness of evening moving to night, the shrunkenness of last embers lying on a bed of cold ashes. Imagine a ruined chapel, its "choirs" (where services would be sung) collapsed, echoing only with the whistle of the wind. See bare branches (like the skeletal remains of "ruined choirs") etched against a gray twilight sky; hear the sound of wind in those branches and, when the wind is still, the silence left by the departure of the birds; feel on your skin the feel of winter in the air. See in the fire your own life, consuming itself with each sustaining breath; sense out the visual image implied in "seals up all in rest." In its series of related images, the poem enacts what it feels like to grow old.

Having reached us through our own senses, Shakespeare can then do what he does in the last two lines, which take a surprising turn. We might have expected him to say: you perceive that I am growing old, which should make your love all the stronger because you know that I won't be around very much longer. For it is the speaker who feels death creeping up, not the listener/reader. Instead, Shakespeare turns the whole thing around: love well now because of what you see in me—a foreshadowing of your own aging and death. Shakespeare can turn the couplet as he does because he has made the listener/reader feel directly the encroachment of age and death through the poem's images. These images touch with the force of experience because we know the feel of what they refer to. Therein lies the power of imagery, a power that you can perhaps tap in the following exercise.

Exercise

Fill in the blanks with concrete words:

    I'd rather be a _____ than a _____;
    I'd rather be a _____ than a _____;
    I'd rather be a _____ than a _____;
    I'd rather be a _____ than a _____.

The context will make your words extended images. So stay with things. Try also to build to a climax and, by choosing related sets of things, to make your four lines together express some overriding wish.

Here are a few examples of what other students have done. The first is somewhat off the mark:

    I'd rather be a comic than a newspaper;
    I'd rather be a toy than a computer;
    I'd rather be a child than an adult;
    I'd rather be free than enslaved.

Abstraction, Concretion, Imagery

Though the poem expresses an overriding wish, the last two lines are highly abstract and the last line is muddy in its thought. Are children really free? Besides, "free" is not a concretion. And why the spelling out in line 3? Concretions would avoid the problems of the last two lines and have far greater impact. Is not the following revision, arrived at in class discussion, more forceful because more tangible?

> I'd rather be a crayon than a checkbook;
> I'd rather be in a puddle than a muddle.

The next two work well throughout. With charm and wit, each builds to a climax and overall gives solid expression to feeling.

> I'd rather be an eider-down jacket than a mink stole;
> I'd rather be Levi's jeans than an ensemble by Pucci;
> I'd rather be a V.W. Bug than a Mercedes-Benz;
> I'd rather be Frye Boots than heels by Gucci.
>
> *Jannette Tadone*

> I'd rather be an eagle than a pigeon;
> I'd rather be a mountain than a skyscraper;
> I'd rather be a forest than a city;
> I'd rather be a wild grape than the Big Apple.
>
> *Peter Konopka*

Imagery and Dimensionality

The distinction between verbal abstractions and concretions is not a distinction between generality and precision. Many abstract words, of course, are general and imprecise: *love, democracy, freedom, fear.* Equally as many, however, are most precise: *diastrophism* (a specific geological process), *aventurine* (a kind of glass), *sclerosis* (a tissue disease). Conversely, a great many concretions are general rather than specific: *bird* (as opposed to *robin* or *eagle*), *tree* (as opposed to *oak* or *maple*), *green* (as opposed to *pea-green* or *chartreuse*). Nor should we think that concretions alone have associational value. Certainly, such words as *love* and *democracy* carry a wealth of associations. But the associations they carry for you are very likely different from the associations they carry for me, whereas the associations—yours and mine—brought up by the word *tiger* are probably fairly similar. Imagery, then, can tap shared experience. It also has "dimensionality." Abstractions like *love* have emotional depth, but lack precision; abstractions like *diastrophism* are precise, but lack depth. Concretions like Shakespeare's "Bare ruined choirs" have a high degree of both. Also, along with other of a poem's elements, imagery allows for the expression of the many-sidedness of emotions in a way that abstraction does not, at least not vividly and concisely. Shakespeare's fading fire in the context of his late autumn evening, for example, expresses coldness and a residue of warmth *simultaneously*. To abstract and say "I feel death (cold) approaching; nevertheless, there is still a bit of life (heat) left to me" is to lose the simultaneity that the image imparts and therefore to lose the edge of experience as we feel it. It is exactly this edge that Robert Frost captures in one of his best known poems, "Stopping by Woods."

Stopping by Woods on a Snowy Evening

Whose woods these are I think I know.
His house is in the village, though;
He will not see me stopping here
To watch his woods fill up with snow.

My little horse must think it queer   5
To stop without a farmhouse near
Between the woods and frozen lake
The darkest evening of the year.

He gives his harness bells a shake
To ask if there is some mistake.   10
The only other sound's the sweep
Of easy wind and downy flake.

The woods are lovely, dark, and deep,
But I have promises to keep,
And miles to go before I sleep,   15
And miles to go before I sleep.

(1923)

We start with a speaker in a frozen landscape. Late in the evening, in the dead of winter ("the darkest evening of the year"), he's on a journey —why, we are not told. In that he thinks he knows the owner of the woods, though, we can say that he is familiar with the region. For some reason he pauses. His pausing, however, seems to cause him to feel much anxiety, evidenced by his concern about being seen and by the judgment he attributes to his horse ("must think it queer"), a judgment surely the speaker's own, projected onto the dumb creature. Then why has he paused? Relate to the image of the "lovely, dark, and deep" woods. Mysterious, peaceful, the woods almost beckon him to come in and rest. There is an odd attraction here, odd in that should the speaker give himself over to the attraction of the frozen scene, he would die. This pervasive fact signals that the imagery (visual, auditory, tactile) of the poem is more than simply descriptive in relevance. So does a probable allusion to a strange, macabre poem about death by Thomas Lovell Beddoes called "The Phantom Wooer" (see page 242): "Young soul, put off your flesh and come/With me into the quiet tomb,/Our bed is lovely, dark, and sweet." Both fact and allusion suggest that the attraction the speaker feels for this winterscape, swept by "easy wind and downy flake" (how beautifully the sound and movement of these words capture what they describe), springs from a deep, dark desire for cessation. Weary, no doubt, from his journey, he momentarily feels the attraction of the end of all journeys. Frost's is no macabre poem, however. The speaker pulls back from the brink (the "But" of line 14 is pivotal) by remembering that he has human commitments. These are not obligations imposed on him, but "promises" that *he* has made and desires to fulfill. He feels an upswelling of a desire for cessation, but at the same time he desires to continue. His literal "miles to go" are wearisome. Nevertheless, he accepts that he has miles (metaphorical) to go before the final sleep of death.

Notice how I have gone about reading the poem. I've stayed with its concretions (its imagery), and by exploring those concretions, felt out the poem's emotional depth and complexity. The speaker feels a normal feeling: the attraction of death (implied by the associations of darkness and winter) in the face of life's burdens. Yet his feeling is not single: he also feels uneasy about his being drawn to the woods, and he feels uneasy about the scene itself—the image of the "dark, and deep" woods is as fearful as it is appealing in its mystery—and he feels strongly the divergent pull of life. Through its concretions and overall structure, the poem gives voice to the layeredness of *human* emotion. (The difference between man and animal on this score is poignantly implied in stanza 3.) It renders with immediacy a sense of the multidimensional nature of human response to the world and to life. In doing the next exercise, see what you can accomplish with respect to voicing your own divergent feelings.

Exercise

Fill in the blanks:
    I wish I were _____,
    For then _____.
    I wish I were _____,
    For then _____.
Lines 1 and 3, at least, should be filled in with images, now contrasting in nature. For in one way or another, your second wish should be contrary to your first. The object is for you to give expression to dual feelings in a way that suggests their simultaneity.

This time I've chosen two examples written by students. The first is somewhat problematic, though instructive; the second, breathtaking.

> I wish I were an airplane,
> For then I could be in view of everyone.
> I wish I were a subway,
> For then I could be hidden from the world.

Well, subways are hidden in a sense; still, they are seen by millions of riders every day. Therefore, though the pair of wishes strikes a chord, the subway image doesn't really work. There is a logic to imagery: an image is expressive only to the extent that what is referred to carries the associations that the writer means to evoke.

> I wish I were curling rings of smoke,
> For then I'd waver and stretch into ribbons of blue ice.
> I wish I were crystal glass,
> For then I'd shatter into pellucid clumps.

> *Ellen Fitzgerald*

"Waver and stretch"—feel in your muscles the sense of physical release that the words embody (the imagery is kinesthetic). Feel out the contrast between "smoke" and glass," connected by the image of "blue ice," which smoke is like on a cold winter's day. The wish is to be totally elastic; yet because no one can so be, there is the alternate wish to be "crystal glass." For if one must be rigid and capable of shattering, as people are metaphorically, how much better to shatter into "pellucid clumps" than into the incomprehensible splinters that people shatter. Much is said here concretely; through her concretions, the poet explores and gives voice to the depth and multiplicity of her feeling. Such is the power of imagery.

OTHER TYPES OF CONCRETION

We have dealt now with one type of concretion—verbal. But there are other types. Indeed, anything in a text that has immediate sensory effect is a concretion. The sounds of words, if their sounds call attention; the ways they move together; the structures they can be used to form—all fall into the realm of concretion, as does the characteristic division of poetry into lines and even, at times, the way a poem lies on a page.[1] These possibilities of words are concretions because they are palpable, physical in appeal. They speak in the way dreams speak.

---

[1] See "Easter Wings" (page 248) and "The Convergence of the Twain," with its shiplike, iceberglike stanzas (page 276).

We shall consider in turn all the other types of concretion, concreteness being the essence of poetry. Let me exemplify, and by exemplifying, give a preview of things to come.

[No Worst, There Is None]

Gerald Manley Hopkins

No worst, there is none. Pitched past pitch of grief,
More pangs will, schooled at forepangs, wilder wring.
Comforter, where, where is your comforting?
Mary, mother of us, where is your relief?
My cries heave, herds-long; huddle in a main, a chief-   5
woe, world-sorrow; on an age-old anvil wince and sing—
Then lull, then leave off. Fury had shrieked 'No ling-
ering! Let me be fell:° force° I must be brief.'   *deadly | perforce*
O the mind, mind has mountains; cliffs of fall
Frightful, sheer, no-man-fathomed. Hold them cheap   10
May who ne'er hung there. Nor does long our small
Durance deal with that steep or deep. Here! creep,
Wretch, under a comfort serves in a whirlwind: all
Life death does end and each day dies with sleep.

(c. 1885)

In the octave (first eight lines) of this sonnet, the speaker is clearly in a state of desperation. There is no "worst" for him, only progressive stages of worse and worse and worse, as the demonlike "pangs" to come learn to wring him all the more terribly from the pangs that have come before. Thus the sense of vertigo, of the speaker's having been "Pitched" into some bottomless pit. He cries out for comfort, but to no avail. His cry is answered only by the contrasting cries of the next four lines, cries wrung out of him by some dreadful "Fury." What is the cause of this agony? The sestet (last six lines) gives an answer.

Visualize the scene: a man has been traveling in some landscape like the moon; losing his way, he falls over the edge of a cliff and hangs there above an unfathomable abyss (the image concretizes the vertigo sensed at the beginning of the poem); feeling that he cannot hang there long and fearing that a whirlwind will shortly blow up and whirl him into oblivion, he searches for a place of safety; he finds one, a crevice in the cliffside into which he can crawl. These images (visual, auditory, tactile, kinesthetic), which communicate sheer terror, are all turned to metaphor: traveling in the mind, or introspection, is like traveling in such a forbidding landscape. In both, one can get hopelessly stranded and fall into dark regions, for the mind, too, has unfathomed depths. It is in a mental landscape that the speaker has gotten lost. There he hangs and fears a renewed whirlwind of self-doubt and accusation (the "pangs," then, are pangs of conscience). So he bids himself to creep into a metaphorical crevice—the comfort that the thought of sleep and, finally, death offers.

There is great power here. With his images and the metaphors they form, Hopkins renders his desperation[2] in a way that an abstraction like "the mind poses its own difficulties" never could. The latter is an observation; the poem is an experience. Hopkins renders his desperation through a host of other concretions as well. The very density of the poem's imagery and metaphors is a concretion, one that carries a sense of density and mental turmoil. The concentration of monosyllables toward the end, each of which is to be stressed, conveys the feel of weariness, yet also mimics a gasping for breath. Breathlessness is the effect, too, of the rhythmic flow of the words. Then there is the supreme awkwardness of the entire poem: the awkward hyphenation of "chief-/woe" and "ling-/ering," and of the internal rhymes "steep . . . deep . . . creep"; the way the lines trip over the edge of their endings and fall into one another; the awkward syntax and elision ("Hold them cheap/May who" instead of "Hold them cheap they may, those who have . . ."). All these concretions embody a sense of the stumbling and groping of a being at odds with itself. Then there are the many plosive sounds of the sonnet (such as *p*) and the harshness of such words as *wretch*. Using words in all their qualities, Hopkins speaks to and through our senses. He communicates on the level of experience through a structure of concretions.

Notice again how I have gone about my reading—particularly how I approach the last six lines of Hopkins's sonnet. They seem almost impenetrable at first sight; but they aren't if we remember to begin with concretions. We start with images, then construct in our minds a situation or narrative. We imagine something happening in the scene, both scene and situation being concretions in that both can be visualized in the imagination. Then we make whatever metaphorical transfer is called for —here, from "mountains" to "mind." We respond as well to the given sounds, rhythms, phrasing. These are the means of a poem, and we must interact with these before moving to interpretation, for these are what we are interpreting.

So much for exemplification and preview; now to a poem assignment, the first of seven such assignments. This one is aimed at leading you

---

[2] Biographically, Hopkins was in a state of desperation when he composed this sonnet, a state caused by introspection. Always severely scrupulous with himself, he evidenced such agitation that his superiors (Hopkins was a Jesuit) ordered him to discontinue the prescribed practice of meditation.

further toward thinking in images. You can do the assignment—and all the other poem assignments—if you let your feelings take shape in concretions and explore those feelings thereby.

POEM ASSIGNMENT

Write a poem of four to eight lines, in which you give voice to some fear through your imagery. Don't write on fear itself, and don't name what it is you fear. Thinking of the poem as being something like a nightmare, perhaps, let the feeling well up in you and take shape in your images and verbal patterns. Remember the one stricture of form: *divided into lines.* Also, give your poem a title.

Division into lines is central to poetry. It is the one thing that all poems have in common and the one thing that most readily demarks poetry from prose. The line breaks that occur in prose at the righthand margin are arbitrary; those of poetry are deliberate and expressive. When writing your poem, decide whether you want short lines or long or a mixture of the two. Question why one is preferable to the other given your purposes in the poem. Question, too, what happens at the end of each line: does the end of a given line coincide with a grammatical pause, or does the sense pull the voice over into the next line without pause? What is the effect in either case? Read the following student samples with an eye especially to line treatment.

The Fear of Death

Although death is inevitable, I fear the mere thought of dying.
I try to visualize life after death, yet darkness and barrenness are all
    I see.
My mind withdraws from its surroundings and becomes infected
    with gruesome ideas.
My insides grow shaky and the palms of my hands begin perspiring.
It is time which allows me to carry on, but once this valuable time is
    out, I will join the other ghosts.   5
I fear the unknown, and surely that is one definition of death.

This piece is of six long lines. Capitalization at the beginning of a line, though not necessary to poetry, is one way a poet can show line divisions. Rather abstract, however, "The Fear of Death" is basically a piece of expository prose divided into lines. It is a commentary as opposed to a dramatic enactment. At least, its material is not realized in poetic terms.

Contrast it with the next three samples. "Sea Gulls" doesn't stand aside and observe; it embodies feeling with immediacy through its imagery of scavenger gulls and cold north, and through the fine line break "and/ Moved on" (which produces a moment of chilling suspension). In "Clock," the abstraction "Time" is blooded by the metaphorical image of the "whore." And "Hospital," through its imagery, carefully calculated line lengths and breaks, and pattern of repetition, *dramatizes* fully the fear it concerns.

Sea Gulls

Annemarie Gannon

They came from the north
Flying in a triangle covering the sky.
They came down as I lay on the beach;
They examined around me, and
Moved on.

Clock

Michael Doyle

Time
    stands flexing like a whore,
    always there for more, boy.
    You can run, hide, or crawl, boy;
    She'll squeeze you till you're dry, boy.
Time

Hospital

Eugene George

Absence of light
Save the narrow shafts in which the dust particles dance
Absence of sound
Save the wild rhythmic pounding of my heart
Absence of motion
Save the twitching and flinching of my nervous limbs
Absence of feeling
Save the sensation that in my last hours I am the target of countless
    piercing eyes.

5

Because you are now to write free verse, read the "Addendum" below before you begin your poem.

ADDENDUM: FREE VERSE AND LINE TREATMENT

Free verse means "unmetered poetry." Free verse can be rhymed (though it usually isn't), but it cannot have a recurrent beat, which is the hallmark of metrical poetry. Both types of verse, however, entail division into lines. Line division—a concretion because division into lines greatly affects how a poem is heard—is an important aspect of all poetry, whether free or metrical. The difference between metrical and free verse on this score is that free verse allows the line to be contracted or expanded at will and broken off at any point. All the preceding student samples are in free verse, as is the following poem. Read it aloud, letting your voice be guided by the shifting lengths of its lines and its line breaks (line treatment—line lengths and breaks—being made possible by line division). Much of the fun of the poem lies in the hearing.

Portrait of a Lady

William Carlos Williams

Your thighs are appletrees
whose blossoms touch the sky.
Which sky? The sky
where Watteau hung a lady's
slipper. Your knees   5
are a southern breeze—or
a gust of snow. Agh! what
sort of man was Fragonard?
—as if that answered
anything. Ah, yes—below   10
the knees, since the tune
drops that way, it is
one of those white summer days,
the tall grass of your ankles
flickers upon the shore—   15
Which shore?—
the sand clings to my lips—
Which shore?

Agh, petals maybe. How
should I know?   20
Which shore? Which shore?
I said petals from an appletree.

(*1915*)

PORTRAIT OF A LADY. 4 and 8. Jean Watteau (1684–1721) and Jean Frago-
nard (1732–1806) were both French painters in the rococo style. The haunt-
ingly erotic painting by Watteau to which the speaker alludes depicts a
beautiful young woman swinging in a swing while her left shoe goes flying
into the air. Fragonard, inspired by Watteau, did a painting of a similar
subject.

Though the speaker sets out to paint a portrait in words (images and
metaphors) of his "Lady," he fails because of her constant interruptions.
Yet the poem manages to paint that portrait by way of those very inter-
ruptions; it also paints its male speaker, who is totally different from the
woman he addresses. He's a moonstruck creature of passion and fancy.
She's an unimpassioned literalist whose attention span seems limited, at
least with respect to the attempts at seduction by the male before her.
The speaker begins by rhapsodically comparing the lady's thighs to apple
trees (she must be rather sturdily built), in lines relatively long and flow-
ing. She, a literalist, picks up on the word *sky* and asks a question of fact:
"Which sky?" That disturbs his concentration—a disturbance reflected by
the shortening of the line and the rough line breaks: "The sky/where"
and "lady's/slipper." But he almost regains his ardor (lines 5–7), when
she throws him again. His reference to Watteau has brought Fragonard
to her mind, and she asks her tangential matter-of-fact question without
regard to context. Her mind is not on the speaker and his desire at all.
Thus his annoyance, which the shortening of the line and the rough line
breaks again betray. The line treatment imparts a sense of tension as the
speaker almost loses his train of thought (suggested by "Ah, yes"). A per-
sistent lover, though, he haltingly regains his composure and again rhap-
sodizes in longer and more even lines (lines 13–15). Then comes her final
outrageous question: "Which shore?" That's the last straw. The sand
pathetically clings to his lips because it is real to him in his imagination.
She, however, is a literalist, and it's not real to her. Feeling now fully
their incompatibility, the speaker ends his attempted seduction in a state
of rage. He can only blurt out choppy little phrases as his voice becomes
rough and cracks with anger. At the end of the poem he remembers his
initial mood, but the mood is gone. So he throws up his hands in comic
despair—comic to the reader, not to him.
    Along with its imagery and implied situation, the line treatment of the

poem lends it concreteness. In doing the first poem assignment, try to give your piece this further dimension. Before you begin, you might want to read a few more poems in free verse (see pages 250–262) to get a feeling for its possibilities.

POEMS FOR FURTHER STUDY

My Papa's Waltz

Theodore Roethke

The whiskey on your breath
Could make a small boy dizzy;
But I hung on like death:
Such waltzing was not easy.

We romped until the pans   5
Slid from the kitchen shelf;
My mother's countenance
Could not unfrown itself.

The hand that held my wrist
Was battered on one knuckle;   10
At every step you missed
My right ear scraped a buckle.

You beat time on my head
With a palm caked hard by dirt,
Then waltzed me off to bed   15
Still clinging to your shirt.

(1948)

Questions
1. What is the scene of the poem? What is its situation?
2. What specific images does it present? What associations do they carry?
3. The mother would have smiled if she could have, but her "countenance/Could not unfrown itself." What does this face tell us about the lives of these people?
4. The poem gives expression to ambivalent (mixed) feelings. What is the ambivalence on the part of the mother? In what respect is the specific memory recounted by the speaker marked by ambivalence?

5. What other concretions has Roethke made use of? (Look, for example, at line length and rhythmic movement.)

Upon Julia's Clothes

Robert Herrick

Whenas in silks my Julia goes,
Then, then, methinks, how sweetly flows
That liquefaction of her clothes.

Next, when I cast mine eyes, and see
That brave vibration, each way free,   5
O, how that glittering taketh me!

(1648)

Questions
1. What scene does the poem ask us to imagine?
2. "Liquefaction" is an abstraction. How does the context breathe life into it and bring out its underlying concreteness?
3. In part, the speaker is describing the clothes of this Julia. But he's also intimating by way of his description things that cannot be seen. What? What is the focus in stanza two? (In this regard, consider the word *brave*, which in the Renaissance meant "boastful," "showy," "challenging.")
4. The speaker also gives voice to his feeling. How? Is "glittering," for example, an image in the narrow sense only or in the extended sense of the word as well?

Ars Poetica

Archibald MacLeish

A poem should be palpable and mute
As a globed fruit,

Dumb
As old medallions to the thumb,

Silent as the sleeve-worn stone   5
Of casement ledges where the moss has grown—

A poem should be wordless
As the flight of birds.

A poem should be motionless in time
As the moon climbs,   10

Leaving, as the moon releases
Twig by twig the night-entangled trees,

Leaving, as the moon behind the winter leaves,
Memory by memory the mind—

A poem should be motionless in time   15
As the moon climbs.

A poem should be equal to:
Not true.

For all the history of grief
An empty doorway and a maple leaf.   20

For love
The leaning grasses and two lights above the sea—

A poem should not mean
But be.

                                                                    (1926)

ARS POETICA. The title means "the art of poetry."

Questions
1. What are the images of this poem?
2. What do they communicate? For example, what feelings does "sleeve-worn stone/Of casement ledges" convey?
3. What abstractions are found in the poem? To what extent are its abstractions grounded in its concretions?
4. How do the images of the poem support its statement? Is there any gap between image and statement? Should there be statements here at all given what is being said about poetry?
5. Poems mean by their being, but they do mean, just as they are made of words and flow in time. MacLeish realizes all this, of course. The poem, then, presents us with a paradox inherent to poetry. But does MacLeish fully dramatize the paradox and give it embodiment, or does he tend more to comment on the complexity of poetic language?

Abstraction, Concretion, Imagery

Domination of Black

Wallace Stevens

At night, by the fire,
The colors of the bushes
And of the fallen leaves,
Repeating themselves,
Turned in the room,   5
Like the leaves themselves
Turning in the wind.
Yes: but the color of the heavy hemlocks
Came striding.
And I remembered the cry of the peacocks.   10

The colors of their tails
Were like the leaves themselves
Turning in the wind,
In the twilight wind.
They swept over the room,   15
Just as they flew from the boughs of the hemlocks
Down to the ground.
I heard them cry—the peacocks.
Was it a cry against the twilight
Or against the leaves themselves   20
Turning in the wind,
Turning as the flames
Turned in the fire,
Turning as the tails of the peacocks
Turned in the loud fire,   25
Loud as the hemlocks
Full of the cry of the peacocks?
Or was it a cry against the hemlocks?

Out of the window,
I saw how the planets gathered   30
Like the leaves themselves
Turning in the wind.
I saw how the night came,
Came striding like the color of the heavy hemlocks.
I felt afraid.   35
And I remembered the cry of the peacocks.

(1923)

Questions

1. Where is the speaker at the beginning of "Domination"? What is he
   looking at?

2. What the speaker is looking at reminds him of other things. What? What is the relationship between what he is actually looking at and what it brings to mind?
3. Green is the color of life, and hemlocks are evergreens. Yet at evening, their dense, shaggy branches look black against the bleakness of the sky. Also, you may remember that the herb hemlock was the poison Socrates drank. Given these associations, what might the poem express about life and death (or their relationship) through its image of hemlocks? Might the poem's central image—its "turning ... flames," its "fire"—be read as expressing the same awareness? (Remember Shakespeare's "fire," "Consumed with that which it was nourished by.")
4. Peacocks, whose cry is a horrendous shriek, symbolized the immortality of the radiant soul in the iconography of the Renaissance. In our more secular age, however, the peacock has come to symbolize much the reverse: this-wordliness as opposed to other-worldliness: ephemerality, and the feelings of sadness and compassion that the awareness of ephemerality brings; the pride of youthful accomplishment or of physical beauty ("as proud as a peacock"—usually said not with condemnation but with affection). In this secular context, what does the "cry of the peacocks" signify? Why might the cry be against not only the "twilight" and the fallen "leaves" but also the "hemlocks" and the whole universe (the "planets gathered")?
5. What other concretions does Stevens use?
6. The next-to-last line amounts to a flat statement of feeling. Does the statement *in its context* seem grounded in concretion?

IDEAS FOR WRITING

1. Write a paraphrase of the piece you did for the first poem assignment. What is lost in the translation? Or, if you feel that nothing is lost, how did you go wrong in doing the assignment? Analyze the concretions in what you wrote.
2.

Why Think? By Thinking You Grow Old

Arthur Hugh Clough

To spend uncounted years in pain,
Again, again, and yet again,
In working out in heart and brain
    The problem of our being here;
To gather facts from far and near,

Upon the mind to hold them clear,
And, knowing more may yet appear,
Unto one's latest breath to fear,
The premature result to draw—
Is this the object, end and law,   10
    And purpose of our being here?

                                     (1869)

WHY THINK?   9. *result:* death.

In what way(s) does "Why Think?" fail? Suggest how it might be
improved. For example, what images might help make it more of an
experience for the reader? If you think the poem a success, defend
your case.
3. Compare "Why Think?" and Hughes's "Harlem." How do the two
differ in language and effect? In a separate paragraph, state your re-
sponse to "Harlem" and the reasons for your response. Do you like it
or not? Why? In your judgment, does it succeed aesthetically or not?
(One's likings and dislikings do not always coincide with one's aes-
thetic judgment. By distinguishing between the two, we can guard
against restricting ourselves to momentary preferences and impeding
growth.)

Harlem

Langston Hughes

What happens to a dream deferred?

Does it dry up
like a raisin in the sun?
Or fester like a sore—
And then run?   5
Does it stink like rotten meat?
Or crust and sugar over—
like a syrupy sweet?

Maybe it just sags
like a heavy load.   10

Or does it explode?

                                     (1951)

4.

Cherry Robbers

D. H. Lawrence

Under the long dark boughs, like jewels red
    In the hair of an Eastern girl
Hang strings of crimson cherries, as if had bled
    Blood-drops beneath each curl.

Under the glistening cherries, with folded wings   5
    Three dead birds lie:
Pale-breasted throstles and a blackbird, robberlings
    Stained with red dye.

Against the haystack a girl stands laughing at me,
    Cherries hung round her ears.   10
Offers me her scarlet fruit: I will see
    If she has any tears.

(1913)

Contrast this poem with the following passage from Lawrence's novel *Sons and Lovers:*

> Miriam came out wondering.
> "Oh!" Paul heard her mellow voice call, "isn't it wonderful?"
> He looked down. There was a faint gold glimmer on her face, that looked very soft, turned up to him.
> "How high you are!" she said.
> Beside her, on the rhubarb leaves, were four dead birds, thieves that had been shot. Paul saw some cherry stones hanging quite bleached, like skeletons, picked clear of flesh. He looked down again to Miriam.
> "Clouds are on fire," he said.
> "Beautiful!" she cried.
> She seemed so small, so soft, so tender, down there. He threw a handful of cherries at her. She was startled and frightened. He laughed with a low, chuckling sound, and pelted her. She ran for shelter, picking up some cherries. Two fine red pairs she hung over her ears; then she looked up again.
>   . . .
> He seemed to be almost unaware of her as a person: she was only to him then a woman. She was afraid.

What are the similarities between the poem and the prose passage? What are the differences? Which seems to capture more fully the dimensionality of youthful sexual feelings? Defend your judgment.

Voice, Tone, Diction
Chapter Three

THE POEM AS UTTERANCE

Of the various concretions that go into the making of poems, perhaps the most obvious, though the one most frequently neglected by beginning students, is **voice**. We say that an image is concrete because it evokes sensation. But the way a poem moves and sounds when read aloud is a concretion still more immediate because we can actually hear it with our ears. One principle, therefore, that should govern your reading of poetry is: *read aloud*. Let the words form in your mouth and echo in your ears. Or, as Hopkins frequently advised his correspondents, "read with your ears," for poetry is in large measure "speech framed to be heard."

Every poem should be heard as an utterance spoken by a speaker to himself in meditation, or to a specified listener, or to the reader, or by two or more speakers to each other. The speaker is to be taken sometimes as the poet; sometimes as an imagined character (or characters); and sometimes as either the one or the other. (The speaker of "Stopping by Woods" could be thought of as the poet himself or as a character—a local doctor, perhaps). Whatever the case, a poem should be regarded as an act of speech, not as some disembodied communication from beyond. Many of the techniques that poets use are aimed specifically to this end—to getting into written language the nuances of spoken language. Meter is often instrumental in establishing the sense of voice. So, too, are the individual sounds of words, when their sounds are used with deliberation, and all matters having to do with line treatment (length and division).

Dramatic monologues illustrate voice well. (A **dramatic monologue** is a poem clearly spoken by an imagined character, often called a "persona.") Read the following monologue aloud; imagine its scene and situation, and concentrate on the voice of the duke (the speaker of this poem). To whom is he speaking? How does he speak—easily or with difficulty or both in turn? What does his manner of speech reveal about him?

My Last Duchess

Robert Browning

FERRARA

That's my last duchess painted on the wall,
Looking as if she were alive. I call
That piece a wonder, now: Frà Pandolf's hands
Worked busily a day, and there she stands.
Will't please you sit and look at her? I said   5
"Frà Pandolf" by design, for never read
Strangers like you that pictured countenance,
The depth and passion of its earnest glance,
But to myself they turned (since none puts by
The curtain I have drawn for you, but I)   10
And seemed as they would ask me, if they durst,
How such a glance came there; so, not the first
Are you to turn and ask thus. Sir, 'twas not

Her husband's presence only, called that spot
Of joy into the Duchess' cheek: perhaps   15
Frà Pandolf chanced to say "Her mantle laps
"Over my lady's wrist too much," or "Paint
"Must never hope to reproduce the faint
"Half-flush that dies along her throat": such stuff
Was courtesy, she thought, and cause enough   20
For calling up that spot of joy. She had
A heart—how shall I say?—too soon made glad,
Too easily impressed; she liked whate'er
She looked on, and her looks went everywhere.
Sir, 'twas all one! My favor at her breast,   25
The dropping of the daylight in the West,
The bough of cherries some officious fool
Broke in the orchard for her, the white mule
She rode with round the terrace—all and each
Would draw from her alike the approving speech,   30
Or blush, at least. She thanked men—good! but thanked
Somehow—I know not how—as if she ranked
My gift of a nine-hundred-years-old name
With anybody's gift. Who'd stoop to blame
This sort of trifling? Even had you skill   35
In speech—which I have not—to make your will
Quite clear to such an one, and say, "Just this
"Or that in you disgusts me; here you miss,
"Or there exceed the mark"—and if she let
Herself be lessoned so, nor plainly set   40
Her wits to yours, forsooth, and made excuse,
—E'en then would be some stooping; and I choose
Never to stoop. Oh sir, she smiled, no doubt,
Whene'er I passed her; but who passed without
Much the same smile? This grew; I gave commands;   45
Then all smiles stopped together. There she stands
As if alive. Will't please you rise? We'll meet
The company below, then. I repeat,
The Count your master's known munificence
Is ample warrant that no just pretense   50
Of mine for dowry will be disallowed;
Though his fair daughter's self, as I avowed
At starting, is my object. Nay, we'll go
Together down, sir. Notice Neptune, though,
Taming a sea-horse, thought a rarity,   55
Which Claus of Innsbruck cast in bronze for me!

                                                    (1842)

MY LAST DUCHESS.   The poem is spoken by Alfonson II d'Este, Duke of Fer-
rara, Italy. Alfonso's first wife, whom he married when she was fourteen,
died in 1561 under suspicious circumstances.

What should catch the ear most about the voice that Browning has
fashioned for his duke is its confidence. The duke is in full possession of
himself and, or so he believes, of the situation. The sense of confidence is
imparted by the poem's overall ease of movement, produced in large part
by what is called **enjambment**—a line is said to be enjambed when it does
not come to a marked pause at the line break (lines that do end with a
marked pause are called **end-stopped**). The majority of Browning's lines
enjamb, and they do so with a strong forward motion (as compared with
the awkward enjambments of Hopkins's "No Worst, There Is None" and
the rough enjambments of Williams's "Portrait of a Lady"). Through a
careful manipulation of caesuras (a **caesura** is a pause within a line), syn-
tax, and meter, Browning makes his lines run quickly on, so quickly that
one might almost not notice that the poem is in rhymed **couplets** (lines
that rhyme two by two). Rhyme here remains in the background, but it
very much contributes to the forward motion of the poem. Everything com-
bines to render the voice exactly; and in and through that voice is to be
heard a man of high refinement, articulate on most subjects, and su-
premely self-assured. The situation of the poem, too, suggests his self-
assurance. The duke is speaking to an envoy of a count whose daughter
he (the duke) hopes to make his next duchess. That the duke reveals what
he does in this circumstance—that he can tolerate no selfhood in a wife
and that he has had his last wife killed ("I gave commands;/Then all
smiles stopped together") because of her youthful exuberance—intimates
self-confidence bordering on egomania. The voice of the poem is certainly
right for such a man.

   Fluidity, of course, is not a necessary nor even a normal attribute of
poetry. Nor is it the only vocal quality to be heard in "My Last Duchess."
Indeed, given his established ease in speaking, it is particularly significant
that the Duke stammers three times during the course of his monologue
(lines 22, 32, and 36) and that he denies his competence in speech (line
36). Refuted by the ease with which he speaks otherwise, his denial, no
doubt, is conventional (the denial of a man who would appear to be
"macho"); still, there is an area in which the duke is not competent, the
area of human relationships. He's a man of high aesthetic sensibility, yet
profoundly amoral. Thus, people are objects to him. (He even refers to
the count's daughter as his "object"—line 53). His judgments are aes-
thetic in nature rather than moral ("Just this/Or that in you disgusts me,"
disgust being a matter of *taste*). Self-centered (observe the poem's last
word), he must own and he must control. As long as he is in control,
he's perfectly articulate and demonstratively magnanimous (witness his

waving aside of protocol and pulling the envoy to his side as they move to leave, lines 53–54). But when faced with the complexity of a human relationship, he loses his composure. When the duke speaks of art (the painting, which he prizes much more than he did the wife), the voice is fluid; when he speaks of matters calling for moral discrimination, his voice is halting. Here is what is meant by "voice": when a poem is working, one can hear in it the wonderful nuances of speech.

Exercise

To better see (hear) Browning's mastery, do as follows: take the opening of "My Last Duchess" and recast it into short lines, with most either end-stopped or roughly enjambed (observe how much end rhyme is responsible for the poem's forward motion) and marked by few internal pauses. Now read both your version and Browning's, and contrast as to effect.

TONE OF VOICE

Voice involves all of the characteristics of a poem that give it the semblance of an utterance, the semblance of someone's actually speaking. An inseparable aspect of this semblance is *tone*—which means nothing more than what is meant by the phrase "tone of voice": the *way* something is said as that *way* reveals the feelings of a speaker about the subject and/or the audience.

Words when spoken mean much more than their denotations (straight dictionary meanings): the quality of the voice, or its tone, is often central to meaning. The sentence "I would love to go," for example, can be said in such a way (i.e., with a sneer) as to communicate the opposite of what the words literally mean (irony is almost always signified by tone when we speak)—in which case the auditor might reply, "I don't like your tone of voice"; or the sentence can be said with enthusiasm so as to communicate genuine desire.

The voice is truly marvelous. It can be formal in tone or intimate, harsh or playful, serious or ironic, condescending, elevated, passionate, comic or solemn; it can run smoothly on or haltingly, crack with a tear or a smile—and thereby reveal the shifts and turns of feeling.

Exercise

Take the following sentence and say it in three or four of the ways indicated above: "I wish I were in Toledo." Contrast the differing ways the sentence can be uttered as to intent and effect.

How to get these various qualities into the written language? The poet's answer is related to the way voice is established to begin with: in poetry, one or another tone is created by the careful manipulation of sound and movement, as well as grammar and syntax; by word choice; by line treatment; and even by the effects of imagery and metaphor.

For instance, in part because of the density of its imagery, "No Worst, There Is None" has a tone of desperation. The tone of "My Last Duchess," on the other hand, is rather calm, though if we listen closely, there is a note of tension to be heard as well in the way the poem (or its voice) stops and starts. Or take "Stopping by Woods" once more. Listen to its opening lines:

> Whose woods these are I think I know.
> His house is in the village though;
> He will not see me stopping here
> To watch his woods fill up with snow.

By implication, there is anxiety to be felt just under the surface of these lines, but their tone is matter-of-fact, as is the tone of the poem right on through line 10. End-stopped, its first ten lines have the ring of a practical man, one who ordinarily does not go in for such diversions as stopping by woods. Then another tone enters with the soft, enjambed "the sweep/Of easy wind and downy flake." The voice becomes hushed and a sense of mystery enters, a sense that carries over to "The woods are lovely, dark, and deep." By enjambing, by softening, by slowing, Frost affects a shift in tone that in and of itself communicates the dimensionality of the speaker's feeling.

As in speech, so in poetry: shifts in tone are always especially revealing. With this in mind, listen to Marvell's "To His Coy Mistress." See if you can spot a shift in tone between each of its three verse paragraphs. What do its shifts in tone tell as to what the speaker is feeling about his subject (time) and his audience (the coy young lady referred to in the title)?

To His Coy Mistress

Andrew Marvell

> Had we but world enough, and time,
> This coyness, lady, were no crime.
> We would sit down, and think which way
> To walk, and pass our long love's day.
> Thou by the Indian Ganges' side

5

Shouldst rubies find; I by the tide
Of Humber would complain. I would
Love you ten years before the flood,
And you should, if you please, refuse
Till the conversion of the Jews.   10
My vegetable love should grow
Vaster than empires and more slow;
An hundred years should go to praise
Thine eyes, and on thy forehead gaze;
Two hundred to adore each breast,   15
But thirty thousand to the rest;
An age at least to every part,
And the last age should show your heart.
For, lady, you deserve this state,
Nor would I love at lower rate.   20
   But at my back I always hear
Time's wingèd chariot hurrying near;
And yonder all before us lie
Deserts of vast eternity.
Thy beauty shall no more be found,   25
Nor, in thy marble vault, shall sound
My echoing song; then worms shall try
That long-preserved virginity,
And your quaint honor turn to dust,
And into ashes all my lust: 30
The grave's a fine and private place,
But none, I think, do there embrace.
   Now therefore, while the youthful hue
Sits on thy skin like morning dew,
And while thy willing soul transpires   35
At every pore with instant fires,
Now let us sport us while we may,
And now, like amorous birds of prey,
Rather at once our time devour
Than languish in his slow-chapped power.   40
Let us roll all our strength and all
Our sweetness up into one ball,
And tear our pleasures with rough strife
Through the iron gates of life:
Thus, though we cannot make our sun   45
Stand still, yet we will make him run.

                                 (1681)

TO HIS COY MISTRESS.   7. *Humber:* The Humber is a river in England, half
a world away from the Ganges. 10. *the conversion of the Jews:* according

to tradition, at the end of time. 11. *vegetable:* steadily growing. 40. *slow-chapped:* slow-jawed, time here envisioned as a monstrous mouth. 42. *one ball:* like the ball of the sun, our measurer of time. 43–44. *tear . . . gates:* As birds or prisoners, perhaps, might tear at things through the bars of their cages or cells? The reference is enigmatic. Another suggestion offered is that the "gates" are metaphorical equivalents of the labia, and that generally the reference is to the entry to the female citadel, specifically to the hymen (for the mistress is a virgin).

The poem presents us with a man attempting the seduction of a rather modest, though perhaps flirtatious, young woman by the force of his argument. This is the situation, which the title does much to establish. Related to the situation of the poem is its theme, of universal appeal and as ancient as mankind: *"carpe diem"* ("seize the day"), "gather ye rosebuds while ye may," "make hay while the sun shines." It is not the appeal of the theme alone, however, that makes the poem arresting. There have been many poor poems on the same theme, and enough good ones to take the luster off any treatment less than extraordinary. What makes this poem exceptional is the way the speaker argues his case and thereby voices the full urgency of his need. For instance, the way he turns the trio "if, but, therefore" (the poem is structured on this trio) to the purposes of seduction is masterful. The argument might not prove logical under analysis; nevertheless, it has the force of a passionately reasoned plea.

But what is most arresting about Marvell's poem is its contrasting tones. In its tonal shifts, which serve to heighten mood as the poem moves on, the poem crystallizes the depth of human need in the face of mortality. We begin with a jaunty tone, suited to the fantasy proposed by the speaker. In the first verse paragraph, the speaker is having a bit of fun fantasizing about life not bound by time, and making a bit of fun as well. The lines "For, lady, you deserve this state,/Nor would I love at lower rate," for example, surely have a mocking tone about them in that no one *deserves* to be lauded for the amount of time specified (30,500 years) and that "rate" carries with it some odd overtones. The speaker is poking fun at this female before him, who, remember, has refused his advances.

Other elements of this first section that create a jaunty, lightly ironic tone—a tone both of playfulness and of mild annoyance—are the feel of the word *vegetable* (hardly an earnest word), the way the lines move (in a breezy manner), and hyperbole (overstatement). The speaker says that he would sit for 30,500 years and sing the praises of this female if that would win her and if he had the time. For all that time, he would be willing to construct a type of poem known as a "blazon"—in which the body of a woman is described from head to toe by way of metaphor. (Remember Williams's "Portrait of a Lady.") Certainly, this is all bantering on his part. The speaker is simply being mildly sarcastic, as he is when he says that "the last age should show your heart" (she doesn't exactly wear her heart on her sleeve).

In the second verse paragraph, he turns away from the mistress (his audience) to the subject of time and mortality, and as his thoughts turn thus, his tone shifts dramatically. For these matters are gravely serious to him, their gravity being highlighted by the shift of tone. Instead of over-statement, we now get understatement: "deserts of vast eternity" is per-haps the best that can be done in describing the infinity of time; still, the image is smaller than what it describes. And the image of "Time's wingèd chariot" resonates with a sense of elevation—unlike "vegetable"—and so strikes a tone and thereby communicates a feeling of dead earnestness, which very much affects the rest of the second section. Remembering that we don't have world enough and time, the speaker turns back to the mis-tress with a different attitude (or tone) entirely. Now he is bitterly ironic. The "grave" might be "a fine and private place"—just what lovers have always sought—yet it is not a place for love making. The very image of skeletons embracing is so chilling as to cancel out any tone of bantering. Now the speaker is supremely serious, supremely in earnest with respect to his need and the plea that he is making.

The third verse paragraph builds on the shift of the second. Address-ing his "mistress" solely again, only now in light of the urgency felt in section two, the speaker drives home his fear and his need. Along with the grim images of time as a great devouring mouth and of the tearing of pleasure through "iron gates," the colloquial language and pounding rhythm of the third section of the poem render an unparalleled sense of urgency. The tone at this point is of a man who desperately believes what he is saying. More, the tone is of one who has moved beyond mere bodily pleasure to a vision of the human condition: to a full realization of the imminence of death and of the consequences that this realization must have on the living.

"To His Coy Mistress" is compelling to the reader because it embraces an extraordinarily wide range of human experience and feeling. It con-cerns much more than seduction. With its shifting tones, it lays bare the terrible burden of our human awareness of mortality. And in its shifting tones, it embodies the full range of our emotional possibilities: comic, serious, and tragic.

WORDS AS THINGS

Both voice and its various tones are affected by a great many of the ele-ments that go into the making of a poem: line treatment, sound, move-ment, and so forth. One of these elements is especially important in speech and poetry and prose alike. This is **diction,** the selection of words, or the kind of words selected, in a given passage or utterance (different kinds having different effects).

Words have many qualities other than their dictionary meanings. The sound of a word sometimes communicates as much as its lexical meaning. And often a word or phrase affects us because of the kind of word or phrase it is, kind being determined by history and usage.

For example, here's a poem with four distinct voices and several contrasting tones created primarily by diction. See if you can spot the shifts of each.

Reason

Josephine Miles

Said, Pull her up a bit will you, Mac, I want to unload there.
Said, Pull her up my rear end, first come first serve.
Said, Give her the gun, Bud, he needs a taste of his own bumper.
Then the usher came out and got into the act:

Said, Pull her up, pull her up a bit, we need this space, sir.   5
Said, For God's sake, is this still a free country or what?
You go back and take care of Gary Cooper's horse
And leave me handle my own car.

Saw them unloading the lame old lady,
Ducked out under the wheel and gave her an elbow,   10
Said, All you needed to do was just explain;
Reason, Reason is my middle name.

                                                      (*1955*)

REASON. " 'Reason' is a favorite one of my poems because I like the idea of speech . . . as the material from which poetry is made"—Miles's note.

"Pull her up . . . , Mac"—we know immediately that the speaker is a truck or taxi driver because of usage. (We associate "Mac" with truck drivers and cabbies, not with nuns or doctors.) "Pull her up my rear end" —the second speaker (the obstinate driver of the first vehicle) is angry, his tone being established by the kind of words he uses as much as by their referential meaning. (Compare "Pull her up my rear end" with "I choose to remain stationary.") "Give her the gun, Bud"—the third speaker, probably a male passer-by (for few women in the 1950s would have said "Bud"), is angry as well. Then comes the usher—"pull her up a bit, we need the space, sir." His formal "sir" is of a different tone entirely. "Mac . . . my rear end . . . Bud . . . sir"—much of the meaning of the poem lies in the dictional qualities of its words.

Because of their histories and areas of usage no less than their sounds, words themselves are things in a way, mental objects that have differing weights and textures. Again, we're not speaking of dictionary definitions, but of coloration and resonance, properties that words have as words apart from what they refer to. The following quartet, for instance, all denote or point to the same generalized object: *food, grub, cuisine, edibles.* Although they point to the same object, however, they express quite different attitudes toward what they name. They differ in weight and texture. In relation to one another, words have many possible qualities; sound aside, it is these qualities that diction covers, diction being something like the body language of words.

Exercise

Take the following and find three or four denotative equivalents: *white male/black male, female, residence, fat* (as an adjective), *hurry* (a verb). What are the different qualities of the different equivalents of each? If stuck, use a thesaurus. The thesaurus, however, treats words as though they were equivalent. Because of diction, no two words in the language are really synonymous.

The Categories of Diction

Words, then, exhibit diction. They fall into different categories as to kind and have different effects depending on what categories they fall into. We've dealt with two such categories already: verbal abstractions and concretions. To judge individual words as being relatively abstract or relatively concrete is to categorize them according to diction and thus effect. "Connotation" and "denotation" are two other categories of diction that words fall under. Some words are highly connotative (emotive), some highly denotative (explicit and nonemotive). This judgment, too, is relative, although certain words in certain contexts can be all but devoid of denotation. "Brillig" and "slithy toves" in Lewis Carroll's " 'Twas brillig, and the slithy toves" are almost purely connotative. In contrast, "electrical circuit," "economic development," and "theatrical management" are highly denotative.

It is important, incidentally, to distinguish between the pairs abstract/concrete and connotative/denotative: *they should not be thought of as equivalent.* Though many abstract words are also denotative—thus their attraction to the scientist—and many concrete words are highly connotative, such is not necessarily the case. Take the trio "a white man/a Caucasian *Homo sapiens*/whitey." "A white man" is both denotative and relatively concrete; "a Caucasian *Homo sapiens*" is denotative and abstract; "whitey" is highly connotative, yet also somewhat abstract (more conceptual than perceptual). Here again are words or phrases similar in reference yet that have completely different auras. Their weights and textures—derived from their histories and areas of usage—communicate as much as their referential meanings.

So, every word falls into different categories of diction at once. One word might be both abstract and denotative; another, abstract and connotative. There are many other categories of diction as well. One supercategory involves the origins or etymologies (histories) of words. The English language derives its word stock mainly from two diverse languages: Latin and Anglo-Saxon. Our Latin-based words tend to have one set of qualities, and our Saxon another. A heavily Latinate vocabulary would tend to be technical and/or formal ("file for permanent deposition"); a heavily Saxon vocabulary would be common and colloquial ("throw into the wastebasket"). "Technical/common" and "formal/colloquial" are themselves categories of diction, as are "literal/figurative," "archaic/barbaric," "elevated/homely," and "mature/childish" when meant as judgments of vocabulary. If a thirty-five-year-old man should say that he stepped into some "doggie dodo," we'd pronounce his words and him "childish," unless we had reason to take his phrase as ironic. All these pairs are categorizations of words according to their effects, effects to which we respond constantly whether we know it or not. For instance, students often say that they don't like one or another poem because it seems "flowery." "Flowery" is a judgment of diction. And these possible effects of words all serious writers weigh carefully, choosing their words to establish the desired qualities of voice and tone.

1. For instance, take the first line of Donne's "The Canonization": "For God's sake hold your tongue and let me love." What kind of words are these? They're plain, colloquial, mainly Saxon. (Our Saxon words are usually short; our Latin words are more often long.) What is their effect? Read the sentence aloud as you might say it to someone chiding you about your financée (rather formal and French in diction) or your steady (the word sounds old-fashioned, which is also a matter of diction). Just by the kind of words they are, Donne's words communicate anger. The meaning of the sentence suggests anger, too. But so does the abstracted meaning of the following sentence, which, however, does not strike a tone of anger: "For God's benefit, contain yourself, deriding not my known affection."

2. Who speaks the following poem by Blake?

The Lamb

Little Lamb, who made thee?
Dost thou know who made thee?
Gave thee life & bid thee feed,
By the stream & o'er the mead;
Gave thee clothing of delight,   5
Softest clothing wooly bright;
Gave thee such a tender voice,
Making all the vales rejoice!
   Little Lamb who made thee?
   Dost thou know who made thee?   10

Little Lamb I'll tell thee,
Little Lamb I'll tell thee!
He is callèd by thy name,
For he calls himself a Lamb:
He is meek & he is mild,   15
He became a little child:
I a child & thou a lamb,
We are callèd by his name.
   Little Lamb God bless thee.
   Little Lamb God bless thee.   20

(1789)

The speaker is identified in stanza 2 as a child. We don't need the identification, though, to hear a child speaking. In its simplicity of diction, the poem speaks with the voice of a child.

3. Contrast the diction of "The Lamb" with that of the opening lines of Wallace Stevens's "On the Manner of Addressing Clouds":

Gloomy grammarians in golden gowns,
Meekly you keep the mortal rendezvous,
Eliciting the still sustaining pomps
Of speech which are like music so profound
They seem an exaltation without sound.

Whatever else one might say about this passage, one can say with certainty that it is not spoken by a child. Highly Latinate, formal, abstract, the diction of these lines mimics that of dry academics ("grammarians"), whom Stevens imagines as having died (they've kept the "mortal rendezvous") and, in heaven, being like clouds in their academic/angelic "gowns." But how are we to take these lines, or their tone? The cumulative effect of diction here, I suggest, is ironic. Stevens is having fun with his grammarians, or poking fun at their dryness and love of abstraction (diction is an agent of characterization). For the diction of the passage goes beyond bounds, and so comes off as being pompous and silly. I've said that poets veer toward what is concrete in language. Nonetheless, abstraction can serve as well, especially when it is used for the effect of its dictional qualities—such effect, paradoxically, having a concreteness about it.

Shifts in Diction

My examples so far have each been homogeneous in diction. But just as a shift in tone is always important, so is a shift in diction. A shift in diction, indeed, usually signals a shift in tone. In "To His Coy Mistress," the shifts in diction—"vegetable" and "rate" to "wingèd chariot" to "tear . . . with rough strife"—go into the making of the shifts in tone. The same principle applies to the poems that follow.

Methought I Saw

John Milton

Methought I saw my late espousèd saint
   Brought to me like Alcestis from the grave,
   Whom Jove's great son to her glad husband gave,
   Rescued from Death by force, though pale and faint.
Mine, as whom washed from spot of child-bed taint   5
   Purification in the Old Law did save,
   And such, as yet once more I trust to have
   Full sight of her in heaven without restraint,
Came vested all in white, pure as her mind.
   Her face was veiled; yet to my fancied sight   10
   Love, sweetness, goodness, in her person shined
So clear as in no face with more delight.
   But O, as to embrace me she inclined,
   I waked, she fled, and day brought back my night.

(c. 1658)

METHOUGHT I SAW. 1. *saint:* Milton's "saint" (which means "a soul in heaven") is his second wife, who died in 1658, less than two years after her marriage (thus, "late espousèd"). In that Milton had become blind in 1651, he probably had never seen his second wife. 2. *Alcestis:* Admetus's wife, brought back from the dead by Hercules ("Jove's great son") in Euripides' play *Alcestis*. 5–6. *Mine . . . save:* Milton's wife died in childbirth and was purified according to the rituals prescribed by Hebrew law.

Like Milton's diction generally, and, indeed, like the standard diction (of prose as well as poetry) of his age, the diction of the first thirteen lines of Milton's sonnet is Latinate and formal. The effect of Milton's diction, however, is quite different from that of Stevens in "On the Manner of Addressing Clouds," for there is no disparity between matter and manner in Milton's poem, as there is in Stevens's. Stevens uses a seemingly grand diction for a less than grand subject, and thereby produces a mocking tone; Milton's diction, on the other hand, is commensurate with his subject. He's describing a noble, elevated dream of great dignity; and his diction, because of its formality, establishes the right tone, a tone dignified and elevated. But observe what happens in line 14. There's a shift in diction to monosyllabic, simple, Saxon words. More than anything else, this shift makes the poem memorable: waking from a visionary dream, the blind poet painfully realizes the harshness of his waking reality. His pain is communicated by the tone of the last line, a tone established by diction and dictional contrast. To be sure, while Milton's diction overall is in keeping with his subject, it is also in keeping with the preference of his age. When reading poems from past periods, we must often allow for linguistic habits different from our own, or exercise what Eliot called the "historical imagination" by taking into account the cultural background of both poet and poem.

Chaos Staggered Up the Hill

A. R. Ammons

Chaos staggered up the hill
and got the daisies dirty
that were pretty along the road:
messy chaos I said
but then in cooler mind saw   5
incipient eyes revolving in it
with possibly incipient sorrow
and had to admire how
it got along at all
in its kind of weather: 10
passing, it engulfed me
and I couldn't know dissolving
it had rhizobia with it
to make me green some other place.

(*1955*)

The contrast in diction here is between "dirty . . . pretty . . . messy" and "incipient . . . revolving . . . admire . . . engulfed . . . dissolving . . .

rhizobia." The first three are the highly connotative words of a child, and have a childish quality about them; in contrast, the six words of the second list are denotative and rather scientific, the words of an educated adult. In this shift lies the meaning of the poem. Seeing a personified Chaos staggering (how else could Chaos move?), the speaker responds initially out of some childish depth. Then his more mature self takes hold and he accepts the inevitability of the chaos of life, which at the last seems even to have design. Through diction, the poem suggests growth in its speaker from the limited awareness of the child to the more encompassing awareness of the adult. Of course, diction is not necessarily as prominent a means in other poems as it is here. We pay attention to what is marked; it is what is marked that must be felt as to effect.

In this regard, consider the word *diurnal* in the context of the second stanza of Wordsworth's "A Slumber Did My Spirit Seal":

> No motion has she now, no force;
> She neither hears nor sees;
> Rolled round in earth's diurnal course,
> With rocks, and stones, and trees.

Because of its formality in this otherwise colloquial passage, "diurnal," clearly, is marked. To my ear, the word carries an aura of grandeur or sublimity, suggesting a widening of perspective—from agonized recognition to an acceptance of mortality. Yet other readers find the word icy, as icy as the fact of death. In its diction as well as its imagery, then, the closure of the poem seems to offer at least two divergent, though not necessarily mutually exclusive, possibilities. But whatever the interpretation, the diction of "diurnal" must be taken into account.

Or take the closure of Hopkins's sonnet "To R[obert] B[ridges]." In the lines that precede, Hopkins says that he is dry, inspirationless, prosaic in frame of mind. Then he concludes:

> My winter world, that scarcely breathes that bliss
> Now, yields you, with some sighs, our explanation.

The marked words here are "our explanation." "Our" (in place of "my") is cold and official; "explanation" is dry, prosaic, bloodless. Under what circumstance would you use the word? Would you use it in a valentine?

> I love you beyond all imagination.
> Let me give you my explanation.

No, surely not. Yet for Hopkins it is the perfect word, the most poetic (powerful), though the least poetical (pretty). For it dramatically captures in its own paleness all that the poet says he has now become.

From this last example we can glean a principle: any word can be poetic if it is the right word for the purpose at hand. Some people have always felt that poets should use only certain words: pretty, flowery, "poetical" words. That's nonsense, at least to anyone who believes that poetry does or should render experience powerfully. To restrict diction is to restrict content, for to restrict diction is to limit the effects that a poem can have. To this extent, diction and content are one. Thus poets have always been particularly concerned with all matters that bear on diction.

Levels of Diction

All of us have expectations about diction, or about the propriety or decorum of word choice. Certainly, for instance, it would seem odd should the president of a college begin a commencement address with: "This guy flopped into my joint" or "A male *Homo sapiens* crossed my threshold." We also constantly guard our own diction and most often bring it into line with our immediate circumstance. We choose our words, that is, according to audience and occasion, or according to the *level of diction* appropriate at the moment.

Exercise

You've just flunked an exam. How would you express your feelings about the exam to a friend in private? How would you express yourself to your teacher? How to the dean of your school? Write a sentence for each, and compare and contrast the diction and effect of each.

There is a relationship between diction and audience/occasion, or we expect there to be a relationship. Exactly the same is true of poetry: we expect a certain diction for certain subjects. For example, we'd expect a poem on the death of John Kennedy to be rather formal in diction, elevated and austere. Should it contain slang and a sprinkling of four-letter Saxon words, we would surely be jarred and possibly even outraged by the diction and the attitude it would betray.

Often, however, poets deliberately violate our expectations to achieve an effect—irony, perhaps, or pathos. To see what the poet is doing, we must always judge diction against matter. Take the following lines from Alexander Pope's "The Rape of the Lock" (1714):

> Not with more glories, in the ethereal plain,
> The sun first rises o'er the purpled main,
> Than, issuing forth, the rival of his beams
> Launched on the bosom of the silver Thames.

> Fair nymphs and well-dressed youths around her shone,
> But every eye was fixed on her alone.
>
>   . . .
>
> If to her share some female errors fall,
> Look on her face, and you'll forget 'em all.

Matter and manner here are not in accord. Pope is merely describing a boat ride taken by a pretty, empty-headed young woman named Belinda. The grandeur of the diction hardly matches the triviality of the event. Why? Because the passage is tongue in cheek. Given that Pope was a poet who knew exactly what he was doing with words, the mismatch is our clue to an ironic intent. There are other clues as well. The phrases "ethereal plain," "purpled main," and "silver Thames" are too grand for the occasion and yet they are also terribly trite. Pope would never have used them except for the purposes of irony. Then, the mundane epithet "well-dressed" seems completely out of keeping with the diction of the four preceding lines. The shift in diction is jarring. Most important is what happens in the last two lines quoted. The descent into a diction close to slang—"you'll forget 'em all"—undercuts any possibility of a nonironic intent on Pope's part and underscores that the passage as a whole is mocking in tone.[1]

If some of this seems too subtle, take heart: the more you read, the more obvious these effects will become. Granted, we must read with care and pay attention to the language of a poem. But what the poet would have us do is nothing more than we do automatically every time we speak or listen to someone else speaking. The poet simply asks us to be a little more conscious of the language than we normally are. At each turn, poets ask themselves, "Why this word rather than that or the other?" So must readers. Part of living through a poem is asking this question. The following exercise should help you as reader to weigh words with greater deliberation and thus help prepare you for the second poem assignment.

Exercise

Go back to Milton's "Methought I Saw" (p. 57). Find more colloquial— even slangy—words for: "espousèd" (line 1), "vested" (line 9), and "embrace me she inclined" (line 13—e.g., "bent down to hug me"). Find (1) more formal and (2) slang equivalents for: "fled" and "night" (line 14). Now read the poem with your various substitutes in mind. Weigh each as to effect, and judge each against the words Milton chose.

---

1 Notice that I have not been dealing with the poet's intent directly, but rather with intent as implied by the givens of the text—by its mismatch of diction and occasion, and the effects of its marked shifts in diction.

POEM ASSIGNMENT

Write a poem of, say, six to eight lines spoken by a speaker *not* yourself. Put your speaker in a situation, perhaps, as Frost does his in "Stopping by Woods." You might also have him/her address someone else (look again at "To His Coy Mistress" and "My Last Duchess"). Remember that your primary object will be to reveal the nature of your speaker. Once more, watch your line treatment as you now apply what we've said about voice, tone, and diction, and give your poem a title.

Before you begin, look over the following student samples. Work into the poems and take them as models when you write your poem.

POEMS FOR FURTHER STUDY

Of Three Minds

John Farina

That is such a pesty weed
  (Very difficult to get its root out);
My lawn should look much better without it.
    . . .
There is Taraxacum Officinale,
  With its jagged lobed leaves;   5
Its long taproot grows deep.
    . . .
What yellow flowers,
What toothy leaves!
You are welcome, dandy lion, to stay.

Questions
1. Contrast the diction of each stanza.
2. Characterize the voice of each.
3. Who speaks each?

The Machine

Stephen Maher

Let 'em off,
keep it moving,
watch the closing doors . . .
next stop Bleeker.

Can't ya see the sign, lady?   5
"Please Keep Hands Off Doors."
People like you
Screw everything up.

Questions
1. What kind of diction is marked here?
2. What tone results from the poem's diction?
3. What effect does line treatment have?
4. Characterize the speaker with respect to the voice created by the poem.

Lily's Lament

Frank Scheller

Buzzing, buzzing of his eminent approach
   Toward my pristine goblet.
I run with the wind from him,
   To and fro I go
   Trying to get free.   5
To no avail! He persists
   To rape my sweet honey.

Questions
1. What is the situation of the poem? Who speaks it?
2. The image of a "pristine goblet" says much. What? (For example, what sex can we impute to the speaker?)
3. Consider the diction of the piece. What is its effect given the poem's situation and speaker?

Opening Night

Elaine Kauschinger

At the moment, your world is flooded with the gaze of amazed eyes;
You command your audience with bursts of trivia.
You, with sudden unannounced explosions of attentiveness, are
    expectingly appeased
By multitudes of swaying, servantile arms.
Patience—I will wait until I reign again.

Questions

1. What is the situation of the poem? To whom are the speaker's thoughts addressed?
2. What might be the profession of the speaker? What does the word *reign* imply?
3. Here there is a concentration of certain sounds: sibilants (*s, z*), dentals (*d, t*), plosives (*p, b*), and the low-frequency vowel *u* (as in *"flooded"* and *"amazed"*). What effect on tone does this concentration have?
4. "Servantile" is what Lewis Carroll called a "portmanteau word"—a coinage made by a fusion of two or more words into which much connotative meaning is packed. What meanings does the word suggest? That the speaker should have to coin a word suggests something, too. What?

IDEAS FOR WRITING

1.

Naming of Parts

Henry Reed

Today we have naming of parts. Yesterday,
We had daily cleaning. And tomorrow morning,
We shall have what to do after firing. But today,
Today we have naming of parts. Japonica
Glistens like coral in all of the neighboring gardens,   5
   And today we have naming of parts.

This is the lower sling swivel. And this
Is the upper sling swivel, whose use you will see,
When you are given your slings. And this is the piling swivel,
Which in your case you have not got. The branches   10
Hold in the gardens their silent, eloquent gestures,
   Which in our case we have not got.

This is the safety-catch, which is always released
With an easy flick of the thumb. And please do not let me
See anyone using his finger. You can do it quite easy   15
If you have any strength in your thumb. The blossoms
Are fragile and motionless, never letting anyone see
   Any of them using their finger.

And this you can see is the bolt. The purpose of this
Is to open the breech, as you see. We can slide it   20

Voice, Tone, Diction

Rapidly backwards and forwards: we call this
Easing the spring. And rapidly backwards and forwards
The early bees are assaulting and fumbling the flowers:
   They call it easing the Spring.

They call it easing the Spring: it is perfectly easy   25
If you have any strength in your thumb: like the bolt,
And the breech, and the cocking-piece, and the point of balance,
Which in our case we have not got; and the almond-blossom
Silent in all of the gardens and the bees going backwards and
    forwards,
   For today we have naming of parts.   30
                      (1946)

There are two distinct voices in Reed's "Naming of Parts," one of a drill instructor, the other of a green recruit. Decide where the first ends and the second begins in each stanza. Now discuss the tonal differences between the two voices and how these differences are established. (Consider abruptness of movement as opposed to smoothness; end-stopping as opposed to enjambment; marked shifts in diction.) In a separate paragraph, discuss your response to this poem and the reasons why you so respond.

2. Diction is an aspect of every human utterance, of speech as well as of writing, of prose as well as of poetry. Though diction may be more pointed in poetry than in prose, the prose writer as much as the poet is aware of diction and its effects. Take a passage from this book, specify the passage you've chosen, and analyze its diction and tone.

3.

To a Friend Whose Work Has Come to Triumph

Anne Sexton

Consider Icarus, pasting those sticky wings on,
testing that strange little tug at his shoulder blade,
and think of that first flawless moment over the lawn
of the labyrinth. Think of the difference it made!
There below are the trees, as awkward as camels;   5
and here are the shocked starlings pumping past
and think of innocent Icarus who is doing quite well:
larger than a sail, over the fog and the blast
of the plushy ocean, he goes. Admire his wings!
Feel the fire at his neck and see how casually   10

he glances up and is caught, wondrously tunneling
into that hot eye. Who cares that he fell back to the sea?
See him acclaiming the sun and come plunging down
while his sensible daddy goes straight into town.

(*1962*)

TO A FRIEND.   Compare this poem with Yeats's "To a Friend Whose Work
Has Come to Nothing" (page 329). 1. *Icarus:* A figure in Greek mythology,
Icarus is the son of Daedalus, who fashioned two pairs of wings out of
feathers and wax. Daedalus warned his son not to fly too high (too close to
the sun); but Icarus failed to heed the warning, so his wings melted and he
plunged into the sea. 4. *labyrinth:* Daedalus also engineered the great laby-
rinth of Crete. Ironically, both he and his son were subsequently imprisoned
in it, the only way out being up (thus the invention of the wings).

There is a marked shift in diction between lines 13 and 14 in Sexton's
poem. Discuss the tone of the poem regarding Icarus and the shift in
tone, related to a shift in focus, that the diction of the last line
suggests.

4.

from **The Dream Songs**

John Berryman

I

Huffy Henry hid   the day,
unappeasable Henry sulked.
I see his point,—a trying to put things over.
It was the thought that they thought
they could *do* it made Henry wicked & away.   5
But he should have come out and talked.

All the world like a woolen lover
once did seem on Henry's side.
Then came a departure.
Thereafter nothing fell out as it might or ought.   10
I don't see how Henry, pried
open for all the world to see, survived.

What he has now to say is a long
wonder the world can bear & be.
Once in a sycamore I was glad   15
all at the top, and I sang.
Hard on the land wears the strong sea
and empty grows every bed.

(*1964*)

from THE DREAM SONGS. 5. *do it:* comfort Henry. "They" seem to be relatives and friends gathered for the funeral of the one who has departed (line 9). 9. *departure:* "Henry" is an imagined figure, the main persona of *The Dream Songs.* Still, the "departure" here suggests a departure that greatly affected Berryman's life: the suicide of his father.

Phrasing, which involves grammar and syntax (the ordering of words in a sentence), affects voice and tone as much as anything else. Comment on the oddities of Berryman's phrasing. What qualities of voice do these oddities help establish?

5.

Dolor

Theodore Roethke

I have known the inexorable sadness of pencils,
Neat in their boxes, dolor of pad and paper-weight,
All the misery of manilla folders and mucilage,
Desolation in immaculate public places,
Lonely reception room, lavatory, switchboard,   5
The unalterable pathos of basin and pitcher,
Ritual of multigraph, paper-clip, comma,
Endless duplication of lives and objects.
And I have seen dust from the walls of institutions,
Finer than flour, alive, more dangerous than silica,   10
Sift, almost invisible, through long afternoons of tedium,
Dropping a fine film on nails and delicate eyebrows,
Glazing the pale hair, the duplicate gray standard faces.

(1948)

DOLOR. *Dolor* means "sadness," with perhaps a pun on "dollar."

The diction of this poem is abstract and concrete in turn, formal and colloquial, connotative and denotative. Which words are which? Draw up three double-columned lists of the poem's main words labeled according to the pairs just suggested. Then, in a few sentences, describe the effect of this mixture. Does it raise the mundane to the tragic, or drag down the tragic to the mundane? Or both?

6. Analyze the diction and tone of your own poem written for the second poem assignment. What effects were you trying to achieve and how were you trying to achieve them? Read your poem aloud. Does it achieve what you had in mind? Discuss.

7.

The World Is Too Much with Us

William Wordsworth

The world is too much with us; late and soon,
Getting and spending, we lay waste our powers;
Little we see in Nature that is ours;
We have given our hearts away, a sordid boon!
This Sea that bares her bosom to the moon,   5
The winds that will be howling at all hours,
And are up-gathered now like sleeping flowers,
For this, for everything, we are out of tune;
It moves us not.—Great God! I'd rather be
A Pagan suckled in a creed outworn;   10
So might I, standing on this pleasant lea,
Have glimpses that would make me less forlorn;
Have sight of Proteus rising from the sea;
Or hear old Triton blow his wreathèd horn.

(1807)

THE WORLD IS TOO MUCH WITH US.   5. *This:* The use of the demonstrative
adjective suggests that Wordsworth means us to visualize his speaker as
standing on a "lea" and pointing to sea and sky. 13. *Proteus:* In Greek
mythology, Proteus is a sea god who can change his shape at will, and so a
figure of the vitality of natural process. 14. *Triton:* With his conch-shell
trumpet, Triton is the messenger of Poseidon, chief god of the sea and a
symbol of life because of his domain—water.

Why the word "pleasant"? Consider in what context you would use
the word; then discuss the dictional qualities of the word and the
effect of those qualities on meaning. ("I'd rather be" means that "I
am not and thus cannot . . . ," and "less forlorn" means that the
speaker is forlorn.) In a separate paragraph, discuss your response to
the poem and why you respond as you do.

Figurative Language
Chapter Four

THE LITERAL AND THE FIGURATIVE

When speaking of imagery (Chapter 2) and of diction (Chapter 3), I distinguished in passing between literal and figurative uses and types of words. As we approach the subject of figurative language, we need to consider the distinction more closely.

A **literal** statement means what it means "to the letter" ("literal" comes from the Latin for "letter"), whereas a **figurative** statement ("figurative" means "given form to") would be absurd if interpreted to the letter. "It's time to get to work" is literal; "It's time to get hopping" is figurative. Let's pursue the distinction by the (figurative) route of a few more examples.

Take the grade-school motto "Clean Hands, Clean Heart, Clean Mind." "Clean Hands" is literal: one *can* literally scrub one's hands, and the phrase means nothing other than that one *should* scrub one's hands. "Clean Heart, Clean Mind," on the other hand, is figurative. One cannot literally scrub either one, and both phrases mean other than what they literally suggest: "Clean Mind," for example, means that one should not entertain "dirty" thoughts.

My two-year-old son says, "[I want] nuts." My wife, annoyed, says, "You're driving me nuts." Annoyed by my wife's annoyance, I say to her, "Nuts to you"; to my son, I say, "Here are some nuts." This hypothetical dialogue moves from the literal to the figurative and back from the figurative to the literal.

What is literal and what figurative in the following poem by Robert Frost?

Fire and Ice

Some say the world will end in fire,
Some say in ice.
From what I've tasted of desire
I hold with those who favor fire.
But if it had to perish twice,   5
I think I know enough of hate
To say that for destruction ice
Is also great
And would suffice.

(1923)

There's an easy commerce here between the literal and the figurative; clearly, "fire" and "ice" are at first literal and then, associated with "desire" and "hate," figurative. (Note how the figures *give form to* what is intangible.)

This brings us to another principle: the distinction between the literal and the figurative is usually a matter of context. A hunter who returns home after a hunting trip and says that his "dogs are tired" is probably speaking literally; when a policeman returns home after a hard day on the (figurative) beat and says the same thing, he is speaking figuratively.

By the same (figurative) token, to say that a prisoner about to be shot is "on the firing line" is painfully (to the prisoner) literal; when a talk-show host speaks of a guest the same way, he is speaking figuratively.

SOME TYPES OF FIGURATION

Any meaningful statement that is not literal is, necessarily, figurative. Marvell's "Time's wingèd chariot" and "Deserts of vast eternity," for instance, cannot be literal, since, though it flies, time does not really drive a chariot, and eternity is a measure of time, whereas deserts are geographical places. Therefore, the phrases are figurative and must be interpreted accordingly. There are a number of types of figuration, known as *figures of speech*. You're probably familiar with most figures of speech (though you may not know their names), since they occur frequently in speech as well as writing.

Personification

We speak of cancer as a "killer" and of justice as "blind," and we invoke the "long arm of the law." We say bears "hug," a storm "rages," and spring "promises." All these phrases are figurative, and the figure in each instance is **personification**—a figure of speech in which a human quality, motive, or capacity is attributed to an abstraction, an inanimate object, an animal, or whatever.

Cancer is not literally a "killer"; it is a disease that "strikes" (figuratively) without motive. The statement "cancer is a killer," therefore, is not a statement of fact, but a figure of speech meant to communicate feeling—our feeling about the disease. Like all figures, it gives form to what is formless (feeling).

Now look at a sonnet by Sir Philip Sidney addressed to sleep and pick out instances of personification. What human qualities are attributed to the nonhuman agents of the poem? What feelings on the part of the speaker are thereby expressed?

from **Astrophel and Stella**

39

Come sleep! Oh sleep, the certain knot of peace,
The baiting place of wit, the balm of woe,
The poor man's wealth, the prisoner's release,
The indifferent judge between the high and low;
With shield of proof shield me from out the prease   5

Figurative Language

Of those fierce darts Despair at me doth throw;
Oh make in me those civil wars to cease;
I will good tribute pay, if thou do so.
Take thou of me smooth pillows, sweetest bed,
A chamber deaf to noise and blind to light,   10
A rosy garland and a weary head;
And if these things, as being thine by right,
Move not thy heavy grace, thou shalt in me,
Livelier than elsewhere, Stella's image see.

(1591)

from ASTROPHEL AND STELLA. 2. *baiting place:* feeding or resting place, and
perhaps also the place (or time) where the barb of "wit" is baited. 5. *of
proof:* of proven strength; *prease:* crowd. 14. *Stella:* the speaker's beloved,
who is the cause of his sleeplessness.

Hyperbole and Understatement

Hyperbole, or exaggeration, and its opposite—**understatement**—are fig-
ures of speech in that neither is intended to be taken literally. "I won the
race by a mile," you may say. If you did in fact win by a mile, your state-
ment is literal. But if, as is usually the case, you won by only a few yards,
your statement is figurative, meant to communicate feeling rather than
fact. (A lie, incidentally, is not an example of hyperbole, since it is meant
to be taken as fact.) In literature, as in life, hyperbole can serve various
ends. It can contribute to an ironic tone, as it does in the first section of
Marvell's "To His Coy Mistress" (Chapter 3); or it can suggest the magni-
tude of a speaker's feeling, as in Sidney's "prease [crowd]/Of . . . fierce
darts" (lines 5–6) and Lady Macbeth's mournful "Here's the smell of the
blood still: all the perfumes of Arabia will not sweeten this little hand."

If you say, "I won the race by a nose," when actually you won by two
feet, you are again speaking figuratively, and again you mean to com-
municate feeling rather than fact. Now, however, your figure of speech
is understatement, which also has a variety of possible effects. Under-
statement is often ironic, as the following sentence from Swift's *A Tale
of a Tub* attests: "Last week I saw a woman flayed, and you will hardly
believe how much it altered her person for the worse." Understatement
can also serve to give a statement the ring of sincerity and to arouse a
sense of pathos. Such is the effect of the following lines from Wordsworth's
poem "Michael": "many and many a day he thither went/And never lifted
up a single stone." Michael and his son had begun building a sheepfold
out of stone when the son was young; at the end of the poem, the son has
departed, the sheepfold remains unfinished, and Michael is old and broken-
hearted. Wordsworth could have had him rave and rant; how much more
effective, however, is the bare, understated second line above.

Synesthesia
Synesthesia is another common figure of speech. The term refers to speaking of one sensation in terms of another, or speaking of something in terms of a sensory mode not actually appropriate to it. A classic example is the phrase *the blues:* music is sound, not color; and sound affects the ears, not the eyes. Because "sweet" is a word literally appropriate to the sensation of taste, "sweetest bed" (Sir Philip Sidney) is also synesthetic. To be sure, the bed could smell sweet, yet the application of the word *sweet* to smell is itself synesthetic. Indeed, language is marked by thousands of examples of synesthesia: for example, a cool green, a hot red, a dull orange; a loud jacket, a quiet tie; a hard word, a soft job; a light rosé, a hefty Burgundy, a dry martini. At times, it seems, we can speak of one sense only in terms of another.

Exercise

Make a list of ten more such turns of phrase, and in each case identify the sensory mode literally appropriate to the noun and the sensory mode evoked by the adjective. Label each noun and adjective accordingly. Next, pick out the synesthetic figures in the following lines by Keats. What effect does Keats achieve by means of these figures?

> O, for a draught of vintage! that hath been
>   Cooled a long age in the deep-delvèd earth,
> Tasting of Flora and the country green,
>   Dance, and Provençal song, and sunburnt mirth!
> O for a beaker full of the warm South,
>
>   . . . .

Metonymy and Synecdoche
As common as synesthesia are the two related figures of speech called **metonymy** and **synecdoche**.

   Metonymy refers to calling a thing by the name of something else with which it is closely associated. For example, "the White House" is used to mean "the President," a male athlete is called a "jock," and someone from Texas may be known as "Tex." "Bluegrass music" and "Little Red Riding Hood" are also examples of metonymy.

   Synecdoche refers to calling a thing by the name of one of its parts or attributes. For example, workmen are called "hands," a dog a "bow-wow," and a car "wheels." Consider also "Goldilocks" and the nickname "Smiley."

Exercise

Draw up a list of five common metonymies and five common synecdoches. Then identify the metonymies and synecdoches in the following lines from T. S. Eliot's "The Lovesong of J. Alfred Prufrock," a poem in which Eliot makes extensive use of both figures. (You might also read the poem, on pages 423–427 in the Anthology, and consider the effect of these figures in the context of the poem.)

> The muttering retreats
> Of restless nights in one-night cheap hotels
> And sawdust restaurants with oyster shells; (lines 5–7)
>   . . . .
> To prepare a face to meet the faces that you meet; (line 27)
>   . . . .
> The eyes that fix you in a formulated phrase, (line 56)
>   . . . .
> I should have been a pair of ragged claws, (line 73)

In literature, these related figures are both prime tools for particularizing the general, or speaking of a class of things (the abstract) in terms of one of its members (always concrete). For example, Shakespeare's kings usually refer to themselves and their power, or the power of the state (an abstraction), as "the Crown." This metonymous figure gives form to the intangible (power). The same function is served by the synecdoches in Yeats's poem "The Dolls." Read the poem, identify its synecdoches, and decide what they serve to embody.

The Dolls

W. B. Yeats

> A doll in the doll-maker's house
> Looks at the cradle and bawls:
> 'That is an insult to us.'
> But the oldest of all the dolls,
> Who had seen, being kept for show,   5
> Generations of his sort,
> Out-screams the whole shelf: 'Although
> There's not a man can report
> Evil of this place,
> The man and the woman bring   10
> Hither, to our disgrace,

A noisy and filthy thing.'
Hearing him groan and stretch
The doll-maker's wife is aware
Her husband has heard the wretch,   15
And crouched by the arm of his chair,
She murmurs into his ear,
Head upon shoulder leant:
'My dear, my dear, O dear,
It was an accident.'   20

(1914)

Yeats's dolls are figurative—both a personification and a synecdoche. The personification is clear. But in what way is the image a synecdoche: what is the whole of which the dolls are a part and for which they stand? In that dollmaking is a handicraft and dolls are artifacts, the general class of things to which dolls belong is Art. By asking us to generalize (if we did not generalize in this way, the poem would simply have no meaning), "The Dolls" establishes a contrast between Art and Life—of which the implied baby (implied by the metonymy "cradle") is a synecdoche—and, further, between the ideal and the real.

What does Yeats want us to understand about the polarities figured (given form) in the poem? Though based on life, as dolls are modeled on babies, art is ordered, potentially perfectible, seemingly permanent, and above all consciously willed and controlled by human purpose—a doll under the doll-maker's hand. In contrast, life (the baby) is "noisy and filthy," flawed, impermanent, and always an "accident" (because we cannot choose our children's attributes or our own, as the doll-maker, a type of artist, can choose those of the dolls he makes). These differences are concretized by and explored through the poem's synecdoches.

Its synecdoches have a further purpose as well. Why dolls? One reason, certainly, is that dolls are modeled on babies. So Yeats's personified image (the dolls) lends irony to the poem and underscores the paradoxical nature of the relationship between life and art. Still, dolls are hardly the most significant of human artifacts. And no sane human being would consider a doll of greater value than a baby. Yeats's *chosen* images not only concretize the abstractions Art and Life, then, but also embody and direct attitude and feeling. They imply that whatever the circumscribing limitations of life, its dynamism—as opposed to any static perfection we can imagine—is the ground of all value. Human beings have often preferred their imagined heavens to the necessities of reality. In "The Dolls," though with some ambivalence, Yeats opts for life; he would have us "choose necessity," as he wrote in another context. But the power of the poem lies in its figuration. Abstractions are fleeting; concretions remain in their solidity to haunt the mind.

METAPHOR (THE PRIME FIGURE)

We have thus far discussed seven types of figure, six in this chapter. Imagery, too, as we discussed in Chapter 2, is figurative when used to embody feeling. Images also play a part in many of the other figures of speech, as we have just witnessed in "The Dolls." Specifically, images are the stuff of which metaphors are typically constructed. Take, for example, Marvell's "Deserts of vast eternity." "Deserts" is an image meant to evoke feeling; all its associations (dryness, sterility, fear) are to be carried over to the abstraction "eternity," which is defined and concretized by the analogy. "Analogy" is the operative word: metaphor always involves analogy. A **metaphor**, then, is any figurative construction that entails an analogy— whether explicit or implicit—between two terms.

The object of metaphor, and metaphor making, is definition: definition of something *in terms of* something else. The term metaphor derives from a Greek word meaning "to transfer" or "carry over," which is exactly what every metaphor asks us to do: to transfer meaning from one term (the **vehicle**) to the other (the **tenor**). The vehicle, like all vehicles, carries something—specifically, a load of meaning. But the tenor, like the tenor in an opera, holds the dominant part in that the vehicle serves only to define the tenor. With "Deserts of vast eternity," for instance, our response to "Deserts" is transferred to "eternity."

We could diagram the metaphor thus:

Eternity : Tenor
↑ *Deserts* : Vehicle

The arrow indicates the starting-point and the direction of interest. By feeling out the associations of the vehicle (usually a known entity and a concretion), we grasp what is being said about the tenor (usually an unknown and/or an abstraction). Like a match put to a stick of dynamite, the terms of a metaphor come together and explode into meaning (to draw on Samuel Johnson, who called metaphor an "explosion").

Exercise

Collect a handful of clearly metaphorical turns of phrase (for our purposes, ten is a handful) and write them down. You shouldn't have to look very far. Any sports page is loaded with metaphors; and popular songs are a mine: "You are the sunshine of my life"; "C'mon baby, light my fire"; "Life is a cabaret"; "Let's all get stoned." In choosing your examples, remember to distinguish between the literal and the figurative: "Life is a cabaret" is figurative (metaphorical); "Murder is a crime" is not.

I call metaphor the prime figure because of its pervasiveness. One could even make a case that all figures are metaphorical, since language itself, as we'll see shortly, is essentially metaphorical. Of all linguistic phenomena, metaphor (along with rhythm) lies nearest to the heart of poetry. Indeed, poems frequently have their genesis in metaphor. As often as not, poets start with a single metaphor; in exploring it, they begin to explore themselves and what they have to say.

Metaphor is our prime way of putting feeling into words. "How does it feel?" we ask. "It feels like . . . ," we answer. Feeling has no form, but only by giving it form can we hope to express it. So we almost always use metaphor when under the pressure of strong feeling: "you leech, you devil, you scum"; "my sweetheart, my angel, my dreamboat." But metaphor is not only a way of speaking; it is also a way of thinking and of knowing, as Aristotle suggests in *The Rhetoric*: ". . . midway between the unintelligible and the commonplace, it is metaphor that most produces knowledge." When the steam engine came on the scene, for example, someone coined the metaphor "horsepower." That coinage was an act of knowing. We can witness another such act in the following poem.

from **Out of Our Blue**

John Fandel

A cloverleaf
where the long-stemmed violets
used to be . . .

Under the willows,
they were a blue lake   5
we waded in,
the ripples the willow turned light to,
the waters of the violets.

How cool
to dip into the green   10
current of leaves,
to bring up
five petals of water
from the blue blue lake.

(1977)

from OUT OF OUR BLUE. Like all the poems in *Out of Our Blue,* this poem is untitled. 5. *they:* the violets. 6–7. I.e., "We waded in light turned into ripples by the willows."

Language is our tool for knowing. But language is always tending to lose its edge; and when it does, it gives us merely the illusion of knowing —because words then lack the authenticity of experience. The creation of new metaphors gives knowledge because it makes us see anew. That's what happens in the cloverleaf poem. The speaker sees anew a moment in spring, and by seeing it freshly makes it his own. The poem begins matter-of-factly, in the language of observation, not of knowledge. Then, as memory intervenes (this kind of seeing is usually a matter of hindsight), metaphor forms and brings with it that sense of firsthandedness that is the mark of genuine knowledge. "The waters of the violets"—yes, a patch of violets in spring *is* like a lake. Suddenly, wires cross, sparking recognition. By experiencing the metaphor on which the poem is built, the reader, too, is made to see anew.

METAPHOR, THE EVOLUTION OF LANGUAGE, AND THE SELF

We can go further: metaphor is the primary way of knowing because language formation is essentially a matter of metaphor-making. The abundance of **dead metaphor** in the language (any metaphorical phrase that has been used so often that it seems literal) suggests as much. Think of all of the common metaphors (so common as to have become labels) drawn from the human body: *head* of state, of a table, of steam; *face* of a clock; *eye* of a needle or a storm; *lip* of a cup; *teeth* of a comb and *tongue* of a shoe; *leg* of a chair or a journey; *foot* of a bed or a mountain; *heart* of the matter; and so on and on.

That metaphor is the spring of language is also revealed by **etymology** (the study of the origins and historical development of words). Although we know comparatively little about how language began, we do know that it became an affair of metaphor-making early in its evolution. We know as well that language development and metaphor-making are in a chicken-egg relationship with man's evolving knowledge—that is, knowledge is advanced mainly by the discovery of new metaphors. As one astute student of these matters observes:

It is by metaphor that language grows. The common reply to the question "what is it?" is, when the reply is difficult or the experience unique, "well, it is like——." In laboratory studies, both children and adults describing nonsense objects [(tenors)] . . . to others who cannot see them use [vehicles] . . . that with repetition become contracted into labels. This is the major way in which the vocabulary of language is formed. The grand and vigorous function of metaphor is the generation of new language as it is needed. . . .

A random glance at the etymologies of common words in a dictionary will demonstrate this assertion.[1]

Exercise

Duplicate the laboratory experiment described above by attempting, perhaps with some friends, to describe a nonsense object, such as a piece of twisted wire stuck in a glob of plaster. As long as you don't settle for calling it "twisted wire in a glob of plaster," you will find that you cannot proceed except by way of metaphor.

You might also glance through a good dictionary to check Jaynes's (and my) assertion that most words are metaphorical in terms of their etymologies.

The examples are legion. In fact, almost every word, no matter how abstract in current usage or ostensibly literal, originated in the physical and came to mean what it now means by a gradual process of metaphorical adaptation and extension. Remember, for example, the physical basis of the word *abstraction*: "to remove from." And the word *literal* itself is metaphorical in that it derives from the Latin *littera* ("letter"). Etymologies are genuinely poetic. I'd even go so far as to say that every word, understood fully, is a poem in miniature. In other words, poetry is the spring of language.

Consider the words we commonly use to express both thought and emotion. All are metaphors, many drawn from the body and the senses: "I *feel* happy"; "I *sense* that you are feeling *overburdened*"; "I *see* your *point*" (seeing in this sense is related to "insight," "foresight," "hindsight," and "oversight"); I am *touched* and *moved* by your kindness"; "It's right on the *tip of my tongue*"; "My *taste* is as good as anybody's"; "You *hurt* my feelings"; "I feel *torn apart* and *pulled in all directions*"; "I am *wounded* by those *biting* words that you spoke off the *top of your head*." Thus Jaynes says: "Every conscious thought that you [have]... can ... be traced back to concrete actions in a concrete world." [2]

Consciousness, in other words, is tied to language and its slow accretion of metaphors. Without language, we might still feel and think and know, but we could not think about thought or know that we know or feel that we feel. We "come to consciousness" only through the acquisition of language and its metaphors. To the extent that metaphor-making is poetry, therefore, poetry is indeed the source of language and in turn of self, which is the creation of language and its metaphors.

[1] Julian Jaynes, *The Origin of Consciousness in the Breakdown of the Bicameral Mind* (Boston: Houghton Mifflin, 1977), p. 49.

[2] Ibid., p. 61.

TYPES OF METAPHOR

Given our working definition of metaphor, many of the phrases characterized above as metaphorical might seem problematic. Though clearly figurative (words, for example, are not literally "biting"), most do not involve analogy directly. We need to return to the definition, therefore, both to consolidate what has been said thus far and to explore the subject further. Again, a metaphor is a figurative construction that entails an analogy—whether explicit or implicit—between two terms (tenor and vehicle). Broadly speaking, then, there are two types of metaphor: **explicit** and **implicit**.

Explicit Metaphor and Simile

A metaphor is explicit if both tenor and vehicle are expressed: "*Deserts* of vast *eternity*"; Stevie Wonder's "*You* are the *sunshine* of my life"; "*mother* *nature.*" In each case, expressed tenors ("eternity," "you," "nature") are defined by expressed vehicles ("Deserts," "sunshine," "mother"). As always, we must distinguish between the literal and the figurative; many similar phrases are not figurative and thus not metaphorical: "Deserts of sand"; "You are my girlfriend"; "mother McCree."

A **simile** is an explicit metaphor made logical by the introduction of "as" or "like" or sometimes the suffix -*y* (for example, "a piggy little boy").[3] To say "My love is like a red, red rose" is to say "I observe several points of similarity between a red rose and my love." There's nothing at odds with logic here, whereas the statement "My love is a red, red rose" is, strictly speaking, nonlogical. Because "as" and "like" can be used in literal as well as figurative constructions (such as, "Every house on this street is like every other house"), we must once again be careful to distinguish between the literal and the figurative.

As long as we make this crucial distinction, explicit metaphors are usually easy enough to recognize. Once recognized, however, they require some living with and living through: we must actively feel out the associations of a given vehicle and then carry over the relevant associations (relevance is determined by context) to the tenor. Hamlet's "a sea of troubles," for instance, asks us to feel in the vehicle "sea" immensity and fearsomeness (not the pleasures of a seaside vacation) and to transfer these relevant associations to the tenor "troubles." The following poem is rich in explicit metaphor. Read it through with an eye to its metaphors. Pick

---

[3] "Made logical by"—this is, no doubt, the reason why the simile was the dominant figurative mode of the eighteenth century (commonly called "The Age of Reason"). I am speaking not of occasional use, but of a characteristic preference (of prose writers as well as poets). Given that the simile is the most logical of figures, the preference of eighteenth-century writers for it attests to, as it derives from, the broader values of the period as a whole. This point illustrates a fundamental principle of poetry: figures of speech are not mere ornaments; they are modes of feeling and thinking and being.

out a few and identify the vehicle and tenor of each. Be aware, too, that the poem turns on one prime metaphor of some complexity. What is it? What is the vehicle and what the tenor? Live with the vehicle for awhile, letting its associations expand as they will. Then carry over the relevant associations to the tenor. By way of its prime metaphor, the poem probes, explores, and crystallizes its strikingly prophetic theme. The way into the poem is through that metaphor.

The Purse-Seine

Robinson Jeffers

Our sardine fishermen work at night in the dark of the moon; day-
    light or moonlight
They could not tell where to spread the net, unable to see the phos-
    phorescence of the shoals of fish.
They work northward from Monterey, coasting Santa Cruz; off New
    Year's Point or off Pigeon Point
The look-out man will see some lakes of milk-color light on the sea's
    night-purple; he points, and the helmsman
Turns the dark prow, the motorboat circles the gleaming shoal and
    drifts out her seine-net. They close the circle   5
And purse the bottom of the net, then with great labor haul it in.

                        I cannot tell you
How beautiful the scene is, and a little terrible, then, when the
    crowded fish
Know they are caught, and wildly beat from one wall to the other of
    their closing destiny the phosphorescent
Water to a pool of flame, each beautiful slender body sheeted with
    flame, like a live rocket   10
A comet's tail wake of clear yellow flame; while outside the nar-
    rowing
Floats and cordage of the net great sea-lions come up to watch,
    sighing in the dark; the vast walls of night
Stand erect to the stars.

             Lately I was looking from a night mountain-top
On a wide city, the colored splendor, galaxies of light: how could I
    help but recall the seine-net   15
Gathering the luminous fish? I cannot tell you how beautiful the
    city appeared, and a little terrible.

I thought, We have geared the machines and locked all together into
    interdependence; we have built the great cities; now
There is no escape. We have gathered vast populations incapable of
    free survival, insulated
From the strong earth, each person in himself helpless, on all depen-
    dent. The circle is closed, and the net
Is being hauled in. They hardly feel the cords drawing, yet they
    shine already. The inevitable mass-disasters   20
Will not come in our time nor in our children's, but we and our
    children
Must watch the net draw narrower, government take all powers—or
    revolution, and the new government
Take more than all, add to kept bodies kept souls—or anarchy, the
    mass-disasters.

                These things are Progress;
Do you marvel our verse is troubled or frowning, while it keeps its
    reason? Or it lets go, lets the mood flow   25
In the manner of the recent young men into mere hysteria, splin-
    tered gleams, crackled laughter. But they are quite wrong.
There is no reason for amazement: surely one always knew that cul-
    tures decay, and life's end is death.

                                      (1937)

THE PURSE-SEINE. A purse-seine is a fish net shaped like a bag. 2. *unable to
see:* [if] unable to see. 3. places in California.

The first half of the poem (lines 1–13) is ostensibly descriptive. In long
yet supple lines, Jeffers presents a sweeping panorama—the lines them-
selves seem sweeping—of sea, ships, fishermen, and phosphorescent shoals
of fish. He cannot simply tell us his response to the scene, however ("How
beautiful the scene is, and a little terrible"): feeling must be fleshed out
to be communicated. So, like all of us at moments of true feeling, he
shifts into metaphor. The water becomes "a pool of flame, each beautiful
slender body sheeted with flame"; and the flame in turn becomes "a live
rocket," and then immediately "A comet's tail" against "the vast walls of
night." Thus we are made to see the splendor of the scene and also to
feel the terror of the thrashing fish. We are made to feel the walls of net
closing in.
    The second half of the poem also presents us with a double perspective
arising from the conjunction of beauty and terror. The scene shifts: the
poet is looking at the panorama of a "wide city" with its "galaxies of
light." Meditating, he makes a pivotal connection: "how could I help

but recall the seine-net (line 15). This is the prime metaphor of the poem, from which its second half flows: the city is a net; its lights, the phosphorescence of the fish; its crowds, the "crowded fish" (line 8), encircled and being drawn in. Again, the poet says that he cannot simply tell us how beautiful and terrible the scene is. In so saying, he underscores the function of his dominant metaphor. The whole first section of the poem is vehicle; the second section, tenor: the function of the analogy is to make us see and feel the beauty and plight of the people as we have seen and felt the beauty and terror of the fish. The city, which comes to symbolize industrial culture generally, is indeed beautiful, its lights shimmering like the phosphorescence of the shoals of fish. Yet it is this very phosphorescence that enables the fishermen to net the fish (line 2). However beautiful, the lights of the city will lead us also to doom. By insulating us and making us passive and incapable, our culture is a net walling us in, the ropes pulled by forces as mysterious to us as the fishermen are to the helpless fish. The last lines of the poem, which form a kind of coda, fan out to suggest the inevitability of this process, which the poet accepts with stoic calm.

The poem's metaphorical critique of the industrial world is especially compelling. Written over forty years ago, the poem has proven truly prophetic. How could Jeffers have known what we know now? The answer, I believe, is metaphor. In finding and exploring his metaphor, Jeffers was led to vision. As I have said, metaphor is a way of saying and more: it is also a way of thinking, of feeling, and of knowing.

Implicit Metaphor
A metaphor is implicit when either the vehicle or the tenor or both are not expressed but somehow immediately implied. For example, we say that we "spend time": time (tenor), therefore, is money (implicit vehicle). We also "feed computers," which come in "generations" and "spit out" information: an analogy between computers (tenor) and living creatures (implicit vehicle) is implied here. Similarly, if one's words (tenor) are "sharp" or "biting," they are teeth (implicit vehicle).

"In political life," a political commentator wrote recently, "pygmies abound—giants are rare." Here we have a case of an expressed vehicle (pygmies/giants) and an implied tenor (politicians). Of the same order are most proverbs. Should you have more help than you need, you might say, "Too many cooks spoil the broth." The statement would be literal if you are a cook in a kitchen full of cooks making broth. As soon as the context changes, however, the statement becomes metaphorical, the tenors for the vehicles "cooks" and "broth" being suggested by the new context. Or if you say that you feel "wounded," your feelings (tenor) are like your limbs or torso (vehicle), and whatever has offended you (tenor) is like a knife or a bullet (vehicle).

It is in this way that language works. Even when we are not fashioning explicit metaphors, implicit metaphor lurks behind our words. The difference between ordinary discourse and poetry is that metaphors in poetry —whether explicit or implicit—are deliberate. Poets choose their words with care so as to squeeze out of them as much meaning as possible. For instance, the implicit metaphor of Jeffers's "crowded fish" (line 8) brims with meaning in the context of the second part of "The Purse-Seine." And, as I have said, metaphor is to the poet a means of exploring as well as of speaking. Let me illustrate this point again, now by way of a poem whose metaphors are basically implicit. This poem, which is rather metaphysical in its conceits (a **metaphysical conceit** is a metaphor whose analogy is unexpected, even shocking), had its genesis in my discovery of the word *brainpan* (a more vivid, because more clearly metaphorical, term for the cranium).

New Uses for Old Utensils

Edward Proffitt

Your cauliflower served
my brainpan
death
with housewife fingers
and economy   5
will plant you deep
with daffodils
the rose-roots twining round
caressing
every blossom grounded there   10
my flowerpot.

(1976)

If the part of the skull that holds the brain is a pan, I thought, it holds (given the look of the brain) a cauliflower. "Cauliflower" and "brainpan" are expressed vehicles, then, and "brain" and "cranium" the implicit tenors. My chance find of the word *brainpan* led me to see the brain as a cauliflower; the domesticity of the imagery led me in turn to envision death (personified) as a housewife—here, a careful housewife who wastes nothing. Again, the metaphor is implicit: I do not call death a housewife directly, but imply the analogy in the phrase "housewife fingers/and economy," which suggests that death, like a good housewife, is frugal and inventive. Just as a good housewife would find a use for an old pan, my housewife (death) will find a use for this brainpan once its time is past—

that is, once the cauliflower brain is "served" by death to the waiting worms. A housewife might use such a pan as a flowerpot; death will do the same with this brainpan (once again, the metaphor is implicit). In the grave, it will be planted "with daffodils"; itself planted deep, it will be entwined by "rose-roots" (personified in passing by "caressing").

The playful conceits of the poem add up to a way of conceiving death and of thinking through the conception. It is the playfulness of the conceits, indeed, that does the work. Death is domesticated: the metaphors say that death is no terrible thing, but only part of the process of life, the part on which all new life depends ("every blossom grounded there"). In them, I voice a conception; through them, I offer a possible path to acceptance.

The Symbol

The **symbol** can be thought of as belonging to the category of implicit metaphor in which the vehicle is expressed and the tenor implied. But there is a crucial difference between the symbol and the implicit metaphors we have already looked at: its tenor is *not immediately* implied. That is, the vehicle—the symbol—stands alone in its immediate context, and can be understood only in light of some broader context: the piece of writing in which the symbol occurs and/or the entire body of a writer's work and/or the general cultural context of both the work and the writer. What brings to our attention the possibility that a given element (such as an image, a situation, or a structure) of a piece of writing is symbolic is its elaboration and/or repetition and/or significant placement. Sometimes, too, we come to recognize that an element is symbolic by tacitly asking the question "If not symbolic, what?"

We recognize nonliterary symbols in exactly the same way. The symbols of dreams, for instance, establish themselves by elaboration, repetition, placement, and especially by the nagging feeling that our dream-images are not strictly literal. And they yield to interpretation only by being considered in the context of the dream, the dreamer, and the culture of the dreamer. Or, from the myriad symbols of everyday life, take clothing. A professor wearing jeans in the garden is simply being practical; the same professor wearing the same jeans to class is probably making a symbolic statement. Placement is our clue, and context our means of interpretation. Clothing is in the second case a vehicle expressing a complex tenor involving discontent and rebelliousness.

We are not always conscious of the symbols in daily life, of course, nor of the symbols in literature. To become fully responsive readers, however, we need to become more sensitive to the symbolic elements operative in texts because these elements are always of particular significance. The final lines of "My Last Duchess," for example, are especially significant when seen as having symbolic weight:

> Notice Neptune, though,
> Taming a sea horse, thought a rarity,
> Which Claus of Innsbruck cast in bronze for me!

The very fact that the poem ends with the word *me* seems symbolic, the mode of closure here being a vehicle that serves further to reinforce our sense of the egomania of the duke. But I'm thinking primarily of the image of the statue of Neptune taming a sea horse. Prominent because of its position at the end of the poem, the image calls attention to itself; and in doing so, it asks to be read as more than a descriptive detail. Taken in the context of the poem as a whole, the closing image capsulizes the essence of the speaker, who would tame a wife as he would a dumb creature.

We might call such a symbol "reinforcing": in its context, it serves to deepen and enrich, but the symbol can be missed and the poem nevertheless be meaningful. Some poems, however, operate wholly at the symbolic level. The following poem by Blake is of this order:

The Sick Rose

William Blake

> O Rose, thou art sick.
> The invisible worm
> That flies in the night
> In the howling storm
>
> Has found out thy bed   5
> Of crimson joy,
> And his dark secret love
> Does thy life destroy.

(1794)

If not symbolic, what? On a literal level, the poem offers a lesson in gardening: if you want to keep your roses from getting sick, watch out for invisible worms that fly in the night. But—and this is the point—there is no literal level here. Unlike Browning's image of the statue of Neptune, which in context is both literal and symbolic, Blake's images are wholly symbolic.

How are we to go about interpreting Blake's symbolic images, vehicles that stand alone in the immediate context: a *rose* in a *crimson* rose *bed* made sick by a *worm* that enters by *night* in a *storm* and invisibly bores from within? It would help to have read other poems by Blake, and to place this poem in the larger context of the poet's whole body of work.

Still, some general knowledge of the cultural context (necessary in this instance for full comprehension) combined with a bit of sensitivity on our part can take us far. Associate with the images in the poem, and bring your knowledge of their cultural significance to bear: rose—soft, delicate, feminine, and symbolic in Western culture of romantic (that is, sexual) love; bed—roses grow in beds, and beds are also places where people copulate; worm—masculine, and also suggestive of disease and deceit (the worm in the apple, symbol of the Fall of Man); crimson—the color associated with prostitution (implied as well by "secret love"); night—the time for lovers, yet also a time universally symbolic of death, as storms universally symbolize evil (thus their prevalence in horror movies). Putting all of this together suggests that *in part* Blake is making a statement about sick sexuality, or sexuality in a culture that represses healthy sexual impulses and drives them underground. With his frighteningly vivid and hauntingly dreamlike images, he embodies a wealth of feeling in such a way as to touch the unconscious, which conceives in symbols alone.

I say "in part" because symbols (as opposed to signs) do not resolve themselves into neat equivalents, like x equals y. A symbol is like a prism, which radiates different colors when turned in the light. The very attraction of the symbol is that it allows much meaning to be packed into little space. What I have said about "The Sick Rose," therefore, is not meant as definitive, but only as one way to approach the poem, whose full meaning seems to shimmer just beyond the reach of the rationalizing intellect and to defy translation into other terms. Certainly other approaches suggest themselves when the poem is considered in the larger context of *Songs of Innocence and of Experience* ("The Sick Rose" is a song of experience) and of Blake's other work. The possible interpretations are not infinite, but reading the poem in its various contexts suggests that it is richer than any single interpretation.

The definition of the symbol I offered above is not to be taken as definitive either. One way of conceptualizing the symbol is as a metaphor whose tenor is not immediately implied. Another equally valid way is to think of the symbol, as did Coleridge, as a *complex* synecdoche or metonymy in which a concrete agent comes to stand for the more general and inclusive class of which it is a part or with which it is associated. Or perhaps this is another type of symbol, exemplified by Marilyn Monroe taken as a symbol of 1950s-era femininity (one woman fleetingly embodying a complex concept of womanhood) or by the rose taken as a symbol of romantic love (the rose having been long associated with this amorphous concept). In this light, the dolls and the baby in "The Dolls" could be thought of as symbols—synecdoches of sufficient complexity to be more than simple names. Just as much as "The Sick Rose," "The Dolls" prompts us to ask the question "If not symbolic, what?" And like the images of "The Sick Rose," those of "The Dolls" carry wide significance.

The city in Jeffers's "The Purse-Seine" is also symbolic: by the end of the poem, Jeffers's city has come to stand for the whole complex of industrial culture; what is said of the one city is meant to be applied to the culture at large.

In sum, however we conceptualize them, symbols are concretions that fan out to signify far more than what they are literally or bring to mind by virtue of their inherent characteristics alone. They suggest larger realms of abstraction—which cannot be thought about succinctly in any other way—and yield their meanings by being considered in connection with the larger literary and/or cultural context.

METAPHORICAL EXTENSION

Though poets are always aware of the relationship of their metaphors and the possible extensions of each, the vehicles of a great many poems, or the realms from which their vehicles are drawn, change as the thought-and-feeling of the poem shifts and develops. For instance, "O My Luve's like a red, red rose,/That's newly sprung in June," says Robert Burns; and then, "O My Luve's like the melodie/That's sweetly played in tune." The tenor ("My Luve") remains the same, but the vehicles shift; there-fore, the metaphors are discrete. The same is true of many of the meta-phors in the first part of "The Purse-Seine": for example, "each beautiful slender body sheeted with flame, like a live rocket/A comet's tail wake. . . ."

In contrast, the second part of "The Purse-Seine" develops via **meta-phorical extension**. Everything in the second part, in other words, is to be thought of *in terms of* the one vehicle established by the clause "how could I help but recall the seine-net." The metaphor is sustained for the rest of the poem. Many poems proceed in this way: in such poems, the poet extends a prime metaphor by staying with one vehicle or by drawing all subsequent vehicles from the same general area. The final lines of Donne's "A Valediction: Forbidding Mourning," whose male speaker is about to leave his beloved and go on a long journey, is a classic example:

> Our two souls therefore, which are one,
>   Though I must go, endure not yet
> A breach, but an expansion,
>   Like gold to airy thinness beat.
>
> If they be two, they are two so   25
>   As stiff twin compasses are two;
> Thy soul, the fixed foot, makes no show
>   To move, but doth, if th' other do.

And though it in the center sit,
    Yet when the other far doth roam,   30
It leans and hearkens after it,
    And grows erect, as that comes home.

Such wilt thou be to me, who must
    Like th' other foot, obliquely run;
Thy firmness makes my circle just,   35
    And makes me end where I begun.

                           (1633)

A VALEDICTION: FORBIDDING MOURNING.   26. *compasses:* V-shaped instruments consisting of two "legs" or "feet" used to draw circles or measure distances on a globe. 35. *just:* true, complete.

The metaphysical conceit (Donne was a leading Metaphysical poet) of the lover's souls being "stiff twin compasses" (lines 25–26) structures and underlies the concluding ten lines. All the metaphors that follow derive from and expand on the initial (prime) figure; together, they work to make the end of the poem graceful, yet highly charged.

That his prime metaphor works so well in extension is a result of Donne's skill. Extension is a tricky business: it requires tact and vigilance on the part of the writer, who must control the extension by careful word-choice (diction) so as to block the ludicrous associations that can easily creep in. One example should prove the point. This is the conclusion of an appeal for a college scholarship fund (the "he" referred to is a dead minister who had worked for the fund):

> When he died, his shoes were worn-out. Full of holes, broken shoelaces. Scuffed and scarred by the daily trudge.
> When his will was probated, his widow, looking at that pair of worn-out shoes, decided to give the little that he had left where it would do the most good.
> "I want others to walk in his shoes," she said.
> College students have been walking in others' shoes for a long time. Tuition is high. Yes. But it is still only 58% of the cost of education. Forty-two percent comes from others' "shoes."
> But there's not enough to go around. We need more shoes.

It is easy to be original when constructing and extending a metaphor. The art of using metaphor lies in being original (and thereby having impact on the reader) and apt at the same time, and in knowing when a metaphor in extension is becoming **mixed** (that is, not working).

Enamored by his own cleverness, perhaps, the male author of the fund appeal failed to see the ineptitude of his prime metaphor and of its extension.

One mark of the poet is that he/she does not fail in this way. Sensitive to the tricks that language can play, the poet thinks through every metaphor in extension (whether or not the metaphor is extended in the poem) and in relation to every other figure being used. The sensitive reader, in turn, comes to appreciate a poem by going through a similar process. In order to consolidate what has been said about metaphor generally and about metaphorical extension, let us carry a poem through this process.

To R. B.

Gerard Manley Hopkins

The fine delight that fathers thought; the strong
Spur, live and lancing like the blowpipe flame,
Breathes once and, quenchèd faster than it came,
Leaves yet the mind a mother of immortal song.

Nine months she then, nay years, nine years she long   5
Within her wears, bears, cares and combs the same:
The widow of an insight lost she lives, with aim
Now known and hand at work now never wrong.

Sweet fire the sire of muse, my soul needs this;
I want the one rapture of an inspiration.   10
O then if in my lagging lines you miss

The roll, the rise, the carol, the creation,
My winter world, that scarcely breathes that bliss
Now, yields you, with some sighs, our explanation.

(c. 1889)

TO R. B.   R. B. is Robert Bridges, a well-known poet himself. This poem is the last Hopkins wrote; he died a few months after its completion.

The octave (first eight lines) of Hopkins's sonnet is carefully built on two related metaphors, the first quatrain on a metaphor of insemination and the second on one of gestation. "Delight" is a father that impregnates the mother mind with "thought." "Delight" is also a "Spur"—an instrument for pricking, a stimulus (catch the suggestion of a penis)—and a "blowpipe flame," as sharp and "lancing" as a spur. "Spur" gives rise to "lancing," and "flame" arises out of the "-light" of "delight." As "Spur," delight lances; as "flame," it "Breathes" (a flame can be said to breathe) and is "quenchèd." Both flame and breath, it should be noted, are pervasive romantic symbols of "inspiration" (which means, etymologically, "to breathe into"), as delight is renamed later in the poem (line 10). All in all, father delight lances the mother mind with its flame, spurs it into thought and then is "quenchèd faster than it came" (line 3, I suggest, concerns the orgasm of delight): delight or inspiration, like sexual ecstasy, is fleeting. Yet from the action of delight conception results—conception of "thought," the embryo song, and thence "immortal song" itself.

Having been conceived by the action of delight (or inspiration) on the mind, the song then gestates, not for the nine months required for mortal birth, but, because the song is to be immortal, for "nine years" (the amount of time specified by the Latin poet Horace as necessary for poetic creation). The mind ("she") carries her immortal fetus "Within her" for nine years; for nine years she "wears, bears, cares and combs" her fetal song ("the same"). Both growth and the effort needed for creation are suggested. "Bears" grows out of "wears" and "cares" out of "bears" by rhyme. Then, with a sense of strain in the voice, "cares" yields by alliteration to "combs" (whose primary meaning in this context is "to cleanse"). As a womb "wears, bears, cares and combs" a fetus (the vehicle), the mind sifts and sorts (another meaning of "combs" is "searches systematically") its material in the long gestation of poetic creation (the tenor). Hopkins has now moved from the ecstasy of a fleeting inspiration to the difficulty of the creative process. The insemination of delight is prime, but after it must follow hard labor. Delight impregnates the mind, which is then left (because delight is "quenchèd") a "widow of an insight lost" (emotional insight, equivalent to delight). Because impregnated, however, she now has "aim." Like a mother preparing for the birth of her child, the mind proceeds in her metaphorical pregnancy with the calm certainty of an inevitable result.

Inspiration and craftsmanship, then, are the parents of immortal song. But, though the poet possesses the latter, he lacks the spur of the former. "Sweet fire the sire of muse" (a restatement of "The fine delight that fathers thought")—that is what his soul needs, "the one rapture of an inspiration." ("Rapture" is derived from *rapere*—to seize—and so is an etymological cousin of "rape.") Though his womblike mind is prepared for impregnation, there is no "fire" in his life now (note how "fire" extends the flame imagery of the first quatrain). His is a "winter world," lacking springtime fever, a world that "scarcely breathes that bliss." There is no delight now, no breath of inspiration. And so, after the rising, climactic "the roll, the rise, the carol, the creation," the poem falls into anticlimax. "Winter" connotes infertility, sterility, and barrenness, and underlying the image (in conjunction with the mother metaphor of the octave) is the frustration of a childless woman longing to give birth. Because of this implied extension, which results from association, the sestet (last six lines) of the sonnet is in sad contrast with the octave. The poet has resigned himself (thus only "some sighs") to barrenness. His world "yields" no fruit, only an "explanation." Abstract, matter-of-fact, dry, "explanation" is the perfect word. Its diction sadly captures all that the poet feels he has become.

POEM ASSIGNMENT

Write a poem of at least four lines built on one prime metaphor. Like Donne, you might start with an explicit metaphor (such as a simile) and extend it by careful choice of subsequent metaphors, or, like Hopkins, you might imply a metaphor and extend it by verbal association. However you establish your prime metaphor, be sure either to stay with its vehicle throughout or to draw all subsequent vehicles from the same general realm. A word of caution: watch out for mixed metaphors (metaphors that in extension or combination don't work) and be mindful of the logic of metaphor. What is said of tenor or vehicle must be true of both. As always, give your poem a title.

In the following student sample, the metaphor breaks down because the vehicle in extension does not apply to the tenor.

> The land is a tool
> Used and re-used,
> Set aside, ignored,
> Thrown out when broken.

Yes, land can be used and re-used, and it can be said to be set aside and ignored. Unlike tools, however, it cannot be "Thrown out when broken." The extension at this point doesn't work. What about the next poem?

> Deeply rooted in our own tracks,
> Running to and fro, stopping only
> To empty and refill,
> Rushing noisily,
> Seeing the light only as we near   5
> The yard.

Human life can be seen as analogous to the trip of a train. Do we necessarily see the light, though, as we reach the end of our journey ("The yard")? On the level of vehicle, how does "Seeing the light" apply to a

train? How can one be "Deeply rooted in . . ." and "Running to and fro"
at the same time? And can a train be "Deeply rooted in [its] own tracks"?
Clearly, the metaphors are mixed from the start.

> My dog's fur is velvet;
> his paws are tiny pillows;
> he has a nose of coal;
> his ears are flags;
> his tail wags often,   5
> and his eyes open wide to greet me.

Terribly maudlin, this poem does not proceed by metaphorical extension.
Though lines 1–4 are metaphorical, the metaphors are discrete (an error
in the context of this assignment, though not otherwise). Also, the last
two lines are basically literal.

Now let us turn to a few successful poems, meant to be taken as
models. Live through the prime metaphor of each and then observe how,
by extending the given metaphor, each author finds expression and comes
to insight.

Winter Birds

Teresa Vara

> Like winter birds,
> your eyes dart and land,
> fluster and flee,
> certain only
> of their   5
> hunger.

A Joke

Raymond Carthy

Laughter tastes of orange soda
Bubbling all the way down,
Then exploding through your nose.
Later, hiccups of remembrance are flat Kool-Aid.

Self-Revelation

Thomas Lesser

I, a dodder,* have no chlorophyll.
My tendrils penetrate deep
And absorb the energies of other lives.
I am destructive of anything cultivated.

* Any plant of a genus of leafless parasites with threadlike stems.

The Skirt

Daniel McKessy

The mighty schooner battles the stormy seas,
Its sails fluttering in the high gales;
All hands are below, the hatches are fastened;
Still, the lovely lady cannot conquer the nasty wind.

POEMS FOR FURTHER STUDY

Strange Fruit

Lewis Allan

(as sung by Billie Holiday)

Southern trees bear a strange fruit
Blood on the leaves and blood at the root
Black fruit swinging in the Southern breeze
Strange fruit, hanging from the poplar trees.

Pastoral scene of the gallant South   5
The bulging eyes, the twisted mouth
Smell of magnolias, sweet and fresh
Then the sudden smell of putrid flesh.

Here is a fruit for the crows to pluck
For the rain to gather, for the wind to suck   10
For the sun to rot, for the tree to drop
Here is a strange and bitter crop.

(1941)

Figurative Language

Questions
1. Stanzas one and three of this lyric are built on an implicit metaphor. What is the implied tenor for the vehicle "strange fruit"?
2. How do we come to recognize what the tenor is?
3. What does Allan gain by keeping the tenor implicit?
4. A **pastoral** is a poem set in an idyllic landscape; traditionally, it evokes nostalgia for the beauty and peace of (idealized) nature. How and for what purpose does Allan make use of the pastoral? Is there symbolic weight in the juxtaposition of "Pastoral scene" and "bulging eyes"?
5. Stanzas one and three proceed by metaphorical extension. What words establish the extension?
6. In terms of metaphor, stanza two seems different from stanzas one and three. How so? What is the effect of Allan's positioning stanza two between the highly metaphorical stanzas that precede and follow it?

Wants

Philip Larkin

Beyond all this, the wish to be alone:
However the sky grows dark with invitation-cards
However we follow the printed directions of sex
However the family is photographed under the flagstaff—
Beyond all this, the wish to be alone.   5

Beneath it all, desire of oblivion runs:
Despite the artful tensions of the calendar,
The life insurance, the tabled fertility rites,
The costly aversion of the eyes from death—
Beneath it all, desire of oblivion runs.   10

(*1955*)

Questions
1. Analyze the details of the poem with regard to metaphor.
2. The repetitions in this poem themselves seem metaphorical. What does the repetitive structure of the poem imply?
3. What are "the artful tensions of the calendar"? Is the phrase figurative? How so?
4. "Run" can be traced back to the Sanskrit word *arnas*, meaning "stream," and we still speak of water as "running." Given this etymology, there is an implicit metaphor in the poem's last line. What is the metaphor? What does it suggest in extension?

[I Taste a Liquor Never Brewed]

Emily Dickinson

I taste a liquor never brewed–
From Tankards scooped in Pearl–
Not all the Frankfort Berries
Yield such an Alcohol!

Inebriate of Air–am I–   5
And Debauchee of Dew–
Reeling–thro endless summer days–
From inns of Molten Blue–

When "Landlords" turn the drunken Bee
Out of the Foxglove's door–   10
When Butterflies–renounce their "dram"–
I shall but drink the more!

Till Seraphs swing their snowy Hats–
And Saints–to windows run–
To see the little Tippler   15
From Manzanilla come!

(c. 1860)

[I TASTE A LIQUOR NEVER BREWED]. 3. *Frankfort Berries:* grapes used to
make Rhine wine. 16. *Manzanilla:* a sherry wine from a region in Spain of
the same name.

Questions
1. "I Taste a Liquor" exhibits a number of different figurative types.
   What type of figure is "Molten Blue"? What type is "inns of Molten
   Blue"?
2. What other figures does Dickinson use?
3. What is the prime metaphor of the poem? How is the metaphor es-
   tablished?
4. What words and phrases serve to extend the metaphor?

Sonnet 65

William Shakespeare

Since brass, nor stone, nor earth, nor boundless sea,
But sad mortality o'ersways their power,
How with this rage shall beauty hold a plea,

Figurative Language

Whose action is no stronger than a flower?
Oh, how shall summer's honey breath hold out   5
Against the wrackful siege of battering days,
When rocks impregnable are not so stout,
Nor gates of steel so strong, but Time decays?
O fearful meditation! Where, alack,
Shall Time's best jewel from Time's chest lie hid?   10
Or what strong hand can hold his swift foot back?
Or who his spoil of beauty can forbid?
   Oh, none, unless this miracle have might,
   That in black ink my love may still shine bright.

(1609)

Questions

1. What is the synesthetic figure in line 5?
2. What abstractions are personified in this poem?
3. Underlying the poem is an extended metaphor. What is this metaphor? What words accomplish the extension?
4. Diction is central to metaphorical extension; it also shapes tone and directs attitude. Consider the phrase "spoil of beauty" (line 12). Why did Shakespeare choose the word "spoil" rather than "catch" or "loot"?

London

William Blake

I wander thro' each charter'd street,
Near where the charter'd Thames does flow,
And mark in every face I meet
Marks of weakness, marks of woe.

In every cry of every man,   5
In every Infant's cry of fear,
In every voice, in every ban,
The mind-forg'd manacles I hear.

How the Chimney-sweeper's cry
Every blackning Church appalls;   10
And the hapless Soldier's sigh
Runs in blood down Palace walls.

Figurative Language

But most thro' midnight streets I hear
How the youthful Harlot's curse
Blasts the new-born Infant's tear,   15
And blights with plagues the Marriage hearse.

(1794)

LONDON. 1. *charter'd:* legally defined. 7. *ban:* a law or public notice commanding or forbidding some action. 16. *plague:* venereal disease.

Questions
1. There are synecdoches in the first and last stanzas of "London." What are they?
2. At the end of the last line there is an implicit metaphor. What is it?
3. The images and implicit metaphors of stanza three are **surrealistic** (bizarre, nightmarish). What is the effect of the surrealism of the stanza?
4. "Blasts" and "blights" in the last stanza are both metaphorical. What vehicles do they suggest for the tenors "infant" (implied by "Infant's tear") and "husband and wife" (implied by "Marriage hearse")?
5. With "London" in mind, reread "The Sick Rose" (page 86). What are the similarities between the two poems? How does the context provided by "London" (also a song of experience) aid us in reading "The Sick Rose"?
6. Blake's London seems symbolic—a complex synecdoche and/or a vehicle whose tenor is understood by considering the poem in its larger cultural context. What does London as portrayed in Blake's poem symbolize?

IDEAS FOR WRITING

1. Consult a good standard dictionary or, better yet, a dictionary of word origins (etymologies) to identify the metaphorical bases of each of the following words: discover, bombast, disaster, catastrophe, mull, wisdom, fathom. Is there any relationship between "science" and "scissors"? Choose a few words of your own and see what you can find. Write up what you discover.
2. Analyze the poem you wrote for the poem assignment in the present chapter with regard to metaphor. What is your prime metaphor? How have you extended that metaphor? What does your poem as a whole express through its figures?
3. In a clearly metaphorical statement, what is doing the work (the vehicle) and what is being defined (the tenor) are most often relatively easy to determine. Sometimes, however, a poet will deliberately confuse the two. Consider the following satirical poem in this light.

The Brides

A. D. Hope

Down the assembly line they roll and pass
Complete at last, a miracle of design;
Their chromium fenders, the unbreakable glass,
The fashionable curve, the air-flow line.

Grease to the elbows Mum and Dad enthuse,   5
Pocket their spanners and survey the bride;
Murmur: "A sweet job! All she needs is juice!
Built for a life-time—sleek as a fish. Inside

"He will find every comfort: the full set
Of gadgets; knobs that answer to the touch   10
For light or music; a place for his cigarette;
. Room for his knees; a honey of a clutch."

Now slowly through the show-room's flattering glare
See her wheeled in to love, console, obey,
Shining and silent! Parson with a prayer   15
Blesses the number-plate, she rolls away

To write her numerals in his book of life;
And now, at last, stands on the open road,
Triumphant, perfect, every inch a wife,
While the corks pop, the flash-light bulbs explode.   20

Her heavenly bowser-boy assumes his seat;
She prints the soft dust with her brand-new treads,
Swings towards the future, purring with a sweet
Concatenation of the poppet heads.

(1951)

This poem clearly proceeds by metaphorical extension. But is "brides"
the tenor and "automobiles" the vehicle, or is "brides" the vehicle
and "automobiles" the tenor? Or are both both, the thrust of the
poem being two-edged? Discuss, keeping in mind the poem's cultural
context. How were automobiles advertised in the 1950s—that is, what
metaphor underlay those advertisements (and many such advertise-
ments today)? What did most young women in the 1950s have to look
forward to? What was the social status of the new bride? In a separate
paragraph, discuss your response to this poem.

4. Analyze the following passage from Dickens's *Hard Times* with re-
   gard to metaphor. Point out the metaphorical phrases, the relation-
   ship of the metaphors, and their effect. Finally, taking the passage
   as a whole, suggest what possible symbolic weight Dickens's town
   (called "Coketown") might have.

   > It was a town of red brick, or of brick that would have been red
   > if the smoke and ashes had allowed it; but as matters stood it
   > was a town of unnatural red and black like the painted face of
   > a savage. It was a town of machinery and tall chimneys, out of
   > which interminable serpents of smoke trailed themselves for ever
   > and ever, and never got uncoiled. It had a black canal in it, and
   > a river that ran purple with ill-smelling dye, and vast piles of
   > buildings full of windows where there was a rattling and a trem-
   > bling all day long, and where the piston of the steam engine
   > worked monotonously up and down, like the head of an ele-
   > phant in a state of melancholy madness. It contained several
   > large streets all very like one another, and many small streets
   > still more like one another, inhabited by people equally like one
   > another. . . .

5. I once heard Robert Frost talk on the subject of walls. I don't recall
   his exact words, but I remember their gist: we deceive ourselves with
   sentimental hogwash if we think that walls, boundaries, and the like
   aren't necessary. I also remember him using as an analogy: the body's
   cell walls, without which there would be no life. These remarks elu-
   cidate "Mending Wall," one of Frost's best-known and most often
   misread poems. Read it in light of the above.

Mending Wall

Something there is that doesn't love a wall,
That sends the frozen-ground-swell under it
And spills the upper boulders in the sun,
And makes gaps even two can pass abreast.
The work of hunters is another thing: 5
I have come after them and made repair
Where they have left not one stone on a stone,
But they would have the rabbit out of hiding,
To please the yelping dogs. The gaps I mean,
No one has seen them made or heard them made,   10
But at spring mending-time we find them there.
I let my neighbor know beyond the hill;

And on a day we meet to walk the line
And set the wall between us once again.
We keep the wall between us as we go.   15
To each the boulders that have fallen to each.
And some are loaves and some so nearly balls
We have to use a spell to make them balance:
'Stay where you are until our backs are turned!'
We wear our fingers rough with handling them.   20
Oh, just another kind of outdoor game,
One on a side. It comes to little more:
There where it is we do not need the wall:
He is all pine and I am apple orchard.
My apple trees will never get across   25
And eat the cones under his pines, I tell him.
He only says, 'Good fences make good neighbors.'
Spring is the mischief in me, and I wonder
If I could put a notion in his head:
'*Why* do they make good neighbors? Isn't it   30
Where there are cows? But here there are no cows.
Before I built a wall I'd ask to know
What I was walling in or walling out,
And to whom I was like to give offense.
Something there is that doesn't love a wall,   35
That wants it down.' I could say 'Elves' to him,
But it's not elves exactly, and I'd rather
He said it for himself. I see him there
Bringing a stone grasped firmly by the top
In each hand, like an old-stone savage armed.   40
He moves in darkness as it seems to me,
Not of woods only and the shade of trees.
He will not go behind his father's saying,
And he likes having thought of it so well
He says again, 'Good fences make good neighbors.'   45

                                               (*1914*)

Now write a paper on Frost's wall. Taking the wall as a symbol, feel out
the areas of human experience symbolized. Then consider what attitude
we are to take toward all of this. In doing so, question Frost's speaker.
Are we to take him at his word? Or might he be guilty of some degree
of self-deception? After all, it is he who initiates the wall-mending (line
12), and he doesn't think very highly of his neighbor (lines 40–43). Per-
haps he is best separated from this man "who moves in darkness," though
the wall-mending itself, ironically, bonds them in a common task. Do the
poem's concretions, then, give voice to a depth of mixed feelings?

Rhythm & Meter
Chapter Five

SOUND AND SENSE

In spoken language, the relation between sound and sense is immediate. When we're excited, for example, we communicate our excitement vocally by raising the volume of our voices and speaking rapidly; conversely, when we're melancholy, we lower our volume and speak, for instance, in long, drawn-out phrases. The relationship of sense to sound is fundamental to speech, and fundamental to poetry as well. The poet strives to tap all the resources of language, and the way words sound when put together into lexically and grammatically meaningful units is a prime resource. We are turning now to a matter as central to poetry as is metaphor—the subject of rhythm, which takes us back to the subject of voice just as metaphor took us back to imagery. The principle is simple: however a poet chooses finally to shape a poem, everything in the poem that involves sound figures in the making of rhythm. This is what line length and division are about; line treatment is a technique for suggesting the rhythms of a speaker's voice. The same is true of meter, rhyme, alliteration, and all other aspects of the sound of poetry. All enter into the making of exact rhythms—the more exact, the more expressive, because the more intimately linked to sense.

RHYTHM: AN OVERVIEW

A central goal of the poet is to capture in print the effects of the speaking voice—the way it moves and pauses, shouts or whispers, rises and falls, stresses and slurs; in short, the way it reflects the immediate and ongoing thought and feeling of a speaker. To be more specific, there are five basic attributes of English speech that impart meaning:

accentuation stress or emphasis on one syllable as opposed to another.
inflection the degree of stress (though many words in a given utterance are stressed, some will be stressed more heavily than others).
volume the loudness or softness of the voice.
pace the rapidity or slowness of an utterance.
pause the points at which the voice rests so the body can breathe or the mind gather its thoughts.

These are the qualities of the spoken language, qualities that affect meaning as decisively as do the dictionary definitions of words. Put these qualities together and you have **rhythm:** the way words move (*rhythm* comes from a Greek word meaning "to flow") as determined by the variables of the five basic qualities of speech enumerated above.

In that these qualities affect how a statement is interpreted, rhythm is a prime determinant of meaning. In speech, rhythm can communicate as much as the denotations of words. Indeed, we can often grasp the import of someone's words even when we cannot hear the words distinctly. We know when someone is angry by the inflection, volume, and pace of the person's voice, even if we cannot make out a single word uttered. When someone is happy, the voice tends to skip along, the way the words move—their rhythm and resultant tone—indicating the feeling of the speaker. (Recall what we have already said about tone, therefore, in light of the present discussion of rhythm.) What is true of speech is also true of poetry, whatever the specific techniques used by a poet to impart the flavor of the speaking voice. A poet uses the tools at hand to sculpt rhythm; when the poet succeeds, we say that the finished poem is exact, meaning that the poet has gotten into the written language the crucial qualities of spoken language. If we remember to hear as we read, a poem should speak to us with all the subtlety and force of a spoken utterance.

How does a poet manage this miraculous trick? Again, rhythm equals accentuation, inflection, volume, pace, and pause. A poet specifies each of these qualities by means of the tools of the craft: meter, rhyme, alliteration, consonant and vowel manipulation, line length and division, and the like. These tools, some of which go into the making of every poem (though all are not necessarily operative in any given poem), are specifically those of the poet. In previous chapters we have dealt with aspects of language that characterize both prose and poetry. Now we shall look at linguistic phenomena that by and large are peculiar to poetry alone and that constitute the formal difference between poetry and prose.

METER AND METRICS

Meter as Rhythmic Recurrence

The first such phenomenon is **meter,** the regular recurrence of some rhythmic configuration or pulse. Consider the words *although* and *today*. We pronounce both in a set way, as we do all **polysyllabic** words, or words of more than one syllable. These two we pronounce with a **stress** (accent or special emphasis) on the second syllables and no stress (or slack) on the first (˘ indicates slack; ´ indicates stress):

ălthóugh, tŏdáy

Each constitutes a little rhythmic unit or pulse. If we choose words so as to create a pulsating pattern of slack and stress, or stress and slack, we would have a meter:

Ălthóugh/Ĭ dó/ĭnténd/tŏ cóme/tŏdáy . . .

Note how the rhythmic configuration ˘ ´ is made to recur by the selection and ordering of words. When a pulse is made to recur in this way, we speak of the unit of recurrence as a **foot** or a **beat.** The above phrase has five feet or beats. A poet writing metrically chooses words so that they will form the desired pattern of recurrence.

The Meter of English Verse

Though meter always involves rhythmic recurrence, different languages have given rise to different types of meter. Though poets writing in English have experimented with many, the type most characteristic of English verse from Chaucer to the present is **accentual-syllabic;** as we shall see, this type is closest to (and based on) the patterns of English speech. In English poetry generally, the sense of rhythmic recurrence springs from the number of syllables per line *and* the number of stresses, a set number of stressed syllables alternating with a set number of slack (unstressed) syllables. In other words, rhythmic recurrence, or meter, is tied to the repetition of a set number of feet or beats per line. For example, consider the last stanza of "Stopping by Woods":

> Thĕ woŏds/arĕ lóve/lў, dárk,/ănd déep,
>
> Bŭt Í/hăve próm/isĕs/tŏ kéep,
>
> Ănd mílĕs/tŏ gó/bĕfóre/Ĭ sléep,
>
> Ănd mílĕs/tŏ gó/bĕfóre/Ĭ sléep.

Each line contains eight syllables, four stressed and four slack, with unstressed and stressed syllables alternating to form a pulsating pattern of four beats per line.

Metrical Terminology

If a given rhythmic configuration recurs in a piece of writing, it has a meter, describable with respect to the kind of beat that recurs and the number of recurrences of that beat per line (a beat normally consists of one stressed syllable—the beat itself—and one or two unstressed syllables). The basic beats and patterns of recurrence characteristic of modern English metrics are:

Beats	Recurrences
iamb/iambic: ălthóugh, tŏdáy	*tri*meter: three, the root meaning
trochee/trochaic: móthĕr, fáthĕr	of *tri-*
anapest/anapestic: ĭn thĕ héat/ŏf	*tetr*ameter: four, the root mean-
thĕ níght (because of the nature	ing of *tetr-*
of English, no single word exem-	*pent*ameter: five, the root mean-
plifies the anapest well)	ing of *pent-*
dactyl/dactylic: fámĭlў, élĕphănt	*hex*ameter: six, the root meaning
	of *hex-*

There are a number of other beats, as well as other possible patterns of recurrence. There are, for example, beats called amphibrachs and amphimacers, and there are dimeters, heptameters, octameters, and so on. But these other possible beats are almost never recurrent in English verse, and in practice we rarely find lines shorter than three beats or longer than six. Two other feet, though, should be noted:

spondee/spondaic: hátráck,   *pyrrhic:* ĭn thĕ/bĕgín/nĭng Gód
fóotbáll

The spondaic foot contains two stressed syllables; the pyrrhic, two unstressed. Though not recurrent, both are frequent deviants in a metrical context.

Exercise

Compile a list of five words or phrases exemplifying each of the four primary beats. If you get stuck, open your dictionary at random and look at words of two or more syllables. What about your own name? Next, write two or three lines in which one of the primary beats recurs a fixed number of times per line:

Cŏnstrúct/sŏme línes/ĭn whích//ă chó/sĕn béat/rĕcúrs (these two are in iambic trimeter).

These, then, are our terms for naming and analyzing what happens in a piece of metrical writing. When approaching a metered poem, we first *scan* it ("to scan" means to divide a line into syllables and then to indicate which syllables receive stress and which do not) and then observe what type of beat recurs and how many recurrences there are per line. Finally, we name the meter accordingly: for example, the passage from "Stopping by Woods" scanned above is in iambic tetrameter. Theoretically, any combination of type of beat and number of beats per line is possible. We could find or invent samples of trochaic trimeter, for instance, or anapestic hexameter:

Flýĭng/dówn tŏ/Rĭŏ; Wĭth ă báng/ănd ă bóom/ŏf thĕ bíg/gĕst ŏf
bómbs/wĕ bĕgán/tŏ bĕgín.

If a piece of writing as a whole exhibits recurrence of this sort, or is describable in these terms, it is **verse** in the usual sense of the term at present.

Verse, however, is not necessarily poetry. Many poems are nonmetrical (free verse), and many pieces of verse are actually mere metered prose. A number of television ads are in verse, but few would call them poems. Look at the following (sung to the tune of "Rock of Ages"):

> Chámbĕrs cáskĕts áre jŭst fíne,
>
> Máde ŏf sándlĕwoŏd ŏr píne.
>
> Íf yŏur lóved ŏnes háve tŏ gó,
>
> Díal Cólúmbŭs 9–6–0.
>
> Íf yŏur lóved ŏnes páss ăwáy,
>
> Háve thĕm páss thĕ Chámbĕrs' wáy.
>
> Chámbĕrs' cŭstŏmĕrs ăll síng,
>
> Déath, ŏh Déath, whĕre ĭs thy stíng?

This advertisement for a funeral home is a piece of verse, but surely it is not a poem. When something is said to be "in verse," all that is meant is that it is characterized by rhythmic recurrence or meter.

One more bit of terminology can be useful: iambic and anapestic meters, which are related, are often called **rising,** because the beat of each comes at the end of the foot; conversely, trochaic and dactylic meters, also related, are called **falling.** These terms can be particularly useful in characterizing metrical effect. For example, the last line of Wallace Stevens's "Sunday Morning" begins with a falling feeling and ends on a rising note:

> Dównwărd tŏ dárknĕss ŏn ĕxténdĕd wíngs.

We could analyze this mixed line as containing two dactyls followed by two iambs, or a dactyl and a trochee followed by an anapest and an iamb. In either case, falling yields to rising, and the shift is very much in keeping with what is being expressed: that we all go down to death (falling), but that we can do so with grace and purpose (rising). There are no rules specifying the difference in effect between rising and falling meters, since their effects depend entirely on context. Still, there is a difference, and poets exploit that difference for their purposes.

VERSE AND THE STRUCTURE OF THE BRAIN

We have just touched on a matter that may have been nagging at you. Why would anyone go to such a lot of trouble, adding to the difficulty of writing a poem the further difficulty of creating a metrical pattern? I offer two answers to this question, one rather theoretical and the other quite practical. As to the first, my own theory has to do with the fact, discussed in Chapter 1, that the brain is divided into two hemispheres: the verbal left hemisphere, adept at abstraction, and the nonverbal right hemisphere, grounded in the physically concrete. My theory is that verse, which is temporally *measured* language, arises from and stimulates the right hemisphere. Therein lies its power.

Because of the structure of the brain, verse has the power to bypass the more strictly rational faculties and touch us deeply. Thus Julian Jaynes queries:

> Why has so much of the textual material we have used as evidence in earlier chapters been poetry [by which Jaynes means poetry in verse]? And why, particularly in times of stress, have a huge portion of the readers of this page written poems? What unseen light leads us to such dark practice? And why does poetry flash with recognitions of thoughts we did not know we had, finding its unsure way to something in us that knows and has known all the time . . . ?[1]

The most sensuous way that words can be put together, verse arises from and reaches back to our more primitive, physical selves. Mimicking the beating heart, perhaps, or the pulsations of our breathing and walking, a metrical beat is immediately sensory. I have called poetry experience because it both stimulates and evokes sensation: it evokes sensation through its imagery; it stimulates sensation through its sound. Meter has the latter kind of appeal: its sensory effect is immediate. Here is the source of the potential power of verse, a power exhibited in the chants of children and religionists alike (Hare Krishna chants), the carefully contrived jingles of Madison Avenue, and the strongly pulsating beat of popular song lyrics.

METER AS TOOL: THE PRINCIPLE

As to the practical rationale for meter, it can be a very useful tool for the attainment of what all poets strive for: exactness of statement, or reproducing in written language the rhythmic exactnesses of the spoken. Meter can serve this end in two ways.

First, because a metrical pattern provides a norm, it allows for syncopation, or meaningful deviation from the norm. When we name the meter of a given poem in verse, we are naming the norm. Every line does not necessarily adhere exactly to the established metrical pattern, however. Few poems lack significantly deviant beats—deviant when measured against the metrical norm. Here we confront a human paradox: there must be a norm for there to be deviation. In large part, what leads a poet to write verse is the opportunity it allows for deviation.

Second, a metrical pattern can help establish **rhetorical stress.** Note that there are three kinds of stress:

[1] Julian Jaynes, *The Origin of Consciousness in the Breakdown of the Bicameral Mind* (Boston: Houghton Mifflin, 1977), p. 361.

lexical   the stress placed on syllables in polysyllabic words, as indicated by the dictionary.

metrical   the stress or pattern of stress established in verse by the metrical norm.

rhetorical   the stress thrown by the voice for the purposes of emphasis and delineation.

This third kind of stress is a fundamental quality of speech, often crucial to meaning. Look, for example, at the following sentence, as flat and simple a sentence as I can think of: "I shall go at noon." Nevertheless, depending where the stress is thrown, there are at least four distinct ways these five words can be said, and therefore four distinct meanings possible:

Í shăll gó at nóon—a statement of intention.

Ĭ shăll gŏ ăt nóon—a response to the question "What time are you going?"

Í shŭ gŏ ŭt nŏon—as opposed to you or someone else.

Ĭ sháll gŏ ŭt nŏon—despite your opposition.

Each has a different rhythmic swing, and each a different **meaning**.

Exercise

Write down a statement you've recently made with feeling. Indicate which words you stressed and decide why you stressed those words and not others. Now read what you've written in another way. Compare the meanings of the two versions.

Accentuation (as well as inflection) is an integral aspect of how we mean when we speak. Thus there is a great difference between

"Whére dŏ yŏu thĭnk yŏu're góĭng?"

and

"Whére dŏ yŏu thĭnk yóu're góĭng?"

The first is a query about intention, the second an expression of hostility. But how can this crucial quality of speech, this basic dimension of the way words mean when spoken, be reproduced in print? For the poet, meter can be part of the answer. Through verse, a poet can suggest accentuation—that is, what is to be stressed and what is not to be stressed.

In sum, meter can be a powerful tool because it allows for deviation and because a poet can use it to suggest with immediacy the pattern of accentuation desired, and thus the rhetorical emphasis of a speaker's voice. Some examples should help to clarify the basic principle (that meter is a tool) and to suggest how metrical considerations bear on interpretation generally.

METER AS TOOL: EXAMPLES

Meaningful Deviation

Paradoxically, one of the main reasons for scanning a poem is to see where deviations occur. (Scansion is never an end in itself.) Having established where deviations occur, the reader should then try to account for them by relating what has been observed about a poem's metrics to overall interpretation. But how does one know when the verse is deviating? The answer has largely to do with polysyllabic words, or the lexical stress that characterizes such words. Although a poet can wrench an accent or slur it—both of which we do occasionally in speech—poets almost always respect the lexical stress of polysyllabic words, just as we almost always do in speech. In other words, when the lexical and metrical stress *do not coincide,* we favor the lexical stress, establishing thereby deviations from the metrical pattern. For example, should you find the words "although" and "ribbon" in a poem, they are to be pronounced "althóugh" and "ríbbon," not "álthough" and "ribbón." Read the following poem with this in mind and try to hear where enforced deviations (enforced by lexical stress) from the iambic norm occur.

Delight in Disorder

Robert Herrick

A sweet disorder in the dress
Kindles in clothes a wantonness.
A lawn about the shoulders thrown
Into a fine distractiön;
An erring lace, which here and there   5
Enthralls the crimson stomacher;
A cuff neglectful, and thereby
Ribbons to flow confusedly;
A winning wave, deserving note,
In the tempestuous petticoat;   10
A careless shoestring, in whose tie
I see a wild civility;
Do more bewitch me than when art
Is too precise in every part.

(1648)

DELIGHT IN DISORDER. 3. *lawn:* a piece of fine, sheer linen or cotton. 4. *distraction:* pronounced as having four syllables, like other "-ion" words of the time. But in the present context, the elongation is itself something of a distraction. 6. *stomacher:* an ornamental garment worn under the open (and often laced) front of a bodice.

Though in iambic tetrameter overall, the poem does not adhere to the norm throughout: the verse deviates at certain key points, namely lines 2, 4, 8, and 10. "Kíndlĕs," "Íntŏ," and "Ríbbŏns" in lines 2, 4, and 8 are trochaic intrusions into the iambic pattern (again, when lexical and metrical stress do not coincide, we respect the lexical). Line 10 could be scanned

$$\text{Ĭn thĕ́ tĕmpéstŭŏus pĕ́tticóat}$$

or

$$\text{"Ĭn thĕ tĕmpéstŭŏus pĕ́tticóat"}$$

or, as I prefer,

$$\text{"Ĭn thĕ́ tĕmpéstŭŏus pĕ́tticóat."}$$

I prefer the third scansion because the first does not seem rhetorically apt (this is a matter of judgment) and the second has only three stresses (usually, though not always, the established number of stresses per line is a constant, however deviant a line otherwise). Also, the third scansion makes the first two beats of the line dactylic, and thus brings them into relationship with the poem's trochaic deviations (trochaic and dactylic beats, remember, are related); it also makes the line strongly syncopated. To be sure, there is room for variation in scansion. And often we should hear a latent alternative scansion playing itself off against the scansion that seems primary—the result being a lively sense of counterpoint. In any case, line 10 is deviant.

Having noted the poem's deviations, we next should try to account for them. Herrick's poem is built on **oxymoron** (ŏk′sĭ·mō′ rŏn)—a phrase consisting of two terms that in ordinary usage are contradictory. There are three strategically placed oxymorons in this poem: "sweet disorder," "fine distraction," and, most important, "wild civility." Together, these oxymorons convey that the speaker desires neither order nor disorder, neither wildness nor civility, but a fine balance of these contrary qualities. In particular, the speaker would like to see such a balance in female dress, which he describes, blazon-fashion, as in his imagination his eyes move down a woman clothed to his taste. In general, clothing here is a synecdoche of the more inclusive "art," which includes poetry and the poem at hand. He would have all art imitate such balance—as his poem does in its metric, which is neither wild nor too regular. It is marked by a strong beat, but also by strong deviations (the trochaic and dactylic beats in an iambic context are strong deviants, whereas an anapest would be a weak deviant because it too is rising).

The poem's deviations serve still another purpose. Look at where they come—in the lines containing the "wild" words of the poem: "wantonness," "distraction," "confusedly," and "tempestuous." The metrical deviations are at one with meaning and help to make meaning vivid. But the effect is possible mainly because of the regularity of the context as a whole. Again, one can attain deviation only in the presence of a norm.

Rhetorical Stress

To the writer striving to catch the exactness of speech, monosyllabic words pose a special problem. Because they lack built-in stress, we have no way of knowing exactly how to say a train of such words in a nonmetrical context. Granted, there is a normal way of stressing: we usually stress nouns and verbs, and rarely stress articles or prepositions. Indeed, this tendency to stress certain parts of speech and not others explains how one establishes a beat in a monosyllabic line.

$$\breve{I} \; \acute{w}ent \; t\breve{o} \; g\acute{e}t \; th\breve{e} \; c\acute{a}r \; b\breve{u}t \; f\acute{o}und \; \breve{i}t \; g\acute{o}ne.$$

This is an iambic pentameter line because the words we normally stress alternate with the words we normally do not stress. Having no reason to read it in some other way, we read it normally and an iambic beat is established. But sometimes, for rhetorical purposes, we do not stress normally:

$$\breve{I} \; s\breve{a}id \; \acute{i}n \; th\breve{e} \; c\acute{a}bin\acute{e}t \; \breve{a}nd \; n\breve{o}t \; \acute{o}n \; \breve{i}t.$$

The problem is how to get this kind of a rhythm into the written language. Here again, meter can be the answer, or part of it.

By working in a metrical framework, a poet can suggest that we stress certain words we might not usually stress and the reverse. Rhetorical stress *always coincides* with metrical stress; consequently, the metrical pattern becomes our guide to the rhetorical emphasis of the voice speaking a poem. The principle is this: once a beat has been established, we continue the pattern (another reason to scan a poem in verse) unless we have reason to deviate from it (such as the placement of a polysyllabic word in a position that would require us to violate its lexical stress for the pattern to be maintained). A powerful instance of the coincidence of rhetorical and metrical stress is the fifth line of Sidney's sonnet on sleep (page 71): "With shield of proof shield me from out the prease." In a nonmetrical context, we would almost certainly read the line as follows:

$$W\breve{i}th \; sh\acute{i}eld \; \breve{o}f \; pr\acute{o}of \; sh\acute{i}eld \; m\breve{e} \; fr\breve{o}m \; \acute{o}ut \; th\breve{e} \; pr\acute{e}ase.$$

The metrical context of Sidney's poem, however, points to another reading. Having no reason to deviate from the established iambic norm, we should try, given the context, to maintain the beat:

With shield ŏf próof shiĕld mé frŏm óut thĕ préase.

That's it. With the stress on "me," the line explodes into meaning. Sleep, the speaker says in the preceding lines, comes to everyone else. Then he virtually screams out in desperation, "Why not to mé?" In the rhetorical stress suggested by the metrical, there can be heard all the isolation and frustration that the insomniac feels as he struggles for sleep late at night. By focusing our attention in this way and asking us to choose one reading over another, verse brings out *exact* meanings. Now let us look at a whole poem from the point of view of rhetorical stress.

Where the Bee Sucks

William Shakespeare

Where the bee sucks, there suck I:
In a cowslip's bell I lie;
There I couch when owls do cry.
On the bat's back I do fly
After summer merrily.   5
Merrily, merrily shall I live now
Under the blossom that hangs on the bough.

(1623)

First we must determine what the metrical norm is. In order to do so, we must inspect the words, especially of the opening lines: the norm of a poem is usually established at the beginning. Since the iambic beat is the fundamental beat of the language, we might try line 1 as iambic:

Whĕre thé bĕe súcks, thĕre súck Ĭ.

No, that will not do. We simply do not speak our language this way. What about this?

Whĕre thĕ bĕe súcks, thĕre súck Í.

This reading is certainly much better: it is more speechlike and it sets up a meaningful conjunction between "bee" and "I." Still, we have missed something. There is an internal rhyme here, which should serve on second reading to throw stress on "Where" (as we'll see later, rhyme tends to draw stress to itself). Everything suggests that the line is trochaic, with an added stressed syllable at the end:

Whére thĕ bée sŭcks, thére sŭck Í.

Having at this point tentatively established the metrical norm, we must read on to see if the poem adheres by and large to the norm. And so it does: lines 2–4 can be read very nicely as trochaic trimeters with an added stressed syllable per line (a frequent pattern in Renaissance poetry), and this is the only pattern possible for line 5.

We have thus arrived at a tolerable scansion of the poem's first five lines:

Whére thĕ bée sŭcks, thére sŭck Í:

Ín ă cówslĭp's béll Ĭ líe;

Thére Ĭ cóuch whĕn ówls dŏ cry.

Ón thĕ bát's băck Í dŏ flý

Áftĕr súmmĕr mérrĭlý.

Yet our task is not complete. The question remains, "Why this scansion rather than another?" The reason, I submit, is rhetorical stress. Notice that the proposed trochaic pattern makes us stress certain words we would normally not stress: "Where," "there," "In," "There," and "On." If our scansion is to be valid, we must account for this. Why would the speaker of the poem throw his stress on these words? The poem, from *The Tempest,* is spoken by a sprite named Ariel, who has been under the power of a magician named Prospero for many years. At the point in the play when the song is sung, Prospero has promised Ariel his freedom. Contemplating his freedom, though still in bondage, Ariel sings this song. Think of yourself as a prisoner. What would you not be able to do? To *go* where you liked. So, thinking of freedom, Ariel stresses place—the whereness, thereness, inness, and onness of things. That's where the voice of a prisoner would throw stress; the rhythm created by the meter is right. The metrical norm as I hear it conveys rhetorical emphasis, which, because psychologically significant, is integral to the meaning of the poem.

Finally, the last two lines of the poem take us back to the subject of deviation. Trying to retain the trochaic beat, we might at first read them this way:

Mérrĭlý, mérrĭly̆ shall Í live nŏw/Úndĕr thĕ blóssŏm thăt hángs ŏn

thĕ bóugh.

Having discarded that reading, we should observe that line 7 does not really offer much possibility of variance. It is pretty clearly a dactylic trimeter with an added stressed syllable:

Únder thĕ blŏ́ssŏm thăt hángs ŏn thĕ bóugh.

Given that the last two lines are printed as a unit, we should next read back to see if line 6 can be read in the same manner. And so it can:

Mérrĭlў, mérrĭlў shắll Ĭ lĭve nów.

Though this is not the only possible reading, and though we should no doubt hear other contrapuntal patterns in the background, I suggest that this is the reading of choice. This scansion brings out a nice rhetorical stress on the word "now," which rhymes with the clearly stressed "bough." It also brings the line into relationship with both line 7 and lines 1–5, in that the dactyl and the trochee are related and that reading the last two lines as dactylic retains the same number of beats per line throughout the poem.

Still, lines 6 and 7 are deviant in the context of lines 1–5, and again the question is "Why?" Remember the situation of the poem: Ariel, a prisoner, contemplating his coming freedom. Read as trochaic trimeters, the first five lines move slowly, and thus have the effect of serious contemplation. In contrast, lines 6 and 7 move to a dancelike beat, as though Ariel suddenly realizes fully what freedom means. The shift is not violent (the dactyl and trochee are related beats), nor should it be, given that lines 6 and 7 amount to an emotional realization of what has been contemplated in lines 1–5. Yet there is a change: the poem itself breaks into a little dance of jubilation as its singer dances off the stage (as Ariel does at the end of the song). The deviation from the norm—allowed for by the norm—creates the sense of a sudden release of desire and joy. Multiple in meaning, both the norm as it suggests rhetorical stress and the deviation work to convey emotional significance that the denotation of words alone could never fully convey.

METER AND THE ELEMENTS OF RHYTHM

So meter can be a terribly useful tool. Meter can help a poet reproduce in the written language the nuances and gradations of meaning we take for granted when we speak. To put the matter another way, with meter a poet can create rhythms as exact as those of speech. As we've seen, a metrical norm suggests accentuation. In allowing for deviation, it also serves to suggest inflection (the degree of stress): since things that are deviant always call attention to themselves, a deviant beat will tend to draw heavier stress than a nondeviant beat. The use of meter to suggest inflection is illustrated by the following lines from Pope's "The Rape of the Lock":

> "Restore the Lock!" she cries; and all around
> "Restore the Lock!" the vaulted roofs rebound.
> Not fierce Othello in so loud a strain
> Roared for the handkerchief that caused his pain.

"Roared for" is an **inverted foot** (trochaic rather than iambic in this otherwise iambic context). The deviation puts special emphasis on "Roared," which is thus more heavily inflected than the other stressed words in the line. Because of its positioning, the word roars all the more, and, in consequence, rises in volume as well.

In discussing meter, I have concentrated on the role meter plays in suggesting accentuation and, to a lesser degree, inflection. These are the elements of rhythm most strikingly affected by meter. That meter can also affect volume, though, leads to another point: meter can help a poet create exact rhythms because it touches all the elements of rhythm (volume, pace, and pause as well as accentuation and inflection). Free verse has its advantages: it is more pliable than verse proper, and so lends itself more readily to a radical shortening or lengthening of the line. Therefore, it can render more easily a sense of the erratic breath units of a speaker. But it is never as exact as verse proper with respect to all five elements of rhythm.

We have just seen that a deviant beat attracts greater stress, and so tends to be of greater volume, in a metrical context than the surrounding regular beats. Pace, too, is affected by deviation in that we tend to slow up at a deviant beat. This is the effect, I think, of the metrical deviation in the second line of "Delight in Disorder":

Ă sweét dĭsórdĕr ín thĕ dréss / Kíndlĕs ĭn clóthĕs ă wántŏnnéss.

A slight slowing up occurs at "Kindles"—enough of a slowing to let the metaphor take hold (a kindling moment, if you will). Pace is also affected by the initial choice of meter: a trimeter will tend to move more rapidly than a pentameter, and an anapestic or dactyllic line will normally be of greater speed than an iambic or trochaic line. In this regard, compare the first five lines of "Where the Bee Sucks" with the last two. Marked by a heavy trochaic beat (once that beat is heard), the first five lines move slowly, their effect being that of contemplation; the last two lines, dactylic in feel, move to the more rapid beat of a joyful dance.

Finally, pause is affected by meter in that a heavily inflected syllable will make for pause in a metrical context. Once we have discerned the preferred reading, surely, we pause after the "me" of Sidney's "With shield of proof shield me from out the prease," and in pausing throw all the more emphasis on "me." Similarly, the voice automatically pauses slightly after "Roared" in Pope's "Roared for the handkerchief that caused him pain," thereby further emphasizing the roaring quality of the word.

Verse is indeed an extremely useful tool. It is not, however, the poet's only tool for sculpting rhythms, and cannot finally be considered in isolation from the other elements that contribute to the overall sound and movement of a poem. In Chapter 6 we shall look into the interaction of a poem's elements with regard to rhythm. For the moment, let us consolidate what has been said about scansion generally and consider the relation between scansion and oral interpretation.

SCANSION: GUIDELINES AND APPLICATION

Scansion is not the easiest of matters, and it takes time to sensitize the ear. There are, though, guidelines that can help heighten one's capacity to hear. First of all, when reading verse, don't forget what I have said about polysyllabic words. You know how to scan these: simply pronounce them the way you always do and scan them accordingly. As to monosyllabic words, try to maintain a given beat when reading unless a phrase deviates radically from normal speech; then speech takes precedence. We must not forget, of course, that since the origin of modern English around the fourteenth century, our language has undergone a series of changes with respect to diction, syntax, and pronunciation. When reading poems from periods other than our own, as I have said, we must allow for speech patterns that may differ from our own, patterns reflected in the treatment of verse. Here, incidentally, is further evidence of the intimate relation between verse and the spoken language: our best indication of how the language was spoken (that is, its rhythms) before the introduction of mechanical recording (which has helped make free verse attractive in our century) is the verse characteristic of given a period.

How does one go about determining the basic beat (the norm) of a poem in verse? Remember that a beat or foot will usually contain one stressed syllable and one or two unstressed syllables, which can either precede or follow the stressed syllable. I would judge the following sentence, for example, to be an iambic pentameter:

$$\text{Remém/ber éve/rythíng/you héard/todáy.}$$

This sentence suggests, too, the importance of polysyllabic words in establishing a basic beat. Most of the words in it must be pronounced as I have indicated; therefore, an iambic beat is clearly marked. Because any single line can be deviant, however, one must take more than one line into account in determining the metrical norm of a poem. Look at an entire poem, or a number of lines from a longer poem, before making a final determination.[2] Scan a poem quickly on first reading to see what kind of beat occurs most often, or recurs. Then, maintaining the beat as much as possible but allowing for deviation when indicated, read the poem in light of your initial scansion. When scanning, keep in mind that certain words will tend to attract stress to themselves—nouns, verbs, and words that rhyme, for instance. One more point: usually a poet will maintain a set number of stresses per line, whatever the other deviations. This is by no means a hard-and-fast rule, however. Indeed, we're not dealing with rules at all, only with guidelines.

Nothing I have said is meant to suggest that there is no room for variation. Though all skilled readers will agree on the metrical norm of a given poem in verse, no two are likely to scan a piece of verse with identical interpretative emphasis. Here we are in a most delicate area, or an area that calls for delicacy of judgment. Scansion affects interpretation, yet interpretation carries back and affects scansion in turn. It would certainly not be wrong, for instance, to scan the sixth line of "Where the Bee Sucks" as follows:

Mérrily, mérrily shall I líve now (instead of "líve now").

One might easily feel "live" to be the stronger word rhetorically, and stress it for reasons of interpretation. There is room for variation in scansion, then, though not as much room as prose allows for. One could read the last phrase, for example, in any number of ways:

though not as much room as prose allows for;

though not as much room as prose allows for;

though not as much room as prose allows for;

though not as much room as prose allows for;

though not as much room as prose allows for;

and so on. The beauty of verse is that, by limiting possibilities, it moves us to make choices consciously; thus it is rhetorically more exact than nonverse. Nevertheless, many lines of verse allow for variation in scansion.

But however you finally decide to scan and thereafter to read a given line, there is one major principle of verse that should guide you: when reading a poem in verse, one should have a reason for scanning as one does. The reason for scanning most polysyllabic words in a given way, for instance, is that that is the way they are pronounced. One tries to

---

[2] I am speaking here of the typical poem in verse: a poem whose lines are all more or less the same length and, on the whole, composed of the same kind of beat. There are poems in verse composed of variable lines and even of shifting meters (examples are to be found in the Anthology). Usually, though, poems of this sort establish a pattern of variation stanza by stanza, a pattern that careful scansion will reveal.

maintain a beat, or at least a given number of stresses per line, because one is dealing with verse in the first place. Yet a beat should never be maintained rigidly—deviation must be allowed for—and, because both norm and deviations are often clues to meaning, we should keep questioning (reasoning with) the choices the verse points us toward. If our interpretation calls for some shift of stress, our reason for scanning as we do is interpretative emphasis. Whatever the case may be, it is the reasoning that counts. Verse asks us to choose; and asking us to choose, it asks us to justify our choice on the basis of meaning.

At this point we shall take one more poem and carry it through the process of scansion. This will take us, too, to the matter of oral interpretation.

The Oven Bird

Robert Frost

There is a singer everyone has heard,

Loud, a mid-summer and a mid-wood bird,

Who makes the solid tree trunks sound again.

He says that leaves are old and that for flowers

Mid-summer is to spring as one to ten.   5

He says the early petal-fall is past

When pear and cherry bloom went down in showers

On sunny days a moment overcast;

And comes that other fall we name the fall.

He says the highway dust is over all.   10

The bird would cease and be as other birds

But that he knows in singing not to sing.

The question that he frames in all but words

Is what to make of a diminished thing.

(1916)

Read the poem aloud; then mentally divide all polysyllabic words into syllables and place a mark of slack or stress above each syllable. Now, looking for some recurrent pattern, place a mark of slack or stress over all monosyllabic words you feel sure of. Next, take one line whose beat seems clear (line 8, perhaps) and count the number of beats it contains.

Iambic pentameter would seem to be the norm. Try out the whole poem with this norm in mind. Most of the lines do fall easily into an iambic pentameter pattern, which helps to create rhetorical stress on the bird's saying ("says") and on the important "not" of line 12. Not all the lines are strict, though. Lines 4 and 7 have an additional unstressed syllable each; line 2 doesn't fit the pattern at all; and line 1 might be read with a deviant beat at the start. Taking the poem as a dramatic utterance— visualizing its speaker as standing in the place he's speaking of and pointing at a bird—I hear the first foot as inverted and stress "There" rather than "is." Line 2 is much more emphatically deviant. We certainly would not want to read it as follows:

Loud, a mid-summer and a mid-wood bird.

By virtue of its sense and of its being set off by a comma, "Loud" should surely be stressed. The rest of the line is metrically rather ambiguous, even awkward. Should we scan it this way?

Loud, a mid-summer and a mid-wood bird.

Or this way?

Loud, a mid-summer and a mid-wood bird.

Whatever we decide, the line is entirely deviant *given the context generally*. The fairly strict regularity of the rest of the poem, indeed, gives the first two lines an arresting quality and underscores the haltingness of line 2, which in its awkwardness and ambiguity imitates what it is about: the rasping bird and, symbolically, the modern poet—the "singer" whose plight is analogous to that of the bird.

But when reading Frost's poem (preferably aloud) or any poem in verse, one should not overemphasize its regularity. A metrical pattern is a kind of foundation; it supports from below and should remain below. The *rule* is this: read as naturally as possible. Remembering the guidelines we've discussed, try to read a poem in verse with its meter in mind, once you have determined the norm; but never force a pattern. Let the verse deviate where it will, and never read mechanically: daDEE daDEE daDEE daDEE daDEE. Don't forget that *all stresses are not of the same weight* (that is what "inflection" means). Although we do not normally indicate differences of stress when we scan a poem, there are at least four degrees of stress audible to the English ear. In Shakespeare's line "Where the bee sucks, there suck I," inflection is as important as simple accentuation: because of the rhyme, "Where" and "there" receive heavier stress than "bee" and "I." Or the "a" of the last line of "The Oven Bird" should be given only the slightest degree of stress.

When reading, pause where pause is indicated (after "Loud" in line 2 of Frost's poem, for example, and after "He says" in line 10). Pause, which greatly affects the movement of a line, works against the mechanical, as do deviation and the possibility of alternate scansions. To put it succinctly, never read a poem faster than you can naturally speak it. Try to make your reading sound like lively English speech. If the way you read a poem doesn't have this sound, something is wrong.

FREE VERSE AND BLANK VERSE

Before we conclude, two more matters need attention: free verse as it relates to meter, and blank verse. As we discussed in Chapter 2, free verse is nonmetrical. It is verse in the older sense of the word: "verse" comes from the Latin meaning "to turn," and etymologically suggests only division into lines. Line division alone, that is, is the defining element of free verse. However, though a poem in free verse is a poem in which no metrical pattern is strictly operative, many free-verse poems do seem to play against some metrical norm. We might call such poems *structured* free verse. T.S. Eliot was a master of this kind of line, as the beginning of *The Waste Land* testifies:

> April is the cruelest month, breeding
> Lilacs out of the dead land, mixing
> Memory and desire, stirring
> Dull roots with spring rain.
> Winter kept us warm, covering   5
> Earth in forgetful snow, feeding
> A little life with dried tubers.

This would have to be called free verse, yet it has a definite falling feel to it and seems to play against (or with) a trochaic beat. To be sure, not even the most structured free verse is as structured as verse proper, and most free verse is much more erratic than these lines. When reading free verse, though, you should not put aside entirely what you have learned about metrics; often a knowledge of metrics can help bring to the surface the more elusive rhythms of free verse.

Finally, there is blank verse, which must be clearly distinguished from free verse. (Because of the similarity of terms, beginning students sometimes confuse the two.) **Blank verse** is verse that consists of lines in *iambic pentameter* that are *unrhymed* ("blank" means "unrhymed"). Blank verse was the primary medium of Shakespeare, Milton, Wordsworth, Browning, and Stevens, to name only its major practitioners. All wrote rhymed verse and verse in other meters, and Stevens wrote much free verse too. But for their most ambitious poems, all five turned to blank verse. Why? I believe the reason is that the blank-verse line is very close in patterning to English speech. As research using the oscillograph has demonstrated, native speakers of English tend to speak in a rising pattern and in breath units of about ten syllables. So it is that a great many ordinary English sentences are strict iambic pentameters. Consider the following, gleaned from commercials, newspapers, songs, and conversations:

> I hate to see that evenin' sun go down.
> He drank the beer so fast he barfed for days.
> And solitaire's the only game in town.
> What kind of flowers do you think she'd like?
> I can be very friendly, yes I can.
> The cat jumped up and scratched me on the face.
> The impact of the rebate may be great.
> The day will come when all will turn to God.
> Be foxy and fantastic wearing Scholls.
> I went downstairs to see if she was there.
> The man returned to find an empty house.
> I can't afford to waste my time like that.
> It gets the dirt the others leave behind.
> Enjoyment is a low-tar cigarette.
> Don't tell your friends about the two of us.
> The paper said the weather would be fine.
> Serve Kraft Velveeta when you're having guests.
> At last he came to see that he was wrong.
> You care enough to send the very best.
> I wish I were an Oscar Meyer frank.

In pattern, if not in meaning (would anyone really want to be a frankfurter?), none of these statements seems out of keeping with ordinary speech. Yet they are iambic pentameters all.

Exercise

Compose or find (not in poems but in newspapers, commercials, songs, and the like) five sentences that seem ordinary enough in pattern, but on analysis prove to be iambic pentameters. Write down each and its scansion. Now turn to the Anthology, find five poems in iambic pentameter, and list their titles.

Perhaps because the blank-verse line is so close to the essense of English speech patterns, blank verse has proven particularly supple—another reason for its extensive use. In the hands of Shakespeare, who typically used common diction and straightforward syntax, it has the effect of vigorous speech. Milton, whose diction and syntax are more Latinate, created the effect of prophetic speech, or speech heightened to the dignity of prophetic pronouncement. If we allow for the changes in vocabulary between Shakespeare's time and ours, Shakespeare sounds like us; Milton sounds like some Old Testament prophet speaking the words of Yahweh. Wordsworth lies somewhere in between. Though he could and did write blank verse with the flavor of the commonest speech, his single greatest poem, *The Prelude,* is more heightened. In *The Prelude,* Wordsworth's blank verse has the overall effect of a very serious talk, or of a mind in the act of articulating its thought to itself. To see the suppleness of blank verse, and the great variety of effects that it makes possible, turn to pages 337–358 in the Anthology. Read aloud a passage from each of the selections of blank verse gathered there.

POEM ASSIGNMENT

Write a poem in blank verse. Remember the definition of blank verse: *lines in iambic pentameter that are unrhymed.* You will ultimately have ten syllables per line, five slack syllables alternating with five stressed syllables. Even deviant lines should normally contain five stressed syllables. But deviate only when you have clear reason to do so. Try to make most of your lines strict, though as natural-sounding to your own ear as possible. Important monosyllabic words should fall on the beat itself, as should the accented syllables of polysyllabic words. This assignment will take thought and rewriting, since writing in verse is not like making cookies: one doesn't impose a pattern from the outside, as one does with a cookie-cutter, but chooses words so they will naturally form the pattern. Incidentally, your lines need not be end-stopped; your grammar may be such that they enjamb. Once again, ground your thought in the concretions of situation, imagery, metaphor, and give your poem a title.

The first student sample is not quite in accord with the assignment, though rather nice in and of itself:

Gap

James Zwanzig

She said that life is short and that
You don't yet know how fast it goes.
But I don't care 'cause I'm so young,
And she was old and oh so gray.

The problem with this poem, in light of the assignment, is that it is in iambic tetrameter, not pentameter. With a little bit of rewriting, however, it can easily be turned into blank verse:

> She slowly said that life is short and that
> You someday will find out how fast it goes.
> But I don't care because I'm very young,
> And she was old and oh so very gray.

The next samples fulfill the pattern perfectly, though, because of other variables, their effects differ. "Dampened Spirits" resembles everyday speech; with its more heightened diction and tone, "On Viewing Ancient Lands" is more like a eulogy spoken over a grave; heavily enjambed, "Down the Road" has the feel of meditation.

Dampened Spirits

Jeannette Tedone

How can I answer this demand he writes?
My thoughts are scattered like the drops outside.
They should be pooled together to make sense,
But mine just fall on rooftops aimlessly.

On Viewing Ancient Lands

Joseph Capitani

The olive trees of ancient lands produce
No more for peasant hands to harvest home.
Etruscan might of days long past is gone,
With nothing left but tracks of meager grains.
And now I shed a bitter tear for them;   5
But they'll not hear the hollow cry "Absurd!"
For they are only compost that were men,
And deeper settle with each putrid rain.

Down the Road

Gerald Pearce

With haunted hearts and vacant eyes we stare
while riding into space. We never thought
that we'd grow old. We talked and joked and sang
while riding west. We rode our last ride down.

Finally, a poem I find a sheer delight. Its simplicity of diction and syntax, and its pleading tone, impart a childlike flavor (as does the failure of the speaker to distinguish as to sex—Hildegard is a female name). But the child is growing in the ways of reality, as is suggested by the prosaic elongation—made possible by the verse context—of the last line, along with the contrasts between the fantasy name "Hildegard" and the mundane "Fred" and between bird and toad.

Hildegard

Jarlath Duffy

I had a little bird and kept it caged.
I liked him and I called him Hildegard.
I gave him food and water every day,
As much of each as he could ever want.
But then one day I opened up the door   5
To see my bird just up and fly away.
Oh Hildegard! I gave you all I had!
You left me here all stranded by myself.
So now I have to find another friend.
I think today I'll get a toad and call him Fred.   10

POEMS FOR FURTHER STUDY

The Pleasures of Merely
Circulating

Wallace Stevens

The garden flew round with the angel,
The angel flew round with the clouds,
And the clouds flew round and the clouds flew round
And the clouds flew round with the clouds.

Is there any secret in skulls,   5
The cattle skulls in the woods?
Do the drummers in black hoods
Rumble anything out of their drums?

Mrs. Anderson's Swedish baby
Might well have been German or Spanish,   10
Yet that things go round and again go round
Has rather a classical sound.

                                                          (1935)

Questions
1. Scan the poem.
2. What is its basic beat?
3. How does Stevens keep that beat from becoming monotonous?
4. In what way is the meter of the poem appropriate to its subject matter?
5. What effect does meter have here on rhythmic movement and thence on tone?
6. Compare the effect of "The Pleasures of Merely Circulating" with that of the following poem by Tennyson.

Tears, Idle Tears

Alfred, Lord Tennyson

Tears, idle tears, I know not what they mean,
Tears from the depth of some divine despair
Rise in the heart, and gather to the eyes,
In looking on the happy autumn-fields,
And thinking of the days that are no more.   5

Fresh as the first beam glittering on a sail,
That brings our friends up from the underworld,
Sad as the last which reddens over one
That sinks with all we love below the verge;
So sad, so fresh, the days that are no more.   10

Ah, sad and strange as in dark summer dawns
The earliest pipe of half-awakened birds
To dying ears, when unto dying eyes
The casement slowly grows a glimmering square;
So sad, so strange, the days that are no more.   15

Dear as remembered kisses after death,
And sweet as those by hopeless fancy feigned
On lips that are for others; deep as love,
Deep as first love, and wild with all regret;
O Death in Life, the days that are no more!   20

(1847)

TEARS, IDLE TEARS. 7. *from the underworld:* from below the horizon.

Questions
1. Scan the poem.
2. What is its basic meter? In that the poem is not rhymed, what kind of verse is this?
3. Many of the lines of this poem begin with metrical inversions. How do these deviations affect our reading?
4. Where might one choose to deviate for interpretive emphasis? To what effect?
5. How does the overall rhythmic movement of the poem reflect mood?

That the Night Come

W. B. Yeats

She lived in storm and strife,
Her soul had such desire
For what proud death may bring
That it could not endure
The common good of life,   5
But lived as 'twere a king
That packed his marriage day
With banneret and pennon,
Trumpet and kettledrum,
And the outrageous cannon,   10
To bundle time away
That the night come.

(1914)

Questions
1. Scan the poem.
2. What is its basic meter?
3. This poem concerns a woman who lived with urgency, as a king might on his wedding day. How does Yeats's choice of line express that urgency?

4. Contrast the effects of Yeats's relatively short lines and Tennyson's much longer lines.
5. What is the effect of the metrical deviations of lines 9 and 12?
6. What is the effect of the shortening of line 12?

Terrible Dactyl, Son of Rodan

Edward Proffitt

As I was walking on iambic feet
At dusk, as is my wont, along a street
Of fine poetic structures, old but meet,
Terrible Dactyl came beating around,
Clumsily pounding with hideous sound. 5
I mustered my forces and gave the sign
To an army of anapests manning the line.
But no use! All was in deepening disarray
Till I remembered the Japanese way.
Grabbing at once for any old haiku, 10
I shortened the line
And pelted out petals—
Numberless petals
Brushed with the russet color
Of the sinking sun. 15
The monster was undone.
I then returned to where I had begun.

(*1977*)

Questions
1. Scan the poem.
2. Many different metrical effects operate here. What are they? (Contrast with regard to meter lines 1–3, 4–5, 6–7, 8–12, 13–15, and 16–17).
3. A haiku is a nonmetrical Japanese form consisting of three lines of 5–7–5 syllables respectively. Haikus usually concern the more delicate aspects of nature. What lines comprise the haiku here? With respect to metrics, why would writing a haiku help the speaker defeat Terrible Dactyl? In what other way is a haiku an appropriate weapon with which to defeat this monster?
4. Aside from the echo of "pterodactyl" (a prehistoric reptilian bird) in "Terrible Dactyl," why is the dactyl cast in the role of a monster (as "Son of Rodan," a monster who appears in a number of Japanese monster movies)? How would a persistent dactylic beat affect a poem

in iambics, which the speaker indicates he was trying to write at the outset? What is the difference in effect between the two beats?

IDEAS FOR WRITING

1. Paraphrase Tennyson's "Tears, Idle Tears," and then discuss the difference between paraphrase and poem. (What is lost in the bare paraphrase?)
2. Scan Wordsworth's "Lines Written in Early Spring":

> I heard a thousand blended notes,
> While in a grove I sate reclined,
> In that sweet mood when pleasant thoughts
> Bring sad thoughts to the mind.
>
> To her fair works did Nature link   5
> The human soul that through me ran;
> And much it grieved my heart to think
> What man has made of man.
>
> Through primrose tufts, in that green bower,
> The periwinkle trailed its wreaths;   10
> And 'tis my faith that every flower
> Enjoys the air it breathes.
>
> The birds around me hopped and played,
> Their thoughts I cannot measure—
> But the least motion which they made,   15
> It seemed a thrill of pleasure.
>
> The budding twigs spread out their fan,
> To catch the breezy air;
> And I must think, do all I can,
> That there was pleasure there.   20
>
> If this belief from heaven be sent,
> If such be Nature's holy plan,
> Have I not reason to lament
> What man has made of man?

(1798)

LINES WRITTEN IN EARLY SPRING.   10. *periwinkle:* a trailing evergreen ground cover with blue flowers in the spring (called "myrtle" in many parts of the United States).

First determine what the norm is and where deviations occur. Now discuss the rhetorical effects the norm allows for and the reasons for Wordsworth's deviations from that norm. What, for example, is the effect of the shortening of the fourth line of each stanza? In a separate paragraph, discuss your response to the poem.

3. I have suggested that there will normally be a given number of stresses per line, whatever the other deviations. This too, however, is only a norm: many poems contain lines with more or fewer stresses than the norm, though every line should be read against the norm if one is suggested. What about John Donne's Sonnet 14 (from "Holy Sonnets") in this regard?

> Batter my heart, three-personed God; for You
> As yet but knock, breathe, shine, and seek to mend;
> That I may rise and stand, o'erthrow me, and bend
> Your force to break, blow, burn, and make me new.
> I, like an usurped town, to another due,   5
> Labor to admit You, but O, to no end;
> Reason, Your viceroy in me, me should defend,
> But is captived, and proves weak or untrue.
> Yet dearly I love You, and would be lovèd fain,
> But am betrothed unto Your enemy.   10
> Divorce me, untie or break that knot again;
> Take me to You, imprison me, for I,
> Except You enthrall me, never shall be free,
> Nor ever chaste, except You ravish me.
>
> *(1633)*

The beat is iambic, and pentameter is the norm. Yet there is much deviation here, and some lines contain more than five stresses. Scan the poem and account for your scansion.

4. William Carlos Williams's "The Dance," which describes a lively painting by Breughel (1520–1569) called *The Kermess,* would be hard to label as to meter. Nevertheless, it has about it a clear feeling of rhythmic recurrence and a sense of deviation from a norm as well. Scan the poem and give a label to the norm: is it rising or falling, anapestic or dactylic? Read the poem with your choice in mind; then read it in light of the opposite possibility. Live with the poem for a few days, and live through its sensuous patterns. Finally, discuss the overall effect of its metrical ambiguity and the highly contrapuntal rhythms produced by that ambiguity.

The Dance

W. C. Williams

In Breughel's great picture, The Kermess,
the dancers go round, they go round and
around, the squeal and the blare and the
tweedle of bagpipes, a bugle and fiddles
tipping their bellies (round as the thick-   5
sided glasses whose wash they impound)
their hips and their bellies off balance
to turn them. Kicking and rolling about
the Fair Grounds, swinging their butts, those
shanks must be sound to bear up under such   10
rollicking measures, prance as they dance
in Breughel's great picture, The Kermess.

(1944)

Rhythm & Other Constituents of Voice
Chapter Six

SOUND AND SENSE

There's an old Yiddish story about a man who puzzles over why noodles are called "noodles." After much internal debate, he concludes matter-of-factly: "Ehh, they're called 'noodles' because they look like noodles." That the story translates as well as it does lends validity to its underlying assumption about words: that they are intimately tied to the things they mean. The English word *noodle is* noodlely, ending as it does with a little curl of sound.

But we know better. Unlike more primitive peoples, who believe that words are potent with the reality they name, we of the scientific world are nominalists: our knowledge of history leads us to see words as arbitrary signs. So, that noodles are called "noodles" is only an historical accident. There is no innate link between a word's sound and its sense. Of course, one could compile a long list of words that do seem to suggest a link. For example, 90 percent of the English words that end in *-sh* involve violent action (*bash, lash, gash, mash*); the word *sneer* has a sneering quality, for when it is said emphatically, it curls the lip and wrinkles the nose; the *-mm* sound in *mother* seems related to infant nurturing. Then there are **onomatopoetic** (on'o · mat'o · po · et"ik) words—words whose sounds imitate the sounds of what they name (*buzz, splash, cock-a-doodle-doo*). Still, we know that other languages have completely different words for the same auditory phenomena. And for every word that somehow sounds like what it means, there are ten that don't.

It would seem, then, that we are left with a language of sterile signs—sterile because not expressive, not expressive because arbitrary. However, we use words not one by one but rather in patterns of our own making. That is, whatever history has given us by way of vocabulary, we can make our words expressive—or unite sound and sense—by *choice* and *patterning*. We do so automatically at moments of genuine feeling, when, modulating our voices in one way or another, we make our words fall into patterns expressively distinctive in rhythm. When we're angry, our words pound out; when we're happy, they elide and skip along; and when we speak love, we speak low. And poets do the same; by deliberate choice and patterning, they shape from the arbitrary signs of language a unity of sound and sense, a language potent and dense with meaning. In our discussion of meter we saw (or heard) poets doing this. Now we shall turn to the other possible tools that go into the making of exact rhythms.

SYNTAX

English is a syntactical language: our words mean what they mean in sentences primarily by virtue of positioning. "Dog bites man," therefore, means one thing, and "man bites dog" another. Also a matter of syntax are the different patterns of phrasing possible in English. One could say, "I earn my money before I spend it," or, "Before I spend my money, I earn it." Each has a different rhythm and a slightly different effect. The first, rapid and matter-of-fact, is unemphatic. The second, slower and more strongly inflected at the end, is more emphatic because it builds to a climax (that is, we wait until the end to find out the central information).

Rhythm & Other Constituents of Voice

Emphasis is also often achieved by simple syntactical **inversion:** e.g., "My money, I earn." To invert normal syntax in this way is to put special weight (also a matter of rhythm) on the inverted word or phrase.

Because syntax affects rhythm and voice, a poet's choice of one pattern over another is often significant. I am thinking in particular of Milton, one of the great masters of syntax as a medium of meaning. One can open *Paradise Lost* to almost any page and find examples of such use of syntax:

> Others apart sat on a hill retired,
> In thoughts more elevate, and reasoned high
> Of providence, foreknowledge, will, and fate,
> Fixed fate, free will, foreknowledge absolute,
> And found no end, in wandering mazes lost.
>
> *(Book II, lines 557–561)*

Here Milton describes a band of fallen angels engaging in the intricate theological disputes of his own day. With much wit (after all, he was not of the devil's party), Milton makes a syntactical maze of his words, thereby dramatically suggesting the maziness of the labyrinthine dispute. Even the minor inversion "Others apart sat" carries meaning: by separating subject and verb, Milton produces a sense of apartness. Just a few lines earlier there occurs another instance:

> The song was partial, but the harmony
> (What could it less when Spirits immortal sing?)
> Suspended Hell. . . .
>
> *(lines 552–554)*

The positioning of the parenthesis—a matter of syntax—creates an almost muscular sense of suspension, embodying the suspension described.

Over and above such local effects as these, the pervasive syntax of *Paradise Lost* as a whole carries a weight of meaning. Consider the opening sentence of the poem:

> Of man's first disobedience, and the fruit
> Of that forbidden tree whose mortal taste
> Brought death into the world, and all our woe,
> With loss of *Eden,* till one greater Man
> Restore us, and regain the blissful seat,　　　　　5
> Sing, Heavenly Muse. . . .
>
> *(Book I, lines 1–6)*

The pattern of these lines—not typical of English, though to be heard against the norm—is characteristic of the entire poem. Milton's syntax, which involves the positioning of the main elements of each sentence at its end, creates a rhythm we might call a "rhythm of climax." We are pulled on inexorably, sentence by sentence, as though adrift at sea and pulled by the tide to some fated rendezvous. Cumulatively, the syntax of *Paradise Lost* (together with its diction) creates a voice elevated and stately, as befits Milton's subject matter; it also produces what one of Milton's most perceptive critics calls a sense "less [of] a destination than a destiny." [1] The characteristic syntax of *Paradise Lost* is one with the grand design of the work as a whole, a design announced in its first sentence: to trace the fall of man, but always in light of the race's ultimate redemption, beckoning at the end of history just as Milton's main subjects and verbs beckon at the ends of his sentences.

With respect to syntax and its effect on rhythm and voice, how utterly different from Milton's stately progress is the movement of Hopkins's last sonnets—called "terrible" because of the agony they express. Marked by a wrenching awkwardness of syntax, as we've seen in "No Worst, There Is None" (page 31), these sonnets move with a rhythm of desperation. Clearly, such is the effect on rhythm of Hopkins's syntactical choices in another late sonnet:

[I Wake and Feel the Fell of Dark]

I wake and feel the fell of dark, not day.
What hours, O what black hoürs we have spent
This night! what sights you, heart, saw; ways you went!
And more must, in yet longer light's delay.

With witness I speak this. But where I say   5
Hours I mean years, mean life. And my lament
Is cries countless, cries like dead letters sent
To dearest him that lives alas! away.

I am gall, I am heartburn. God's most deep decree
Bitter would have me taste: my taste was me;   10
Bones built in me, flesh filled, blood brimmed the curse.

Selfyeast of spirit a dull dough sours. I see
The lost are like this, and their scourge to be
As I am mine, their sweating selves, but worse.

(c. 1885)

[I WAKE AND FEEL THE FELL OF DARK]. 1. *fell:* As a noun, "fell" means "the hide of an animal" and, in an older sense, "bitterness, gall." As an adjective, it means "savage, cruel."

[1] Christopher Ricks, *Milton's Grand Style* (London: Oxford University Press, 1963), p. 30.

Hopkins could have written "what sights you saw, my heart, what ways you went." He wrote, instead, "what sights you, heart, saw; ways you went!" because he did not want the smoothness and sense of calm implicit in the alternate phrasing; he wanted the awkwardness of his chosen pattern because it makes the voice seem strained and, rhythmically, lends the feel of tumult. The same feel is imparted by every grammatical choice the poet made. "My lament/Is cries countless," for instance, is a most ungainly construction (singular subject, copulative verb, plural complement). Yet in the present context it is perfect. The single lament is magnified by the verb of being into "cries countless," the very ungainliness of the construction suggesting the agony of the multiplication. Notice, too, that as the poem unfolds, it is composed increasingly of short, choppy phrases. The sestet (last six lines) is especially halting, and thus renders a voice not of meditation but of gasping pain. Then there is the powerful syntactical inversion "Bitter would have me taste." The wrenched repositioning of the word "Bitter" (which would normally come after "taste") makes it rub off on "decree" as well as on "me": the taste of "me" might be bitter, yet so is the "decree" that would have me taste of that bitterness. In other words, the inversion makes the word "Bitter" serve double duty; Hopkins's syntactical choice also throws special weight on "Bitter" (as does the metrical inversion introduced by the word). Finally, there is the syntactical ambiguity of "but worse." Who is "worse," the "I" or the "lost" in hell? The ambiguity underscores the speaker's agonized puzzlement.

How utterly different are the following lines from John Denham's *Cooper's Hill* (1655):

> O could I flow like thee, and make thy stream
> My great example, as it is my theme!
> Though deep, yet clear; though gentle, yet not dull;
> Strong without rage, without o'erflowing full.

The effect of these lines is that of grace and balance, gained through syntax. Denham used every device at hand to pattern his lines so they would move as they do. First, there is **zeugma** (a syntactical yoking): for instance, "example" and "theme" of line 2 are yoked by their mutual dependence on "stream." Then there is **chiasmus** (a sequence of phrases basically parallel in syntax but with some element reversed): for example, the pattern of the last line, which is framed by its key adjectives. Finally, there is straight syntactical parallelism, particularly in line 3 (note the similarity of pattern between "Though deep, yet clear" and "though gentle, yet not full"). These syntactical devices serve to bind the lines together and make them move with ease and grace, even though lines 1, 2, and 4 break into two rhythmic units each by virtue of the central caesura each contains (a **caesura** is a strong pause within a line enforced by its grammar), and line 3 breaks into four units. But Denham's syntactical patterning, together with the regularity of his caesuras (that is, where they fall) gives the lines an effect far different from that of Hopkins's sonnet. Indeed, Denham's lines are far removed both from the spiritual turmoil of Hopkins and from the spiritual elevation of Milton. Here is the rational mind seeking the classical golden mean. Rationality, grace, balance—these were to become the values of the "Age of Reason." And these secular values underlie Denham's lines and are reflected in their syntax and resultant rhythmic balance and grace.

Exercise

Recast Denham's lines syntactically so as to disturb their balanced movement (for example, "Without rage, strong; full, yet not o'erflowing"). Now contrast the effect of the lines as recast and as Denham wrote them.

END-LINE PHENOMENA

As important as syntax with respect to rhythm, and very much related to syntax, is poetry's division into lines, which makes for a host of possible effects. We have seen, for instance, that division into lines makes it possible for a poet to choose long lines or short, or some mixture of the two, and that different line lengths have different rhythmic potentials. We have discussed the relation between division into lines and meter (meter in English, you will recall, involves in part the number of syllables *per line*), as well as how crucial line division is to free verse. Deliberate line division—perhaps the essential concretion—lends to a poem a muscular dimension: the eyes are pulled forward and backwards, and because of that pulling, the body tenses and relaxes rhythmically. Line division also allows a poet to impart a sense of balance, as Denham does in the lines quoted above largely by virtue of their central caesuras. Observe how grammatical pause is made to fall at the center of each line (each line having a center precisely because it is a line). Conversely, a poet can heighten tension by making caesuras fall unevenly, as Hopkins often does. Finally, line division makes possible what I am now calling "end-line phenomena." What happens at the end of a line is usually of particular importance; obviously, what happens can happen only because a piece is divided into lines.

Specifically, there are four things that can happen at the end of a line. It can end with a marked pause enforced by punctuation, in which case it is called **end-stopped;** or, because of its syntax, it can end with barely the hint of a pause or no pause at all, in which case it is called **enjambed.** And it can end on a stressed syllable or an unstressed syllable, which we

shall call **strong** and **weak** endings respectively.[2] The first five lines of
Keats's *Endymion* (1818) exemplify the various possibilities:

> A thing of beauty is a joy forever:
> Its loveliness increases; it will never
> Pass into nothingness; but still will keep
> A bower quiet for us, and a sleep
> Full of sweet dreams. . . .

The first line is end-stopped and has a weak ending ("forever"); the sec-
ond line has a weak ending and enjambs; line 3 enjambs and has a strong
ending; and line 4 has a strong ending and is, to my ear, end-stopped.
Like meter, line division often asks us to make choices (such as whether to
pause or enjamb) dependent on interpretative emphasis. Indeed, one of
the functions of line division in the first place is to heighten our aware-
ness of the choices to be made. In all of its aspects, thus, line division is
intimately linked to interpretation and meaning.

End-line phenomena in particular open out a variety of possibilities
in that what happens at the end of a line can affect all five elements of
rhythm (accentuation, inflection, volume, pace, and pause). A poet can
slow the pace of a poem, for instance, by constructing lines that are all
end-stopped. Conversely, a poet can speed up pace by constructing lines
that all enjamb easily. By end-stopping with a stressed syllable, a poet can
suggest greater stress (inflection) and heighten volume by virtue of the
pause. Conversely, a poet can soften and diminish volume by enjambing
after a weak ending. What happens at the line break, then, very much
affects rhythm and voice; it also affects tone. Depending on other factors
(such as diction), a series of end-stopped lines can, for example, have a
matter-of-fact tone. This is the effect of Frost's line treatment in "Stop-
ping by Woods" (see page 28). Also depending on other factors (such as
the kind of grammatical element split), lines that enjamb can do so awk-
wardly, creating a tone of agitation. Whatever the case, the fundamental
principle is: a poet can work either with the line or against it. Because
the natural tendency is to pause at the end of a line, a poet is working
with the line when a grammatical pause falls at its end, and against it in
one way or another when it enjambs.

John Berryman is clearly working against the line in the following:

> I don't see how Henry, pried
> open for all the world to see, survived.

---

2 What I am here calling "strong" and "weak" endings are usually called "masculine"
and "feminine" endings respectively. It is time to change terms. I bring up the matter
only because "masculine" and "feminine" are still the standard terms in critical discourse.

Graceless, the enjambment underscores the gracelessness of the syntax of the two lines. The effect of the break is a kind of stutter, which is apt in that the poem expresses the inability of this Henry to express his grief. That it is line division in particular that creates this effect can be seen, I think, by re-lining. Compare the lines as Berryman wrote them with the following re-lining:

> I don't see how Henry,
> pried open for all the world to see,
> survived.

Enjambment need not be awkward, however. Keats's "it will never/Pass into nothingness" enjambs easily and in so doing quickens the pace.

Line division and what happens at the break can also be agents of humor, and are often agents of suspense and the unexpected. Take a passage from Byron's *Don Juan:*

> And then this best and meekest woman bore
>   With such serenity her husband's woes,
> Just as the Spartan ladies did of yore,
>   Who saw their spouses killed, and nobly chose
> Never to say a word about them more.

The slight pause after "chose" creates a moment of suspense: chose what? Something noble, one supposes. We then rush on as the line enjambs to have our momentary expectations undercut by the comic twist of the last line. The same device can be made to work for noncomic effects. Consider these lines from Stevens's "Sunday Morning":

> Divinity must live within herself:
> Passions of rain, or moods in falling snow;
> Grievings in loneliness, or unsubdued
> Elations when the forest blooms; gusty
> Emotions on wet roads on autumn nights.

There is just enough of a pause after "gusty," though the line enjambs, for "Emotions" to have about it a sense of the unexpected (we had expected, perhaps, "Wind"). With this little shock, heightened by the enjambment, Stevens clinches his meaning: that divinity springs only from life, and that emotions must be one with what gives them birth—the earth.

Another advantage of line division is that it enables a poet to suggest a strong pause not suggested by grammar and syntax. Wordsworth achieves a little miracle in this regard:

> Then sometimes, in the silence while he hung
> Listening, a gentle shock. . . .

The significant suspension is produced by line division alone. Equally significant as to end-stopping is a moment in Hamlet's "To be or not to be" soliloquy:

>   . . . to die—to sleep—
> No more . . . .

"To die—to sleep" is conventional, death being traditionally thought of as a sleep. If we pause, as Shakespeare indicates we should, all the conventional associations flood into the mind. Then comes the dramatic reversal "No more." With that reversal, underscored by the strong pause suggested, Shakespeare departs from the conventional entirely and moves into another dimension of meaning.

That it is dimensions of meaning we are talking about can perhaps be borne home by way of a contrast.

> April is the cruelest month, breeding
> Lilacs out of the dead land, mixing
> Memory and desire, stirring
> Dull roots with spring rain.
> Winter kept us warm, covering   5
> Earth in forgetful snow, feeding
> A little life with dried tubers.

The insistence of the rather flabby enjambments of this, the opening of T. S. Eliot's *The Waste Land,* coupled with the weak endings and falling rhythmic feel, imparts a sense of aimlessness to the voice. In contrast, the opening lines of *Paradise Lost* have the feel of firmness and resolve:

> Of man's first disobedience, and the fruit
> Of that forbidden tree whose mortal taste
> Brought death into the world, and all our woe,
> With loss of *Eden,* till one greater Man   5
> Restore us, and regain the blissful seat,
> Sing, Heavenly Muse. . . .

Aimlessness versus the firmness of resolve—that is exactly the difference in meaning between the two poems generally, a difference embodied in the divergent ways the line is treated by each poet and the ways the lines move because of what happens at the line breaks.

Exercise

Re-line both of the above passages. Make the lines from *The Waste Land* all end-stopped ("April is the cruelest month,/Breeding lilacs...") and the lines from *Paradise Lost* enjamb arbitrarily ("...and the/Fruit of that forbidden tree whose/mortal..."). Then read aloud the originals and your revisions. What is lost in the re-linings? You might also write out each passage as though it were prose—straight across the page. Now what's lost? Finally, compare each of the following passages with regard to line treatment and effect (such as easy versus awkward enjambment). See, too, if you can detect contrasting movements created by line treatment (end-stopping here, enjambment there) within each passage.

> And after she was dead, and he had paid
> The singers and the sexton and the rest,
> He packed a lot of things that she had made
> Most mournfully away in an old chest
> Of hers, and put some chopped-up cedar boughs
> In with them, and tore down the slaughter-house.
>
> *E. A. Robinson*

> He gives his harness bells a shake
> To ask if there is some mistake.
> The only other sound's the sweep
> Of easy wind and downy flake.
>
> *Robert Frost*

> Ah, yes—below
> the knees, since the tune
> drops that way, it is
> one of those white summer days,
> the tall grass of your ankles
> flickers upon the shore—
> Which shore?—
> the sand clings to my lips—
> Which shore?
> Agh, petals maybe. How
> should I know?
>
> *W. C. Williams*

> But if it had to perish twice,
> I think I know enough of hate
> To say that for destruction ice
> Is also great
> And would suffice.
>
> *Robert Frost*

Full fathom five thy father lies;
   Of his bones are coral made;
Those are pearls that were his eyes:
   Nothing of him that doth fade,
But doth suffer a sea change   5
Into something rich and strange.
Sea nymphs hourly ring his knell:
   Ding-dong.
Hark! now I hear them—Ding-dong, bell.

(1623)
William Shakespeare

CONSONANTS AND VOWELS

Consonants and vowels, when carefully patterned, also affect rhythm and participate in the design of a poem's meaning. I am not speaking now of words as such, but of the sounds of the English language in themselves. English consonants fall roughly into ten categories: the fricatives "f" and "v," and the affricative "j"; the nasals "m" and "n"; the sibilants "s" and "z"; the plosives "b" and "p" and the related dentals "d" and "t"; the gutturals "g" (as in "god"), "k," "q," and "x"; the aspirate "h"; the glides or rolls "r" (as in "rough"), "w," and "y"; and the liquids "l" and "r" (as in "tiger"). There are also consonantal sounds, produced by the combining of consonants, called "blends" and "digraphs": for example, "ng," "sh," "sp," "cl," "th," "str," "ch." Our vowel sounds, of which there are at least sixteen in standard English plus diphthongs (such as "ai" as in "day" and "ou" as in "how"), can be long or short ("sāy" versus "săt") and differ in frequency or pitch. Look at the following chart of selected vowel sounds arranged in descending steps as to pitch:

  ē (see)
    ā (say)
      ī (sigh)   ĭ (sit)
          ĕ (set)
            ă (sat)   ŭ (suds)
                ô (saw)
                   ŏ (sot)   ŏo (schnook)
                        ō (shone)
                        ōo (shoe)

There is some subjectivity involved in one's perception of descent of pitch.³ But surely there is a clear difference in pitch between the extremes (ē and ōō), just as there is a clear difference in quantity (the length of time it takes to say a vowel) between long and short vowels (such as ē versus ĕ).

At any rate, these are our basic consonantal and vowel sounds, which, because they involve the mouth and tongue in different motions, have different feelings (literally and metaphorically) about them. The nasals (m, n) are easier to say and softer in feel than the gutturals (g, k, q, x); the aspirate "h" is much quieter than the affricative "j"; the liquids (l, r) are much more fluid than the plosives (b, p), which are more explosive. As for vowels, the long vowels do take longer to say than the short vowels (this quantitative difference very much affects rhythm), and the high-pitched vowels are somewhat brighter or more piercing than the duller low-pitched vowels. Individual words, however, do not necessarily reflect their senses in their sounds. It has been held, for instance, that in terms of sound alone, the most melodious word in English is "diarrhea."

What counts in poetry is the sound of words in context and the patterns that can be made of carefully chosen words in combination—patterns that can reflect meaning in that they exploit the different innate qualities of sounds (the sounds of consonants and vowels). For instance, a concentration of long and/or low vowels will have a different effect from a concentration of high and/or short vowels: "No motion has she now, no force" versus "Hail to thee, blithe Spirit" or "Variety is the spice of life"; "moaning low" versus "Better get up." Similarly, a line with a marked recurrence of aspirates and liquids will be quite different in feel and movement from a line characterized by a recurrence of affricatives and dentals: "Home is where the heart is" versus "Judge not lest ye be judged." The first is hushed and even in movement, its one sharp sound (the "t" of "heart") softened by elision with the vowel that follows; the second is loud and abrupt, not an exhalation of sentimental feeling but a stern command. The pattern of each is deliberate and meaningful (or a dimension of meaning). That's why phrases of this sort stick in the mind: their words, however arbitrary individually, are expressive in the patterns they form.

There are so many possible patterns of vowels and vowels, consonants and consonants, and consonants and vowels that it would be impossible to name them all. There are, however, four general terms that can be useful: assonance, vowel gradation, consonance, alliteration.

---

³ In fact, however, the wavelengths of high-frequency vowels, which are formed in the front of the mouth, are shorter and more intense than those of low-frequency vowels, which come from the back of the mouth. Thus there is a physical basis to the distinction.

Assonance is the repetition of similar vowel sounds in a sequence of words: "Thou still unravished bride of quietness,/Thou foster child of silence and slow time" (John Keats); "near the winter river with silt like silver" (William Stafford). Such repetition can have a number of different effects on rhythm and voice, effects already illustrated in passing (for example, "No motion has she now, no force"). If the vowels of a line are mostly long, they tend to slow the pace; if they are mostly short, they tend to quicken it. If the vowels are mainly low-pitched, they tend to deepen and darken; if they are mainly high-pitched, they tend to lighten or give the voice a sharp edge. If the vowels are short and high-pitched, they quicken and lighten; if they are long and low-pitched, they slow and darken. Equally marked in effect is **vowel gradation,** the step-by-step shifting of vowels from high to low or low to high. The first line of the old blues song "St. Louis Blues" is a striking example of purposeful vowel gradation: "I hate to see that evenin' sun go down." Look at the line's main vowels: ī, ā, ē, ŭ, ō, ä/ōō (for the diphthong "ou" of "down"). There is a clearly gradated movement from high-pitched to low-pitched vowels, a movement reflected in the song's melody line and reflective of the sinking the line describes.

The opposite of assonance is **consonance,** the repetition of a sequence of consonants with a change in the intervening vowels—for example, "tick/tock," "life/loaf," "breed/bread." The primary effect of consonance is dissonance, since words in consonantal relationship are so close that their internal differences tend to grate. Wilfred Owen, the foremost poet of the First World War, developed the technique of consonance to a high degree and used it to give voice to his disgust:

Arms and the Boy

Wilfred Owen

Let the boy try along this bayonet-blade
How cold steel is, and keen with hunger of blood;
Blue with all malice, like a madman's flash;
And thinly drawn with famishing for flesh.

Lend him to stroke these blind, blunt bullet-heads   5
Which long to nuzzle in the hearts of lads,
Or give him cartridges of fine zinc teeth,
Sharp with the sharpness of grief and death.

For his teeth seem for laughing round an apple.
There lurk no claws behind his fingers supple;   10
And god will grow no talons at his heels,
Nor antlers through the thickness of his curls.

(1920)

ARMS AND THE BOY. Owen alludes to the first line of Vergil's *Aeneid:* "I sing of arms and the man."

Like rhyme, consonance tends to draw attention—and thus stress—to itself. This is why "Arms and the Boy" seems as dissonant as it does. At the point where we might expect the resolution of rhyme—at the crucial end-line position—we encounter words enough alike to draw attention to themselves; yet we are led to feel difference rather than similarity, and so denied a sense of resolution. The effect of Owen's "blade/blood," "flash/flesh," "-heads/lads," and so on, is like the effect in a piece of music of a strongly dissonant chord just when we expect a return to the tonic (an harmonious chord that provides resolution). Both tend to set the teeth on edge and make one feel uncomfortable. This is the effect, too, of internal consonance ("blind, blunt bullet-"); the poem's concentration of plosives (b, p), dentals (d, t), and gutturals ("cartridges of fine zinc"); and its insistent lack of assonance. (The lines of the poem exhibit a minimum of vowel repetition—"And thinly drawn with famishing for flesh.") All these elements work together to produce a voice bitterly ironic in tone.

Finally, there is **alliteration:** the repetition of a consonantal sound, placed conspicuously at the beginning of a word or of an internal stressed syllable, in a sequence of nearby words. (Words that exhibit consonance, then, also alliterate.) You are surely already familiar with alliteration, since we all delight in and make use of it constantly. Just think of the thousands of trite phrases that stick in the mind only because they alliterate: "tried and true," "fit as a fiddle," "wit and wisdom," "vim and vigor" (the word "vim" has been retained in the language only by this phrase), "part and parcel," "crystal clear," "fabulous 50's," "neither rhyme nor reason," "last but not least," and so on.

Exercise

Compile a list of five to ten familiar alliterative phrases. You might also add a few phrases marked by assonance ("a stone's throw," "a golden oldie") and consonance ("pitter-patter"). This exercise should cause you no trials or tribulations—just listen carefully to your own and other people's ordinary speech.

Such trite phrases are to be avoided in writing (when writing, one can take time to avoid the worn). Nevertheless, they do persist. Why? Again, the right hemisphere of the brain seems to love linkages of any sort. There is another reason as well: alliterative linkages draw weight to themselves and thus serve to emphasize—which is their main function in poetry.

Saxon "stress metrics"—a type of meter based on the number of stressed syllables per line—is a case in point. Another name for this type of meter is "alliterative meter," since the words to be stressed usually alliterate: for example, "In a <u>s</u>omer <u>s</u>eason, whan <u>s</u>oft was the <u>s</u>onne." The pattern of stress here is established by alliteration. The underlying principle still holds true: we tend to stress alliterated words and syllables, and, indeed, to stress them more heavily than nonalliterated words. Because we do, alliteration is a tool with which a poet can suggest both deviant stress and inflection. Listen to Keats's "Thou foster chi<u>l</u>d of <u>s</u>ilence and <u>s</u>low time." Because of the alliteration, we would not read the end of the line this way:

$$\breve{\text{o}}\text{f s}\acute{\text{i}}\text{lence }\acute{\text{a}}\text{nd sl}\breve{\text{o}}\text{w t}\acute{\text{i}}\text{me.}$$

The alliteration causes "slow" to be stressed and heavily inflected, introducing deviance into the meter (a pyrrhic and a spondee) and greatly affecting the movement of the line (reinforced by the long "ō" sound, the slowing is marked). The same is true of Marvell's "Thus, though we cannot make our <u>s</u>un/<u>St</u>and <u>st</u>ill, yet we will make him run." Alliteration reinforces the effects of caesural pause, syntax, and line division to create metrical deviation and rhythmic alteration.

Just as alliteration can affect voice by affecting rhythm, it can affect or be a constituent of tone. Heavy alliteration, especially of certain consonants, can make a passage comic or derisive:

> In verses wil<u>d</u> with motion, <u>f</u>ull of <u>d</u>in,
> Lou<u>d</u>ened by <u>c</u>ries, by <u>c</u>lashes, qui<u>ck</u> and su<u>r</u>e
> As the <u>d</u>ea<u>d</u>ly though<u>t</u> of men a<u>cc</u>omplishing
> Their <u>c</u>urious <u>f</u>a<u>t</u>es in wa<u>r</u>, <u>c</u>ome, <u>c</u>eleb<u>r</u>ate
> The <u>f</u>aith of <u>f</u>or<u>t</u>y, wa<u>r</u>d of <u>C</u>upi<u>d</u>o.
>
> *Wallace Stevens*

There is just too much alliteration here for comfort (and I have noted only the main instances), especially of the hard guttural "k" and the dentals "d" and "t." But that is the point: we are not meant to be comfortable, for the speaker is mocking the very thing he is saying (as his diction also suggests). Owen achieves a similar effect with his "<u>bl</u>in<u>d</u>, <u>bl</u>un<u>t</u> <u>b</u>u<u>ll</u>e<u>t</u>-hea<u>d</u>s," as does Tennyson in the line "On the <u>b</u>ald s<u>t</u>ree<u>t</u> <u>br</u>ea<u>k</u>s the blan<u>k</u> <u>d</u>ay." In both, alliteration serves to guide the voice with regard to stress and creates a tone of derisive pain.

In contrast, alliteration that is somewhat less obtrusive can produce, given the right consonants, an even flow and a mellow tone. This is very much the effect of the conjunction of "m," "n," "r," and "z" sounds in the opening lines of Keats's "To Autumn":

> Season of mists and mellow fruitfulness,
>> Close bosom-friend of the maturing sun;
> Conspiring with him how to load and bless
>> With fruit the vines that round the thatch-eaves run;
> To bend with apples the mossed cottage-trees,
>> And fill all fruit with ripeness to the core.

At work here too are assonance and vowel-patterning: the passage is composed largely of muted vowels (of Keats's sixty vowel sounds, only six are high-pitched) and soft consonants. It is also carefully constructed with regard to a phenomenon that has no name but is as important to rhythm as anything we have taken up: what happens *between* words when they are formed in the mouth. Read Tennyson's line aloud and notice what happens in your mouth and neck: "On the bald street breaks the blank day." This line is hard to say because its word-end/word-beginning sounds cannot be elided; to speak the words, one must pause after each and re-shape the mouth: "On the bal<u>d</u> <u>s</u>tree<u>t</u> <u>b</u>reaks the blan<u>k</u> <u>d</u>ay." Contrast Tennyson's straining pattern with Keats's "Season of mists and mellow fruitfulness." Keats's words almost melt into one another with no strain whatsoever.

All of this leads us to a most important point: the things we have been speaking of do not operate in isolation, but in consort and in a context. This is why the possible patterns and their effects are infinitely various. For example, a concentration of high-pitched vowels in a context of many nasals and liquids and much elision will have a strikingly different feel and rhythmic effect from a concentration of high-pitched vowels in a context of many gutturals and plosives and minimal elision. End-line phenomena, too, have differing effects depending on the context, as do rhyme, syntax, and even meter. Each is affected by all: a given passage depends for its final effect on the interaction of all its elements.

I am not saying that a reader need be aware of everything going on in the language of a poem for its language to work. The brain takes in a great deal more than we are usually conscious of. My claim is merely that, whether or not we know it, the things we have been discussing do have effect. The following two passages should serve to underscore the point:

About suffering they were never wrong,
The Old Masters:* how well they understood
Its human position; how it takes place
While someone else is eating or opening a window or just walking
    dully along.

                                                            W. H. Auden

* *Old Masters:* the great Flemish painters of the Renaissance.

                In Xanadu did Kubla Khan
                A stately pleasure dome decree:
                Where Alph, the sacred river, ran
                Through caverns measureless to man
                    Down to a sunless sea.

                                        Samuel Taylor Coleridge

These passages are totally different in effect, and even without knowing
why, few readers would fail to feel the difference. With its long lines and
many caesural pauses, its flat diction, almost unheard rhyme ("wrong/
along"), and lack of obvious alliteration and assonance (but Auden's
vowels are quite important—notice his five dull "ŭ" sounds), the first pas-
sage is deliberately prosaic, as prosaic as Auden is saying life really is.
With its shorter lines and heavy metrical beat, its pronounced rhymes,
concentration of alliterative and assonantal sounds, and ease of movement
with respect to word-ends and word-beginnings, the second passage is in-
cantatory (chantlike) and lyrical (songlike). (In general, the heavier the
concentration of rhyme, assonance, and alliteration, the more lyrical a
poem will be.) Auden would bring us down to earth; Coleridge would
hypnotize us and lead us into the realm of the sacred. In each passage,
sound and sense are one.

As we have just seen, final effect depends on the interaction of all of a
poem's elements. Let us look at one more poem by way of consolidation.
Recall what has been said earlier (pages 90–92) about Hopkins's "To
R.B."; now read it again with an ear to its syntax, movement, and sound.

            The fine delight that fathers thought; the strong
            Spur, live and lancing like the blowpipe flame,
            Breathes once and, quenchèd faster than it came,
            Leaves yet the mind a mother of immortal song.

            Nine months she then, nay years, nine years she long   5
            Within her wears, bears, cares and combs the same:
            The widow of an insight lost she lives, with aim
            Now known and hand at work now never wrong.

Sweet fire the sire of muse, my soul needs this;
I want the one rapture of an inspiration.　　　　　　　　10
O then if in my lagging lines you miss

The roll, the rise, the carol, the creation,
My winter world, that scarcely breathes that bliss
Now, yields you, with some sighs, our explanation.

Marked by intricate though unobstrusive patterns of assonance and alliteration, the octave (first eight lines) moves with certainty and strength. The poet knows whereof he speaks: that delight gives rise to song and that, given the moment of delight, song will take shape. All of the lines have strong endings, and all but three are end-stopped. Of the three that enjamb, two do so gracefully (lines 5—whose enjambment suggests extension—and 7), and the third (line 1) moves with sureness, in part because of alliteration and the stress thrown on "Spur" by alliteration and syntax. Hopkins's treatment of syntax, line endings, assonance, and alliteration is such that the first eight lines are lively (also a result of metrical deviation) and firm.

The same is more or less true of the next four lines, which rise to a climax with the gradated "The roll, the rise, the carol, the creation." (Notice the shift from the low "ō" of "roll" to the high-pitched "ē" and "ā" of "creation.") The poet still knows whereof he speaks: what it is that his lagging lines miss. What he does not know is why—why delight has fled, why his is now a winter world. Especially because of their rhythmic haltingness (which results from the awkwardness of their syntax), the anticlimactic last two lines voice the poet's quandary. That they are anticlimactic in itself says a great deal: the anticlimax dramatically reflects the poet's feeling about his potential as a poet, and about his failed life generally. But the tone is muffled. The poet is no longer screaming out in his darkness, as he did in "I Wake and Feel the Fell of Dark" (page 135). The regularity of the meter and the gentle quality of the alliteration impart a tone of resignation. There are still "some sighs" left, sighs to be felt in the haltingness of the lines and the stumbling overflow of "bliss/ now" (compare the much firmer enjambment "with aim/Now known and hand"). The poet may be in a quandary, but his muffled tone speaks an acceptance of his bleak state as a permanent condition.

Finally, there is the masterstroke of the poem—the single word *explanation,* which seems particularly anticlimactic coming where it does. Flat, dry, bloodless, the word is cold (as is the official "our") and has about it a sense of canceling out ("ex-"); yet, because of its weak ending, it trails off into a diminuendo in the soft nasal "n." (The poem would not be nearly as effective, I think, had it ended with a crisp dental or a plosive.) Everything about the last two lines works to communicate a sense of waning and diminishment, of a life that is, almost beyond regret, draining out. But how poetically splendid! These are not just words on a page. Made to be what they are about, they allow us to hear a unique human voice in all its poignancy. We can hear the rhythm of that voice, and feel the being that its rhythm reflects. This is the triumph of poetry.

RHYME

I have saved rhyme for last because it is one of the odder aspects of poetry. Not that poems have to rhyme: half the greatest poems in the language do not. Still, half do. Why, one might wonder, would a poet choose to impose the limits that rhyming entails, especially when poetry does not have to rhyme to be poetry?

In part, like versifying, rhyming is a game. Frost compared it to the net in tennis: it is an obstacle, and one of the delights of reading poetry can be watching how that obstacle is skillfully overcome and turned to advantage. Another attraction of rhyme, and the source of its power, is that it has a way of reaching beyond the rational self and engaging the non-rational side of the being. We are not, after all, strictly rational creatures. So it is that children love rhyme and advertisers use rhymed jingles. Because of the nature of the brain, we delight in rhyme, and phrases that rhyme tend to stick in the mind.

Exercise

Jot down willy-nilly a few of the trite rhymed phrases one hears and uses repeatedly: "fat cat," "prime time," "boob tube," "hot shot," "jet set," "pooper scooper," "a blast from the past," "loose as a goose," "drunk as a skunk," "made in the shade," "knock your block off," "by hook or by crook." That phrases of this sort persist suggests that rhyme does indeed have appeal.

Rhyme also appeals to the poet because, sensuous and aurally concrete, it adds another dimension of physicality to a poem. Whatever else poetry is, it is language constructed so as to touch the reader physically as well as mentally. Rhyme, certainly, is on the physical side of things. Most important, rhyme can be an extremely useful tool. A poet can use it, for instance, to devise stanzaic patterns, rhyme being by and large what defines stanzas.[4] More to the point here is that rhyme affects rhythm, voice, and tone. It can therefore be another tool for shaping the movement of a poem and imparting the vocal qualities desired by the poet for the pur-

---

[4] Chapter 7 will be entirely devoted to this matter. A further reason for line division, incidentally, is that it makes possible end rhyme and thence stanzaic patterns.

pose at hand. Like the effects of line division and end-line phenomena, the possible effects of rhyme are widely diverse. A few examples should be enough to suggest this diversity of possible effect and to clarify my premise that rhyme in poetry is functional.

1. First of all, rhyme can be fun, imparting a tone of lightness and levity. Take Arlo Guthrie's "I don't want a pickle,/Just want to ride on my motorsickle." For some reason, polysyllabic rhymes ("pickle/sickle") tend to be comic in English (though not in other languages). At least, such rhyming is found primarily in our comic poetry, where it is an agent of humor. Byron, a master of the polysyllabic rhyme, provides examples galore:

> Sagest of women, even of widows, she
>   Resolved that Juan should be quite a paragon,
> And worthy of the noblest pedigree,
>   (His Sire was of Castile, his Dam from Aragon):
> Then, for accomplishments of chivalry,
>   In case our Lord the King should go to war again,
> He learned the arts of riding, fencing, gunnery,
> And how to scale a fortress—or a nunnery.
>
> *(from* Don Juan)

2. The fun of rhyme makes it a fine tool for the writer of comic or satirical poetry, both of which almost always rhyme. Consider the effect of rhyme in the following comic poem:

A Reasonable Affliction

Matthew Prior

On his deathbed poor Lubin lies;
    His spouse is in despair:
With frequent sobs, and mutual cries,
    They both express their care.

"A different cause," says parson Sly,   5
    "The same effect may give:
Poor Lubin fears that he shall die;
    His wife, that he may live."

(1709)

The humor here lies mainly in the unexpectedness of the ending, an unexpectedness the rhyme itself has much to do with; and it is certainly the rhyme that creates the comic tone. Just try the second stanza without rhyme:

> "A different cause," says Parson Sly,
>   "The same effect may give:
> Poor Lubin fears that he shall fail;
>   His wife, that he may not."

A similar effect is gained by Pope in the following satirical couplet from "The Rape of the Lock":

> Now lapdogs give themselves the rousing shake,
> And sleepless lovers just at twelve awake.

Maneuvered into climactic position, the word *awake* gives the lie to convention: though these lovers conventionally protest that they could not sleep a wink, they have slept long and well. Pope's mocking of conventionality is greatly heightened by the position of the word *awake* (which gives it the twist of the unexpected) and by the rhyming itself, because of which *awake* carries punch. In satire, such rhyming is like the final twist of a knife: it delivers the satirical deathblow.

3. More generally, rhyme tends to bring us up short, especially when lines are end-stopped. Partly by enforcing a pause following the rhyme word, rhyme can heighten climax, provide a sort of emotional punctuation, and create a sense of resolution. Climax is attained, for example, by the rhyme at the end of Hughes's "Harlem" (page 42): "Maybe it just sags/like a heavy load./*Or does it explode?*" Similarly, Blake's ironic rhyme "joy/destroy," the only rhyme in "The Sick Rose" (page 86), acts as an emotional exclamation point, underscoring the bitter irony of the poem as a whole. As for resolution, listen to the concluding couplet from the first section of Pope's "An Essay on Man":

> And, spite of pride, in erring reason's spite,
> One truth is clear, WHATEVER IS, IS RIGHT.

The rhyme is like the final chord in a symphony or like a tumbler falling in a lock, locking in the truth of the statement. Even though intellectually I do not agree with Pope, his rhyme convinces me of the truth of his statement to him.

4. The lyric qualities of rhyme offer yet another dimension of possible effect. Can you think of a popular song whose words do not rhyme? Nor are there many truly lyric poems that do not. Rhyme can impart a singing tone to the voice. The *chime* (another word for rhyme) carries with it, or can, the lilt of a melody. A fine lyric poem by Pound should speak for itself on this score:

Alba

Ezra Pound

When the nightingale to his mate
Sings day-long and night late
My love and I keep state
In bower,
In flower,   5
'Till the watchman on the tower
Cry:

"Up! Thou rascal, Rise,
I see the white
Light   10
And the night
Flies."

(1915)

ALBA. A song sung at dawn by one lover to another warning that they
must flee.

5.   Pound's "Alba" also suggests the single most important effect of
rhyme in poetry: its effect on rhythm. As I have said in passing, rhyme
tends (we are dealing always and only with tendencies), in drawing atten-
tion to itself, to draw stress to itself. We have seen this in Shakespeare's
"Where the Bee Sucks": the internal rhyme of the first line ("Where the
bee sucks, there suck I") helps to establish the basic meter of the poem.
Both internal rhyme and end rhyme affect accentuation and inflection.
End rhyme also makes for pause: a half pause in expectation of the chime,
a full pause with the chime. Pound's rhymes, for instance, make us pause
a little and linger over their sounds—and thus the lyric quality of the
whole. Pause is also suggested by rhyme at the end of Frost's "Fire and
Ice":

But if it had to perish twice,
I think I know enough of hate
To say that for destruction ice
Is also great
And would suffice.

Created by line division and by rhyme, the pause after "ice" lends the
voice an ironic crackle and carries with it a special twist of meaning re-
siding in the silence of the pause.

6.   Finally, deliberate deviation, or violation of the expectations rhyme sets up, can have a number of possible effects. For example, though rhyme tends to make for pause, a poet can undercut this tendency by marked enjambment and make rhyme work for speed by virtue of its pull. Browning does this in "My Last Duchess":

> That's my last Duchess painted on the wall,
> Looking as if she were alive. I call
> That piece a wonder now: Frà Pandolf's hands
> Worked busily a day, and there she stands.
> Will't please you sit and look at her? I said
> "Frà Pandolf" by design, ...

Browning makes use of rhyme to structure, but works against his rhyme by enjambment to achieve two rather different effects: first, a sense of fluidity; second, a sense of tension in the voice, created by the subtle tension between strong end rhymes (all of the poem's lines have strong endings) and enjambment.

Another possible deviation is **off-rhyme** (sometimes called "slant rhyme"). "Frown" and "down" rhyme; "soon" and "noon" rhyme; but "down" and "noon" do not rhyme, though they are close to being rhymes. Their very closeness accentuates their difference, a difference that can be used, like consonance, to create a dissonant effect. Emily Dickinson loved off-rhyme for this capacity. In the first stanzas of "It Was Not Death," the effect is clear enough:

> It was not Death, for I stood up,
> And all the Dead, lie down–
> It was not Night, for all the Bells
> Put out their Tongues, for Noon.
>
> It was not Frost, for on my Flesh   5
> I felt Siroccos–crawl–
> Nor Fire–for just my Marble feet
> Could keep a Chancel, cool–
>
> And yet, it tasted, like them all,
> The Figures I have seen   10
> Set orderly, for Burial,
> Reminded me, of mine–

Dickinson sets up the expectation of rhyme (by means of stanzaic division) and then delivers its opposite. By so doing, she creates and heightens dissonance: something bitter tastes all the more bitter if we had expected something sweet.

Expectation can also be violated by simple absence:

The Lover Mourns for the Loss of Love

W. B. Yeats

Pale brows, still hands, and dim hair,
I had a beautiful friend
And dreamed that the old despair
Would end in love in the end:
She looked in my heart one day   5
And saw your image was there;
She has gone weeping away.

(*1899*)

Something is missing—an eighth line to complete the expected pattern. In that the poem concerns loss, this absence embodies, ironically, all that Yeats is saying.

Exercise

The better to hear the effect of rhyme on movement, as well as its potential lyric qualities, go back to Pound's "Alba" and substitute words that don't rhyme for all those in the poem that do (such as "spouse" for "mate"). Read the poem as written and then as rewritten. Compare and contrast.

POEM ASSIGNMENT

Write a poem of from four to eight lines (or more, if you wish), making use of one or another—if not all—of the tools discussed in this chapter. You might try rhyme, for instance, or see what effect you can create with concentrations of consonants and vowels. Your aim should be to make form generally (sound, syntax, and the like) a function of content. Remember to give your poem a title.

The first student sample exploits the lyric potential of rhyme; the second, its potential for satiric thrust.

Garden of Night

Robert Leddy

Before we drift off into sleep,
There's a tree for us to climb
In a garden of delight—
The night will give us time.

Show me your garden now   5
And the rosebuds of your eyes;
Let me climb the tree to my dream;
Hold me as it shakes and cries.

When we tire of the night
And have no more tears to weep,   10
We'll sing a lullaby
And drift off into sleep.

4th Row, 5th Seat

John McMaster

A Number, just a Number . . .
Robots in a class.
4th row, 5th seat.
They only notice you
If you cheat.   *   5
Numbers for a grade—
If you're good, you get aid.
4th row, 5th seat.
As a teacher, a computer can't be beat.
But it cannot understand you don't understand.   10
Understand!
It's so simple, yet
4th row, 5th seat.
A student dies, but the computer does not overheat.

The overall effect of the next poem results from the interaction of
line division, dissonance ("along/torn," "torn/upon," "go/alone"), and a

concentration of low-frequency vowels. Metaphor, too, plays its part. Agents of mood and meaning, the elements of the poem conspire to give shape to the speaker's desolation.

The Road and I

William Vahey

As I walked along
all tattered and torn,
the road came up to greet me.
It was parched and
dirty and dry.   5

We were much the same,
the road and I,
all dirty and torn
and tread upon,
where not even the dogs   10
care to go.

We were all alone
and all but forgotten.

Finally, a poem that makes expressive use of enjambment, parallel phrasing (a matter of syntax and line division), and, especially, alliteration (of the plosive "p" and the sibilant "s"). The title alludes to James Joyce's *Portrait of the Artist as a Young Man,* of which the poem is reminiscent.

Portrait

Michael Doyle

I secretly laugh while
 Pious Priests press empty prophecies.
I smile seductively as
 Swanky Sluts besiege my fancies.
But we don't talk, we just dance.

POEMS FOR FURTHER STUDY

from An Essay on Criticism

Alexander Pope

'Tis not enough no harshness gives offense,
The sound must seem an echo to the sense.   365
Soft is the strain when Zephyr gently blows,
And the smooth stream in smoother numbers flows;
But when loud surges lash the sounding shore,
The hoarse, rough verse should like the torrent roar.
When Ajax strives some rock's vast weight to throw,   370
The line too labors, and the words move slow;
Not so when swift Camilla scours the plain,
Flies o'er the unbending corn, and skims along the main.

(*1711*)

Questions
1. The basic meter of this passage is iambic pentameter. But there is considerable deviation. Scan the passage and note the differing effects with respect to inflection, volume, and pace of the metrical deviations.
2. What consonantal sounds does Pope make use of and what are their differing effects in combination?
3. What vowel sounds does Pope exploit and to what end?
4. Read the passage aloud with some deliberation and feel what happens as your mouth forms and reforms. Which combinations of word-end/word-beginning sounds are difficult to say? Which combinations are easy to say (because their sounds elide)? What are the effects on rhythm of these combinations? How do they further embody meaning?

from The Eve of St. Agnes

John Keats

And still she slept an azure-lidded sleep,
In blanchèd linen, smooth, and lavendered,
While he from forth the closet brought a heap
Of candied apple, quince, and plum, and gourd;   265
With jellies soother than the creamy curd,

And lucent syrups, tinct with cinnamon;
Manna and dates, in argosy transferred
From Fez; and spicèd dainties, every one,
From silken Samarcand to cedared Lebanon.   270

(1820)

from THE EVE OF ST. AGNES. 266–269: jellies creamier ("soother") than the curds of cream, clear ("lucent") syrups edged ("tinct") with the sharp taste of cinnamon, and sweet gums ("manna") and dates carried by some great merchant ship ("argosy") from Morocco ("Fez").

Questions

1. Seven lines of this lush descriptive stanza are end-stopped. What is the effect of the end-stopping?
2. Two lines enjamb significantly. Do they do so gracefully or awkwardly? Why the enjambment at these two points?
3. What is the overall effect of the combinations of words Keats chose— that is, the effect of the consonants and vowels of those words in combination? Are there any contrasting sounds (for example, consider "tinct")? What momentary effects do such contrasts have?
4. The following is from Keats's manuscript of "The Eve of St. Agnes."

~~But~~
~~And still she slept:~~
And still she slept an azure-lidded sleep
   In blanched linen smooth and lavender'd;
While he from forth the closet brought a heap

~~fruits~~
Of candied ~~sweets sweets with~~ and plumb and gourd
   apple   Quince
               creamed
With jellies soother than the ~~dairy~~ curd
      tinct
And lucent syrups ~~smooth~~ with crannamon

~~And sugar'd dates from that o'er Euphrates fard~~
    ~~in Brigantine transferred~~
              ~~transferred~~
Manna and daites in Bragine ~~wild transferrd~~
    ~~and Manna~~
~~And Manna wild and~~   ~~Bragentine~~
        ~~sugar'd~~ dates transferrd

  argosy
  ~~In Brigantine from Fez~~
From fez—and spiced danties every one
  ~~glutted~~
From ~~wealthy~~ Salmarchand to cedard lebanon
   silken

Try to account for the revisions (such as "silken" rather than "glutted," "tinct" rather than "smooth").

Slow, Slow, Fresh Fount

Ben Jonson

Slow, slow, fresh fount, keep time with my salt tears;
Yet slower, yet, O faintly, gentle springs!
List to the heavy part the music bears,
Woe weeps out her division, when she sings.
   Droop herbs and flowers;   5
   Fall grief in showers;
Our beauties are not ours. O, I could still,
Like melting snow upon some craggy hill,
   Drop, drop, drop, drop,
Since nature's pride is now a withered daffodil.   10

(1600)

SLOW, SLOW, FRESH FOUNT.   This song, from Jonson's play *Cynthia's Revels*, is sung by the Greek demi-deity Echo, who wasted away to an echo because of her love for Narcissus. Narcissus fell in love with his own reflection in a pool of water and, according to one version of the myth, was changed into the flower that bears his name. The daffodil (line 10) is a variety of narcissus. 4. *division:* a section or part of a song.

Questions
1. What vowel sounds are concentrated in this poem? To what end?
2. What about word-end/word-beginning sounds? What about medial consonants (consonants found in the middle of words)?
3. What is the effect of the many caesural pauses of the poem and of its end-stopping?
4. I once tried my hand at an exercise involving Jonson's song. Contrast the effects of my efforts with those of the original.

     Hurry on, fresh fount, and wash away old stings;
     Quickly now, ye newly rising springs!
     Hear the happy part the music brings
     And dance to Love's division as she sings.
        Bloom, herbs and flowers;   5
        Spring joy in bowers,

> Our beauties now are ours.
>   For I can still
> (Like melting snow upon a sun-crowned hill)
>   Run and laugh from rill to rill: 10
> All nature has become a daffodil.

With regard to vowels and consonants, what was the point of my
exercise? I tried to keep caesuras to a minimum and to elide when-
ever possible. To what effect? I could have kept Jonson's "tears" and
"bears." Why did I not? What was I aiming at in my rhyming? To
what extent did I succeed overall? (You need not be overgenerous in
your judgment.)

from **Commander Lowell**

Robert Lowell

Having a naval officer
for my Father was nothing to shout
about to the summer colony at "Matt."   20
He wasn't at all "serious,"
when he showed up on the golf course,
wearing a blue serge jacket and numbly cut
white ducks he'd bought
at a Pearl Harbor commissariat . . .   25
and took four shots with his putter to sink his putt.
"Bob," they said, "golf's a game you really ought to know how to
     play,
if you play at all."
They wrote him off as "naval,"
naturally supposed his sport was sailing.   30
Poor Father, his training was engineering!
Cheerful and cowed
among the seadogs at the Sunday yacht club,
he was never one of the crowd.

"Anchors aweigh," Daddy boomed in his bathtub,   35
"Anchors aweigh,"
when Lever Brothers offered to pay
him double what the Navy paid.
I nagged for his dress sword with gold braid,
and cringed because Mother, new   40

caps on all her teeth, was born anew
at forty. With seamanlike celerity,
Father left the Navy,
and deeded Mother his property.

He was soon fired. Year after year,   45
he still hummed "Anchors aweigh" in the tub—
whenever he left a job,
he bought a smarter car.

(1959)

from COMMANDER LOWELL. 20. *"Matt"*: Mattapoisett, Massachusetts—a
summer resort.

Questions
1. "Commander Lowell" is uneasy in its movement, no doubt because
   the poem expresses ambivalence, and somewhat bitter in its tone.
   How does syntax help create a sense of uneasiness (as in "because
   Mother, new/caps on all her teeth, was born anew")?
2. Characterize Lowell's line treatment generally with regard to enjamb-
   ment. How does the type of enjambment Lowell exploits ("shout/
   about," "to pay/him") help to embody a sense of discomfort?
3. Does enjambment have any shock effect here? (Consider, for example,
   "because Mother, new/caps on all her teeth.") Does enjambment con-
   tribute to the subdued bitterness of tone?
4. What about rhyme and off-rhyme ("cut/bought," "tub/job") in this
   regard? Though colloquial, the passage is highly wrought with respect
   to both, which play off against each other. How so?
5. The passage is also highly wrought with respect to its consonants and
   vowels, though its concentrations of sounds are in no way obtrusive.
   What consonants mark the passage? What vowels? To what effect?
   And what is the effect of Lowell's having kept his concentrations
   unobtrusive?

IDEAS FOR WRITING

1. Though most of the verbal phenomena considered in the last two
   chapters characterize poetry alone, some can be found in prose as
   well. The following passage by Joyce suggests that consonant and
   vowel choice and concentration, along with carefully manipulated
   syntax and phrasing, can indeed be an aspect of prose style.

   He was alone. He was unheeded, happy and near to the wild
heart of life. He was alone and young and wilful and wildhearted,

alone amid a waste of wild air and brackish waters and the seaharvest of shells and tangle and veiled grey sunlight and gayclad lightclad figures, of children and girls and voices childish and girlish in the air . . . .

Note the concentration in this passage of consonantal and vowel sounds—its glides ("w"), aspirates ("h"), and liquids ("l," "r"), and its many high-pitched vowels. Write a paragraph discussing the sound of the passage, and how its form is a dimension of meaning.

2. Reread Williams's "The Dance" (page 131) and write a paragraph on the effects of its end-line phenomena. Two lines are end-stopped. Why these two? The rest of the lines, most of which have weak endings, enjamb. Characterize the enjambments (as, for example, smooth or rough). What is the effect on rhythmic movement of the combination of weak endings and enjambment? How does what happens at the line breaks serve Williams's purpose?

3. Paraphrase the poem you wrote for the last poem assignment. Then discuss what is lost in the translation.

4.

Don Juan

George Gordon, Lord Byron

from Canto II

18

"Farewell, my Spain! a long farewell!" he cried,
   "Perhaps I may revisit thee no more,
But die, as many an exiled heart hath died,
   Of its own thirst to see again thy shore: 140
Farewell, where Guadalquiver's waters glide!
   Farewell, my mother! and, since all is o'er,
Farewell, too, dearest Julia!—(here he drew
Her letter out again, and read it through).

19

"And oh! if e'er I should forget, I swear—   145
   But that's impossible, and cannot be—
Sooner shall this blue ocean melt to air,
   Sooner shall earth resolve itself to sea,
Than I resign thine image, oh, my fair!
   Or think of anything, excepting thee;   150
A mind diseased no remedy can physic—
(Here the ship gave a lurch, and he grew seasick.)

20

"Sooner shall heaven kiss earth—(here he fell sicker)
  Oh, Julia! what is every other woe?—
(For God's sake let me have a glass of liquor;   155
  Pedro, Battista, help me down below.)
Julia, my love—(you rascal, Pedro, quicker)—
  Oh, Julia!—(this cursed vessel pitches so)—
Beloved Julia, hear me still beseeching!"
(Here he grew inarticulate with retching.)   160

21

He felt that chilling heaviness of heart,
  Or rather stomach, which, alas! attends,
Beyond the best apothecary's art,
  The loss of love, the treachery of friends,
Or death of those we dote on, when a part   165
  Of us dies with them as each fond hope ends:
No doubt he would have been much more pathetic,
But the sea acted as a strong emetic.

                                                    (*1824*)

from DON JUAN. Everything in quotes is spoken by Don Juan, on board a
ship sailing from Spain. 144. *Her letter:* The letter is a farewell love note
sent by Julia, a married woman with whom the young Juan was discovered
(thus his exile).

Don Juan, sailing into exile, would play the hero. For the reasons
indicated, he fails. Discuss the effects of syntax and Byron's mode of
rhyming, and how both serve to undercut his "hero" and make him
comic.

5.   **Dover Beach**
_____

Matthew Arnold

The sea is calm tonight.
The tide is full, the moon lies fair
Upon the straits; on the French coast the light
Gleams and is gone; the cliffs of England stand,
Glimmering and vast, out in the tranquil bay.   5
Come to the window, sweet is the night-air!
Only, from the long line of spray
Where the sea meets the moon-blanched land,
Listen! you hear the grating roar

Of pebbles which the waves draw back, and fling,   10
At their return, up the high strand,
Begin, and cease, and then again begin,
With tremulous cadence slow, and bring
The eternal note of sadness in.

Sophocles long ago   15
Heard it on the Aegean, and it brought
Into his mind the turbid ebb and flow
Of human misery; we
Find also in the sound a thought,
Hearing it by this distant northern sea.   20

The Sea of Faith
Was once, too, at the full, and round earth's shore
Lay like the folds of a bright girdle furled.
But now I only hear
Its melancholy, long, withdrawing roar,   25
Retreating, to the breath
Of the night-wind, down the vast edges drear
And naked shingles of the world.

Ah, love, let us be true
To one another! for the world, which seems   30
To lie before us like a land of dreams,
So various, so beautiful, so new,
Hath really neither joy, nor love, nor light,
Nor certitude, nor peace, nor help for pain;
And we are here as on a darkling plain   35
Swept with confused alarms of struggle and flight,
Where ignorant armies clash by night.

(1867)

DOVER BEACH.   23. *like the folds of a bright girdle furled:* like a beautiful sash, girdling and giving support. 28. *shingles:* beaches composed of stones and pebbles.

Choose two or three prominent verbal elements of "Dover Beach" (such as syntax, consonant and vowel concentration, end-line phenomena, rhyme) and write a paper on how they combine to create the qualities of movement and voice that characterize the poem. First specify the qualities you hear; then proceed to discuss how they are established. You might focus on just three or four lines or an entire section. Whatever you choose to do, address yourself to the relation of content and form.

Rhyme Schemes & Formal Designs
Chapter Seven

FORM AND CONTENT

Any matter of form—meter, line division, sound patterning, repetition—
is, or should be, a matter of content as well. Form should not be thought
of as a vase into which content is poured. Rather, the formal features of
a poem are instruments a poet uses to shape the amorphous stuff of feeling
and actualize the intangible qualities of experience. Thus, in a genuine
work of art, *form and content are inseparable.*

The Ballad

Let us look at two anonymous ballads of the fifteenth or sixteenth centuries and try to evaluate them on a formal basis. In other words, let us try to determine in which of the two the formal attributes of the ballad are exploited more fully, or are more fully integral to drama and overall impact. The main formal feature of the ballad is **incremental repetition** —repetition with variation, which introduces enough new information to advance the story (ballads are narratives) step by step. Why ballads should be marked by repetition is not hard to fathom. Folk ballads were (and still are) composed by nonliterate people, who must rely on memory rather than the written word. Repetition is first and foremost an aid to memory. It is also an aid to hearing—if you missed something the first time, you can catch it the second. Ballads are, after all, meant to be sung, and it is sometimes hard to discern words when they are sung. (Popular songs are marked by repetition for much the same reason.)

Still, there are more successful and less successful ballads. "According to what criteria of judgment?" you may ask—this is always the fundamental question with regard to aesthetic discrimination. How closely the words and music correspond is certainly a valid criterion, though not a strictly literary one. A literary criterion would be how integral the repetition is to the import of the given ballad, or to what extent its content is actualized by form. The question to ask of ballads specifically is: does the way the ballad unfolds contribute to its meaning, or does it proceed as it does merely because its author wished to write a ballad and thus had to employ incremental repetition? If the answer is the latter, the poem is a failure in that *form is never self-justifying*. In other words, with regard to the ballad, repetition must serve purposes greater than merely making the poem qualify as a ballad. It must be instrumental to the drama of the poem, or a vehicle of psychological portraiture, or whatever. What, then, of the ballads that follow? One is a very great poem; the other, middling at best. Which is which and why?

Lord Randal

1

"O where ha' you been, Lord Randal, my son?
And where ha' you been, my handsome young man?"
"I ha' been at the greenwood; mother, mak my bed soon,
For I'm wearied wi' huntin', and fain wad° lie down."   *would*

2

"And wha met ye there, Lord Randal, my son?   5
And wha met you there, my handsome young man?"

"O I met wi' my true-love; mother, mak my bed soon,
For I'm wearied wi' huntin', and fain wad lie down."

3

"And what did she give you, Lord Randal, my son?
And what did she give you, my handsome young man?"   10
"Eels fried in a pan; mother, mak my bed soon,
For I'm wearied wi' huntin', and fain wad lie down."

4

"And wha gat your leavin's, Lord Randal, my son?
And wha gat your leavin's, my handsome young man?"
"My hawks and my hounds; mother, mak my bed soon,   15
For I'm wearied wi' huntin', and fain wad lie down."

5

"And what becam of them, Lord Randal, my son?
And what becam of them, my handsome young man?"
"They stretched their legs out and died; mother, mak my bed soon,
For I'm wearied wi' huntin', and fain wad lie down."   20

6

"O I fear you are poisoned, Lord Randal, my son!
I fear you are poisoned, my handsome young man!"
"O yes, I am poisoned; mother, mak my bed soon,
For I'm sick at the heart, and I fain wad lie down."

7

"What d' ye leave to your mother, Lord Randal, my son?   25
What d' ye leave to your mother, my handsome young man?"
"Four and twenty milk kye°; mother, mak my bed soon,   *kine, cattle*
For I'm sick at the heart, and I fain wad lie down."

8

"What d' ye leave to your sister, Lord Randal, my son?
What d' ye leave to your sister, my handsome young man?"   30
"My gold and my silver; mother, mak my bed soon,
For I'm sick at the heart, and I fain wad lie down."

9

"What d' ye leave to your brother, Lord Randal, my son?
What d' ye leave to your brother, my handsome young man?"
"My houses and my lands; mother, mak my bed soon,   35
For I'm sick at the heart, and I fain wad lie down."

10

"What d' ye leave to your true-love, Lord Randal, my son?
What d' ye leave to your true-love, my handsome young man?"
"I leave her hell and fire; mother, mak my bed soon,
For I'm sick at the heart, and I fain wad lie down."   40

Edward

1

"Why does your brand° sae° drap wi' bluid,   *sword* / *so*
    Edward, Edward,
Why does your brand sae drap wi' bluid,
    And why sae sad gang° ye, O?"   *go*
"O I ha'e killed my hawk sae guid,   5
    Mither, mither,
O I ha'e killed my hawk sae guid,
    And I had nae mair° but he, O."   *more*

2

"Your hawke's bluid was never sae reid,°   *red*
    Edward, Edward,   10
Your hawke's bluid was never sae reid,
    My dear son I tell thee, O."
"O I ha'e killed my reid-roan steed,
    Mither, mither,
O I ha'e killed my reid-roan steed,   15
    That erst was sae fair and free, O."

3

"Your steed was auld,° and ye ha'e gat mair,   *old*
    Edward, Edward,
Your steed was auld, and ye ha'e gat mair,
    Some other dule° ye drie,° O."   *grief* / *suffer*   20
"O I ha'e killed my fader dear,
    Mither, mither,
"O I ha'e killed my fader dear,
    Alas, and wae° is me, O!"   *woe*

4

"And whatten° penance wul ye drie for that,   *what sort of*   25
    Edward, Edward?

And whatten penance wul ye drie for that,
   My dear son, now tell me O?"
"I'll set my feet in yonder boat,
   Mither, mither,   30
I'll set my feet in yonder boat,
   And I'll fare over the sea, O."

5

"And what wul ye do wi' your towers and your ha',°   *hall*
   Edward, Edward?
And what wul ye do wi' your towers and your ha',   35
   That were sae fair to see, O?"
"I'll let them stand tul they down fa',
   Mither, mither,
I'll let them stand tul they down fa',
   For here never mair maun° I be, O."   *must*   40

6

"And what wul ye leave to your bairns° and your wife,   *children*
   Edward, Edward?
And what wul ye leave to your bairns and your wife,
   Whan ye gang over the sea, O?"
"The warlde's room, let them beg thrae° life,   *through*   45
   Mither, mither,
The warlde's room,° let them beg thrae life,   *the wide world*
   For them never mair wul I see, O."

7

"And what wul ye leave to your ain mither dear,
   Edward, Edward?   50
And what wul ye leave to your ain mither dear,
   My dear son, now tell me, O?"
"The curse of hell frae° me sall° ye bear,   *from / shall*
   Mither, mither,
The curse of hell frae me sall ye bear   55
   Sic° counsels ye gave to me, O."   *such*

    The majority of my students invariably choose "Lord Randal" as the better poem. And I always dissent. "Edward" is a great poem; "Lord Randal" is mediocre if that. Specific judgment is less to the point, however, than the process of arriving at such a judgment. We need, therefore, to examine the criteria of judgment used. Typically, a number of students answer that "Lord Randal" is better because it is easier to read. The criterion of judgment here is faulty: that something is easier to read than something else does not necessarily make it better. One would not consider a McDonald's hamburger better than a seven-course feast because the hamburger can be eaten more readily. Nor is smoothness a valid criterion. Some of my students always answer something like " 'Edward' is choppier and not as smooth as 'Lord Randal.' Therefore, 'Lord Randal' is better." But many poems of the highest order (such as "Reuben Bright") are not smooth, *nor should they be*. More nearly on target is the answer that "There is more repetition in 'Lord Randal'; therefore, 'Lord Randal' is a better ballad." Nevertheless, the criterion of judgment is still faulty. Quantity is never an apt criterion. The criterion, rather, is *use*—whether or not a given element serves a function. This is what should inform judgment in the main, and this is what we must attend to.

Let us consider "Edward" first. Note the elements that repeat: the names "Edward" and "Mither," the "O's," the pattern of lines—lines 1 and 3, and 5 and 7 repeating within each stanza, and the question-answer format. Is this repetition only a matter of the author's having known that the ballad form requires one to repeat a lot? Or is it functional, a means of establishing character and building drama? I find the latter. To begin with, the poem is a suspenseful psychological drama, a drama that involves a duel between its main characters, Edward and Mither. The repetition of the names serves to keep the two face to face in the mind's eye and to create a sense of psychological maneuvering between the two. Much the same purpose is served by the incremental question-answer format, which also helps to impart a sense of suspense—a sense that builds to the poem's explosive climax, where we discover that Edward has simply been a pawn of his mother in the murder of his father. As to the poem's "O's," the mother's single "O" per stanza is only exclamatory, as in "Oh, I forgot to do that." In contrast, Edward's "O's" express a mounting feeling of remorse. The repetition, therefore, serves the purposes of both characterization and character delineation.

We can be still more specific about the poem's personae. From the curse that ends the poem, we know that up until that moment Edward has been a mama's boy, radically swayed by Mither's will. The repetition of "Edward, Edward" and "Mither, Mither" itself rings with a sense of dependence (it also serves to create a feeling of agitation, which we might correlate with anxiety on the parts of mother and son), as does Edward's compliance—albeit reluctant—with his mother's questioning. Edward has been weak, a passive agent; but during the course of the poem we see him gaining moral strength. From the outset he is full of remorse, which is why he can't come right out and say what he has really done. (He hasn't actually killed his hawk or his steed.) That he cannot at first bring himself to say the truth suggests how terrible it suddenly seems to him. Like Edward's repeated "O's," the two-stanza delay thus helps establish Edward's remorse—another way in which form and content are related. The repeating seventh line in each stanza also seems functional in the same way. At first the repetition, coupled with those repeating "O's," has the quality of lamentation; toward the end, it has the feel of resolve. All of this is validated by the drastic penance Edward intends to endure, a penance entirely self-imposed: now that he is Lord of the Manor, no one will come to punish him. Though only a pawn in the unfolding drama, he takes the guilt on himself. At the end, he finds moral strength.

Mither is a being of a different order—hard, calculating, and devoid of moral fiber. Consider her response to Edward's "O I ha'e killed my reid-roan steed": "Your steed was auld, and ye ha'e gat mair." What a cold, heartless reply! Of course, she knows, or hopes, that Edward has killed neither hawk nor steed, but his father (her husband). So, with little regard for what her son is feeling, she badgers him into his painful confession, badgering being conveyed by the insistence of her questioning (a matter of the poem's format), her exclamatory tone (her "O"), and the nagging repetition of the third line of each stanza. These aspects of form function to convey how she has been able to use Edward's weakness to work her will. Notice also her attempt at self-ingratiation with "your ain mither dear" and the careful climactic ordering of her questions, which build to the question most important to her after Edward's admission of the murder: "And what wul ye leave to your ain mither dear . . . ?" This cold, scheming, evil woman, who has known very well how to manipulate her son, shows not the least sign of remorse or guilt. Indeed, as soon as Edward confesses, she throws the entire blame on him ("And whatten penance wul ye drie for that . . . ?"), though she has been the prime mover and he merely her instrument. This we learn at the poem's climax, toward which the poem moves inexorably, as Edward finally gains the strength to separate himself from his mother.

Because of its intense drama, its psychological subtlety, and its unity of form and content, "Edward" is a little masterpiece, which, like all great poems, suggests reaches of meaning beyond its immediate confines. Here is intimated one of the great tragic themes of Western literature: the question of justice. Is there justice in this world, where the wholly innocent—the wife and children—are to suffer for a crime not theirs, whereas the truly guilty party—the mother—suffers least, if at all? (She has gotten what she wanted, the death of her husband and, with Edward's departure, probably the estates as well.) Maybe there is justice in the next world ("The curse of hell"), the poem suggests with Saxon resignation, but not in this. Certainly, too, there is intimated here one of the deepest of human realities: oedipal terror and guilt. The poem gives shape to basic conflicts in us all, and asks us to explore ourselves by exploring it.

Superficially, "Lord Randal" is much like "Edward." Again mother and son are face to face, and again we encounter structured repetition and a question-answer format. But is there any real drama here? And if so, is the form integral to it? My answer is "no" on both scores. For one thing, the wrong people are face to face: as the poem unfolds, the mother seems quite superfluous to the drama of Randal and his sweetheart. And what an odd pattern of questions. Unless we are to conclude that the mother is an idiot, there is simply no good reason for her delaying her exclamation "O I fear you are poisoned." In "Edward" there is a wealth of psychological meaning in Edward's delayed admission, the patterning of his mother's questions, and the blurted climax. Not so "Lord Randal." Its suspense is superficial—merely contrived—and its format and patterning are arbitrary. There's little reason for the mother's initial questions nor for Randal's bequests. Nor is there much by way of characterization: we learn almost nothing about Randal, his mother, or, most notably, his sweetheart. Why did she poison him? Also, the poem leaves us with little of substance to ponder and no sense of its applicability to the human circumstance. In sum, its form is not integral to its content. Would not the poem have been more penetrating had it begun with a statement of the mother's concern—"O I fear you are poisoned"—and proceeded to unfold the dynamics of the Randal/sweetheart relationship and why the sweetheart did what she did? Had it been so constructed, its incremental repetition might have served to convey, for instance, Randal's reluctance to state the reason for the sweetheart's act (had he betrayed her?)—and the repetition might have been psychologically revealing.

Have I been too hard on "Lord Randal"? Probably. My analysis, however, rests not simply on taste and temperament, though both are always at play under the surface. But both should be informed by reason and allied with valid criteria of judgment. My two criteria have been integration of form and content, and breadth of significance—criteria which go hand in glove: only when content is animated by form can a work be fully expressive and aesthetically satisfying.

Meaningful Deviation
For a work to succeed fully, form and content must be one—as they are in "Edward," which respects the givens of its form meaningfully. ("Lord Randal" respects them too, but not so meaningfully.) We should never forget, however, the possibility of meaningful deviation. Sometimes a poet will deliberately violate one or another aspect of a chosen form in order to achieve expression. There is a paradox here: I am suggesting that union of form and content can sometimes be attained by divergence. The goal, as always, is meaning. If deviation from some aspect of a form is meaningful, then form is being made to serve what form should always serve—content. Therefore, form and content remain indivisible.

Let us pursue this point by considering a specific formal design, the **triolet.** A triolet is a fixed form consisting of two quatrains (four-line units) on two rhymes, the first line repeated as the fourth and seventh lines, and the second line repeated as the last line. This rhyme scheme is signified as *ABaAabAB*.[1] Intricate in its design, the triolet seems inherently playful. So it is that the triolet is associated with light social satire, for which such cleverness of form, if well executed, seems apt.[2] But in the following poem Thomas Hardy deliberately violates the inherent qualities of the form and thus our expectations:

Winter in Durnover Field

SCENE. – A wide stretch of fallow ground recently sown with wheat, and frozen to iron hardness. Three large birds walking about thereon, and wistfully eyeing the surface. Wind keen from north-east: sky a dull grey.

(Triolet)

Rook.—Throughout the field I find no grain;
    The cruel frost encrusts the cornland!
Starling.—Aye: patient pecking now is vain
    Throughout the field, I find . . .
Rook.—   No grain!
Pigeon.—Nor will be, comrade, till it rain,   5
    Or genial thawings loose the lorn land
    Throughout the field.
Rook.—   I find no grain:
    The cruel frost encrusts the cornland!

(1901)

1 Rhyme schemes are characterized by means of letters. For example, *abab* indicates that the first and third lines rhyme, as do the second and the fourth; *abab/cdcd/efef* indicates a repeated *pattern* of rhyme, though the particular rhyme sounds change between stanzas. (If they remained the same, the notation would be: *abab/abab/abab*.) Capital letters are used to signify repetition of an entire line.

2 Here, for example, is a typical triolet:

Circe

Henry Austin Dobson

In the School of Coquettes
    Madam Rose is a scholar—
O, they fish with all nets
In the School of Coquettes!
When her brooch she forgets   5
    'Tis to show her new collar;
In the School of Coquettes
    Madame Rose is a scholar!

(1874)

CIRCE. Circe is a beautiful enchantress in *The Odyssey*.

If we come to Hardy's poem (subtitled "Triolet") knowing the inherent qualities of the form, we will probably feel dislocated. The grave content of this triolet seems out of keeping with the playful, frivolous nature of the triolet generally. But dislocation is precisely the point. Hardy deliberately makes form and content diverge, the result being a sense of irony as bleak and grim as the poem's setting. In that this divergence of form and content is itself a vehicle of meaning, the two here move to the same end and so are, paradoxically, inseparable.

The principle of unity of form and content applies to all formal aspects of a poem, as we have seen when speaking of meter, syntax, sound, and so forth. Whatever patterns the words of a poem make, its patterns will be integral to its statement if the poem succeeds. This principle applies equally to formal designs—verbal structures defined by rhyme—which must also be looked at with function in mind. The question is always whether or not the poet has made use of the innate qualities of a given design, either by exploiting those qualities to achieve the desired end or by meaningfully deviating from them. To make such a judgment, of course, one must know what the potentialities of the various formal designs used by poets are. This chapter will examine the most common recurrent rhyme schemes from the perspective of potentiality.

COUPLETS

A **couplet** is two contiguous lines that rhyme. Consider the following:

On His Books

Hilaire Belloc

When I am dead, I hope it may be said:
"His sins were scarlet, but his books were read."

(1944)

This punny poem is just right. One cannot do a great deal in two lines; one can, though, write an **epigram**—a highly polished little statement, usually witty or satirical, that makes a single point concisely and effectively, and usually has a punch to it (in context, the punch lines of most jokes are epigrammatic). Belloc chose and exploited the couplet in light of its inherent potentiality: a single, self-contained couplet, which seems almost to want to end with a punch (or to ask that some key word be manipulated into the climactic rhyme position), is by nature epigrammatic. The design is right for the purpose at hand.[3]

More important than the single-couplet poem is the longer poem constructed of couplets (denoted *aabbccdd . . .*). We would not speak of the couplets of such a poem as "stanzas"; even the larger subdivisions of poems in couplets are called **verse paragraphs** rather than "stanzas." Still, a poem composed of couplets clearly has a design defined by rhyme. There are two quite different types of couplet—open couplets and closed couplets—and the two differ considerably in potential.

Open Couplets

Open couplets are couplets that do not form self-contained grammatical units. A poem in open couplets necessarily rhymes *aabbccdd*, but can be in any meter, or even in free verse. The attraction of open couplets is that they serve to structure (to give shape and a sense of continuity); yet, handled well, they remain unobtrusive. "My Last Duchess" and "To His Coy Mistress," both of which are in open couplets, are excellent examples. The form also allows for distinct effects of pace and pause, and so can be allied with other elements in a poem to create exact rhythms. This is one of the reasons why I chose to write the following poem in open couplets. Read the poem aloud, letting it pause and enjamb where it will, and listen to the effect of rhyme on both pace and pause. Consider it in light of the discussions of fact and feeling in Chapter One, and of metaphor and self in Chapter Four.

Our Decor

Edward Proffitt

It surely is not a natural thing
To have forsythia except in spring,
Much less to have it spread across the walls
And creep along the ceiling, where it crawls,
Or seems to, into the ceiling light,   5
And lends a sense of life to winter's night.
But there it is, green stems and yellow blooms,
The handiwork of men in their own rooms—
This one my study, where I sometimes sit
Like a tired bird, who having quit   10

[3] Related to its potential for punch is the deviational potential of the single couplet: deliberate anticlimax, such as Pope achieves in his satirical lines about a hack writer who "Rhymes ere he wakes, and prints before term ends,/Obliged by hunger and request of friends."

The air, will settle far from reach or sight
Within the thicket, resting from its flight.
Hard Times lies open on my desk—the stern
Victorians, like brass, pipe up and spurn
My fancy, spring-like, shimmering, a harp   15
Despite the winter's wind and the snow's sharp
Tongue; yet they would cover chair legs from fear
Of metaphor, and thus deprived, not hear
Such music as redeems the waning year.
A rustling in my brain, my thought goes flying: 20
It is for want of this that we are dying:
For want of metaphor as nothing more
Than metaphor, but that enough, a store
To draw on in hard times, or a sudden find
Of seedy semblances to feed the mind,   25
Itself a living part of all it sees,
Its pulses but a startled swarm of bees
Remaking spring, its fashionings, a nest
To settle in and coo, and then to rest.
And so, I am content to nestle here,   30
And harp upon my fancy as the year
Spins out, and feel the branches curling round,
And bear old winter's whistle—it a sound
Of music, too—and ready for another spring,
Myself a whole and wholly natural thing.   35

(1975)

OUR DECOR. 3. *the walls:* I am speaking of wallpaper, an artifact that widens in the course of the poem to include all of man's making. My study is papered, walls and ceiling, in a forsythia pattern. 13–14. Hard Times . . . *Victorians:* An allusion to the following dialogue between teacher and students in Dickens's novel *Hard Times:*

> "Would you paper a room with representations of horses?"
> [Some answer yes and some no.]
> "Of course No. Why wouldn't you?"
> [No response.]
> "I'll explain to you, then. . . . Do you ever see horses walking up and down the sides of rooms in reality—in fact? Do you?"
> "Yes, sir!" from one half. "No, sir!" from the other.
> "Of course, No. . . . Why, then, you are not to see anywhere, what you don't see in fact; you are not to have anywhere, what you don't have in fact. What is called Taste, is only another name for Fact."

17. *cover chair legs:* The "skirt" round the bottom of upholstered pieces of furniture is a product of the period, the best literature of which is remarkably gloomy. It was a characteristic of Victorian interior decoration (and a

symptom of Victorian modesty) to cover chair legs with "skirts" in an effort to nullify the perceived sexual analogy.

Rhyming heightens the sense of the poem as a made thing, yet it moves "naturally" enough—my reason for choosing open couplets. Both purposes correspond to what I'm getting at in the poem. Thus it is that form serves content, and that a poet chooses a given formal design—always to probe, to extend, and to embody.

Closed Couplets

A **closed couplet** is a couplet that is a self-contained grammatical unit (such as the Belloc couplet on page 175). We speak of the couplet that typically ends the Shakepearean sonnet as closed, since it is self-contained. Like open couplets, closed couplets can be used to fashion longer poems in any meter or, theoretically, in free verse. But there is one type of closed couplet whose meter is specified, a type of such importance in English poetry that it has a name of its own: the **heroic couplet** (called "heroic" after the heroic plays of Dryden, who used the design extensively). The heroic couplet is a closed couplet in iambic pentameter (thus both meter and rhyme define the form). We would not speak, however, of a single couplet like Belloc's as "heroic"; the name is reserved for longer poems composed of a series of closed iambic-pentameter couplets. Because most of the finest poems in heroic couplets date from the eighteenth century, we shall turn to this era for illustrations. The following excerpts from longer eighteenth-century poems in heroic couplets should serve to suggest what the form is best suited for.

from **The Choice**

[the last verse paragraph]

John Pomfret

If heaven a date of many years would give,
Thus I'd in pleasure, ease, and plenty live;   155
And as I near approached the verge of life,
Some kind relation, for I'd have no wife,
Should take upon him all my worldly care
While I did for a better state prepare.
Then I'd not be with any trouble vexed,   160
Nor have the evening of my days perplexed;
But by a silent and a peaceful death,
Without a sigh, resign my aged breath:

And when committed to the dust, I'd have
Few tears, but friendly, dropped into my grave.   165
Then would my exit so propitious be,
All men would wish to live and die like me.

(1700)

from **An Essay on Man**

─────────────────────────────────

Alexander Pope

  Know then thyself, presume not God to scan;
The proper study of mankind is Man.
Placed on this isthmus of a middle state,
A being darkly wise, and rudely great:
With too much knowledge for the skeptic side,   5
With too much weakness for the Stoic's pride,
He hangs between; in doubt to act, or rest,
In doubt to deem himself a god, or beast;
In doubt his mind or body to prefer,
Born but to die, and reasoning but to err;   10
Alike in ignorance, his reason such,
Whether he thinks too little, or too much:
Chaos of thought and passion, all confused;
Still by himself abused, or disabused;
Created half to rise, and half to fall;   15
Great lord of all things, yet a prey to all;
Sole judge of truth, in endless error hurled:
The glory, jest, and riddle of the world!

(1733)

from **The Vanity of Human Wishes**

─────────────────────────────────

Samuel Johnson

  Let Observation, with extensive view,
Survey mankind, from China to Peru;
Remark each anxious toil, each eager strife,
And watch the busy scenes of crowded life;
Then say how hope and fear, desire and hate   5
O'erspread with snares the clouded maze of fate,
Where wavering man, betrayed by venturous pride
To tread the dreary paths without a guide,

As treacherous phantoms in the mist delude,
Shuns fancied ills, or chases airy good;   10
How rarely Reason guides the stubborn choice,
Rules the bold hand, or prompts the suppliant voice;
How nations sink, by darling schemes oppressed,
When Vengeance listens to the fool's request.

(1749)

from THE VANITY OF HUMAN WISHES. 14. *When . . . request:* when ven-
geance is ready to be the motive force of political action if the proposals
of fools prevail.

from **Mac Flecknoe**

John Dryden

All human things are subject to decay,
And when fate summons, monarchs must obey.
This Flecknoe found, who, like Augustus, young
Was called to empire, and had governed long;
In prose and verse, was owned, without dispute,   5
Through all the realms of Nonsense, absolute.
This aged prince, now flourishing in peace,
And blest with issue of a large increase,
Worn out with business, did at length debate
To settle the succession of the state;   10
And, pondering which of all his sons was fit
To reign, and wage immortal war with wit,
Cried: " 'Tis resolved; for nature pleads that he
Should only rule, who most resembles me.
Sh——— alone my perfect image bears,   15
Mature in dullness from his tender years:
Sh——— alone, of all my sons, is he
Who stands confirmed in full stupidity.

(1682)

from MAC FLECKNOE. 3. *Flecknoe:* Richard Flecknoe, who died not long
before Dryden wrote this poem, was an Irish poet as prolific as he was
boring. *Augustus:* Caesar Augustus. 15. *Sh———:* Thomas Shadwell (1640–
1692) was a comic playwright of some repute. But by casting him in the
role of Flecknoe's son and heir ("Mac" means "son of"), Dryden satirized
him into oblivion. Catch the scatological implication of Dryden's tongue-in-
cheek attempt at anonymity ("Sh———").

What, then, is the form suited for? It is not generally apt for lyric passion (though, as always, there are significant exceptions) and certainly not for epic grandeur. Instead, because it requires keen powers of precision and conciseness on the part of a poet, it seems a fit vehicle for another kind of passion (as the Pope passage suggests): intellectual passion. It also has the potential for elegance and grace, a potential that springs from the sense of balance innate to the form, as we saw when we glanced at Denham's *Cooper's Hill* (page 136) and as can be seen from Pomfret's charming lines above. Most of all, the form is a superb vehicle for wit and satire—whether straight-faced, like Johnson's, or comic, like Dryden's—because of the epigrammatic feel of the closed couplet generally and the punch it can so readily deliver. So striking are these potentialities that, knowing nothing more about the eighteenth century than that the heroic couplet was its dominant form, one might venture to guess that the age had a bent toward rhetoric and satire, prized balance and grace, and veered toward the intellectual and away from the raw emotions. One would be right on all scores, which suggests a fascinating phenomenon: as I mentioned when discussing the simile, the different periods of history reflect themselves, albeit obliquely, in the differing formal choices made by their artists collectively. Form is, then, the vehicle not only of a given artist's outlook and sensibility but also of the spirit of the times.

POEM ASSIGNMENT

Write at least one closed couplet in iambic pentameter. If you like, write two or three, or attempt a longer poem in such couplets (in which case they—and you—would be "heroic"). It is not easy to write a good closed couplet—one that does not twist the language out of shape. To do so you will have to avoid senseless inversions and, undoubtedly, revise several times (this is what "polishing" means). Remember the prime potentiality of the form: punch. Build your couplet(s) to a climax, witty if possible. Your content, in other words, should be conditioned by the givens of the form.

Decide how well the criteria I have established apply to the following student samples, which might serve as models:

> It is a stupid joke that God hath chose
> To make the world a sewer and me a nose.
>
> > *Howard Bostwick*

> My once so verbal wife lies still in bed,
> The reason being she is oh so dead.
>
> > *Joseph Micali*

The battlefield was hushed with a vicious calm;
He went to a bar, and she went home to mom.

Ann Marie Trentacosti

Although you think you look so sweet and ripe,
I'm sorry honey, you're just not my type.

Thomas Kane

Lord Randal's Lover Speaks
in His Defense

Raymond Carthy

I speak out of the past for I have heard
That you have called my Randal's song a bird.*
You look to Edward's old ballad for joy—
The senseless story of a mama's boy.
The drama, heartache, pain you failed to see   5
Between my love and in-law once to be.
And why, you ask, did I knock him off? You sot.
I had to kill him, else there'd be no plot.

* Overstating my case, I had called "Lord Randal" a "turkey" in class.

A FEW STANZAIC PATTERNS

More elaborate in design than couplets are the many stanzaic patterns
found in English poetry, most of which are defined by rhyme, and some
by meter as well.[4] Stanzas—yet another type of concretion—should be
thought of as building-blocks constructing the larger edifice of the whole
poem. Stanzaic forms have a clear spatial dimension, and may be charac-
terized as right-hemispheric in appeal. But what I wish to stress is, again,
potentiality: why a given stanzaic form is suited to a given purpose. To
do so, we shall focus on four of the many traditional rhymed forms at a
poet's disposal. These four are of special importance because they fre-
quently recur in the corpus of our poetry.

[4] A **stanza** is a grouping of lines usually demarked by spacing, a recurrent rhyme
scheme, and a repeating pattern of lines with reference to number and length. Many
unrhymed poems are also divided into stanzas (demarked by spacing), in which case what
recurs is a set number of lines per stanzaic unit. Some rhymed poems are composed of
variable stanzas (for instance, the irregular ode, such as Wordsworth's "Ode: Intimations
of Immortality").

Terza Rima

Terza rima (tĕr tsa rē´ma) stanzas are **tercets** (tŭr´ sĕts—three-line units) marked by interlinking rhymes: *aba/bcb/cdc/ded* and so on. This rhyme pattern creates a marked pull forward, the *b* rhyme pulling us on from stanza one to stanza two, the *c* rhyme from stanza two to stanza three, and so forth. For this reason, the form is especially suited to narrative poetry, though it also has lyric dimensions. Good narrative, as a rule, has a strong forward motion, which is exactly the innate effect of terza rima. Thus Dante chose terza rima for *The Divine Comedy*, one of the greatest (and longest) narrative poems in any language. In English, terza rima has been used by Milton, Shelley, Byron, MacLeish, Auden, and Eliot, to name only its most prominent practitioners. It also crops up in variation. Think again of Frost's little narrative lyric "Stopping by Woods" (page 28), which proceeds *aaba/bbcb/ccdc/dddd*. Frost used this modified version of terza rima, I think, for the pull of the rhyme and the strong closure his modification allows. As for strict terza rima, the following excerpt from Browning's narrative poem "The Statue and the Bust" well exemplifies the feel of the form:

> So weeks grew months, years; gleam by gleam
> The glory dropped from their youth and love,
> And both perceived they had dreamed a dream;
>
> Which hovered as dreams do, still above—
> But who can take a dream for a truth?   155
> Oh, hide our eyes from the next remove!
>
> One day as the lady saw her youth
> Depart, and the silver thread that streaked
> Her hair, and, worn by the serpent's tooth,
>
> The brow so puckered, the chin so peaked—   160
> And wondered who the woman was,
> Hollow-eyed and haggard-cheeked,
>
> Fronting her silent in the glass—
> "Summon here," she suddenly said,
> "Before the rest of my old self pass,   165
>
> "Him, the Carver, a hand to aid,
> Who fashions the clay no love will change,
> And fixes a beauty never to fade.

(1855)

The Spenserian Stanza

Named after Edmund Spenser, who devised the form, the **Spenserian stanza** is rather elaborate: it is composed of nine lines rhymed *ababbcbcc*, with the first eight lines in iambic pentameter and the ninth, iambic hexameter. (Such a line is called an **alexandrine.**) A good narrative stanza because of its length (it is long enough for a poet to accomplish much in a single stanza), it is especially suited to descriptive poetry, or poetry that involves a good deal of description along with narration. Its sheer luxuriance of sound—with its four *b* and three *c* rhymes—lends itself to descriptive purposes. When handled well, the interweaving rhymes of the stanza add a dimension of tonal depth and coloration that itself works toward descriptive ends. It is probable, incidentally, that Spencer made the last line an alexandrine in order to eliminate even the hint of wit. He wanted the sense of closure that an end couplet brings, and only that. The effect of the added foot is to throw the timing off and, therefore, to undercut the normal potential of the closed couplet.

That the stanza is so well suited to descriptive purposes may be why it became a favorite among such romantic poets as Wordsworth, Byron, Shelley, Keats, and Tennyson. The stanza is supple and rich in sound, and its sound as it cumulates serves to flesh out description. One stanza from Keats's "The Eve of St. Agnes" provides an illustration:

> Anon his heart revives: her vespers done,
> Of all its wreathèd pearls her hair she frees;
> Unclasps her warmèd jewels one by one;
> Loosens her fragrant bodice; by degrees
> Her rich attire creeps rustling to her knees: 230
> Half-hidden, like a mermaid in sea-weed,
> Pensive awhile she dreams awake, and sees,
> In fancy, fair St. Agnes in her bed,
> But dares not look behind, or all the charm is fled.

The warmth of Madeline's (the young woman who undresses) jewels and bodice can almost literally be felt. Over and above Keats's fine adjectives, the stanza form itself has much to do with the palpable quality of the writing—because, simply, there is so much to hear. Its richness of rhyme helps to make vivid the scene being described.

Ottava Rima

The prime potentiality of the **ottava rima** (ō · tǎ′va rē′ma) stanza, which rhymes *abababcc*, is suggested by the couplet with which it closes: wit, humor, satirical thrust. It is for this potential that Byron chose ottava rima for his long comic narrative *Don Juan*. (Like the Spenserian stanza, the ottava rima stanza is long enough for narrative purposes.) Byron exploited the comic potential of the form so well that any poet who used the form after Byron had to be mindful of what he had done with it. Two stanzas, both from Canto One, should suffice to illustrate the innate qualities of the form. The first concerns a search conducted by Julia's husband, Alfonso, for her suspected lover, Don Juan—who has been hiding *in* the bed all along. Finding nothing, Alfonso stands shamefaced and at Julia's mercy—the substance of the second stanza.

Stanza 144

Under the bed they searched, and there they found— 1145
   No matter what—it was not that they sought;
They opened windows, gazing if the ground
   Had signs or footmarks, but the earth said nought;
And then they stared each other's faces round:
   'Tis odd, not one of all these seekers thought, 1150
And seems to me almost a sort of blunder,
Of looking *in* the bed as well as under.

Stanza 180

Alfonso closed his speech, and begged her pardon,
   Which Julia half withheld, and then half granted,
And laid conditions, he thought very hard on, 1435
   Denying several little things he wanted:
He stood like Adam lingering near his garden,
   With useless penitence perplexed and haunted,
Beseeching she no further would refuse,
When, lo! he stumbled o'er a pair of shoes. 1440

Both stanzas exhibit narrative thrust and comic rhyming (rhyming of polysyllabic words), and the closing couplet of each is marked by comic surprise and climax. *Don Juan* is well served by the stanza form Byron chose.

The In-Memoriam Stanza
The single most frequent stanzaic form in English poetry is the quatrain, a four-line stanza that can rhyme *aabb, abab, aaba, abcb* (the scheme usually associated with the ballad), or *abba*. The last—called the

In-Memoriam stanza—is particularly important and particularly instructive with regard to the concept of potentiality. Named after a long poem by Tennyson in which it is exploited fully, the stanza is also called the "envelope" stanza, suggesting something of its nature: there is an innate sense of enclosure and inwardness to the form *abba*. Too short and halting for the purposes of extended narration, too plain and unadorned for elaborate description, the stanza is wonderfully suited to little bursts of lyric passion or quiet moments of meditation. This is certainly why Tennyson turned to the form when he poured out the lyrics that compose *In Memoriam,* an intensely personal poem expressing in bursts the poet's grief over the death of his dearest friend. The following lyric from *In Memoriam,* imbued with deep personal grief, is remarkable for its inwardness and aura of authentic feeling:

Poem No. 7 from *In Memoriam*

Dark house, by which once more I stand
　　Here in the long unlovely street,
　　Doors, where my heart was used to beat
So quickly, waiting for a hand,

A hand that can be clasped no more—　　　　　　5
　　Behold me, for I cannot sleep,
　　And like a guilty thing I creep
At earliest morning to the door.

He is not here; but far away
　　The noise of life begins again,　　　　　　10
　　And ghastly through the drizzling rain
On the bald street breaks the blank day.

　　　　　　　　　　　　　　(1850)

From IN MEMORIAM.　1. *Dark house:* The house of the dead friend, Arthur Hallam.

As for the meditative potential of the *In-Memoriam* stanza, consider next a poem whose surface is as quiet as meditation itself, but that nevertheless finds its closure in a muffled burst of lyric passion:

About My Students

John Fandel

Against the pleated pillars of Old Main,
   Like caryatids in plaids, the coeds lean,
   Loafing in wisdom's porticoes between
Lectures on Aristotle and the Dane.

The heroes of their gaze accord the spring   5
   In rolled-up sleeves, all similar in sweet ease
   And pastimes lackadaisical as the breeze
That stalled the canvas of Mycenae's King.

Ten-minute freedoms in the outdoor sun
   Accommodate their restlessness in class   10
   Where they sit doodling, while professors mass
The facts about Thermopylae and Verdun.

Among their lolling youth my daydreams flit:
   How I, like they, lived once from bell to bell.
   No old accumulated notes can tell   15
Them life is stranger than they fancy it.

(1959)

ABOUT MY STUDENTS. 2. *caryatids:* statues of draped female figures used to support, like columns, the portico of a building of classic design. 4. *the Dane:* Hamlet. 5. *accord:* are in harmony with. 8. *Mycenae's King:* Agamemnon, commander of the Greek forces in the Trojan War. Because the fleet was stalled by a northern breeze, Agamemnon, acting under advisement, sacrificed his daughter Iphigenia to the gods. The allusion, which brings to mind the tragedy of the Trojan War, serves to underpin the statement made in the poem's last stanza. 12. *Thermopylae and Verdun:* the two great battles that frame Western history.

The quietness and reflectiveness of the poem impart the feel of meditation, the inwardness of memory. Its stanzaic form also contributes to voice. Its slow-moving stanzas have about them the halting wistfulness of age (as opposed to the impetuous rush of youth). From whatever angle we look at the poem, its form bears its content—always the mark of a poem that works.

Fixed Forms

In conjunction with or in addition to stanzaic patterns, rhyme (and sometimes meter and/or line repetition) defines a number of fixed forms, such as the sestina, the rondeau, the rondel, the triolet, the limerick, the

villanelle. Take, for instance, the villanelle. The scheme of the **villanelle**
(vĭl´an·ĕl´´) is *ABA'/abA/abA'/abA/abA'/abAA'* (lines *A* and *A'*, which
rhyme, repeat word for word). Like the triolet, the villanelle is usually
associated with light verse. But it can be turned to other ends, as Dylan
Thomas turns it in his poem about the imminent death of his father:

Do Not Go Gentle into That Good Night

Do not go gentle into that good night,
Old age should burn and rave at close of day;
Rage, rage against the dying of the light.

Though wise men at their end know dark is right,
Because their words had forked no lightning they   5
Do not go gentle into that good night.

Good men, the last wave by, crying how bright
Their frail deeds might have danced in a green bay,
Rage, rage against the dying of the light.

Wild men who caught and sang the sun in flight,   10
And learn, too late, they grieved it on its way,
Do not go gentle into that good night.

Grave men, near death, who see with blinding sight
Blind eyes could blaze like meteors and be gay,
Rage, rage against the dying of the light.   15

And you, my father, there on the sad height,
Curse, bless, me now with your fierce tears, I pray.
Do not go gentle into that good night.
Rage, rage against the dying of the light.

(1952)

The poem is paradoxical: Thomas calls death a "good night" and
"right," but insists that one must resist it. To affirm life one must both
resist death (not want to die) and accept it at the last as right (because
it is a given of life). Thomas expresses this paradoxical aspect of hu-
man awareness in the texture of his almost surrealistic imagery and in
his initial choice of form. The form—generally associated, as I have
said, with light verse—serves here to lighten the tone of the poem, and
thereby to create a tension between form and content that embodies the

paradoxical attitude toward life and death that Thomas would have his father take. The principle, once again, is that form is either meaningfully respected or meaningfully deviated from—and sometimes both at once, as in "Do Not Go Gentle."

The Sonnet

Of all the fixed forms established over the centuries, none has proven as enduring and as pliable as the **sonnet**—a fourteen-line poem usually in iambic pentameter. There are several types of sonnet, foremost among which are the **Petrarchan** (pē · trar′ kan) and the **Shakespearean** (each named after its creator). The rhyme schemes and formal divisions of each are:

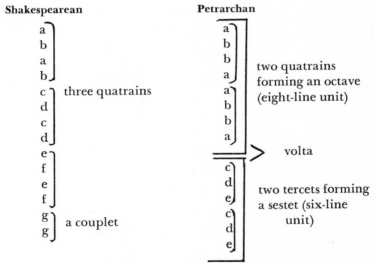

Each form has particular potentialities. Though some sonnets of the first type seem to divide themselves into octave and sestet (see Shakespeare's sonnets 29 and 146, pages 397 and 399), the fundamental potential of the Shakespearean form is three steps in an argument and a summation, or three parallel statements and a conclusion, which (summation or conclusion) often entails a pointed reversal (the inherent inclination of the closed couplet). By virtue of its innate division into octave and sestet, the Petrarchan sonnet offers broader possibilities: question and answer; generalization and particularization, or particularization and generalization; statement and modification or full counterstatement. Contrasts are also possible between the quatrains of the octave and even between the tercets of the sestet. (There are many Petrarchan sonnets, however, in which the rhyme scheme of the sestet is varied. The *cde/cde* pattern is the norm to the extent that there is a norm.)

We have already encountered a good example of the Shakespearean sonnet in "That Time of Year Thou Mayst in Me Behold" (page 25), which consists of three parallel statements and a conclusion, startling because unexpected. You might look now at sonnets 30 and 130 in the Anthology (page 130), both of which follow the pattern of parallel statements and reversal. We shall see the alternate pattern of three-step argument and summation in sonnet 129, which we'll look at in some detail in Chapter 8.

But however finely wrought by its originator, the Shakespearean sonnet has proven less popular than the Petrarchan with the major latter-day practitioners of the sonnet: Milton, Wordsworth, and Hopkins. The reason the Petrarchan sonnet has dominated English poetry is, I believe, that its many internal divisions allow for and underscore contrast. Division is the nature of the Petrarchan form; for a poem in the form to succeed fully, the poet must somehow make use of its basic divisions, especially between octave and sestet—where we should expect some sort of a shift, called a *volta*. Hopkins sums up the matter:

> Now it seems to me that this division [between octave and sestet] is the real characteristic of the sonnet and that what is not so marked off and moreover has not the octet [another word for "octave"] again divided into quatrains is not to be called a sonnet at all.[5]

In other words, rhyme scheme alone does not define a Petrarchan sonnet; to be worthy of the name, a poem in the form must exploit it for what it is, as does the following sonnet by Hopkins. Note especially the contrast between the quatrains and the shift (volta) into the sestet. The meaning of the poem lies especially in the contrasts made possible by its formal design; to live through the poem thus means, in part, to respond to that design.

God's Grandeur

The world is charged with the grandeur of God.
  It will flame out, like shining from shook foil;
  It gathers to a greatness, like the ooze of oil
Crushed. Why do men then now not reck his rod?
Generations have trod, have trod, have trod;   5
  And all is seared with trade; bleared, smeared with toil;
  And wears man's smudge and shares man's smell: the soil
Is bare now, nor can foot feel, being shod.

[5] *The Correspondence of G. M. Hopkins and R. W. Dixon*, 2nd ed., ed. C. C. Abbott (London: Oxford University Press, 1955), p. 71.

And for all this, nature is never spent;
   There lives the dearest freshness deep down things;
And though the last lights off the black West went
   Oh, morning, at the brown brink eastward, springs—
Because the Holy Ghost over the bent
   World broods with warm breast and with ah! bright wings.

                                   10

(c. 1877)

GOD'S GRANDEUR. 1. *charged:* as a battery is charged. 2. *shook foil:* In the Leyden jar experiment, a piece of gold foil suspended in a bell jar in which a vacuum has been created will, if fur is rubbed on the outside of the jar, spark with static electricity. 4. *Crushed:* Highly viscous oil will, if pressed ("crushed") with a finger, gather back on itself because of its surface tension. 6. *seared . . . toil:* The point of contrast is that the very things—"flame" and "oil"—that in their natural state reveal God serve in the hands of man to conceal Him (thus "seared" and "bleared, smeared"). 9. *spent:* as a battery is said to be "spent" (see, too, Wordsworth's "Getting and spending" below). 14. *broods:* as a bird (specifically, a dove) broods on an egg.

Again, we cannot overlook the possibility of meaningful deviation. Wordsworth, for instance, deviates most meaningfully from the expectations of the Petrarchan form in "The World Is Too Much With Us" (against which "God's Grandeur" should be read—the two poets make similar judgments of the modern world, though the poems diverge in terms of focus). Observe what happens between the octave and sestet (lines 8–9):

The world is too much with us; late and soon,
Getting and spending, we lay waste our powers;
Little we see in Nature that is ours;
We have given our hearts away, a sordid boon!
This Sea that bares her bosom to the moon,   5
The winds that will be howling at all hours,
And are up-gathered now like sleeping flowers,
For this, for everything, we are out of tune;
It moves us not.—Great God! I'd rather be
A Pagan suckled in a creed outworn;   10
So might I, standing on this pleasant lea,
Have glimpses that would make me less forlorn;
Have sight of Proteus rising from the sea;
Or hear old Triton blow his wreathèd horn.

                                (1807)

The octave rises to a climax with the sweeping indictment of its eighth line, and then falls into anticlimax with the tagged-on "It moves us not." If we know the form and come to Wordsworth's sonnet with the proper expectations, the slopping over of the octave into the sestet should serve to put us off guard. We expect a volta but get, it seems, its opposite. So we relax for just a moment. Then Wordsworth lets us have it: the voice rises to the pitch of passion as the delayed volta ("Great God!") hits us in the solar plexus. By this subtle deviation, Wordsworth gains tremendous power.

Much more deviant, though its rhyme scheme is clearly Petrarchan (the *cdcdcd* scheme of the sestet is a common variant), is the following late sonnet by Hopkins:

[Thou Art Indeed Just, Lord]

Justus quidem tu es, Domine, si disputem tecum:
verumtamen justa loquar ad te:
Quare via impiorum prosperatur? etc.

Thou art indeed just, Lord, if I contend
With thee; but, sir, so what I plead is just.
Why do sinners' ways prosper? and why must
Disappointment all I endeavour end?
   Wert thou my enemy, O thou my friend,   5
How wouldst thou worse, I wonder, than thou dost
Defeat, thwart me? Oh, the sots and thralls of lust
Do in spare hours more thrive than I that spend,
Sir, life upon thy cause. See, banks and brakes
Now, leavèd how thick! lacèd they are again   10
With fretty chervil, look, and fresh wind shakes
Them; birds build—but not I build; no, but strain,
Time's eunuch, and not breed one work that wakes.
Mine, O thou lord of life, send my roots rain.

(c. 1889)

[THOU ART INDEED JUST, LORD]. *Epigraph:* "Righteous art thou, O Lord, when I complain to thee; yet I would plead my case before thee. Why does the way of the wicked prosper?" (Jeremiah 12:1). What follows in Jeremiah is also relevant: "Why do all who are treacherous thrive? Thou plantest them and they take root; they grow and bring forth fruit; thou art near in their mouth and far from their heart." 9. *brakes:* clumps of fern. 11. *fretty:* fretted. Chervil is a spring herb.

Beginning by paraphrasing Jeremiah's question, though with two signifi-
cant differences—Hopkins's God seems sterner ("sir") than Jeremiah's
(who calls God by the familiar "tu"), and Hopkins's concern is much more
personal ("I")—Hopkins makes the Petrarchan form implode by collaps-
ing the octave into the sestet. This collapse is purposeful: it is dramati-
cally at one with the emotional collapse of the poet himself in the latter
part of the poem. The formal collapse of the poem echoes and makes
vivid the corresponding emotional collapse, rendering form and content
inseparable. To return to the paradox of deviation, the poem is a perfect
Petrarchan sonnet because Hopkins has turned the form into a vehicle of
meaning.

Deviation is not always meaningful, though; there is always the possi-
bility of ineptness. By way of illustration, let us look at a sonnet that is of
some historical interest because its author is no less a poet than Words-
worth:

The Stepping-Stones

The struggling Rill insensibly is grown
Into a Brook of loud and stately march,
Crossed ever and anon by plank or arch;
And, for like use, lo! what might seem a zone
Chosen for ornament—stone matched with stone   5
In studied symmetry, with interspace
For the clear waters to pursue their race
Without restraint. How swiftly have they flown,
Succeeding—still succeeding! Here the Child
Puts, when the high-swoln Flood runs fierce and wild,   10
His budding courage to the proof; and here
Declining Manhood learns to note the sly
And sure encroachments of infirmity,
Thinking how fast time runs, life's end how near!

(1820)

THE STEPPING-STONES. 1. *Rill:* the source of the river Duddon, the subject
of the sonnet sequence of which this sonnet is number 9. 3. *arch:* bridge.
8. *they:* the waters—though, deliberately vague, "they" could refer to in-
crements of time as well.

Though the end is lovely and the poem as a whole isn't bad (especially
nice is the link of water and running time), one wonders why Wordsworth
chose to cast his material in this form. He violates the divisions of the

form at each turn without apparent reason. All one can conclude is that Wordsworth had decided to write a series of sonnets, and that "The Stepping-Stones" therefore had to be a sonnet. Aesthetically, however, that is an insufficient reason—which is why, though pleasant, the poem is not compelling. To make such a judgment, one has to know the inherent qualities and potentialities of a given form, as one must to discern when a poem is working.

Exercise

Nearly everyone knows the **limerick**—a form associated with light verse that rhymes *aabba* and more or less conforms to the metrical pattern of the following example:

Relativity

There was a young lady named Bright,
Who travelled much faster than light;
   She started one day
   In the relative way,
And returned on the previous night.

With these formal strictures in mind, try your hand at a limerick, or gather a few friends together and write a limerick communally. Part of the fun lies in seeing what can be done within the givens of the form. The same is true, of course, of any fixed form. You might also see what you can do with one of the other forms we have looked at, such as the ottava rima stanza or, if the muse is upon you, the sonnet.

POEMS FOR FURTHER STUDY

Down, Wanton, Down

Robert Graves

Down, wanton, down! Have you no shame
That at the whisper of Love's name,
Or Beauty's, presto! up you raise
Your angry head and stand at gaze?

Poor bombard-captain, sworn to reach 5
The ravelin and effect a breach—
Indifferent what you storm or why,
So be that in the breach you die!

Love may be blind, but Love at least
Knows what is man and what mere beast; 10
Or Beauty wayward, but requires
More delicacy from her squires.

Tell me, my witless, whose one boast
Could be your staunchness at the post,
When were you made a man of parts 15
To think fine and profess the arts?

Will many-gifted Beauty come
Bowing to your bald rule of thumb,
Or Love swear loyalty to your crown?
Be gone, have done! Down, wanton, down! 20

(1933)

Questions
1. What is the stanzaic form of Graves's droll offering?
2. What is the rhyme scheme of each stanza? What do we call lines rhymed in this way?
3. The poem is epigrammatic, which seems suited to its content. How so?
4. In what way does the formal design of "Down, Wanton, Down!" contribute to its overall effect? In other words, what is the effect on tone of the poem's design?

Acquainted with the Night

Robert Frost

I have been one acquainted with the night.
I have walked out in rain—and back in rain.
I have outwalked the furthest city light.

I have looked down the saddest city lane.
I have passed by the watchman on his beat 5
And dropped my eyes, unwilling to explain.

I have stood still and stopped the sound of feet
When far away an interrupted cry
Came over houses from another street,

But not to call me back or say good-by; 10
And further still at an unearthly height
One luminary clock against the sky

Proclaimed the time was neither wrong nor right.
I have been one acquainted with the night.

(1928)

Questions
1. What is the formal pattern of Frost's poem?
2. What does Frost accomplish by his chosen form?
3. Frost seems to allude to another fixed form we have considered, his allusion serving to give the poem a further degree of solidity. What form am I speaking of? (Count the number of lines.)
4. Frost's love of traditional forms of all sorts has been called his "stay against confusion." The comment sheds light on the poem at hand. How so? That is, in the face of the kind of universe depicted in this poem, what purely human desire does formal design serve to concretize here?

La Belle Dame sans Merci

John Keats

O what can ail thee, Knight at arms,
  Alone and palely loitering?
The sedge has withered from the Lake
  And no birds sing!

O what can ail thee, Knight at arms, 5
  So haggard, and so woebegone?
The squirrel's granary is full
  And the harvest's done.

I see a lily on thy brow
  With anguish moist and fever dew, 10
And on thy cheeks a fading rose
  Fast withereth too.

I met a Lady in the Meads,°   *meadows*
    Full beautiful, a faery's child,
Her hair was long, her foot was light   15
    And her eyes were wild.

I made a Garland for her head,
    And bracelets too, and fragrant Zone;°   *girdle*
She looked at me as she did love
    And made sweet moan.   20

I set her on my pacing steed
    And nothing else saw all day long,
For sidelong would she bend and sing
    A faery's song.

She found me roots of relish sweet,   25
    And honey wild, and manna dew,
And sure in language strange she said
    "I love thee true."

She took me to her elfin grot
    And there she wept and sighed full sore,   30
And there I shut her wild wild eyes
    With kisses four.

And there she lullèd me asleep,
    And there I dreamed, Ah Woe betide!
The latest° dream I ever dreamt   *last*   35
    On the cold hill side.

I saw pale Kings, and Princes too,
    Pale warriors, death-pale were they all;
They cried, "La belle dame sans merci
    Thee hath in thrall!"   40

I saw their starved lips in the gloam
    With horrid warnings gapèd wide,
And I awoke, and found me here
    On the cold hill's side.

And this is why I sojourn here,   45
    Alone and palely loitering;
Though the sedge is withered from the Lake
    And no birds sing.

                                                      (1820)

LA BELLE DAME SANS MERCI. "The beautiful lady without pity." The title helps lend the poem the aura of a medieval troubadour song.

Questions
1. Keats's poem is a type known as a *literary ballad*—a ballad written not by one of the folk, but by a highly sophisticated poet in imitation of the folk ballad. What ballad elements does Keats make use of?
2. Why did Keats choose to cast *this* material into a ballad? That is, how is form here integral to content?

Playboy

Richard Wilbur

High on his stockroom ladder like a dunce
The stock-boy sits, and studies like a sage
The subject matter of one glossy page,
As lost in curves as Archimedes once.

Sometimes, without a glance, he feeds himself.   5
The left hand, like a mother-bird in flight,
Brings him a sandwich for a sidelong bite,
And then returns it to a dusty shelf.

What so engrosses him? The wild décor
Of this pink-papered alcove into which   10
A naked girl has stumbled, with its rich
Welter of pelts and pillows on the floor,

Amidst which, kneeling in a supple pose,
She lifts a goblet in her farther hand,
As if about to toast a flower-stand   15
Above which hovers an exploding rose

Fired from a long-necked crystal vase that rests
Upon a tasseled and vermilion cloth
One taste of which would shrivel up a moth?
Or is he pondering her perfect breasts?   20

Nothing escapes him of her body's grace
Or of her floodlit skin, so sleek and warm
And yet so strangely like a uniform,
But what now grips his fancy is her face,

And how the cunning picture holds her still   25
At just that smiling instant when her soul,
Grown sweetly faint, and swept beyond control,
Consents to his inexorable will.

(1969)

PLAYBOY.   4. *Archimedes:* Greek mathematician (287?–212 B.C.).

Questions
1. What stanzaic form goes into the making of Wilbur's poem?
2. How is this form (as opposed to some other form) appropriate to the situation of the poem?
3. Given that the young man described in the poem is rather shallow and empty-headed, there also seems an ironic intent in Wilbur's choice. How so? (Remember what has been said about the inwardness and meditative potentiality of the stanza form in question.)

IDEAS FOR WRITING

1.

Surprised by Joy

William Wordsworth

Surprised by joy—impatient as the Wind
I turned to share the transport—Oh! with whom
But thee, deep buried in the silent tomb,
That spot which no vicissitude can find?
Love, faithful love, recalled thee to my mind—   5
But how could I forget thee? Through what power,
Even for the least division of an hour,
Have I been so beguiled as to be blind
To my most grievous loss!—That thought's return
Was the worst pang that sorrow ever bore,   10
Save one, one only, when I stood forlorn,
Knowing my heart's best treasure was no more;
That neither present time, nor years unborn
Could to my sight that heavenly face restore.

(1815)

SURPRISED BY JOY.   3. *thee:* the poet's daughter Catherine, who died in 1812 at age four.

After clarifying for yourself its various shifts in time and perspective, paraphrase this sonnet. Then discuss Wordsworth's use of Petrarchan form. Does he respect its divisions? If not, why not? In a separate paragraph, discuss your response to the poem.

2. Paraphrase Graves's "Down, Wanton, Down!" Then discuss what is lost in the translation. What is your response to this poem?

3. Write a ballad about some school-related matter that concerns you. Remember that your poem will be a narrative of sorts that proceeds in increments. Imitate the stanzaic form of Keats's "La Belle Dame sans Merci."

4. Read "The Eve of St. Agnes" (pages 383–394) and write a paper on the function of its framing stanzas (stanzas 1–3 and 42). The poem begins and ends with the Beadsman. Why? How does the frame of the poem condition the romance of its narrative? You might also consider Keats's use of the Spenserian stanza, especially in the framing stanzas. There is a good deal of tension between form and content in these stanzas. How does this tension serve to underscore the many other tensions of the poem—in particular, the tension between its narrative and its frame?

5.
Leda and the Swan

W. B. Yeats

A sudden blow: the great wings beating still
Above the staggering girl, her thighs caressed
By the dark webs, her nape caught in his bill,
He holds her helpless breast upon his breast.

How can those terrified vague fingers push   5
The feathered glory from her loosening thighs?
And how can body, laid in that white rush,
But feel the strange heart beating where it lies?

A shudder in the loins engenders there
The broken wall, the burning roof and tower   10
And Agamemnon dead.
                    Being so caught up,
So mastered by the brute blood of the air,
Did she put on his knowledge with his power
Before the indifferent beak could let her drop?

(1924)

LEDA AND THE SWAN. According to Greek myth, Zeus descended to earth as a swan and raped Leda, who then gave birth to four children, among them Helen (of Troy) and Clytemnestra. This rape thus resulted in the Trojan War (referred to in line 10) and subsequent murder (line 11) of Agamemnon at the hands of his wife, Clytemnestra.

Do some research on this poem and see what its critics have to say. Ask your librarian how to use the *MLA Bibliography*. You might also consult Joseph M. Kuntz, *Poetry Explication,* rev. ed. (Chicago: Swallow Press, 1962). Work up a bibliography first; then read five to ten critical analyses of the poem; finally, write a paper on the poem as sonnet. What contrast does Yeats draw between the quatrains of the octave? Though the sonnet is Petrarchan, the octave rhymes *abab/cdcd.* Might there be a reason (in terms of contrast) for this deviation? What about the poem's volta? And why the division in the sestet? "Leda" has been called "an almost perfect sonnet." What grounds would lead one to this conclusion? Some of your research will be directly applicable to the task at hand, and some will not. Use what is pertinent to bolster your own analysis. But the interpretation should be yours. Don't just summarize what others have said; instead, use your research to stimulate you into insight.

Approaching Definition
Chapter Eight

WHAT IS POETRY?

Attempting something like a definition of poetry, Emily Dickinson wrote: "If I feel physically as if the top of my head were taken off, I know that is poetry." A. E. Housman concurred: "Experience has taught me, when I am shaving, to keep watch over my thoughts, because, if a line of Poetry strays into my memory, my skin bristles so that the razor ceases to act." Most of us have had similar experiences at one time or another: suddenly a turn of phrase strikes home with peculiar force. Still, this approach to definition is inadequate, because it unduly limits one's scope. Some readers, basing their sense of poetry on the vagaries of personal taste (which does come from somewhere—usually from the cultural milieu of one's childhood), have pronounced Pope not a poet at all; others have felt the same way about Wordsworth, or Whitman, or Eliot. To judge poets and poetry thus is to confine one's understanding to the preferences of the moment, and therefore to limit the possibility of growth.

Should we go to the opposite pole and assent to Frost's maxim that "poetry is the kind of thing that poets write"? The openness of Frost's approach is refreshing, but not particularly helpful when we undertake the sorting of our experiences that understanding requires. We need a definition less wide and value-free than Frost's, but not as narrow and prone to personal and cultural whim as Dickinson's or Housman's. On the one hand, we do need some sense of delimitation; on the other, we should not allow ourselves to be beguiled by the judgments of taste alone, thereby cutting ourselves off from the wonderful diversity of poetry.[1] Our interest should be twofold: to discover who we are at the moment, yet to permit the self to grow beyond the conditioning of its background to the point that we each can say with the Roman playwright Terence, *humani nil a me alienum* ("nothing human is alien to me").

A TENTATIVE ANSWER

I have postponed attempting a definition of poetry, first because I believe that evidence should precede conclusions, and second because I am forced by the nature of the evidence to agree with the poet Howard Nemerov when he defines poetry as "an activity resistant to definition." Nevertheless, there is an answer to the question before us. In her superb book on poetics, Winifred Nowottny says that "the poem is not a collection of phrases, but a dramatic action, the actors being such things as metrics, alteration of tone and so on."[2] Here is the answer. A poem is a verbal construct that means by what it is.

Dylan Thomas gave eloquent expression to this conception of poetry:

The body, its appearance, death, and disease, is a fact, sure as the fact of a tree. It has its roots in the same earth as the tree.... All thoughts and actions emanate from the body. Therefore the description of a thought or action—however abstruse it may be—can be beaten home by bringing it onto a physical level. Every idea, intuitive or intellectual, can be imaged and translated in terms of the

---

[1] This diversity is exemplified by the poems gathered in the Anthology under the heading "Paired Poems."

[2] Winfred Nowottny, *The Language Poets Use* (London: Athlone Press, 1962), p. 111.

body, its flesh, skin, blood, sinews, veins, glands, organs, cells, or senses.

Through my small, bonebound island I have learnt all I know, experienced all, and sensed all. All I write is inseperable [sic] from the island. . . . therefore, I employ the scenery of the island to describe the scenery of my thoughts, the earthquake of the body to describe the earthquake of the heart.[3]

In sum, poetry is thought made palpable, the body of feeling. The question always is: how to speak the unspeakable? Some have thought it impossible to do so. The twentieth-century philosopher Ludwig Wittgenstein, for instance, held that "What we cannot speak about we must consign to silence." Yet what we cannot speak about is precisely what is most important to us. Must we remain dumb, possessed only of a language unfit to bear the weight of our experience? I think not, though I agree with Nowottny's observation that "a vocabulary however extensive can do nothing of itself to communicate the particularity and concretion of living experience." [4] That is, it is not so much the meanings of words that allow us to speak and to penetrate our experience as it is what Nowottny calls "the silent touch of enactment." [5] The paradox implicit in calling poetry "silent" was expressed succinctly by Wallace Stevens when, alluding to Shakespeare, he defined poetry as "excellent dumb discourse." As Stevens wrote elsewhere: "The poet, the musician, both have explicit meanings but they express them in the forms these take and not in explanation."

This view of poetry was articulated first by Coleridge, who, believing the aim of poetry to be pleasure (in its broadest sense), wrote that "it [poetry] is discriminated by proposing to itself such delight from the *whole* as is compatible with a distinct gratification from each component *part*," [6] and then went on to note that what makes poetry poetry is "the property of exciting a more continuous and equal attention than the *language* [italics mine] of prose aims at." [7] According to this distinction, the difference between the prose you are reading now and a poem is that you are not required to respond point by point to the language of this book, only to comprehend it on the level of dictionary meaning, as though language were a transparent window through which meaning can

---

[3] *The Selected Letters of Dylan Thomas,* ed. C. FitzGibbon (New York: New Directions, 1965), p. 48.

[4] Nowottny, *The Language Poets Use,* p. 106.

[5] Ibid., p. 116.

[6] S. T. Coleridge, *Biographia Literaria: or Biographical Sketches of My Literary Life,* ed. J. Shawcross (Oxford: Clarendon Press, 1907), II, p. 10.

[7] Ibid., p. 11.

be seen. In contrast, a poem asks first and last that we consider its words in all their particularity (that we attend to diction, sound, and so forth), just as a stained-glass window asks us to look at it, not through it. The various aspects of poetic technique that we have spoken of, then, are *not* embellishments; they are fundamental to what poetry is and the way it works.

It is through its enactment that a poem touches us, if it does—not just our conscious minds, but our psyches and muscles as well. To put this another way, poetry is a mode of exploration through words into the deepest reaches of our being, an exploration beyond intention into discovery. Consequently, poetry has the potential of engaging us in the ongoing process of self-formation. As we saw in Chapter 1, a poem is not merely about experience; it is an experience itself, aimed at tapping and making available the entire self—the right hemisphere as well as the left, the unconscious as well as consciousness, muscles and nerve ends as well as the intellect.

No paraphrase, therefore, can ever replace the poem it translates: a paraphrase always misses the crucial experiential dimension, as mere words always miss the substantiality of life. But substantiality is the very essence of poetry. Read aloud these two lines by Hopkins:

> How to keep—is there any any, is there none such nowhere known
>   some, bow or brooch or braid or brace, láce, latch or catch or
>   key to keep
> Back beauty, keep it, beauty, beauty, beauty, . . . from vanishing
>   away?

In his letters Hopkins speaks of *Back* as having "that sense of physical constraint" which is the meaning of the lines. Everything is designed to embody and palpably impart that sense: the length of the first line (which should be read as spreading unbroken across some enormous page and, from "bow" on, read in one breath); the strong ending of line 1 and the incredible enjambment (which exhausts the breath and the reader); the sound patterning of the whole and the guttural quality of the word *Back* by itself. The lines affect us in the body as much as the head; they involve us in action as much as in thought, or in thought through action.

CONCLUDING

A successful poem, then, is an experience to be lived through with one's full being. The following sonnet by Shakespeare exemplifies as well as any single poem can the nature of poetic enactment.

Sonnet 129

William Shakespeare

Th' expense of spirit in a waste of shame
Is lust in action; and till action, lust
Is perjured, murderous, bloody, full of blame,
Savage, extreme, rude, cruel, not to trust;
Enjoyed no sooner but despisèd straight: 5
Past reason hunted; and no sooner had,
Past reason hated, as a swallowed bait,
On purpose laid to make the taker mad:
Mad in pursuit, and in possession so;
Had, having, and in quest to have, extreme;   10
A bliss in proof, and proved, a very woe;
Before, a joy proposed; behind, a dream.
All this the world well knows; yet none knows well
To shun the heaven that leads men to this hell.

(1609)

SONNET 129.   1. *Th' expense . . . shame:* Without precluding other readings,
I will suggest a possible gloss for this terribly knotty and much disputed
line. "Spirit" commonly meant "semen" in the Renaissance, and ejaculation
was commonly spoken of as an "expending" or a "spending"; "shame" is
the base meaning of the word "pudendum," the anatomical word for the
female genitals. These overtones, together with the suggestion of buying
in the word "expense," connote that someone's been a-whoring—engaged
in an act not worth the shame. 11. *in proof:* in the experience.

At first glance this seems more like a little moral lecture than a poem.
The speaker *is* flatly making a statement, or trying to. And the poem as
a whole has the shape of discourse: three steps in an argument and a
summation. "Isn't Shakespeare simply declaiming against lust?" you ask.
If so, I answer, he's made an awful botch of it. From the perspective of
a moral lecture, the poem is a mess. The knottiness of the first line is
hardly fit for the purposes of a moralist. Then there's the haltingness of
the poem and, most important, its absurd anticlimaxes. "Perjured, mur-
derous, bloody" (a strong word to an Englishman)—fine. But "full of
blame"? The line ends with its weakest epithet. Again, "Savage, extreme,
rude, cruel"—all right, though "extreme" is a bit pallid. But "not to
trust" in the climactic position? (Not only did he run away with my wife
and steal my money, . . . he scratched the right fender of my car as well.)
Finally, "Had, having, and in quest to have [an odd sequence in terms

of time], extreme." "Extreme" again? The poet could not have chosen a more colorless word.

To what are we to attribute all this seeming ineptness? Couldn't Shakespeare find decent rhyme words? Shakespeare?! No, he could have found stronger words had he wished. So we need to look at the poem anew—as a poem. For it is not a little moral lecture at all; it is a dramatic enactment of a very human, highly conflicted state of mind, a state that cannot find adequate expression in mere words. Thus the anticlimaxes: the feeling outpaces the words at every turn. Thus the knottiness of the first line and the illogical sequence of line 10. Thus, too, the haltingness of the poem, especially at the beginning. I suggest that lines 1 and 2 be read as end-stopped; read in this way, they communicate the tone not of a speaker with lecture-notes in hand but of a man struggling to articulate, to define what he's feeling, and pausing before definition to gather his conflicted thoughts. Then the rush to words, which fail miserably, though in their failure the poem succeeds. And, finally, thus the ambiguity of the summary couplet, which does not do what we expect it to do. "Bliss" (which connotes an almost mystical sense of rapture), "joy," "dream" (which hardly counterbalances "joy"), "heaven" are the words not of a moralist summarizing his diatribe against lust, but of a deeply split human being who knows that, whatever the dictates of reason or the depth of his present disgust, he will wind up doing the thing again. He struggles to let reason prevail, to guide his actions by the sure knowledge gained from past experience. He casts his thoughts into a logical pattern and affects the language of discourse (the only full figure in the poem being that of the "bait" in lines 7–8). But his very hissing against desire (note the harsh, spitting sounds of much of the poem) betrays its power to subvert reason. The bait, though known to be poisoned, will once more prove too sweet to be resisted. His only solace is that what he knows of himself, he knows also to be true of the rest of humankind. His attempt at reasoning with himself having failed, he settles for the meager comfort of rationalization.

What we encounter in the poem is an enactment of a very human, highly conflicted state of mind: the id and the superego playing out their battle in the language of the sonnet, or in what the language does. Not a lecture, a poem. The voice is exact, and so, paradoxically, expresses what the speaker fails to say, what cannot be said. There's the splendor of poetry: it speaks what cannot be spoken.

My definition of poetry as an enactment in language is intentionally broad. For poetry always seems to defy set boundaries, and the line between poetry and much of the best prose (to which the epithet "poetic" is often applied because of the nature of its language) is never sharp. The study of poetry should lead to an expanding sense of what it is in itself;

yet our study would be incomplete if it did not also lead us to see the relation of poetry to all human endeavor as that endeavor is revealed in literature and the arts in general. Speaking specifically of poetry, but implying all of literature as well, the distinguished novelist, critic, and poet Robert Penn Warren encapsulates the thrust of my argument:

[In poetry] we find not merely a verbal language, but a primary language of imagery (the image of metaphor or the image of scene), the pre-verbal "language" that reaches back to infancy and the primitive dark; but it still remains the naked language of our emotional life by which we envisage the object of desire, hate, or fear. At the same time, poetry not only utters itself in such a language that reminds us of our deepest being, but embodies ideas and values; and so its images are, in one dimension, a sophisticated dialectic. The poem . . . eventuates in "meaning"—no, *as* "meaning."

Literally, the process of composition is, in one degree or another, a movement toward meaning. The writer (like any artist) is not a carpenter who builds the chicken coop according to a blueprint. If the carpenter has a blueprint he knows exactly what kind of chicken coop will be forthcoming. But the writer, no matter how clear his idea or strong his intuition of the projected work, can never know what it will "be" or "mean" until the last word is in place—for every word, every image, every rhythm participates in the "being," and the "being" is, ultimately, the "meaning." And the reader is made to share in this process.

We are bombarded all day long by abstractions, by the "truths" of the advertising man, the politician, the preacher, and suddenly a good poem . . . reminds us that every truth that is not lived into, not earned out of experience, either literally or imaginatively, is a lie. We are redeemed from all our would-be redeemers—especially from those who would redeem us for their own profit or power—and reminded that we must, after all, redeem ourselves. How? By learning to respect the self and respect experience. Chastened by a keener awareness of human possibility of salvation or disaster, we may be a little more certain of the terms by which the individual fate will be determined. If our current civilization would cut us off from ourselves as well as from nature and other men, we may remember what Henri Bergson says of fiction, and what may be said of all imaginative literature: it "returns us into the presence of ourselves." [8]

8 Robert Penn Warren, "Poetry in a Time of Crack-up," *New York Review of Books*, 15, No. 12 (January 7, 1971), pp. 32–33.

LIVING THROUGH A POEM

One particular idea that Warren touches on has informed our study from the outset: "And the reader is made to share in this process." Reading is a dynamic activity, an experience that takes shape in the dialectic of reader and text, and in the reader's living through all of a poem's elements. Because of the nature of any "study," however, we have had to work sequentially and to look at poems piecemeal, focusing first on one element and then on the next. Now, finally, let us live through a poem entire. Of course, I cannot do the living for you. All I can do is to record how I live through a poem, and thereby perhaps sharpen your response to that poem and, more generally, help you to integrate the many aspects of poetry we have discussed.

A Valediction Forbidding Mourning

Adrienne Rich

My swirling wants. Your frozen lips.
The grammar turned and attacked me.
Themes, written under duress.
Emptiness of the notations.

They gave me a drug that slowed the healing of wounds.   5

I want you to see this before I leave:
the experience of repetition as death
the failure of criticism to locate the pain
the poster in the bus that said:
my bleeding is under control.   10

A red plant in a cemetery of plastic wreaths.

A last attempt: the language is a dialect called metaphor.
These images go unglossed: hair, glacier, flashlight.
When I think of a landscape I am thinking of a time.
When I talk of taking a trip I mean forever.   15
I could say: those mountains have a meaning
but further than that I could not say.

To do something very common, in my own way.

(1971)

A VALEDICTION FORBIDDING MOURNING. The title alludes to Donne's "A Valediction: Forbidding Mourning," whose final four stanzas we looked at in Chapter 4. The complete text is to be found in the Anthology, pp. 315–316. 5. *They gave me ... of wounds:* As well as alluding to Donne, Rich seems to allude at several points to Eliot's *The Waste Land.* In this line, for instance, I catch an echo of the end of Eliot's poem, in which the fisher king Anfortas lies wounded, waiting for what will magically heal him: the simple question "What is wrong?" The "drug" Rich speaks of slows "the healing of wounds" because it numbs and so keeps one from asking this question, from feeling and facing the wound.

"The language is a dialect called metaphor"—in part, Rich's "Valediction" concerns metaphor (language) and its failures. In this regard, her poem is far removed from Donne's, which, through its conceits and elaborate metaphorical extension, suggests confidence in language (metaphor) and, concomitantly, in the self and its purposes. Given Rich's allusion, the very absence of sustained metaphorical extension in her poem is itself perhaps metaphorical, as are its broken syntax and even its look in print, with three of its lines separated out from the rest and made to stand in isolation. At any rate, her title serves to establish the situation of her poem: the parting of lovers (the one of "swirling wants" leaving the one of "frozen lips"). Unlike Donne's speaker, however, Rich's is "taking a trip ... forever." Donne forbids mourning because his lovers cannot be separated; Rich forbids mourning because hers are to make a clean break. Donne's emphasis is on continuance; Rich's is on freedom, the desire for which her speaker can only "attempt" to express.

She knows all too well how language can conceal instead of reveal, freeze into patterns that give only the illusion of meaning. When she says "grammar," she also means herself, her life as defined by other people's language. Her life with the man she is leaving has become a college theme "written under duress," empty of conviction, dry (like footnotes), feelingless, frozen by "repetition." Having come to "experience ... repetition as death," she must break out and feel what she must— first, the depth of her pain. In a long, weary line (line 5) marked by low-pitched vowel sounds, she sums up her life until this moment of departure: drugged—perhaps by the drug of marriage, with its load of conventional definitions, perhaps literally by tranquilizers—she has not felt her wounds. So how could they be healed? Like the characters in *The Waste Land,* she has been insulated from herself. Trapped in the grammar of conventional expectations, she has lost touch with her own needs.

Yet, "swirling," those needs have finally surfaced. She must, therefore, sever this relationship, which has become a relationship only in name. The very grammar of the first line suggests their separateness, the "me" and the "you" isolated in independent sentences and set in opposition by the strong midline caesura. But, however much the poem's speaker now mistrusts language, which has imprisoned her in received definitions, one of her needs ("I want") is to explain why she is leaving. There enters a tone of tenderness, even pity at his dumbfoundedness, and of urgency. She would articulate, both to him and to herself, what has brought her to this leave-taking.

It is the death of possibility—the stifling of growth, the "experience of repetition"—that all the rationalizations of the socialized intellect cannot justify or ease. The pain is there, however concealed; the wound is bleeding internally, however much denied by external patterns of behavior or the characteristic language of the culture at large: the language of commercialism, which saps and devitalizes language, and in so doing cuts us off from understanding our needs. The bus poster for menstruation pills provides a symbolic focal point: *"my bleeding is under control."* Woman, do not bleed; woman, do not need. From all this she would break out, like a potted plant breaking the pot that restricts its growth. Her need is for something real, something felt, even for pain and bleeding if necessary—"A red plant in a cemetery of plastic wreaths."

But how to express in the language of explanation the swirling of the heart? Like J. Alfred Prufrock, Rich's speaker finds it impossible to say just what she means. Her unglossed images remain unglossed. Yet they have a peculiar resonance, as do her metaphors, and a sense of urgency. The swirling heart cries to be free, to have world enough and time to make its own choices. Thus, the trip is to be forever; the break must be clean. The meaning of "those mountains" is freedom— "In the mountains, there you feel free," says a character in *The Waste Land.* Rich's speaker has been in an emotional waste land, but she has awakened to the possibility of a fuller life. More than that she cannot say.

Partly about language, the poem also concerns growth, the pain of endings, the promise of a beginning. Unlike the first speaker of *The Waste Land,* a female who fears growth and would be left dead ("April is the cruellest month," she says), Rich's speaker is in process. Though she has not arrived anywhere, she has begun to allow herself to grow. But she has only begun. While imitating the swirling of the heart, the fragmented form of the poem also suggests that the person of the speaker is not whole. And she has far to go before she is fully in touch with herself. The tonal dryness of much of the poem—created, in part, by severe endstopping, along with syntactical and rhythmical fragmentation—sounds a dichotomy between understanding and feeling. Nevertheless, she has made a start, tentatively, gropingly. Her tentativeness expresses itself in her grammar—"To do" instead of "I shall do." Yet I also hear a firmness of resolve in her end-stopping (as opposed to the insistent enjambment of Eliot's female speaker—see page 140) and especially in the simplicity of the last line and the tonal quality of its last phrase, which strikes a note almost of joy: "in my own way." The bright, high-pitched "ā," the strong ending, and the rhyme (the only rhyme in the poem) convince me of her intent. However painful it is to make an end, she will leave; she will struggle to shed the language that has kept her from growing and grope toward fulfilling in herself the "common" need: the need for *self*-definition.

Like the Shakespeare sonnet we looked at earlier in this chapter, Rich's "Valediction" expresses what its speaker cannot say. Through the resources of the poet, Rich makes vivid the conflicts of her female speaker and the reasons for her departure. By participating in the design of the poem, by living through its images and associations, its metaphors and rhythms, its syntax and form, I am made to feel in myself the common need. Thus, at one and the same time, my self-perception is heightened and my sympathies are enlarged. It is a splendid poem.

POEM ASSIGNMENT—*"To do something very common, in my own way."*

Poets often speak of finding their own "voices," by which they mean finding or forging a language capable of imparting the particular flavor of their individual beings. Finding that language, in turn, strengthens the being by giving it definition. For this final poem assignment I shall set only two restrictions: what you write should be divided into lines and given a title. You might try rhyme and/or meter, or you might concentrate solely on the line as your medium. Whatever you choose to do, avoid the merely poetical and the trite. Your object is to write a poem, which means to fashion from language a language that is yours.

The poems that follow were all written by students to fulfill this assignment. You can do as well, I believe, if you set yourself to it.

Eye of the Shadow

Tom Waddell

Summer's a physical domain;
Winter's the silence;
Autumn's a blanketing of rain;
Spring's by the comet—greening a galaxy light.
Eye of the shadow:
Weather's a hollowing of eyes.

Approaching Definition

Our Poetry Class Was . . .

Raymond Carthy

like an artichoke:
we stripped each leaf to see
the simple structure of its thistled fruit.
Some were distressed at pulling it apart.
Not me: 5
'cause I ate every leaf.

A Letter

Stephen Stout

A folded letter lies upon my desk,
Return addressed to Zainesville, Arkansas;
Its writer begs that I please forgive her.

The pages are scarred by wear and brown tint,
Which colors the eagle of its chic bond . . .
Worn from attempting a reply.

The Regatta

James Petrie

The morning broke as the team began to arrive:
Confusion, decisions, and orders from the coach—the aroma of
   tension;
Last-minute pep-talks, good luck, a cheer from bystanders, then the
   start:
Pushing foot, moving away and keeping the lead, motivation from
   the swain;
Finally the last strokes, the surge of power, . . . muscles glistening
   and exhausted.

Anger

Gerald Fahy

Anger strips man
Dropping like bombs
From a silent sky.
It burns, seethes, devastates,
Leaving after its blast   5
   a calm
Felt only by those
   who were burned.

The 8:36 Express

Paul Gliedman

On the train to
no where
faces stare out grimy windows or
eyes fix in a trance upon some
paper that tells of things a   5
thousand miles away.
Faster we go,
past empty stations, broken fences, rusted autos
on the train to
oblivion.   10

Menagerie

Richard Dryk

I took a drop of water—clear
Yet with a world within its tear.
There isn't a more motley crew
Than in this mini-aqua-zoo.
I saw a shrimp with beady eyes,   5
A tiny cousin of the flies;
The amoeba, with no hands and feet;
A hydra marching to a different beat;
Paramecium whirling like a top—
Bronx Zoo, not in a nutshell but a drop.   10

IDEAS FOR WRITING

1. Take two of the "paired poems" from the Anthology (pages 407–434) and compare and contrast them.

2. Pair two poems yourself and discuss the relevance of the pairing.

3. Choose one of the following topics: diction, imagery, figurative language, rhythm. Develop a thesis about your chosen topic and then write a paper supporting your thesis. For instance, you could write on how _____ (diction, imagery, figurative language, or rhythm) functions in poetry generally, or the function of _____ in a poem you have read. You need not write on poetry, however. Your thesis could concern _____ as it operates in daily discourse (such as levels of diction in everyday life), or _____ as it relates to some nonliterary realm of human endeavor (such as metaphor and sports) or as an aspect of human life generally (such as imagery and thinking).

4. Write a full analysis of the poem you wrote for the final poem assignment—as reader now, rather than as poet. That is, try to put your intentions aside and look at what you wrote as you would look at a poem by someone else.

5. Choose a poem from the text or Anthology and explain why you think it succeeds or fails. Be sure to make your response to the poem clear and to state your criteria for judging it. (At the end of my analysis of Rich's "Valediction," I judge the poem to be "splendid" on the basis of three stated criteria: (1) it makes vivid the conflicts of its speaker, (2) it heightens my self-perception, and (3) it enlarges my sympathies.)

6. Take any poem that you've read this semester and discuss it in relation to your major field of study. In other words, either use your extra-literary knowledge to elucidate some aspect of the poem or use the poem to say something about some aspect of your field. You may wish to use research materials from your field, in which case quote and note accordingly.

Anthology

Chapter One

United 555

Richard Eberhart

St. Paul never saw a sight like this.
Seven miles up, fifty five below outside,
Wide open flat top of cloud vista to the far horizon,
As the sun descends reddening the upworld spectacle.

St. Paul never got off the ground, and, for that matter,   5
Christ was nailed to a Cross a few feet above the earth.
Here I sit seven miles up feeling nothing,
No visceral reaction, dollar martini, endless vista.

I must say it could not be more beautiful.
O think of Akhnaton, who never got off the ground either.   10
Raciest to think of the baboons in East Africa at Treetops,
Who could not imagine to come to such a pass as this.

Christ and Paul never knew what height is,
They never polluted the atmosphere.
I am Twentieth Century Man riding high,   15
Going into the sunset, Seven Up, feeling no pain.

(1976)

UNITED 555. 10. *Akhnaton:* Egyptian pharaoh (c. 1375–1358 B.C.) who held that there was one god—the sun—and who gave rise to a cult of nature worship.

The Pardon

Richard Wilbur

My dog lay dead five days without a grave
In the thick of summer, hid in a clump of pine
And a jungle of grass and honeysuckle-vine.
I who had loved him while he kept alive

Anthology

Went only close enough to where he was   5
To sniff the heavy honeysuckle-smell
Twined with another odor heavier still
And hear the flies' intolerable buzz.

Well, I was ten and very much afraid.
In my kind world the dead were out of range   10
And I could not forgive the sad or strange
In beast or man. My father took the spade

And buried him. Last night I saw the grass
Slowly divide (it was the same scene
But now it glowed a fierce and mortal green)   15
And saw the dog emerging. I confess

I felt afraid again, but still he came
In the carnal sun, clothed in a hymn of flies,
And death was breeding in his lively eyes.
I started in to cry and call his name,   20

Asking forgiveness of his tongueless head.
. . . I dreamt the past was never past redeeming:
But whether this was false or honest dreaming
I beg death's pardon now. And mourn the dead.

(1950)

Western Wind

Anonymous

Western wind, when will thou blow,
  The small rain down can rain?
Christ, if my love were in my arms
  And I in my bed again!

(15th cen.)

WESTERN WIND. *Western wind:* a wind both of autumn and of spring.

Bells for John Whiteside's Daughter

John Crowe Ransom

There was such speed in her little body,
And such lightness in her footfall,
It is no wonder her brown study
Astonishes us all.

Her wars were bruited in our high window.   5
We looked among orchard trees and beyond
Where she took arms against her shadow,
Or harried unto the pond

The lazy geese, like a snow cloud
Dripping their snow on the green grass,   10
Tricking and stopping, sleepy and proud,
Who cried in goose, Alas,

For the tireless heart within the little
Lady with rod that made them rise
From their noon apple-dreams and scuttle   15
Goose-fashion under the skies!

But now go the bells, and we are ready,
In one house we are sternly stopped
To say we are vexed at her brown study,
Lying so primly propped.   20

(*1924*)

BELLS FOR JOHN WHITESIDE'S DAUGHTER.   3. *brown study:* serious expression.
5. *bruited:* reported (by way of echo).

Disillusionment of Ten O'Clock

Wallace Stevens

The houses are haunted
By white night-gowns.
None are green,
Or purple with green rings,
Or green with yellow rings,   5

Or yellow with blue rings.
None of them are strange,
With socks of lace
And beaded ceintures.
People are not going   10
To dream of baboons and periwinkles.
Only, here and there, an old sailor,
Drunk and asleep in his boots,
Catches tigers
In red weather.   15

(1923)

DISILLUSIONMENT OF TEN O'CLOCK.   9. *ceintures:* belts, strings, girdles.

Song from a Country Fair

Leonie Adams

When tunes jigged nimbler than the blood
And quick and high the bows would prance
And every fiddle string would burst
To catch what's lost beyond the string,
While half afraid their children stood,   5
I saw the old come out to dance.
The heart is not so light at first,
But heavy like a bough in spring.

(1954)

The Centaur

May Swenson

The summer that I was ten—
Can it be there was only one
summer that I was ten? It must

have been a long one then—
each day I'd go out to choose   5
a fresh horse from my stable

which was a willow grove
down by the old canal.
I'd go on my two bare feet.

But when, with my brother's jack-knife,   10
I had cut me a long limber horse
with a good thick knob for a head,

and peeled him slick and clean
except a few leaves for the tail,
and cinched my brother's belt   15

around his head for a rein,
I'd straddle and canter him fast
up the grass bank to the path,

trot along in the lovely dust
that talcumed over his hoofs,   20
hiding my toes, and turning

his feet to swift half-moons.
The willow knob with the strap
jouncing between my thighs

was the pommel and yet the poll   25
of my nickering pony's head.
My head and my neck were mine,

yet they were shaped like a horse.
My hair flopped to the side
like the mane of a horse in the wind.   30

My forelock swung in my eyes,
my neck arched and I snorted.
I shied and skittered and reared,

stopped and raised my knees,
pawed at the ground and quivered.   35
My teeth bared as we wheeled

and swished through the dust again.
I was the horse and the rider,
and the leather I slapped to his rump

spanked my own behind.   40
Doubled, my two hoofs beat
a gallop along the bank,

the wind twanged in my mane,
my mouth squared to the bit.
And yet I sat on my steed   45

quiet, negligent riding,
my toes standing the stirrups,
my thighs hugging his ribs.

At a walk we drew up to the porch.
I tethered him to a paling.   50
Dismounting, I smoothed my skirt

and entered the dusky hall.
My feet on the clean linoleum
left ghostly toes in the hall.

Where have you been? said my mother.   55
Been riding, I said from the sink,
and filled me a glass of water.

What's that in your pocket? she said.
Just my knife. It weighted my pocket
and stretched my dress awry.   60

Go tie back your hair, said my mother,
and *Why is your mouth all green?*
*Rob Roy, he pulled some clover
as we crossed the field,* I told her.

                                                               (1958)

THE CENTAUR. *Centaur:* a mythic creature, half man and half horse.

Danse Russe

W. C. Williams

If when my wife is sleeping
and the baby and Kathleen
are sleeping

and the sun is a flame-white disc
in silken mists   5
above shining trees,—
if I in my north room
dance naked, grotesquely
before my mirror
waving my shirt round my head   10
and singing softly to myself:
"I am lonely, lonely.
I was born to be lonely,
I am best so!"
If I admire my arms, my face,   15
my shoulders, flanks, buttocks
against the yellow drawn shades,—

Who shall say I am not
the happy genius of my household?

(1917)

DANSE RUSSE.   19. *genius:* local spirit, household deity.

Root Cellar

Theodore Roethke

Nothing would sleep in that cellar, dank as a ditch,
Bulbs broke out of boxes hunting for chinks in the dark,
Shoots dangled and drooped,
Lolling obscenely from mildewed crates,
Hung down long yellow evil necks, like tropical snakes.   5
And what a congress of stinks!
Roots ripe as old bait,
Pulpy stems, rank, silo-rich,
Leaf-mold, manure, lime, piled against slippery planks.
Nothing would give up life: 10
Even the dirt kept breathing a small breath.

(1948)

As Near to Eden

Robert Francis

Hearing the cry I looked to see a bird
Among the boughs that overhung the stream.
No bird was there. The cry was not a bird's.
Then I looked down and saw the snake and saw
The frog. Half of the frog was free to cry.   5
The other half the snake had in its jaws.
The snake was silent as the sand it lay on.

I ran to blast the thing out of my sight,
But the snake ran first (untouched) into the water
Fluid to fluid and so disappeared   10
And all I saw and heard was flowing water.

I dipped a foot in slowly and began
To saunter down the stream a little way
As I had done so many times before
That summer. Now I went more cautiously   15
Watching the water every step, but water
Had washed the thing away and washed it clean.

Over the stream I had a kind of bed
Built of an old smooth board and four large stones
And there between the sun and water I   20
Would often spend an early afternoon.
It was as near to Eden as I knew—
This alternating cool and warm, this blend
Of cool and warm, of water-song and silence.
No one could see me there and even insects   25
Left me alone.
                    I turned upon my face
And so had darkness for my eyes and fire
On my back. I felt my breathing slacken, deepen.
After a time I reached a hand over
And let the fingertips trail in the water.   30

Strange, strange that in a world so old and rich
In good and evil, the death (or all but death)
Of one inconsequential squealing frog
Should have concerned me so, should for the moment
Have seemed the only evil in the world   35
And overcoming it the only good.

But they were symbols too, weren't they? the frog,
The snake? The frog of course being innocence
Sitting with golden and unwinking eyes
Hour after hour beside a water-weed   40
As rapt and meditative as a saint
Beneath a palm tree, and the snake being—well,
That's all been told before.
                        A pretty contrast,
Yet even under the indulgent sun
And half asleep I knew my picture false.   45
The frog was no more innocent than the snake
And if he looked the saint he was a fake.
He and the snake were all too closely kin,
First cousins once removed under the skin.
If snakes ate frogs, frogs in their turn ate flies   50
And both could look ridiculously wise.
But neither one knew how to feed on lies
As man could do; that is, philosophize.
And having reached that point I closed my eyes,
Rhyming myself and sunning myself to sleep.   55

And while I slept my body was a sundial
Casting its moving, slowly moving shadow
Across the moving, swiftly moving water.
When I awoke I had one clear desire:
The coolness of that swiftly moving water.   60
Yet still I waited, it was so near, so sure,
The superfluity of heat so good.

And then I sat straight up having heard a sound
I recognized too well. It was no bird.
Slipping and splashing as I went I ran   65
Upstream. I couldn't see, I didn't need
To see to know. So all the time I'd slept
And sunned myself and entertained myself
With symbolizing and unsymbolizing
Good and evil, *this* had been going on.   70

They were hidden now among the roots of a tree
The stream had washed the soil from. I found a stick
And jabbed it in as far as I could reach
Again and again until I broke the stick.
But still I kept it up until the snake   75

Having disgorged slipped out and got away.
And still I kept it up until the frog
Must have been pulp and ground into the sand.
The stick, all that was left, I threw as far
As I could throw.
                    Then I went home and dressed.   80
Eden was done for for one day at least.

                                                  (*1944*)

Red-Tail Hawk and Pyre
of Youth

Robert Penn Warren

1

Breath clamber-short, face sun-peeled, stones
Loose like untruth underfoot, I
Had just made the ridge crest, and there,
Opening like joy, the unapprehensible purity
Of afternoon flooded, in silver,   5
The sky. It was
The hour of stainless silver just before
The gold begins.

            Eyes, strangely heavy like lead,
Drew down to the .30/30 hung on my hand   10
As on a crooked stick, in growing wonder
At what it might really be. It was as though
I did not know its name. Nor mine. Nor yet had known
That all is only
All, and part of all. No wind   15
Moved the silver light. No movement,

            Except for the center of
That convex perfection, not yet
A dot even, nameless, no color, merely
A shadowy vortex of silver. Then,   20
In widening circles—oh, nearer!
And suddenly I knew the name, and saw,
As though seeing, coming toward me,
Unforgiving, the hot blood of the air:
Gold eyes, unforgiving, for they, like God, see all.   25

2

There was no decision in the act,
There was no choice in the act—the act impossible but
Possible. I screamed, not knowing
From what emotion, as at that insane range
I pressed the cool, snubbed   30
Trigger. Saw
The circle
Break.

3

Heart leaping in joy past definition, in
Eyes tears past definition, by rocky hill and valley   35
Already dark-devoured, and with the bloody
Body already to my bare flesh embraced, cuddled
Like babe to heart, and my heart beating like love:
Thus homeward. But nobody there. So at last
I dared stare in the face—the lower beak drooping,   40
As though from thirst, eyes filmed.
Like a secret, I wrapped it in newspaper quickly
And hid it deep
In the ice chest.

Too late to start now.   45

4

Up early next morning, with
My father's old razor laid out, the scissors,
Pliers and needles, waxed thread,
The burlap and salt, the arsenic and clay,
A roll of steel wire, and glass eyes gleaming yellow—oh, yes, 50
I knew my business. And at last a red-tail—

Oh, king of the air!

And at that miraculous range.

How my heart sang!

Till all was ready—skull now well scraped   55
And with arsenic dried, and all flesh joints, and the cape
Like a carapace feathered in bronze, and naturally anchored
At beak and at bone joints, and steel

Driven through to sustain wing and bone
And the clay-burlap body built there within.   60
It was molded as though for that moment to take to the air—though,
In God's truth, the chunk of poor wingless red meat,
The model from which all was molded, lay now
Forever earthbound, fit only
For dog tooth, not sky.   65

5

Year after year, in my room, on the tallest of bookshelves,
It was regal, perched on the bough-crotch to guard
Blake and "Lycidas," Augustine, Hardy, and "Hamlet,"
Baudelaire and Rimbaud, and I knew that the yellow eyes,
Unsleeping, stared as I slept.   70

Till I slept in that room no more.

6

Years pass like a dream, are a dream, and time came
When my mother was dead, father bankrupt, and whiskey
Hot in my throat while there for the last

Time I lay, and my heart   75
Throbbed slow in the
Meaningless motion of life, and with
My eyes closed I knew
That yellow eyes somewhere, unblinking, in vengeance stared.

Or *was* it vengeance? What could I know?   80

Could Nature forgive, like God?

7

In the lumber room that night, late,
I found him—the hawk, feathers shabby, one
Wing bandy-banged, one foot gone sadly
Askew, one eye long gone—and I reckoned   85
I knew how it felt with one gone.

And all relevant items I found there: my first book of Milton,
The "Hamlet," the yellow, leaf-dropping Rimbaud, and a book

Of poems friends and I had printed in college, not to mention
The collection of sexual Japanese prints—strange sex   90
Of mechanical sexlessness. And so made a pyre for
The hawk that, though gasoline-doused and wing-dragging,
Awaited, with what looked like pride,
The match.

8

Flame flared. Feathers first, and I flinched, then stood   95
As the steel wire warped red to defend
The shape designed godly for air. But
It fell with the mass, and I
Did not wait.

          What is left   100
To do but walk in the dark, and no stars?

9

Some dreams come true, some no.
But I've waked in the night to see
High in the late and uncurdled silver of summer
The pale vortex reappear—and you come,   105
And always the rifle again swings up, though
With the weightlessness now of dream,
The old .30/30 that knows
How to bind us in air-blood and earth-blood together
In our commensurate fate,   110
Whose name is a name beyond joy.

10

And I pray that, in some last dream or delusion,
While hospital wheels creak beneath
And the nurse's soles make their *squeak-squeak* like mice,
I'll again see the first small, silvery swirl   115
Spin outward and downward from sky-height
To bring me the truth in blood-marriage of earth and air—
And all will be as it was
In that paradox of unjoyful joyousness,
Till the dazzling moment when I, a last time, flinch   120
From that regally feathered gasoline flare
Of youth's poor, angry, slapdash, and ignorant pyre.

                                                    (*1977*)

The Animals

Edwin Muir

They do not live in the world,
Are not in time and space.
From birth to death hurled
No word do they have, not one
To plant a foot upon,   5
Were never in any place.

For with names the world was called
Out of the empty air,
With names was built and walled,
Line and circle and square,   10
Dust and emerald;
Snatched from deceiving death
By the articulate breath.

But these have never trod
Twice the familiar track,   15
Never never turned back
Into the memoried day.
All is new and near
In the unchanging Here
Of the fifth great day of God,   20
That shall remain the same,
Never shall pass away.

On the sixth day we came.

                                          (1949)

THE ANIMALS. 20. *fifth great day:* the fifth day of creation (see Genesis 1:20–25).

"Long Live the Weeds"

Theodore Roethke

Long live the weeds that overwhelm
My narrow vegetable realm!
The bitter rock, the barren soil

That force the son of man to toil;
All things unholy, marred by curse,   5
The ugly of the universe.
The rough, the wicked, and the wild
That keep the spirit undefiled.
With these I match my little wit
And earn the right to stand or sit,   10
Hope, love, create, or drink and die:
These shape the creature that is I.

(1941)

"LONG LIVE THE WEEDS." The title comes from Hopkins's "Inversnaid":
"Long live the weeds and the wilderness yet."

[There's a Certain Slant of Light]

Emily Dickinson

There's a certain Slant of light,
Winter Afternoons–
That oppresses, like the Heft
Of Cathedral Tunes–

Heavenly Hurt, it gives us–   5
We can find no scar,
But internal difference,
Where the Meanings, are–

None may teach it–Any–
'Tis the Seal Despair–   10
An imperial affliction
Sent us of the Air–

When it comes, the Landscape listens–
Shadows–hold their breath–
When it goes, 'tis like the Distance   15
On the look of Death–

(c. 1861)

[After Great Pain]

Emily Dickinson

After great pain, a formal feeling comes–
The Nerves sit ceremonious, like Tombs–
The stiff Heart questions was it He, that bore,
And Yesterday, or Centuries before?

The Feet, mechanical, go round–   5
Of Ground, or Air, or Ought–°   *nothing*
A Wooden way
Regardless grown,
A Quartz contentment, like a stone–

This is the Hour of Lead–   10
Remembered, if outlived,
As Freezing persons, recollect the Snow–
First–Chill–then Stupor–then the letting go–

(c. 1862)

Chapter Two

The Death of the Ball Turret Gunner

Randall Jarrell

From my mother's sleep I fell into the State,
And I hunched in its belly till my wet fur froze.
Six miles from earth, loosed from its dream of life,
I woke to black flak and the nightmare fighters.
When I died they washed me out of the turret with a hose.

(1945)

THE DEATH OF THE BALL TURRET GUNNER. *BALL TURRET:* "A ball turret was a plexiglass sphere set into the belly of a B-17 or B-24, and inhabited by two .50 caliber machine-guns and one man, a short small man. When this gunner tracked with his machine guns a fighter attacking his bomber from below, he revolved with the turret; hunched upside-down in his little sphere, he looked like the foetus in the womb. The fighters which attacked him were armed with cannon firing explosive shells. The hose was a steam hose"—Jarrell's note.

from Six Significant Landscapes

Wallace Stevens

VI

Rationalists, wearing square hats,
Think, in square rooms,
Looking at the floor,
Looking at the ceiling.
They confine themselves
To right-angled triangles.

5

If they tried rhomboids,
Cones, waving lines, ellipses—
As, for example, the ellipse of the half-moon—
Rationalists would wear sombreros.   10

(*1923*)

from SIX SIGNIFICANT LANDSCAPES.   1. *square hats:* such as the hats worn by
academics at graduation exercises.

The Eagle: A Fragment

Alfred, Lord Tennyson

He clasps the crag with crooked hands;
Close to the sun in lonely lands,
Ringed with the azure world, he stands.

The wrinkled sea beneath him crawls:
He watches from his mountain walls,   5
And like a thunderbolt he falls.

(*1851*)

Preludes

T. S. Eliot

1

The winter evening settles down
With smell of steaks in passageways.
Six o'clock.
The burnt-out ends of smoky days.
And now a gusty shower wraps   5
The grimy scraps
Of withered leaves about your feet
And newspapers from vacant lots;
The showers beat
On broken blinds and chimney-pots,   10
And at the corner of the street
A lonely cab-horse steams and stamps.
And then the lighting of the lamps.

2

The morning comes to consciousness
Of faint stale smells of beer   15
From the sawdust-trampled street
With all its muddy feet that press
To early coffee-stands.
With the other masquerades
That time resumes,   20
One thinks of all the hands
That are raising dingy shades
In a thousand furnished rooms.

3

You tossed a blanket from the bed,
You lay upon your back, and waited;   25
You dozed, and watched the night revealing
The thousand sordid images
Of which your soul was constituted;
They flickered against the ceiling.
And when all the world came back   30
And the light crept up between the shutters
And you heard the sparrows in the gutters,
You had such a vision of the street
As the street hardly understands;
Sitting along the bed's edge, where   35
You curled the papers from your hair,
Or clasped the yellow soles of feet
In the palms of both soiled hands.

4

His soul stretched tight across the skies
That fade behind a city block,   40
Or trampled by insistent feet
At four and five and six o'clock;
And short square fingers stuffing pipes,
And evening newspapers, and eyes
Assured of certain certainties,   45
The conscience of a blackened street
Impatient to assume the world.

I am moved by fancies that are curled
Around these images, and cling:
The notion of some infinitely gentle   50
Infinitely suffering thing.

Wipe your hand across your mouth, and laugh;
The worlds revolve like ancient women
Gathering fuel in vacant lots.

(1917)

Clean Curtains

Carl Sandburg

New neighbors came to the corner house at Congress and Green
streets.

The look of their clean white curtains was the same as the rim of a
nun's bonnet.

One way was an oyster pail factory, one way they made candy, one
way paper boxes, strawboard cartons.

The warehouse trucks shook the dust of the ways loose and the
wheels whirled dust—there was dust of hoof and wagon wheel
and rubber tire—dust of police and fire wagons—dust of the
winds that circled at midnights and noon listening to no prayers.

"O mother, I know the heart of you," I sang passing the rim of a
nun's bonnet—O white curtains—and people clean as the prayers
of Jesus here in the faded ramshackle at Congress and Green.

Dust and the thundering trucks won—the barrages of the street
wheels and the lawless wind took their ways—was it five weeks or
six the little mother, the new neighbors, battled and then took
away the white prayers in the windows?

(1918)

[A Narrow Fellow in the Grass]

Emily Dickinson

A narrow Fellow in the Grass
Occasionally rides–
You may have met Him–did you not
His notice sudden is–

The Grass divides as with a Comb– 5
A spotted shaft is seen–
And then it closes at your feet
And opens further on–

He likes a Boggy Acre
A Floor too cool for Corn– 10
Yet when a Boy, and Barefoot–
I more than once at Noon
Have passed, I thought, a Whip lash
Unbraiding in the Sun
When stooping to secure it 15
It wrinkled, and was gone–

Several of Nature's People
I know, and they know me–
I feel for them a transport
Of cordiality– 20

But never met this Fellow
Attended, or alone
Without a tighter breathing
And Zero at the Bone–

(c. 1866)

The Road Not Taken

Robert Frost

Two roads diverged in a yellow wood,
And sorry I could not travel both
And be one traveler, long I stood
And looked down one as far as I could
To where it bent in the undergrowth; 5

Then took the other, as just as fair,
And having perhaps the better claim,
Because it was grassy and wanted wear;
Though as for that, the passing there
Had worn them really about the same, 10

And both that morning equally lay
In leaves no step had trodden black.
Oh, I kept the first for another day!
Yet knowing how way leads on to way,
I doubted if I should ever come back.   15

I shall be telling this with a sigh
Somewhere ages and ages hence:
Two roads diverged in a wood, and I—
I took the one less traveled by,
And that has made all the difference.   20

(1916)

Thirteen Ways of Looking at a Blackbird

Wallace Stevens

I

Among twenty snowy mountains,
The only moving thing
Was the eye of the blackbird.

II

I was of three minds,
Like a tree   5
In which there are three blackbirds.

III

The blackbird whirled in the autumn winds.
It was a small part of the pantomime.

IV

A man and a woman
Are one.   10
A man and a woman and a blackbird
Are one.

V

I do not know which to prefer,
The beauty of inflections,
Or the beauty of innuendoes,   15
The blackbird whistling
Or just after.

VI

Icicles filled the long window
With barbaric glass.
The shadow of the blackbird   20
Crossed it, to and fro.
The mood
Traced in the shadow
An indecipherable cause.

VII

O thin men of Haddam,   25
Why do you imagine golden birds?
Do you not see how the blackbird
Walks around the feet
Of the women about you?

VIII

I know noble accents   30
And lucid, inescapable rhythms;
But I know, too,
That the blackbird is involved
In what I know.

IX

When the blackbird flew out of sight,   35
It marked the edge
Of one of many circles.

X

At the sight of blackbirds
Flying in a green light,
Even the bawds of euphony   40
Would cry out sharply.

XI

He rode over Connecticut
In a glass coach.
Once, a fear pierced him,
In that he mistook   45
The shadow of his equipage
For blackbirds.

XII

The river is moving.
The blackbird must be flying.

XIII

It was evening all afternoon.   50
It was snowing
And it was going to snow.
The blackbird sat
In the cedar-limbs.

(1923)

THIRTEEN WAYS OF LOOKING AT A BLACKBIRD. "This group of poems is not
meant to be a collection of epigrams or of ideas, but of sensations [Stevens,
Letters, p. 251]." 25. *Haddam:* a town in Connecticut. Of the passage
Stevens wrote: "The thin men of Haddam are entirely fictitious. . . . I just
like the name. It is an old whaling town, I believe. In any case, it has a
completely Yankee sound [*Letters,* p. 786]." 38–41. "What was intended by
x was that the bawds of euphony would suddenly cease to be academic and
express themselves sharply: naturally, with pleasure, etc. [*Letters,* p. 340]."

The Phantom Wooer

Thomas Lovell Beddoes

A ghost, that loved a lady fair,
Ever in the starry air
    Of midnight at her pillow stood;
And, with a sweetness skies above
The luring words of human love,   5
    Her soul the phantom wooed.
Sweet and sweet is their poisoned note,
The little snakes of silver throat,
In mossy skulls that nest and lie,
Ever singing, "Die, oh! die."   10

Young soul put off your flesh, and come
With me into the quiet tomb,
    Our bed is lovely, dark, and sweet;
The earth will swing us, as she goes,
Beneath our coverlid of snows,   15
    And the warm leaden sheet.
Dear and dear is their poisoned note,
The little snakes of silver throat,
In mossy skulls that nest and lie,
Ever singing, "Die, oh! die."   20

(1850)

Song

Edmund Waller

   Go, lovely rose!
Tell her that wastes her time and me
   That now she knows,
When I resemble° her to thee,   *compare*
How sweet and fair she seems to be.   5

   Tell her that's young,
And shuns to have her graces spied,
   That hadst thou sprung
In deserts, where no men abide,
Thou must have uncommended died.   10

   Small is the worth
Of beauty from the light retired;
   Bid her come forth,
Suffer herself to be desired,
And not blush so to be admired.   15

   Then die! that she
The common fate of all things rare
   May read in thee;
How small a part of time they share
That are so wondrous sweet and fair!   20
                                    (1645)

Bright Star

John Keats

Bright star, would I were steadfast as thou art—
   Not in lone splendor hung aloft the night
And watching, with eternal lids apart,
   Like nature's patient, sleepless Eremite,°   *hermit*
The moving waters at their priestlike task   5
   Of pure ablution° round earth's human shores, *cleansing*
Or gazing on the new soft fallen mask
   Of snow upon the mountains and the moors—
No—yet still steadfast, still unchangeable,
   Pillowed upon my fair love's ripening breast,   10

To feel forever its soft fall and swell,
   Awake forever in a sweet unrest,
Still, still to hear her tender-taken breath,
And so live ever—or else swoon to death.

(c. 1819)

Ode on Melancholy

John Keats

1

No, no, go not to Lethe, neither twist
   Wolfsbane, tight-rooted, for its poisonous wine;
Nor suffer thy pale forehead to be kissed
   By nightshade, ruby grape of Proserpine;
Make not your rosary of yew-berries,   5
   Nor let the beetle, nor the death-moth be
      Your mournful Psyche, nor the downy owl
A partner in your sorrow's mysteries;
   For shade to shade will come too drowsily,
      And drown the wakeful anguish of the soul.   10

2

But when the melancholy fit shall fall
   Sudden from heaven like a weeping cloud,
That fosters the droop-headed flowers all,
   And hides the green hill in an April shroud;
Then glut thy sorrow on a morning rose,   15
   Or on the rainbow of the salt sand-wave,
      Or on the wealth of globèd peonies;
Or if thy mistress some rich anger shows,
   Imprison her soft hand, and let her rave,
      And feed deep, deep upon her peerless eyes.   20

3

She dwells with Beauty—Beauty that must die;
   And Joy, whose hand is ever at his lips
Bidding adieu; and aching Pleasure nigh,
   Turning to Poison while the bee-mouth sips:

Aye, in the very temple of Delight 25
    Veiled Melancholy has her sov'reign shrine,
        Though seen of none save him whose strenuous tongue
Can burst Joy's grape against his palate fine;°   *sensitive*
His soul shall taste the sadness of her might,
    And be among her cloudy trophies hung. 30
                                (1820)

ODE ON MELANCHOLY. 1. *Lethe:* the river of forgetfulness in Hades, the underworld in Greek mythology. 2. *Wolfsbane:* a poisonous plant. 4. *nightshade:* a poisonous plant. *Proserpine:* goddess of the underworld in Greek mythology. 5. *yew-berries:* a traditional symbol of death. 6. *beetle:* the Egyptian scarab, a usual item found in Egyptian tombs. 7. *Psyche:* the Greek equivalent of the soul, often represented as a moth departing from the mouth of a dying person. 8. *mysteries:* secret religious rites. 21. *She:* Melancholy. 30. *trophies hung:* a reference to the practice of the Greeks and Romans of hanging trophies in the temples of their gods.

On My First Son

Ben Jonson

Farewell, thou child of my right hand, and joy;
My sin was too much hope of thee, loved boy:
Seven years thou'wert lent to me, and I thee pay,
Exacted by thy fate, on the just day.
O could I lose all father now! for why 5
Will man lament the state he should envý,
To have so soon 'scaped world's and flesh's rage,
And, if no other misery, yet age?
Rest in soft peace, and asked, say, "Here doth lie
Ben Jonson his best piece of poetry." 10
For whose sake henceforth all his vows be such
As what he loves may never like too much.
                                (1616)

ON MY FIRST SON. 1. *child of my right hand:* the literal translation of the Hebrew name "Benjamin," the boy's first name. 4. *just day:* Jonson's son died on his seventh birthday in 1603. 5. *lose all father:* give up any thoughts of being a father. 12. *too much:* cf. line 2.

Sonnet 138

William Shakespeare

When my love swears that she is made of truth,
I do believe her, though I know she lies,
That she might think me some untutored youth,
Unlearned in the world's false subtleties.
Thus vainly thinking that she thinks me young,   5
Although she knows my days are past the best,
Simply I credit her false-speaking tongue:
On both sides thus is simple truth suppressed.
But wherefore says she not she is unjust?°   *unfaithful*
And wherefore say not I that I am old?   10
Oh, love's best habit° is in seeming trust,   *appearance*
And age in love loves not to have years told.
Therefore I lie with her and she with me,
And in our faults by lies we flattered be.

(1609)

Crazy Jane Talks with the Bishop

W. B. Yeats

I met the Bishop on the road
And much said he and I.
"Those breasts are flat and fallen now,
Those veins must soon be dry;
Live in a heavenly mansion,   5
Not in some foul sty."

"Fair and foul are near of kin,
And fair needs foul," I cried.
"My friends are gone, but that's a truth
Nor grave nor bed denied,   10
Learned in bodily lowliness
And in the heart's pride.

"A woman can be proud and stiff
When on love intent;
But Love has pitched his mansion in   15

The place of excrement;
For nothing can be sole or whole
That has not been rent."

(1932)

CRAZY JANE TALKS WITH THE BISHOP. 10. *grave nor bed:* That friends depart is learned from death and detumescence. 16. *place of excrement:* "For I will make their places of love, and joy excrementious [Blake, *Jerusalem*]."

Bitter-Sweet

George Herbert

Ah, my dear angry Lord,
Since thou dost love, yet strike;
Cast down, yet help afford;
Sure I will do the like.

I will complain, yet praise;   5
I will bewail, approve;
And all my sour-sweet days
I will lament and love.

(1633)

Adam's Curse

W. B. Yeats

We sat together at one summer's end,
That beautiful mild woman, your close friend,
And you and I, and talked of poetry.
I said: "A line will take hours maybe;
Yet if it does not seem a moment's thought,   5
Our stitching and unstitching has been naught.
Better go down upon your marrowbones
And scrub a kitchen pavement, or break stones
Like an old pauper, in all kinds of weather;
For to articulate sweet sounds together   10
Is to work harder than all these, and yet
Be thought an idler by the noisy set

Of bankers, schoolmasters, and clergymen
The martyrs call the world."

                      And thereupon   15
That beautiful mild woman for whose sake
There's many a one shall find out all heartache
On finding that her voice is sweet and low
Replied: "To be born woman is to know—
Although they do not talk of it at school—   20
That we must labor to be beautiful."

I said: "It's certain there is no fine thing
Since Adam's fall but needs much laboring.
There have been lovers who thought love should be
So much compounded of high courtesy   25
That they would sigh and quote with learned looks
Precedents out of beautiful old books;
Yet now it seems an idle trade enough."

We sat grown quiet at the name of love;
We saw the last embers of daylight die,   30
And in the trembling blue-green of the sky
A moon, worn as if it had been a shell
Washed by time's waters as they rose and fell
About the stars and broke in days and years.

I had a thought for no one's but your ears: 35
That you were beautiful, and that I strove
To love you in the old high way of love;
That it had all seemed happy, and yet we'd grown
As weary-hearted as that hollow moon.

                                     (1903)

ADAM'S CURSE. See Genesis 3:17–19. Evicted from Eden, Adam was cursed
by God to a life of pain and hard work.

Easter Wings

George Herbert

Lord, who createdst man in wealth and store,°   *abundance*
    Though foolishly he lost the same,
        Decaying more and more
           Till he became
           Most poor: 5

With   thee

O   let   me   rise

As   larks,   harmoniously,

And sing this day thy victories:

Then shall the fall further the flight in me.   10

My tender age in sorrow did begin;

And still with sicknesses and shame

Thou didst so punish sin,

That I became

Most thin.   15

With   thee

Let me combine,

And feel this day thy victory;

For, if I imp my wing on thine,

Affliction shall advance the flight in me.   20

(*1633*)

EASTER WINGS. 18. *this day:* Easter. 19. *imp:* a term from falconry: extra feathers were "imped" (grafted) onto the wings of a hawk to improve its speed and power.

Badger

John Clare

When midnight comes a host of dogs and men
Go out and track the badger to his den,
And put a sack within the hole, and lie
Till the old grunting badger passes by.
He comes and hears—they let the strongest loose.   5
The old fox hears the noise and drops the goose.
The poacher shoots and hurries from the cry,
And the old hare half wounded buzzes by.
They get a forkèd stick to bear him down
And clap the dogs and take him to the town,   10
And bait him all the day with many dogs,
And laugh and shout and fright the scampering hogs.
He runs along and bites at all he meets:
They shout and hollo down the noisy streets.

He turns about to face the loud uproar   15
And drives the rebels to their very door.

The frequent stone is hurled where'r they go;
When badgers fight, then everyone's a foe.
The dogs are clapped and urged to join the fray;
The badger turns and drives them all away.   20
Though scarcely half as big, demure and small,
He fights with dogs for hours and beats them all.
The heavy mastiff, savage in the fray,
Lies down and licks his feet and turns away.
The bulldog knows his match and waxes cold,   25
The badger grins and never leaves his hold.
He drives the crowd and follows at their heels
And bites them through—the drunkard swears and reels.

The frighted women take the boys away,
The blackguard laughs and hurries on the fray.   30
He tries to reach the woods, an awkward race,
But sticks and cudgels quickly stop the chase.
He turns again and drives the noisy crowd
And beats the many dogs in noises loud.
He drives away and beats them every one,   35
And then they loose them all and set them on.
He falls as dead and kicked by boys and men,
Then starts and grins and drives the crowd again;
Till kicked and torn and beaten out he lies
And leaves his hold and crackles, groans, and dies.   40

(c. 1835)

Free Verse and Line Treatment

Beat! Beat! Drums!

Walt Whitman

Beat! beat! drums!—blow! bugles! blow!
Through the windows—through doors—burst like a ruthless force,
Into the solemn church, and scatter the congregation,
Into the school where the scholar is studying;
Leave not the bridegroom quiet—no happiness must he have now
   with his bride,   5

Nor the peaceful farmer any peace, ploughing his field or gathering
   his grain,
So fierce you whirr and pound you drums—so shrill you bugles blow.

Beat! beat! drums!—blow! bugles! blow!
Over the traffic of cities—over the rumble of wheels in the streets;
Are beds prepared for sleepers at night in the houses? no sleepers
   must sleep in those beds,   10
No bargainers' bargains by day—no brokers or speculators—would
   they continue?
Would the talkers be talking? would the singer attempt to sing?
Would the lawyer rise in the court to state his case before the judge?
Then rattle quicker, heavier drums—you bugles wilder blow.

Beat! beat! drums!—blow! bugles! blow!   15
Make no parley—stop for no expostulation,
Mind not the timid—mind not the weeper or prayer,
Mind not the old man beseeching the young man,
Let not the child's voice be heard, nor the mother's entreaties,
Make even the trestles to shake the dead where they lie awaiting
   the hearses,   20
So strong you thump O terrible drums—so loud you bugles blow.

(1867)

Cinderella

Olga Broumas

> *. . . the joy that isn't shared*
> *I heard, dies young.*
> Anne Sexton, 1928–1974

Apart from my sisters, estranged
from my mother, I am a woman alone
in a house of men
who secretly
call themselves princes, alone   5
with me usually, under cover of dark.   I am the one allowed in

to the royal chambers, whose small foot conveniently
fills the slipper of glass.   The woman writer, the lady
umpire, the madam chairman, anyone's wife.
I know what I know.   10
And I once was glad

of the chance to use it, even alone
in a strange castle, doing overtime on my own, cracking
the royal code.   The princes spoke
in their fathers' language, were eager to praise me   15
my nimble tongue.   I am a woman in a state of siege, alone

as one piece of laundry, strung on a windy clothesline a
mile long. A woman co-opted by promises: the lure
of a job, the ruse of a choice, a woman forced
to bear witness, falsely   20
against my kind, as each
other sister was judged inadequate, bitchy, incompetent,
jealous, too thin, too fat.   I know what I know.
What sweet bread I make
for myself in this prosperous house   25
is dirty, what good soup I boil turns
in my mouth to mud.   Give
me my ashes.   A cold stove, a cinder-block pillow, wet
canvas shoes in my sisters', my sisters' hut.   Or I swear

I'll die young   30
like those favored before me, hand-picked each one
for her joyful heart.

                                                        (*1977*)

from **The Black Riders**

Stephen Crane

3

In the desert
I saw a creature, naked, bestial,
Who, squatting upon the ground,
Held his heart in his hands,
And ate of it.   5
I said, "Is it good, friend?"
"It is bitter—bitter," he answered;
"But I like it
Because it is bitter,
And because it is my heart."   10

                                                        (*1895*)

Theme for English B

Langston Hughes

The instructor said,

> *Go home and write*
> *a page tonight.*
> *And let that page come out of you—*
> *Then, it will be true.*   5

I wonder if it's that simple?
I am twenty-two, colored, born in Winston-Salem.
I went to school there, then Durham, then here
to this college on the hill above Harlem.
I am the only colored student in my class.   10
The steps from the hill lead down into Harlem,
through a park, then I cross St. Nicholas,
Eighth Avenue, Seventh, and I come to the Y,
the Harlem Branch Y, where I take the elevator
up to my room, sit down, and write this page: 15

It's not easy to know what is true for you or me
at twenty-two, my age. But I guess I'm what
I feel and see and hear, Harlem, I hear you:
hear you, hear me—we two—you, me, talk on this page.
(I hear New York, too.) Me—who?   20

Well, I like to eat, sleep, drink, and be in love.
I like to work, read, learn, and understand life.
I like a pipe for a Christmas present,
or records—Bessie, bop, or Bach.
I guess being colored doesn't make me *not* like   25
the same things other folks like who are other races.
So will my page be colored that I write?

Being me, it will not be white.
But it will be
a part of you, instructor.   30
You are white—
yet a part of me, as I am a part of you.
That's American.
Sometimes perhaps you don't want to be a part of me.
Nor do I often want to be a part of you.   35
But we are, that's true!

As I learn from you,
I guess you learn from me—
although you're older—and white—
and somewhat more free.   40

This is my page for English B.

(1959)

THEME FOR ENGLISH B.   7. and 8. *Winston-Salem* and *Durham:* cities in
North Carolina. 9. *college:* Columbia University. 12. *St. Nicholas:* a street
east of Columbia. 24. *Bessie:* Bessie Smith, blues singer (1898?–1937).

Bavarian Gentians

D. H. Lawrence

Not every man has gentians in his house
in Soft September, at slow, sad Michaelmas.

Bavarian gentians, big and dark, only dark
darkening the daytime, torch-like with the smoking blueness of
   Pluto's gloom,
ribbed and torch-like, with their blaze of darkness spread blue   5
down flattening into points, flattened under the sweep of white day
torch-flower of the blue-smoking darkness, Pluto's dark-blue daze,
black lamps from the halls of Dis, burning dark blue,
giving off darkness, blue darkness, as Demeter's pale lamps give off
   light,
lead me then, lead the way.   10

Reach me a gentian, give me a torch!
let me guide myself with the blue, forked torch of this flower
down the darker and darker stairs, where blue is darkened on
   blueness
even where Persephone goes, just now, from the frosted September
to the sightless realm where darkness is awake upon the dark   15
and Persephone herself is but a voice
or a darkness invisible enfolded in the deeper dark
of the arms Plutonic, and pierced with the passion of dense gloom,
among the splendor of torches of darkness, shedding darkness on
   the lost bride and her groom.

(1932)

BAVARIAN GENTIANS. *Bavarian Gentians:* dark blue fall flowers. 2. *Michael-mas:* the feast of St. Michael, September 29. 4. *Pluto:* Roman god of the underworld. 8. *Dis:* another name for Pluto. 9. *Demeter:* Persephone's mother, goddess of nature's growing cycle. 14. *Persephone:* Abducted by Pluto, Persephone became goddess of the underworld for six months out of every year. According to the myth, she returns every spring to her mother, and departs every fall to Pluto's dark underworld.

Corsons Inlet

A. R. Ammons

I went for a walk over the dunes again this morning
to the sea,
then turned right along
    the surf
                rounded a naked headland   5
                and returned

    along the inlet shore:

it was muggy sunny, the wind from the sea steady and high,
crisp in the running sand,
        some breakthroughs of sun   10
    but after a bit

continuous overcast:

the walk liberating, I was released from forms,
from the perpendiculars,
        straight lines, blocks, boxes, binds   15
of thought
into the hues, shadings, rises, flowing bends and blends
          of sight:

                I allow myself eddies of meaning:
yield to a direction of significance   20
running
like a stream through the geography of my work:
    you can find

in my sayings

swerves of action   25
like the inlet's cutting edge:

there are dunes of motion,
organizations of grass, white sandy paths of remembrance
in the overall wandering of mirroring mind:

but Overall is beyond me: is the sum of these events   30
I cannot draw, the ledger I cannot keep, the accounting
beyond the account:

in nature there are few sharp lines: there are areas of
primrose
        more or less dispersed;   35
disorderly orders of bayberry; between the rows
of dunes,
irregular swamps of reeds,
though not reeds alone, but grass, bayberry, yarrow, all . . .
predominantly reeds: 40

I have reached no conclusions, have erected no boundaries,
shutting out and shutting in, separating inside
        from outside: I have
        drawn no lines:
        as   45

manifold events of sand
change the dune's shape that will not be the same shape
tomorrow,

so I am willing to go along, to accept
the becoming   50
thought, to stake off no beginnings or ends, establish
        no walls:

by transitions the land falls from grassy dunes to creek
to undercreek: but there are no lines, though
        change in that transition is clear   55
        as any sharpness: but "sharpness" spread out,
allowed to occur over a wider range
than mental lines can keep:

the moon was full last night: today, low tide was low:
black shoals of mussels exposed to the risk   60
of air

and, earlier, of sun,
waved in and out with the waterline, waterline inexact,
caught always in the event of change:
    a young mottled gull stood free on the shoals   65
      and ate
to vomiting: another gull, squawking possession, cracked a crab,
picked out the entrails, swallowed the soft-shelled legs, a ruddy
turnstone running in to snatch leftover bits:

risk is full: every living thing in   70
siege: the demand is life, to keep life: the small
white blacklegged egret, how beautiful, quietly stalks and spears
      the shallows, darts to shore
              to stab—what? I couldn't
    see against the black mudflats—a frightened   75
    fiddler crab?

      the news to my left over the dunes and
reeds and bayberry clumps was
      fall: thousands of tree swallows
      gathering for flight: 80
      an order held
      in constant change: a congregation
rich with entropy: nevertheless, separable, noticeable
    as one event,
        not chaos: preparations for   85
flight from winter,
cheet, cheet, cheet, cheet, wings rifling the green clumps,
beaks
at the bayberries
    a perception full of wind, flight, curve,   90
    sound:
    the possibility of rule as the sum of rulelessness:
the "field" of action
with moving, incalculable center:

in the smaller view, order tight with shape: 95
blue tiny flowers on a leafless weed: carapace of crab:
snail shell:
      pulsations of order
      in the bellies of minnows: orders swallowed,
broken down, transferred through membranes   100

to strengthen larger orders: but in the large view, no
lines or changeless shapes: the working in and out, together
     and against, of millions of events: this,
         so that I make
         no form   105
         formlessness:

orders as summaries, as outcomes of actions override
or in some way result, not predictably (seeing me gain
the top of a dune,
the swallows   110
could take flight—some other fields of bayberry
         could enter fall
         berryless) and there is serenity:

         no arranged terror: no forcing of image, plan,
or thought: 115
no propaganda, no humbling of reality to precept:

terror pervades but is not arranged, all possibilities
of escape open: no route shut, except in
    the sudden loss of all routes:

         I see narrow orders, limited tightness, but will   120
not run to that easy victory:
         still around the looser, wider forces work:
         I will try
     to fasten into order enlarging grasps of disorder, widening
scope, but enjoying the freedom that   125
Scope eludes my grasp, that there is no finality of vision,
that I have perceived nothing completely,
     that tomorrow a new walk is a new walk.

                                    (1965)

CORSONS INLET. *Corsons Inlet:* located in southeastern New Jersey. 69. *turnstone:* a seashore bird, like the sandpiper. 83. *entropy:* the process— thought to be a characteristic of the universe—by which energy dissipates into inertia and order to randomness. 96. *carapace:* the shell covering the back.

Portrait of the Artist as a
Prematurely Old Man

Ogden Nash

It is common knowledge to every schoolboy and even every Bachelor
of Arts,
That all sin is divided into two parts.
One kind of sin is called a sin of commission, and that is very
important,
And it is what you are doing when you are doing something you
ortant,
And the other kind of sin is just the opposite and is called a sin of   5
omission and is equally bad in the eyes of all right-thinking
people, from Billy Sunday to Buddha,
And it consists of not having done something you shudda.
I might as well give you my opinion of these two kinds of sin as
long as, in a way, against each other we are pitting them,
And that is, don't bother your head about sins of commission be-
cause however sinful, they must at least be fun or else you
wouldn't be committing them.
It is the sin of omission, the second kind of sin,
That lays eggs under your skin.   10
The way you get really painfully bitten
Is by the insurance you haven't taken out and the checks you haven't
added up the stubs of and the appointments you haven't kept and
the bills you haven't paid and the letters you haven't written.
Also, about sins of omission there is one particularly painful lack of
beauty,
Namely, it isn't as though it had been a riotous red letter day or
night every time you neglected to do your duty;
You didn't get a wicked forbidden thrill   15
Every time you let a policy lapse or forgot to pay a bill;
You didn't slap the lads in the tavern on the back and loudly cry
Whee,
Let's all fail to write just one more letter before we go home, and
this round of unwritten letters is on me.
No, you never get any fun
Out of the things you haven't done,   20
But they are the things that I do not like to be amid,
Because the suitable things you didn't do give you a lot more trouble
than the unsuitable things you did.
The moral is that it is probably better not to sin at all, but if some
kind of sin you must be pursuing,
Well, remember to do it by doing rather than by not doing.

(1931)

Why I Am Not a Painter

Frank O'Hara

I am not a painter, I am a poet.
Why? I think I would rather be
a painter, but I am not. Well,

for instance, Mike Goldberg
is starting a painting. I drop in.   5
"Sit down and have a drink" he
says. I drink; we drink. I look
up. "You have SARDINES in it."
"Yes, it needed something there."
"Oh." I go and the days go by   10
and I drop in again. The painting
is going on, and I go, and the days
go by. I drop in. The painting is
finished. "Where's SARDINES?"
All that's left is just   15
letters, "It was too much," Mike says.
But me? One day I am thinking of
a color: orange. I write a line
about orange. Pretty soon it is a
whole page of words, not lines.   20
Then another page. There should be
so much more, not of orange, of
words, of how terrible orange is
and life. Days go by. It is even in
prose, I am a real poet. My poem   25
is finished and I haven't mentioned
orange yet. It's twelve poems, I call
it ORANGES. And one day in a gallery
I see Mike's painting, called SARDINES.

(1971)

WHY I AM NOT A PAINTER.   4. *Mike Goldberg:* a New York artist (1924–   ).

Penis Envy

Erica Jong

I envy men who can yearn
with infinite emptiness
toward the body of a woman,

hoping that the yearning
will make a child,   5
that the emptiness itself
will fertilize the darkness.

Women have no illusions about this,
being at once
houses, tunnels,   10
cups & cupbearers,
knowing emptiness as a temporary state
between two fullnesses,
& seeing no romance in it.

If I were a man   15
doomed to that infinite emptiness,
& having no choice in the matter,
I would, like the rest, no doubt,
find a woman
& christen her moonbelly,   20
madonna, gold-haired goddess
& make her the tent of my longing,
the silk parachute of my lust,
the blue-eyed icon of my sacred sexual itch,
the mother of my hunger.   25

But since I am a woman,
I must not only inspire the poem
but also type it,
not only conceive the child
but also bear it,   30
not only bear the child
but also bathe it,
not only bathe the child
but also feed it,
not only feed the child   35

but also carry it
everywhere, everywhere . . .

while men write poems
on the mysteries of motherhood.

I envy men who can yearn   40
with infinite emptiness.

(1976)

Chapter Three

Effort at speech between two people

Muriel Rukeyser

Speak to me.   Take my hand.   What are you now?
I will tell you all.   I will conceal nothing.
When I was three, a little child read a story about a rabbit
who died, in the story, and I crawled under a chair   :
a pink rabbit   :   it was my birthday, and a candle   5
burnt a sore spot on my finger, and I was told to be happy.

Oh, grow to know me.   I am not happy.   I will be open:
Now I am thinking of white sails against a sky like music,
like glad horns blowing, and birds tilting, and an arm about me.
There was one I loved, who wanted to live, sailing.   10

Speak to me.   Take my hand.   What are you now?
When I was nine, I was fruitily sentimental,
fluid   :   and my widowed aunt played Chopin,
and I bent my head on the painted woodwork, and wept.
I want now to be close to you.   I would   15
link the minutes of my days close, somehow, to your days.

I am not happy.   I will be open.
I have liked lamps in evening corners, and quiet poems.
There has been fear in my life.   Sometimes I speculate
on what a tragedy his life was, really.   20

Take my hand.   First my mind in your hand.   What are
    you now?
When I was fourteen, I had dreams of suicide,
and I stood at a steep window, at sunset, hoping toward death
if the light had not melted clouds and plains to beauty,
if light had not transformed that day, I would have leapt.   25
I am unhappy.   I am lonely.   Speak to me.

I will be open.   I think he never loved me:
he loved the bright beaches, the little lips of foam
that ride small waves, he loved the veer of gulls:
he said with a gay mouth: I love you.   Grow to know me.   30

What are you now?   If we could touch one another,
if these our separate entities could come to grips,
clenched like a Chinese puzzle . . . yesterday
I stood in a crowded street that was live with people,
and no one spoke a word, and the morning shone.   35
Everyone silent, moving. . . . Take my hand.   Speak to me.

(1935)

The Clod & the Pebble

William Blake

"Love seeketh not Itself to please,
Nor for itself hath any care;
But for another gives its ease,
And builds a Heaven in Hell's despair."

So sang a little Clod of Clay,   5
Trodden with the cattle's feet;
But a Pebble of the brook,
Warbled out these metres meet:

"Love seeketh only Self to please,
To bind another to its delight;   10
Joys in another's loss of ease,
And builds a Hell in Heaven's despite."

(1794)

The Ruined Maid

Thomas Hardy

"O'Melia, my dear, this does everything crown!
Who could have supposed I should meet you in Town?
And whence such fair garments, such prosperi-ty?"
"O didn't you know I'd been ruined?" said she.

"You left us in tatters, without shoes or socks,   5
Tired of digging potatoes, and spudding up docks;
And now you've gay bracelets and bright feathers three!"
"Yes: that's how we dress when we're ruined," said she.

"At home in the barton° you said 'thee' and 'thou,'   *farm*
And 'thik oon,' and 'theäs oon,' and 't'other'; but now   10
Your talking quite fits 'ee for high compa-ny!"
"Some polish is gained with one's ruin," said she.

"Your hands were like paws then, your face blue and bleak
But now I'm bewitched by your delicate cheek,
And your little gloves fit as on any la-dy!"   15
"We never do work when we're ruined," said she.

"You used to call home-life a hag-ridden dream,
And you'd sigh, and you'd sock; but at present you seem
To know not of megrims° or melancho-ly!"   *low spirits*
"True. One's pretty lively when ruined," said she.   20

"I wish I had feathers, a fine sweeping gown,
And a delicate face, and could strut about Town!"
"My dear—a raw country girl, such as you be,
Cannot quite expect that. You ain't ruined," said she.

                                                    (*c. 1886*)

THE RUINED MAID. *Ruined:* in the Victorian sense. 6. *spudding up docks:*
digging up weedy herbs.

Parting

W. B. Yeats

He. Dear, I must be gone
    While night shuts the eyes
    Of the household spies;
    That song announces dawn.
She. No, night's bird and love's   5
    Bids all true lovers rest,
While the loud song reproves
    The murderous stealth of day.
He. Daylight already flies
    From mountain crest to crest.   10

> *She.* That light is from the moon.
> *He.* That bird . . .
> *She.*   Let him sing on,
>   I offer to love's play
>   My dark declivities.   15

(1933)

PARTING. The poem is an alba, or dawn song. Cf. Pound's "Alba" (page 153) and Donne's "Break of Day" (page 271).

Soliloquy of the Spanish Cloister

Robert Browning

1

Gr-r-r—there go, my heart's abhorrence!
   Water your damned flower-pots, do!
If hate killed men, Brother Lawrence,
   God's blood, would not mine kill you!
What? your myrtle-bush wants trimming?   5
   Oh, that rose has prior claims—
Needs its leaden vase filled brimming?
   Hell dry you up with its flames!

2

At the meal we sit together:
   Salve tibi! I must hear   10
Wise talk of the kind of weather,
   Sort of season, time of year:
Not a plenteous cork-crop: scarcely
   Dare we hope oak-galls, I doubt:
What's the Latin name for "parsley"?   15
   What's the Greek name for Swine's Snout?

3

Whew! We'll have our platter burnished,
   Laid with care on our own shelf!
With a fire-new spoon we're furnished,
   And a goblet for ourself,   20
Rinsed like something sacrificial
   Ere 'tis fit to touch our chaps°—   *jaws*
Marked with L for our initial!
   (He-he! There his lily snaps!)

4

Saint, forsooth! While brown Dolores   25
   Squats outside the Convent bank
With Sanchicha, telling stories,
   Steeping tresses in the tank,
Blue-black, lustrous, thick like horsehairs,
   —Can't I see his dead eye glow,   30
Bright as 'twere a Barbary corsair's?
   (That is, if he'd let it show!)

5

When he finishes refection,°   *dinner*
   Knife and fork he never lays
Cross-wise, to my recollection,   35
   As do I, in Jesu's praise.
I the Trinity illustrate,
   Drinking watered orange-pulp—
In three sips the Arian frustrate;
   While he drains his at one gulp.   40

6

Oh, those melons? If he's able
   We're to have a feast! so nice!
One goes to the Abbot's table,
   All of us get each a slice.
How go on your flowers? None double?   45
   Not one fruit-sort can you spy?
Strange! And I, too, at such trouble,
   Keep them close-nipped on the sly!

7

There's a great text in Galatians,
   Once you trip on it, entails   50
Twenty-nine distinct damnations,
   One sure, if another fails:
If I trip him just a-dying,
   Sure of heaven as sure can be,
Spin him round and send him flying   55
   Off to hell, a Manichee?

8

Or, my scrofulous° French novel   *evil*
   On grey paper with blunt type!
Simply glance at it, you grovel
   Hand and foot in Belial's gripe: 60

If I double down its pages
　　At the woeful sixteenth print,
When he gathers his greengages,
　　Ope a sieve and slip it in't?

9

Or, there's Satan! one might venture　　　　　65
　　Pledge one's soul to him, yet leave
Such a flaw in the indenture
　　As he'd miss till, past retrieve,
Blasted lay that rose-acacia
　　We're so proud of! *Hy, Zy, Hine* . . .　　　70
'St, there's vespers! *Plena gratiâ*
　　Ave, Virgo! Gr-r-r—you swine!

(1842)

SOLILOQUY OF THE SPANISH CLOISTER.   No date is given, but we might imag-
ine a medieval setting. 10. *Salve tibi:* "Hail to thee." The words in italics
that follow are Brother Lawrence's. 14. *oak-galls:* abnormal growths on oak
leaves used for tanning. 31. *Barbary corsair:* The Barbary Coast was the
haven for pirates, known for lechery. 39. *Arian:* a Christian heresy that de-
nied the doctrine of the trinity. 49. *Galatians:* In Galatians 15–23, St. Paul
enumerates various "works of the flesh" that can lead to damnation. Our
speaker, perhaps overreading, has found "twenty-nine" possibilities. 56.
Manichee: a reference to the Manichean heresy, which involved the con-
cept that evil is a self-contained force outside of the domain of God. 60.
Belial: one of the chief devils. 69–70. Knowing that he can't touch Law-
rence, the speaker is willing to sell his soul (though he believes himself
clever enough to outwit Satan at the last) to have Lawrence's prize "rose-
acacia" blasted. *Hy, Zy, Hine:* an invocation to the Devil or the grunts of a
madman. 71–72. *Plena gratiâ/Ave, Virgo:* the speaker reverses the opening
words of the *"Ave Maria"* ("Hail Mary, full of grace").

Porphyria's Lover

Robert Browning

The rain set early in tonight,
　　The sullen wind was soon awake,
It tore the elm-tops down for spite,
　　And did its worst to vex the lake:
　　I listened with heart fit to break.　　　　　5
When glided in Porphyria; straight
　　She shut the cold out and the storm,

And kneeled and made the cheerless grate
   Blaze up, and all the cottage warm;
   Which done, she rose, and from her form   10
Withdrew the dripping cloak and shawl,
   And laid her soiled gloves by, untied
Her hat and let the damp hair fall,
   And, last, she sat down by my side
   And called me. When no voice replied,   15
She put my arm about her waist,
   And made her smooth white shoulder bare,
And all her yellow hair displaced,
   And, stooping, made my cheek lie there,
   And spread, o'er all, her yellow hair,   20
Murmuring how she loved me—she
   Too weak, for all her heart's endeavor,
To set its struggling passion free
   From pride, and vainer ties dissever,
   And give herself to me forever.   25
But passion sometimes would prevail,
   Nor could tonight's gay feast restrain
A sudden thought of one so pale
   For love of her, and all in vain:
   So, she was come through wind and rain.   30
Be sure I looked up at her eyes
   Happy and proud; at last I knew
Porphyria worshiped me: surprise
   Made my heart swell, and still it grew
   While I debated what to do.   35
That moment she was mine, mine, fair,
   Perfectly pure and good: I found
A thing to do, and all her hair
   In one long yellow string I wound
   Three times her little throat around   40
And strangled her. No pain felt she;
   I am quite sure she felt no pain.
As a shut bud that holds a bee,
   I warily oped her lids: again
   Laughed the blue eyes without a stain.   45
And I untightened next the tress
   About her neck; her cheek once more
Blushed bright beneath my burning kiss:
   I propped her head up as before,
   Only, this time my shoulder bore   50
Her head, which droops upon it still:

The smiling rosy little head,
So glad it has its utmost will,
    That all it scorned at once is fled,
    And I, its love, am gained instead!   55
Porphyria's love: she guessed not how
    Her darling one wish would be heard.
And thus we sit together now,
    And all night long we have not stirred,
    And yet God has not said a word!   60
                                      (1836)

The Farmer's Bride

Charlotte Mew

Three Summers since I chose a maid,
    Too young maybe—but more's to do
At harvest-time than bide and woo.
    When us was wed she turned afraid
Of love and me and all things human;   5
Like the shut of a winter's day
Her smile went out, and 'twadn't a woman—
    More like a little frightened fay.
        One night, in the Fall, she runned away.

"Out 'mong the sheep, her be," they said,   10
'Should properly have been abed;
But sure enough she wadn't there
Lying awake with her wide brown stare.
So over seven-acre field and up-along across the down
    We chased her, flying like a hare   15
Before our lanterns. To Church-Town
    All in a shiver and a scare
We caught her, fetched her home at last
    And turned the key upon her, fast.

She does the work about the house   20
As well as most, but like a mouse:
    Happy enough to chat and play
    With birds and rabbits and such as they,
    So long as men-folk keep away.
"Not near, not near!" her eyes beseech   25

When one of us comes within reach.
  The women say that beasts in stall
  Look round like children at her call.
  I've hardly heard her speak at all.

Shy as a leveret, swift as he,   30
Straight and slight as a young larch tree,
Sweet as the first wild violets, she,
To her wild self. But what to me?

The short days shorten and the oaks are brown,
  The blue smoke rises to the low grey sky,   35
One leaf in the still air falls slowly down,
  A magpie's spotted feathers lie
On the black earth spread white with rime,
The berries redden up to Christmas-time.
  What's Christmas-time without there be   40
  Some other in the house than we!

  She sleeps up in the attic there
  Alone, poor maid. 'Tis but a stair
Betwixt us. Oh! my God! the down,
The soft young down of her, the brown,   45
The brown of her—her eyes, her hair, her hair!

(1953)

THE FARMER'S BRIDE. 30. *leveret:* a hare in its first year.

Break of Day

John Donne

'Tis true, 'tis day; what though it be?
O wilt thou therefore rise from me?
Why should we rise, because 'tis light?
Did we lie down, because 'twas night?
Love, which in spite of darkness brought us hither,   5
Should in despite of light keep us together.

Light hath no tongue, but is all eye;
If it could speak as well as spy,

This were the worst that it could say,
That being well, I fain would stay,   10
And that I loved my heart and honor so,
That I would not from him, that had them, go.

Must business thee from hence remove?
O, that's the worst disease of love.
The poor, the foul, the false, love can   15
Admit, but not the busied man.
He which hath business, and makes love, doth do
Such wrong, as when a married man doth woo.

                                              (1633)

BREAK OF DAY.   The poem is modeled on the medieval alba, or dawn song
(song of the parting of lovers at dawn). Cf. Pound's "Alba" (page 153)
and Yeats's "Parting" (page 265). "Break of Day" departs from Donne's
usual tone, which is marked by a strong sense of male bravado. In this re-
gard, cf. "Song" (page 372).

So I Said I Am Ezra

A. R. Ammons

So I said I am Ezra
and the wind whipped my throat
gaming for the sounds of my voice
    I listened to the wind
go over my head and up into the night   5
Turning to the sea I said
            I am Ezra
but there were no echoes from the waves
The words were swallowed up
    in the voice of the surf   10
or leaping over the swells
lost themselves oceanward
    Over the bleached and broken fields
I moved my feet and turning from the wind
    that ripped sheets of sand   15
    from the beach and threw them
    like seamists across the dunes
swayed as if the wind were taking me away
and said
            I am Ezra   20

As a word too much repeated
falls out of being
so I Ezra went out into the night
like a drift of sand
and splashed among the windy oats   25
that clutch the dunes
of unremembered seas

(*1955*)

SO I SAID I AM EZRA.   *Ezra:* like some booming-voiced Old Testament prophet.

How Annandale Went Out

E. A. Robinson

"They called it Annandale—and I was there
To flourish, to find words, and to attend:
Liar, physician, hypocrite, and friend,
I watched him; and the sight was not so fair
As one or two that I have seen elsewhere: 5
An apparatus not for me to mend—
A wreck, with hell between him and the end,
Remained of Annandale; and I was there.

"I knew the ruin as I knew the man;
So put the two together, if you can,   10
Remembering the worst you know of me.
Now view yourself as I was, on the spot—
With a slight kind of engine. Do you see?
Like this . . . You wouldn't hang me? I thought not."

(*1910*)

HOW ANNANDALE WENT OUT.   13. *engine:* a hypodermic needle.

from The Dream Songs

John Berryman

14

Life, friends, is boring. We must not say so.
After all, the sky flashes, the great sea yearns,
we ourselves flash and yearn,

and moreover my mother told me as a boy
(repeatingly) 'Ever to confess you're bored   5
means you have no

Inner Resources.' I conclude now I have no
inner resources, because I am heavy bored.
Peoples bore me,
literature bores me, especially great literature,   10
Henry bores me, with his plights & gripes
as bad as achilles,

who loves people and valiant art, which bores me.
And the tranquil hills, & gin, look like a drag
and somehow a dog   15
has taken itself & its tail considerably away
into mountains or sea or sky, leaving
behind: me, wag.

(1964)

from THE DREAM SONGS. 12. *achilles:* Achilles retired from fighting during
the Trojan War because of a slight from Agamemnon, the Greeks' general.

One Perfect Rose

Dorothy Parker

A single flow'r he sent me, since we met.
    All tenderly his messenger he chose;
Deep-hearted, pure, with scented dew still wet—
    One perfect rose.

I knew the language of the floweret;   5
    "My fragile leaves," it said, "his heart enclose."
Love long has taken for his amulet
    One perfect rose.

Why is it no one has sent me yet
    One perfect limousine, do you suppose?   10
Ah no, it's just my luck to get
    One perfect rose.

(1926)

The Death of a Toad

Richard Wilbur

A toad the power mower caught,
Chewed and clipped of a leg, with a hobbling hop has got
  To the garden verge, and sanctuaried him
  Under the cineraria leaves, in the shade
    Of the ashen heartshaped leaves, in a dim,   5
      Low, and a final glade.

  The rare original heartsblood goes,
Spends on the earthen hide, in the folds and wizenings, flows
  In the gutters of the banked and staring eyes. He lies
  As still as if he would return to stone,   10
    And soundlessly attending, dies
      Toward some deep monotone,

  Toward misted and ebullient seas
And cooling shores, toward lost Amphibia's emperies.
  Day dwindles, drowning, and at length is gone   15
  In the wide and antique eyes, which still appear
    To watch, across the castrate lawn,
      The haggard daylight steer.

                                                        (*1950*)

THE DEATH OF A TOAD.   14. *Amphibia's emperies:* "the land of Amphibia,"
here imagined as the guiding spirit of the toad's (and of all amphibians')
universe. Asked about the phrase, Wilbur said: "I may have found it in
John Donne in the first place, but I think I wanted to use it here as a kind
of confession that I'm doing rather a lot with that toad. I'm turning him
into the primal energies of the world in the course of this poem. And so I
get a little bombastic as a way of acknowledging that I'm going rather far."

We Real Cool

Gwendolyn Brooks

The Pool Players.
Seven at the Golden Shovel.

We real cool. We
Left school. We

Lurk late. We
Strike straight. We

Sing sin. We   5
Thin gin. We

Jazz June. We
Die soon.

(1960)

The Convergence of the Twain

(Lines on the Loss of the Titanic)

Thomas Hardy

1

In a solitude of the sea
Deep from human vanity,
And the Pride of Life that planned her, stilly couches she.

2

Steel chambers, late the pyres
Of her salamandrine fires,   ·   5
Cold currents thrid,° and turn to rhythmic tidal lyres.   *thread*

3

Over the mirrors meant
To glass the opulent
The sea-worm crawls—grotesque, slimed, dumb, indifferent.

4

Jewels in joy designed   10
To ravish the sensuous mind
Lie lightless, all their sparkles bleared and black and blind.

5

Dim moon-eyed fishes near
Gaze at the gilded gear
And query: "What does this vaingloriousness down here?"   15

6

Well: while was fashioning
This creature of cleaving wing,
The Immanent Will that stirs and urges everything

7

Prepared a sinister mate
For her—so gaily great—   20
A Shape of Ice, for the time far and dissociate.

8

And as the smart ship grew
In stature, grace, and hue,
In shadowy silent distance grew the Iceberg too.

9

Alien they seemed to be: 25
No mortal eye could see
The intimate welding of their later history,

10

Or sign that they were bent
By paths coincident
On being anon twin halves of one august event,   30

11

Till the Spinner of the Years
Said "Now!" And each one hears,
And consummation comes, and jars two hemispheres.

(1912)

THE CONVERGENCE OF THE TWAIN (LINES ON THE LOSS OF THE TITANIC). *Ti-tanic:* Called "unsinkable," the *Titanic* went down on its maiden voyage after colliding with an iceberg. 5. *salamandrine fires:* According to fable, the salamander could live in the midst of fire. Analogously, the ship's fire burned on though immersed.

As I Walked Out One Evening

W. H. Auden

As I walked out one evening,
    Walking down Bristol Street,
The crowds upon the pavement
    Were fields of harvest wheat.

And down by the brimming river   5
  I heard a lover sing
Under an arch of the railway:
  "Love has no ending.

"I'll love you, dear, I'll love you
  Till China and Africa meet,   10
And the river jumps over the mountain
  And the salmon sing in the street,

"I'll love till the ocean
  Is folded and hung up to dry
And the seven stars go squawking   15
  Like geese about the sky.

The years shall run like rabbits,
  For in my arms I hold
The Flower of the Ages,
  And the first love of the world."   20

But all the clocks in the city
  Began to whirr and chime:
"O let not Time deceive you,
  You cannot conquer Time.

"In the burrows of the Nightmare   25
  Where Justice naked is,
Time watches from the shadow
  And coughs when you would kiss.

"In headaches and in worry
  Vaguely life leaks away,   30
And Time will have his fancy
  Tomorrow or today.

"Into many a green valley
  Drifts the appalling snow;
Time breaks the threaded dances   35
  And the diver's brilliant bow.

"O plunge your hands in water,
  Plunge them in up to the wrist;
Stare, stare in the basin
  And wonder what you've missed.   40

"The glacier knocks in the cupboard,
    The desert sighs in the bed,
And the crack in the teacup opens
    A lane to the land of the dead.

"Where the beggars raffle the banknotes   45
    And the Giant is enchanting to Jack,
And the Lily-white Boy is a Roarer,
    And Jill goes down on her back.

"O look, look in the mirror,
    O look in your distress;   50
Life remains a blessing
    Although you cannot bless.

"O stand, stand at the window
    As the tears scald and start;
You shall love your crooked neighbor   55
    With your crooked heart."

It was late, late in the evening,
    The lovers they were gone;
The clocks had ceased their chiming,
    And the deep river ran on.   60
                                               (1940)

On First Looking into
Chapman's Homer

John Keats

Much have I traveled in the realms of gold,
    And many goodly states and kingdoms seen;
    Round many western islands have I been
Which bards in fealty° to Apollo hold.   *allegiance*
Oft of one wide expanse had I been told   5
    That deep-browed Homer ruled as his demesne;°   *domain*
    Yet did I never breathe its pure serene°   *atmosphere*
Till I heard Chapman speak out loud and bold:
Then felt I like some watcher of the skies
    When a new planet swims into his ken;   10

Or like stout Cortez when with eagle eyes
　　He stared at the Pacific—and all his men
Looked at each other with a wild surmise—
　　Silent, upon a peak in Darien.

(1816)

ON FIRST LOOKING INTO CHAPMAN'S HOMER. *Chapman's Homer:* translation of the *Iliad* by George Chapman (1559?–1634). 4. *Apollo:* the Greek god of poetic inspiration. 11. *Cortez:* the Spanish conqueror of Mexico. Keats confused him with Balboa, who first sighted the Pacific from the heights of Darien, in Panama. Although the confusion matters not at all to the poem, it has a certain charm, for it suggests that the poem was written by a young man in the heat of discovery.

Jabberwocky

Lewis Carroll

'Twas brillig, and the slithy toves
　　Did gyre and gimble in the wabe:
All mimsy were the borogoves,
　　And the mome raths outgrabe.

"Beware the Jabberwock, my son!　　　　　　　　　5
　　The jaws that bite, the claws that catch!
Beware the Jubjub bird, and shun
　　The frumious Bandersnatch!"

He took his vorpal sword in hand;
　　Long time the manxome foe he sought—　　　　10
So rested he by the Tumtum tree,
　　And stood awhile in thought.

And, as in uffish thought he stood,
　　The Jabberwock, with eyes of flame,
Came whiffling through the tulgey wood,　　　　　15
　　And burbled as it came!

One, two! One, two! And through and through
　　The vorpal blade went snicker-snack!
He left it dead, and with its head
　　He went galumphing back.　　　　　　　　　　　20

Anthology

"And hast thou slain the Jabberwock?
  Come to my arms, my beamish boy!
O frabjous day! Callooh, Callay!"
  He chortled in his joy.

'Twas brillig, and the slithy toves   25
  Did gyre and gimble in the wabe:
All mimsy were the borogoves,
  And the mome raths outgrabe.

(1871)

JABBERWOCKY. 1. *brillig:* In *Through the Looking-Glass,* Alice asks Humpty Dumpty to explain. "Brillig," he tells her, means four in the afternoon, when you begin to boil things for dinner. "Slithy" means "lithe" and "slimy"; "mimsy" means "flimsy" and "miserable." And so on. Portmanteau words all.

The Unknown Citizen

W. H. Auden

(To JS/07/M/378
This Marble Monument
Is Erected by the State)

He was found by the Bureau of Statistics to be
One against whom there was no official complaint,
And all the reports on his conduct agree
That, in the modern sense of an old-fashioned word, he was a saint,
For in everything he did he served the Greater Community.   5
Except for the War till the day he retired
He worked in a factory and never got fired,
But satisfied his employers, Fudge Motors Inc.
Yet he wasn't a scab or odd in his views,
For his Union reports that he paid his dues,   10
(Our report on his Union shows it was sound)
And our Social Psychology workers found
That he was popular with his mates and liked a drink.
The Press are convinced that he bought a paper every day
And that his reactions to advertisements were normal in every way. 15
Policies taken out in his name prove that he was fully insured,
And his Health-card shows he was once in hospital but left it cured.
Both Producers Research and High-Grade Living declare

He was fully sensible to the advantages of the Instalment Plan
And had everything necessary to the Modern Man,   20
A phonograph, a radio, a car and a frigidaire.
Our researchers into Public Opinion are content
That he held the proper opinions for the time of year;
When there was peace, he was for peace; when there was war, he
    went.
He was married and added five children to the population,   25
Which our Eugenist says was the right number for a parent of his
    generation,
And our teachers report that he never interfered with their educa-
    tion.
Was he free? Was he happy? The question is absurd:
Had anything been wrong, we should certainly have heard.

(1939)

---

from **War Is Kind**

Stephen Crane

21

A man said to the universe:
"Sir, I exist!"
"However," replied the universe,
"The fact has not created in me
A sense of obligation."

(1899)

**Thoughts on Looking into
a Thicket**

John Ciardi

The name of a fact: at home in that leafy world
chewed on by moths that look like leaves, like bark,
like owls, like death's heads; there, by eating flowers
and stones with eyes, in that zoo of second looks,
there is a spider, *phrynarachne d.,*   5
to whom a million or a billion years
in the humorless long gut of all the wood
have taught the art of mimicking a bird turd.

"It is on a leaf," writes Crompton, "that she weaves
an irregular round blotch, and, at the bottom,   10
a separate blob in faithful imitation
of the more liquid portion. She then squats
herself in the center, and (being unevenly marked
in black and white), supplies with her own body
the missing last perfection, *i.e.,* the darker   15
more solid central portion of the excreta."

Must I defend my prayers? I dream the world
At ease in its long miracle. I ponder the egg,
like a pin head in silk spit, invisibly stored
with the billion years of its learning. Have angels   20
more art than this? I read the rooty palm
of God for the great scarred Life Line. If you
will be more proper than real, that is your
death. I think life will do anything for a living.

And that hungers are all one. So Forbes reports   25
that seeing a butterfly once poised on a dropping
he took it to be feasting, but came closer
and saw it was being feasted on. Still fluttering,
it worked its woolen breast for *phrynarachne,*
pumping her full. So once I saw a mantis   30
eating a grub while being himself eaten
by a copper beetle. So I believe the world

in its own act and accomplishment. I think
what feeds is food. And dream it in mosaic
for a Church of the First Passion: an ochre sea   35
and a life-line of blue fishes, the tail of each
chained into the mouth behind it. Thus, an emblem
of our indivisible three natures in one:
the food, the feeder, and the condition of being
in the perpetual waver of the sea.   40

I believe the world to praise it. I believe
the act in its own occurrence. As the dead
are hats and pants in aspic, as the red
bomb of the living heart ticks against time,
as the eye of all water opens and closes, changing   45
all that it has looked at—I believe
if there is an inch or the underside of an inch
for a life to grow on, a life will grow there;

if there are kisses, flies will lay their eggs
in the spent sleep of lovers; if there is time,   50
it will be long enough. And through all time,
the hand that strokes my darling slips to bone
like peeling off a glove; my body eats me
under the nose of God and Father and Mother.
I speak from thickets and from nebulae: 55
till their damnation feed them, all men starve.

(1955)

The Canonization

John Donne

For God's sake hold your tongue, and let me love,
  Or chide my palsy, or my gout,
My five gray hairs, or ruined fortune, flout,
    With wealth your state, your mind with arts improve,
      Take you a course, get you a place,   5
      Observe His Honor, or His Grace,
Or the King's real, or his stamped face
  Contemplate; what you will, approve,
  So you will let me love.

Alas, alas, who's injured by my love?   10
  What merchant's ships have my sighs drowned?
Who says my tears have overflowed his ground?
    When did my colds a forward spring remove?
      When did the heats which my veins fill
      Add one more to the plaguy bill?   15
Soldiers find wars, and lawyers find out still
  Litigious° men, which quarrels move,   *contentious*
  Though she and I do love.

Call us what you will, we are made such by love;
  Call her one, me another fly,   20
We're tapers too, and at our own cost die,
    And we in us find the eagle and the dove.
      The phoenix riddle hath more wit
      By us: we two being one, are it.

So, to one neutral thing both sexes fit.   25
  We die and rise the same, and prove
  Mysterious by this love.

We can die by it, if not live by love,
  And if unfit for tombs and hearse
Our legend be, it will be fit for verse;   30
  And if no piece of chronicle we prove,
    We'll build in sonnets pretty rooms;
    As well a well-wrought urn becomes
The greatest ashes, as half-acre tombs,
  And by these hymns, all shall approve   35
  Us canonized for love:

And thus invoke us: You whom reverend love
  Made one another's hermitage;
You, to whom love was peace, that now is rage;
  Who did the whole world's soul contract, and drove   40
    Into the glasses of your eyes
    (So made such mirrors, and such spies,
That they did all to you epitomize)
  Countries, towns, courts: Beg from above
  A pattern of your love!   45

(*1633*)

THE CANONIZATION. 5. *course, place:* I.e., settle yourself in life ("Take a course"); obtain an official appointment ("a place"). 7. *stamped face:* i.e., on coins. 8. *approve:* put to proof; discover by your own experience. 13. *spring remove:* by causing it to freeze up. 15. *the plaguy bill:* Deaths caused by summer plagues were recorded in weekly parish lists. 21. *die:* a common pun in the 17th century for the consummation of sexual intercourse. 22. *eagle:* symbol of strength. *dove:* symbol of purity. 23. *hath more wit:* is made more credible. The phoenix is a mythical bird, of which only one exists. According to the myth, the bird lives for a thousand years, then plunges into its funeral pyre only to rise from the ashes reborn. 45. *pattern of your love:* Turned to saints (both diction and metaphor work to this end), the lovers are to be invoked by the rest of mankind and begged from heaven ("above") to provide a paradigm ("pattern") of love for all. "Countries, towns, courts" are objects of "drove." The idea of lines 40–44 is that the eyes, because they both see and reflect, contract into themselves the essence of the world at large.

Come In

Robert Frost

As I came to the edge of the woods,
Thrush music—hark!
Now if it was dusk outside,
Inside it was dark.

Too dark in the woods for a bird   5
By sleight of wing
To better its perch for the night,
Though it still could sing.

The last of the light of the sun
That had died in the west   10
Still lived for one song more
In a thrush's breast.

Far in the pillared dark
Thrush music went—
Almost like a call to come in   15
To the dark and lament.

But no, I was out for stars:
I would not come in.
I meant not even if asked,
And I hadn't been.   20

(1942)

COME IN.   2. *thrush:* cf. Hardy's "The Darkling Thrush" (page 297).

The Face in the Mirror

Robert Graves

Gray haunted eyes, absent-mindedly glaring
From wide, uneven orbits; one brow drooping
Somewhat over the eye
Because of a missile fragment still inhering,
Skin deep, as a foolish record of old-world fighting.   5

Crookedly broken nose—low tackling caused it;
Cheeks, furrowed; coarse gray hair, flying frenetic;
Forehead, wrinkled and high;
Jowls, prominent; ears, large; jaw, pugilistic;
Teeth, few; lips, full and ruddy; mouth, ascetic.   10

I pause with razor poised, scowling derision
At the mirrored man whose beard needs my attention,
And once more ask him why
He still stands ready, with a boy's presumption,
To court the queen in her high silk pavilion.   15

(1958)

The Good-Morrow

John Donne

I wonder, by my troth, what thou and I
Did, till we loved? Were we not weaned till then,
But sucked on country pleasures, childishly?
Or snorted we in the seven sleepers' den?
'Twas so; But this, all pleasures fancies be.   5
If ever any beauty I did see,
Which I desired, and got, 'twas but a dream of thee.

And now good morrow to our waking souls,
Which watch not one another out of fear;
For love all love of other sights controls,   10
And makes one little room an everywhere.
Let sea-discoverers to new worlds have gone,
Let maps to other, worlds on worlds have shown,
Let us possess one world; each hath one, and is one.

My face in thine eye, thine in mine appears,   15
And true plain hearts do in the faces rest;
Where can we find two better hemispheres
Without sharp North, without declining West?
Whatever dies was not mixed equally;
If our two loves be one, or thou and I   20
Love so alike that none do slacken, none can die.

(1633)

THE GOOD-MORROW. 4. *seven sleepers' den:* According to legend, seven youths of Ephesus, fleeing from persecution, hid in a cave and slept there for 187 years. 13. *other:* i.e., though maps to others ("other" is the older plural form) have shown . . . 15. *appears:* Reflected in the pupils of each other's eyes, the lovers make a world of their own. 19. *not mixed equally:* According to alchemy, mortality results from an imperfect mixture of elements ("not mixed equally"); conversely, a perfect mixture would produce a substance immutable and undying.

The Sorrow of Love

W. B. Yeats

[1912 Edition]

The quarrel of the sparrows in the eaves,
The full round moon and the star-laden sky,
And the loud song of the ever-singing leaves,
Had hid away earth's old and weary cry.

And then you came with those red mournful lips,   5
And with you came the whole of the world's tears
And all the trouble of her labouring ships,
And all the trouble of her myriad years.

And now the sparrows warring in the eaves,
The curd-pale moon, the white stars in the sky,   10
And the loud chaunting of the unquiet leaves,
Are shaken with earth's old and weary cry.

The Sorrow of Love

W. B. Yeats

[1933 Edition]

The brawling of a sparrow in the eaves,
The brilliant moon and all the milky sky,
And all that famous harmony of leaves,
Had blotted out man's image and his cry.

A girl arose that had red mournful lips   5
And seemed the greatness of the world in tears,
Doomed like Odysseus and the labouring ships
And proud as Priam murdered with his peers;

Arose, and on the instant clamorous eaves,
A climbing moon upon an empty sky,   10
And all that lamentation of the leaves,
Could but compose man's image and his cry.

THE SORROW OF LOVE [1933 Edition].   8. *Priam:* the king of Troy at the time of the Trojan War, which was won by the Greeks (e.g., Odysseus, who had to labor to return home to Ithaca).

Dead Boy

John Crowe Ransom

The little cousin is dead, by foul subtraction,
A green bough from Virginia's aged tree,
And none of the county kin like the transaction,
Nor some of the world of outer dark, like me.

A boy not beautiful, nor good, nor clever,   5
A black cloud full of storms too hot for keeping,
A sword beneath his mother's heart—yet never
Woman bewept her babe as this is weeping.

A pig with a pasty face, so I had said,
Squealing for cookies, kinned by poor pretense   10
With a noble house. But the little man quite dead,
I see the forbears' antique lineaments.

The elder men have strode by the box of death
To the wide flag porch, and muttering low send round
The bruit° of the day. O friendly waste of breath!   *news*   15
Their hearts are hurt with a deep dynastic wound.

He was pale and little, the foolish neighbors say;
The first-fruits, saith the Preacher, the Lord hath taken;
But this was the old tree's late branch wrenched away,
Grieving the sapless limbs, the shorn and shaken.   20

(*1927*)

High Windows

Philip Larkin

When I see a couple of kids
And guess he's fucking her and she's
Taking pills or wearing a diaphragm,
I know this is paradise

Everyone old has dreamed of all their lives—   5
Bonds and gestures pushed to one side
Like an outdated combine harvester,
And everyone young going down the long slide

To happiness, endlessly. I wonder if
Anyone looked at me, forty years back,   10
And thought, *That'll be the life;*
No God any more, or sweating in the dark

About hell and that, or having to hide
What you think of the priest. He
And his lot will all go down the long slide   15
Like free bloody birds. And immediately

Rather than words comes the thought of high windows:
The sun-comprehending glass,
And beyond it, the deep blue air, that shows
Nothing, and is nowhere, and is endless.   20

(1974)

Chapter Four

The Cool Web

Robert Graves

Children are dumb to say how hot the day is,
How hot the scent is of the summer rose,
How dreadful the black wastes of evening sky,
How dreadful the tall soldiers drumming by.

But we have speech, to chill the angry day,   5
And speech, to dull the rose's cruel scent.
We spell away the overhanging night,
We spell away the soldiers and the fright.

There's a cool web of language winds us in,
Retreat from too much joy or too much fear: 10
We grow sea-green at last and coldly die
In brininess and volubility.

But if we let our tongues lose self-possession,
Throwing off language and its watery clasp
Before our death, instead of when death comes,   15
Facing the wide glare of the children's day,
Facing the rose, the dark sky and the drums,
We shall go mad no doubt and die that way.

(1927)

[I Know that He Exists]

Emily Dickinson

I know that He exists.
Somewhere–in Silence–
He has hid his rare life
From our gross eyes.

'Tis an instant's play.   5
'Tis a fond Ambush–
Just to make Bliss
Earn her own surprise!

But–should the play
Prove piercing earnest–   10
Should the glee–glaze–
In Death's–stiff–stare–

Would not the fun
Look too expensive!
Would not the jest–   15
Have crawled too far!

(c. 1862)

To Autumn

John Keats

1

Season of mists and mellow fruitfulness,
   Close bosom-friend of the maturing sun;
Conspiring with him how to load and bless
   With fruit the vines that round the thatch-eaves run;
To bend with apples the mossed cottage-trees,   5
   And fill all fruit with ripeness to the core;
      To swell the gourd, and plump the hazel shells
   With a sweet kernel; to set budding more,
And still more, later flowers for the bees,
Until they think warm days will never cease,   10
      For Summer has o'er-brimmed their clammy cells.

2

Who hath not seen thee oft amid thy store?
   Sometimes whoever seeks abroad may find
Thee sitting careless on a granary floor,
   Thy hair soft-lifted by the winnowing wind;   15
Or on a half-reaped furrow sound asleep,
   Drowsed with the fume of poppies, while thy hook
      Spares the next swath and all its twinèd flowers:

And sometimes like a gleaner thou dost keep
 Steady thy laden head across a brook;   20
Or by a cider-press, with patient look,
  Thou watchest the last oozings hours by hours.

3

Where are the songs of Spring? Aye, where are they?
 Think not of them, thou hast thy music too—
While barred clouds bloom the soft-dying day,   25
 And touch the stubble-plains with rosy hue;
Then in a wailful choir the small gnats mourn
 Among the river sallows, borne aloft
  Or sinking as the light wind lives or dies;
And full-grown lambs loud bleat from hilly bourn;   30
 Hedge crickets sing; and now with treble soft
 The redbreast whistles from a garden croft;
  And gathering swallows twitter in the skies.

(1820)

TO AUTUMN. 15. *winnowing:* blowing the grain clear from the chaff. 17. *hook:* a scythe—a small curved blade used for cutting grain. 28. *sallows:* willow trees. 30. *bourn:* region, locale. 32. *croft:* an enclosed plot of farmland.

Ode to a Nightingale

John Keats

1

My heart aches, and a drowsy numbness pains
 My sense, as though of hemlock I had drunk,
Or emptied some dull opiate to the drains
 One minute past, and Lethe-wards had sunk:
'Tis not through envy of thy happy lot,   5
 But being too happy in thine happiness—
  That thou, light-wingèd Dryad of the trees,
   In some melodious plot
 Of beechen green, and shadows numberless,
  Singest of summer in full-throated ease.   10

2

O, for a draught of vintage! that hath been
 Cooled a long age in the deep-delvèd earth,

Tasting of Flora and the country green,
  Dance, and Provençal song, and sunburnt mirth!
O for a beaker full of the warm South,   15
  Full of the true, the blushful Hippocrene,
    With beaded bubbles winking at the brim,
      And purple-stainèd mouth;
That I might drink, and leave the world unseen,
  And with thee fade away into the forest dim: 20

3

Fade far away, dissolve, and quite forget
  What thou among the leaves hast never known,
The weariness, the fever, and the fret
  Here, where men sit and hear each other groan;
Where palsy shakes a few, sad, last gray hairs,   25
  Where youth grows pale, and specter-thin, and dies;
    Where but to think is to be full of sorrow
      And leaden-eyed despairs,
Where Beauty cannot keep her lustrous eyes,
  Or new Love pine at them beyond tomorrow.   30

4

Away! away! for I will fly to thee,
  Not charioted by Bacchus and his pards,
But on the viewless wings of Poesy,
  Though the dull brain perplexes and retards:
Already with thee! tender is the night,   35
  And haply the Queen-Moon is on her throne,
    Clustered around by all her starry Fays;°   *fairies*
      But here there is no light,
Save what from heaven is with the breezes blown
  Through verdurous° glooms and winding mossy ways.   40
                                               green-foliaged

5

I cannot see what flowers are at my feet,
  Nor what soft incense hangs upon the boughs,
But, in embalmèd° darkness, guess each sweet   *perfumed*
  Wherewith the seasonable month endows
The grass, the thicket, and the fruit tree wild;   45
  White hawthorn, and the pastoral eglantine;
    Fast fading violets covered up in leaves;
      And mid-May's eldest child,
The coming musk-rose, full of dewy wine,
  The murmurous haunt of flies on summer eves.   50

6

Darkling I listen; and for many a time
 I have been half in love with easeful Death,
Called him soft names in many a musèd° rhyme,   *mediated*
 To take into the air my quiet breath;
Now more than ever seems it rich to die,   55
 To cease upon the midnight with no pain,
  While thou art pouring forth thy soul abroad
   In such an ecstasy!
  Still wouldst thou sing, and I have ears in vain—
   To thy high requiem become a sod.   60

7

Thou wast not born for death, immortal Bird!
 No hungry generations tread thee down;
The voice I hear this passing night was heard
 In ancient days by emperor and clown:
Perhaps the selfsame song that found a path   65
 Through the sad heart of Ruth when, sick for home,
  She stood in tears amid the alien corn;°   *wheat*
   The same that ofttimes hath
  Charmed magic casements, opening on the foam
   Of perilous seas, in faery lands forlorn.° *long past* 70

8

Forlorn! the very word is like a bell
 To toll me back from thee to my sole self!
Adieu! the fancy cannot cheat so well
 As she is famed to do, deceiving elf.
Adieu! adieu! thy plaintive anthem° fades   *hymn* 75
 Past the near meadows, over the still stream,
  Up the hill side; and now 'tis buried deep
   In the next valley-glades:
  Was it a vision, or a waking dream?
   Fled is that music:—Do I wake or sleep?   80
                 (1820)

ODE TO A NIGHTINGALE. 4. *Lethe-wards:* toward Lethe, the river of forget-fulness in Hades, the underworld in Greek mythology. 7. *Dryad:* a mytho-logical wood nymph. 13. *Flora:* Roman goddess of flowers: hence, flowers. 14. *Provençal:* Provence is a region in southern France famous in the Mid-dle Ages for its troubadour poets. 16. *Hippocrene:* Hip′ ō · creen—the fountain of the Muses on Mt. Helicon, "blushful" because here its waters of inspiration are associated with a beaker of wine. 33. *Poesy:* i.e., not by getting intoxicated (Bacchus was the Roman god of wine, whose chariot was pulled by leopards), but on the "viewless" (invisible) wings of poetic inspiration or fancy. 46. *eglantine:* honeysuckle. 51. *Darkling:* in the growing dark. 66. *Ruth:* in the Book of Ruth (Old Testament), a young widow who grieved because she was a stranger in a strange land. 71. *Forlorn:* now in the sense of "sorrowful": thus the word itself tolls the speaker back to earth. We are perhaps meant to be reminded, too, of Ovid's tale of the transformation of Philomel into the nightingale, a grisly tale full of pain and sorrow. 73. *fancy:* i.e., poetic inspiration; cf. "the viewless wings of poesy" of line 33.

No Swan So Fine

Marianne Moore

"No water so still as the
   dead fountains of Versailles." No swan,
with swart blind look askance
and gondoliering legs, so fine
   as the chintz china one with fawn-   5
brown eyes and toothed gold
collar on to show whose bird it was.

Lodged in the Louis Fifteenth
   candelabrum-tree of cockscomb-
tinted buttons, dahlias,   10
sea-urchins, and everlastings,
   it perches on the branching foam
of polished sculptured
flowers—at ease and tall. The king is dead.

(1932)

NO SWAN SO FINE. 2. *Versailles:* palace of Louis XV of France. 4. *gondoliering legs:* Venetian gondoliers paddle from the stern. 9. *candelabrum-tree:* "A pair of Louis XV candelabra with Dresden figures of swans belonging to Lord Balfour"—Moore's note. 11. *everlastings:* flowers that when dried retain their form and color.

A Sort of a Song

W. C. Williams

Let the snake wait under
his weed
and the writing
be of words, slow and quick, sharp
to strike, quiet to wait,   5
sleepless.

—through metaphor to reconcile
the people and the stones.
Compose. (No ideas
but in things) Invent!   10
Saxifrage is my flower that splits
the rocks.

(1944)

A SORT OF A SONG.   11. *saxifrage:* Look it up and check its etymology.

The Darkling Thrush

Thomas Hardy

I leant upon a coppice gate
    When Frost was specter-gray,
And Winter's dregs made desolate
    The weakening eye of day.
The tangled bine-stems scored the sky   5
    Like strings of broken lyres,
And all mankind that haunted nigh
    Had sought their household fires.

The land's sharp features seemed to be
    The Century's corpse outleant,   10
His crypt the cloudy canopy,
    The wind his death-lament.
The ancient pulse of germ and birth
    Was shrunken hard and dry,
And every spirit upon earth   15
    Seemed fervorless as I.

At once a voice arose among
  The bleak twigs overhead
In a full-hearted evensong
  Of joy illimited;   20
An aged thrush, frail, gaunt, and small,
  In blast-beruffled plume,
Had chosen thus to fling his soul
  Upon the growing gloom.

So little cause for carolings   25
  Of such ecstatic sound
Was written on terrestrial things
  Afar or nigh around,
That I could think there trembled through
  His happy good-night air   30
Some blessed Hope, whereof he knew
  And I was unaware.

                               (December 31, 1900)

THE DARKLING THRUSH.   1. *coppice:* a thicket or wood consisting of small trees. 5. *bine-stems:* shoots of climbing plants.

Sonnet 116

William Shakespeare

Let me not to the marriage of true minds
Admit impediments. Love is not love
Which alters when it alteration finds,
Or bends with the remover to remove:
Oh, no! it is an ever-fixèd mark,   5
That looks on tempests and is never shaken;
It is the star to every wandering bark,
Whose worth's unknown, although his height be taken.
Love's not Time's fool, though rosy lips and cheeks
Within his bending sickle's compass come;   10
Love alters not with his brief hours and weeks,
But bears it out even to the edge of doom.
If this be error and upon me proved,
  I never writ, nor no man ever loved.

                               (1609)

SONNET 116. 2. *impediments:* an allusion to the Marriage Service: "If any of you know cause or just impediment why these persons should not be joined together . . . ." 8. *height:* Although a star's altitude ("height") may be fixed and used for the practical purposes of navigation, the value ("worth") of the star itself remains a mystery. Note that the second quatrain is built entirely of images and metaphors of seafaring. 11. *his:* i.e., Time's. 12. *edge of doom:* to the very moment of the Last Judgment; perhaps also a reference to the pre-Renaissance belief that the earth is flat, and that by sailing across the ocean, one would reach the edge of the earth and thus one's doom.

Very Like a Whale

Ogden Nash

One thing that literature would be greatly the better for
Would be a more restricted employment by authors of simile and
    metaphor.
Authors of all races, be they Greeks, Roman, Teutons or Celts,
Can't seem just to say that anything is the thing it is but have to go
    out of their way to say that it is like something else.
What does it mean when we are told   5
That the Assyrian came down like a wolf on the fold?
In the first place, George Gordon Byron had had enough experience
To know that it probably wasn't just one Assyrian, it was a lot of
    Assyrians.
However, as too many arguments are apt to induce apoplexy and
    thus hinder longevity,
We'll let it pass as one Assyrian for the sake of brevity.   10
Now then, this particular Assyrian, the one whose cohorts were
    gleaming in purple and gold,
Just what does the poet mean when he says he came down like a
    wolf on the fold?
In heaven and earth more than is dreamed of in our philosophy
    there are a great many things,
But I don't imagine that among them there is a wolf with purple
    and gold cohorts or purple and gold anythings.
No, no, Lord Byron, before I'll believe that this Assyrian was actu- 15
    ally like a wolf I must have some kind of proof;
Did he run on all fours and did he have a hairy tail and a big red
    mouth and big white teeth and did he say Woof woof woof?
Frankly I think it very unlikely, and all you were entitled to say, at
    the very most,

Was that the Assyrian cohorts came down like a lot of Assyrian co-
   horts about to destroy the Hebrew host.
But that wasn't fancy enough for Lord Byron, oh dear me no, he
   had to invent a lot of figures of speech and then interpolate them,
With the result that whenever you mention Old Testament soldiers 20
   to people they say Oh yes, they're the ones that a lot of wolves
   dressed up in gold and purple ate them.
That's the kind of thing that's being done all the time by poets,
   from Homer to Tennyson;
They're always comparing ladies to lilies and veal to venison.
How about the man who wrote,
Her little feet stole in and out like mice beneath her petticoat?
Wouldn't anybody but a poet think twice   25
Before stating that his girl's feet were mice?
Then they always say things like that after a winter storm
The snow is a white blanket. Oh it is, is it, all right then, you sleep
   under a six-inch blanket of snow and I'll sleep under a half-inch
   blanket of unpoetical blanket material and we'll see which one
   keeps warm,
And after that maybe you'll begin to comprehend dimly
What I mean by too much metaphor and simile.   30

                                                    (*1931*)

VERY LIKE A WHALE.   The title is from *Hamlet* (III:ii): pretending mad-
ness, Hamlet likens the shape of a cloud to a whale. "Very like a whale,"
says Polonius, trying to humor the prince. 6. *wolf on the fold:* Nash alludes
to Byron's "The Destruction of Sennacherib" (see page 326). 13. *many
things:* an allusion to Hamlet's "There are more things in heaven and
earth, Horatio,/Than are dreamt of in your philosophy [I:v]."

A Red, Red Rose

Robert Burns

O My Luve's like a red, red rose,
   That's newly sprung in June;
O My Luve's like the melodie
   That's sweetly played in tune.

As fair art thou, my bonnie lass,   5
   So deep in luve am I;
And I will luve thee still, my dear,
   Till a' the seas gang dry.

Till a' the seas gang dry, my dear,
   And the rocks melt wi' the sun: 10
O I will love thee still, my dear,
   While the sands o' life shall run.

And fare thee weel, my only luve,
   And fare thee weel awhile!
And I will come again, my luve,   15
   Though it were ten thousand mile.

(1796)

[The Brain]

Emily Dickinson

The Brain–is wider than the Sky–
For–put them side by side–
The one the other will contain
With ease–and You–beside–

The Brain is deeper than the sea–   5
For–hold them–Blue to Blue–
The one the other will absorb–
As Sponges–Buckets–do–

The Brain is just the weight of God–
For–Heft them–Pound for Pound–   10
And they will differ–if they do–
As Syllable from Sound–

(c. 1862)

For Sale

Robert Lowell

Poor sheepish plaything,
organized with prodigal animosity,
lived in just a year—
my Father's cottage at Beverly Farms
was on the market the month he died.   5

Empty, open, intimate,
its town-house furniture
had an on tiptoe air
of waiting for the mover
on the heels of the undertaker.   10
Ready, afraid
of living alone till eighty,
Mother mooned in a window,
as if she had stayed on a train
one stop past her destination.   15

(*1956*)

I Wandered Lonely as a Cloud

William Wordsworth

I wandered lonely as a cloud
That floats on high o'er vales and hills,
When all at once I saw a crowd,
A host, of golden daffodils;
Beside the lake, beneath the trees,   5
Fluttering and dancing in the breeze.

Continuous as the stars that shine
And twinkle on the milky way,
They stretched in never-ending line
Along the margin of a bay: 10
Ten thousand saw I at a glance,
Tossing their heads in sprightly dance.

The waves beside them danced; but they
Outdid the sparkling waves in glee;
A poet could not but be gay,   15
In such a jocund company;
I gazed—and gazed—but little thought
What wealth the show to me had brought:

For oft, when on my couch I lie
In vacant or in pensive mood,   20
They flash upon that inward eye
Which is the bliss of solitude;
And then my heart with pleasure fills,
And dances with the daffodils.

(*1807*)

[I Like a Look of Agony]

Emily Dickinson

I like a look of Agony,
Because I know it's true–
Men do not sham Convulsion,
Nor simulate, a Throe–

The Eyes glaze once–and that is Death–   5
Impossible to feign
The Beads upon the Forehead
By homely Anguish strung.

(c. 1861)

The Mower's Song

Andrew Marvell

My mind was once the true survey°   *map*
Of all these meadows fresh and gay,
And in the greenness of the grass
Did see its hopes as in a glass;°   *mirror*
When Juliana came, and she,   5
What I do to the grass, does to my thoughts and me.

But these, while I with sorrow pine,
Grew more luxuriant still and fine,
That not one blade of grass you spied,
But had a flower on either side;   10
When Juliana came, and she,
What I do to the grass, does to my thoughts and me.

Unthankful meadows, could you so
A fellowship so true forego,
And in your gaudy May-games meet,   15
While I lay trodden under feet?
When Juliana came, and she,
What I do to the grass, does to my thoughts and me.

But what you in compassion ought,
Shall now by my revenge be wrought;   20
And flowers, and grass, and I, and all
Will in one common ruin fall;
For Juliana comes, and she,
What I do to the grass, does to my thoughts and me.

And thus, ye meadows, which have been   25
Companions of my thoughts more green,
Shall now the heraldry become
With which I shall adorn my tomb;
For Juliana comes, and she,
What I do to the grass, does to my thoughts and me.   30

(1681)

THE MOWER'S SONG. *mower:* Remember what the prophet said: "All flesh
is grass." 15. *gaudy May-games:* wherein boys and girls interweave like
flowers in the meadow. "Gaudy" implies feasting and light spirits.

To Lucasta, Going to the Wars

Richard Lovelace

Tell me not, sweet, I am unkind
That from the nunnery
Of thy chaste breast and quiet mind,
To war and arms I fly.

True, a new mistress now I chase,   5
The first foe in the field;
And with a stronger faith embrace
A sword, a horse, a shield.

Yet this inconstancy is such
As you too shall adore;   10
I could not love thee, dear, so much,
Loved I not honor more.

(1649)

The Fly

Karl Shapiro

O hideous little bat, the size of snot,
With polyhedral eye and shabby clothes,
To populate the stinking cat you walk
The promontory of the dead man's nose,
Climb with the fine leg of a Duncan-Phyfe   5
   The smoking mountains of my food
      And in a comic mood
   In mid-air take to bed a wife.

Riding and riding with your filth of hair
On gluey foot or wing, forever coy,   10
Hot from the compost and green sweet decay,
Sounding your buzzer like an urchin toy—
You dot all whiteness with diminutive stool,
   In the tight belly of the dead
      Burrow with hungry head   15
   And inlay maggots like a jewel.

At your approach the great horse stomps and paws
Bringing the hurricane of his heavy tail;
Shod in disease you dare to kiss my hand
Which sweeps against you like an angry flail;   20
Still you return, return, trusting your wing
   To draw you from the hunter's reach
      That learns to kill to teach
   Disorder to the tinier thing.

My peace is your disaster. For your death   25
Children like spiders cup their pretty hands
And wives resort to chemistry of war.
In fens of sticky paper and quicksands
You glue yourself to death. Where you are stuck
   You struggle hideously and beg   30
      You amputate your leg
   Imbedded in the amber muck.

But I, a man, must swat you with my hate,
Slap you across the air and crush your flight,
Must mangle with my shoe and smear your blood,   35

Expose your little guts pasty and white,
Knock your head sidewise like a drunkard's hat,
   Pin your wings under like a crow's,
      Tear off your flimsy clothes
And beat you as one beats a rat.   40

Then like Gargantua I stride among
The corpses strewn like raisins in the dust,
The broken bodies of the narrow dead
That catch the throat with fingers of disgust.
I sweep. One gyrates like a top and falls   45
   And stunned, stone blind, and deaf
      Buzzes its frightful F
And dies between three cannibals.

                                          (1942)

THE FLY. 5. *Duncan-Phyfe:* 18th-century U.S. cabinetmaker noted for stylistic delicacy. 41. *Gargantua:* a giant of medieval legend. 47. *F:* i.e., the key of.

[I Like to See It Lap the Miles]

Emily Dickinson

I like to see it lap the Miles–
And lick the Valleys up–
And stop to feed itself at Tanks–
And then–prodigious step

Around a Pile of Mountains–   5
And supercilious peer
In Shanties–by the sides of Roads–
And then a Quarry pare

To fit its sides
And crawl between   10
Complaining all the while
In horrid–hooting stanza–
Then chase itself down Hill–

And neigh like Boanerges–
Then–prompter than a Star   15
Stop–docile and omnipotent
At its own stable door–

(c. 1862)

[I LIKE TO SEE IT LAP THE MILES.]   14. *Boanerges:* any loud preacher or orator.

They Flee from Me

Thomas Wyatt

They flee from me, that sometime did me seek,
With naked foot stalking in my chamber.
I have seen them, gentle, tame, and meek,
That now are wild, and do not remember
That sometime they put themselves in danger   5
To take bread at my hand; and now they range,
Busily seeking with a continual change.

Thanked be Fortune it hath been otherwise,
Twenty times better; but once in special,
In thin array, after a pleasant guise,   10
When her loose gown from her shoulders did fall,
And she me caught in her arms long and small,
And therewith all sweetly did me kiss
And softly said, "Dear heart, how like you this?"

It was no dream, I lay broad waking.   15
But all is turned, thorough my gentleness,
Into a strange fashion of forsaking;
And I have leave to go, of her goodness,
And she also to use newfangleness.
But since that I so kindely am served,   20
I fain would know what she hath deserved.

(1557)

THEY FLEE FROM ME.   12. *long and small:* slender and lovely.   19. *new-fangleness:* fickleness, evidently now in fashion.   20. *kindely:* i.e., in the natural way of women—but with irony, given the modern meaning.

Fall In

Lincoln Kirstein

My mother's brother hauled me to the big-boys' club,
   Where they swam nude, drank beer, shared secrecy.
Males young and old held mystic privilege.
   I was condemned to join their mystery.

These men were hairy on belly and groin; 5
   The boys were hairier at least than me,
No boy, no man, a neuter in-between,
   One hairless silly, neither he nor she.

In locker room my uncle stripped me raw.
   My shyness shivered at his shameless, bare, 10
Terrible body. Off he tore my drawers
   And shoved me naked to the brink of where

In a tiled cage they'd sunk their sacred pool,
   Clean as a toilet bowl, its water poison-green;
No mama near to save or cry "Forbear!" 15
   The taste of infamy is sweet chlorine.

I knew that death swam near but hated uncle more.
   If I were doomed, then uncle, he must pay.
I'd scream, I'd make a scene, or the extreme:
   I'd plummet to bottom, midget martyr play 20

Profoundly drowned, which simply took despair
   (Distinct from courage since it involved caprice),
Hold my breath to bursting waiting The End.
   In suicide is blackmail and release.

He tugged me out with terror, even awe. 25
   I felt my fright infect his grizzled chest;
Palpating this drowned rat to retch and drain,
   He knew I knew who'd flunked his foolish test.

Thus one bears fear in action, guilt in pride.
   I was his sister's son, yet still no male. 30
The spineless kin he'd vowed to make a man
   Confounded polity and saw him fail.

The rage of armies is the shame of boys;
  A hero's panic or a coward's whim
Is triggered by nerve or nervousness.   35
  We wish to sink. We do not choose to swim.

(1964)

Sir Gawaine
and the Green Knight

Yvor Winters

Reptilian green the wrinkled throat,
Green as a bough of yew the beard;
He bent his head, and so I smote;
Then for a thought my vision cleared.

The head dropped clean; he rose and walked;   5
He fixed his fingers in the hair;
The head was unabashed and talked;
I understood what I must dare.

His flesh, cut down, arose and grew.
He bade me wait the season's round,   10
And then, when he had strength anew,
To meet him on his native ground.

The year declined; and in his keep
I passed in joy a thriving yule;
And whether waking or in sleep,   15
I lived in riot like a fool.

He beat the woods to bring me meat.
His lady, like a forest vine,
Grew in my arms; the growth was sweet;
And yet what thoughtless force was mine!   20

By practice and conviction formed,
With ancient stubbornness ingrained,
Although her body clung and swarmed,
My own identity remained.

Her beauty, lithe, unholy, pure,   25
Took shapes that I had never known;
And had I once been insecure,
Had grafted laurel in my bone.

And then, since I had kept the trust,
Had loved the lady, yet was true,   30
The knight withheld his giant thrust
And let me go with what I knew.

I left the green bark and the shade,
Where growth was rapid, thick, and still;
I found a road that men had made   35
And rested on a drying hill.

(1941)

SIR GAWAINE AND THE GREEN KNIGHT. The poem is based on a medieval
poem of the same name. Sir Gawaine cuts off the head of the Green Knight,
who picks up his head and tells Gawaine to come in a year to receive a
like blow. One year later, Gawaine arrives and is wooed by the Knight's
lady while he is out hunting. Keeping his trust, Gawaine is allowed to
leave by the Green Knight, a woodsman and figure of the forces of nature.

A Poison Tree

William Blake

I was angry with my friend:
I told my wrath, my wrath did end.
I was angry with my foe:
I told it not, my wrath did grow.

And I waterd it in fears,   5
Night & morning with my tears;
And I sunnèd it with smiles,
And with soft deceitful wiles.

And it grew both day and night,
Till it bore an apple bright.
And my foe beheld it shine,   10
And he knew that it was mine,

And into my garden stole,
When the night had veild the pole;
In the morning glad I see   15
My foe outstretchd beneath the tree.

(1794)

The Tyger

William Blake

Tyger! Tyger! burning bright
In the forests of the night,
What immortal hand or eye
Could frame thy fearful symmetry?

In what distant deeps or skies   5
Burnt the fire of thine eyes?
On what wings dare he aspire?
What the hand, dare seize the fire?

And what shoulder, & what art,
Could twist the sinews of thy heart?   10
And when thy heart began to beat,
What dread hand? & what dread feet?

What the hammer? what the chain?
In what furnace was thy brain?
What the anvil? what dread grasp   15
Dare its deadly terrors clasp?

When the stars threw down their spears,
And water'd heaven with their tears,
Did he smile his work to see?
Did he who made the Lamb make thee?   20

Tyger! Tyger! burning bright
In the forests of the night,
What immortal hand or eye
Dare frame thy fearful symmetry?

(1794)

from **Asphodel, That Greeny Flower**

W. C. Williams

from Book I

Of asphodel, that greeny flower,
    like a buttercup
        upon its branching stem—
save that it's green and wooden—
    I come, my sweet,   5
        to sing to you.
We lived long together
    a life filled,
        if you will,
with flowers. So that   10
    I was cheered
        when I came first to know
that there were flowers also
    in hell.
        Today   15
I'm filled with the fading memory of those flowers
    that we both loved,
        even to this poor
colorless thing—
    I saw it   20
        when I was a child—
little prized among the living
    but the dead see,
        asking among themselves:
What do I remember   25
    that was shaped
        as this thing is shaped?
while our eyes fill
    with tears.
        Of love, abiding love   30
it will be telling
    though too weak a wash of crimson
        colors it
to make it wholly credible.
        There is something   35
        something urgent
I have to say to you
    and you alone
        but it must wait

while I drink in   40
        the joy of your approach,
                perhaps for the last time.
          . . .

I have forgot
        and yet I see clearly enough
             something
central to the sky   55
        which ranges round it.
             An odor
springs from it!
        A sweetest odor!
                Honeysuckle! And now   60
there comes the buzzing of a bee!
        and a whole flood
            of sister memories!
Only give me time,
        time to recall them   65
            before I shall speak out.
Give me time,
        time.

         . . .

It is a curious odor,
        a moral odor,
            that brings me
near to you.   90
        The color
            was the first to go.
There had come to me
        a challenge,
            your dear self,   95
mortal as I was,
        the lily's throat
            to the hummingbird!
Endless wealth,
        I thought,   100
            held out its arms to me.
A thousand topics
        in an apple blossom.
              The generous earth itself
gave us lief.   105
        The whole world
            became my garden!
         . . .

from Book III

For our wedding, too,
        the light was wakened
                and shone. The light!   425
the light stood before us
        waiting!
                I thought the world
stood still.
        At the altar   430
                so intent was I
before my vows,
        so moved by your presence
                a girl so pale
and ready to faint   435
        that I pitied
                and wanted to protect you.
As I think of it now,
        after a lifetime,
                it is as if   440
a sweet-scented flower
        were poised
                and for me did open.
Asphodel
        has no odor   445
                save to the imagination
but it too
        celebrates the light.
                It is late
but an odor   450
        as from our wedding
                has revived for me
and begun again to penetrate
        into all crevices
                of my world.   455

                (1962)

from ASPHODEL, THAT GREENY FLOWER, BOOK I.   14. *hell:* Williams was close
to death when he wrote this poem.

[I Heard a Fly Buzz]

EMILY DICKINSON

I heard a Fly buzz–when I died–
The Stillness in the Room
Was like the Stillness in the Air–
Between the Heaves of Storm–

The Eyes around–had wrung them dry–   5
And Breaths were gathering firm
For that last Onset–when the King
Be witnessed–in the Room–

I willed my Keepsakes–Signed away
What portion of me be   10
Assignable–and then it was
There interposed a Fly–

With Blue–uncertain stumbling Buzz–
Between the light–and me–
And then the Windows failed–and then   15
I could not see to see–

(c. 1862)

A Valediction:
Forbidding Mourning

John Donne

As virtuous men pass mildly away,
    And whisper to their souls to go,
Whilst some of their sad friends do say
    The breath goes now, and some say, No;

So let us melt, and make no noise,   5
    No tear-floods, nor sigh-tempests move,
'Twere profanation of our joys
    To tell the laity our love.

Moving of th' earth brings harms and fears,
    Men reckon what it did and meant;   10

But trepidation of the spheres,
   Though greater far, is innocent.

Dull sublunary lovers' love
   (Whose soul° is sense) cannot admit   *essence*
Absence, because it doth remove   15
   Those things which elemented° it.   *composed*

But we by a love so much refined
   That our selves know not what it is,
Inter-assurèd of the mind,
   Care less, eyes, lips, and hands to miss.   20

Our two souls therefore, which are one,
   Though I must go, endure not yet
A breach, but an expansion,
   Like gold to airy thinness beat.

If they be two, they are two so   25
   As stiff twin compasses are two;
Thy soul, the fixed foot, makes no show
   To move, but doth, if th' other do.

And though it in the center sit,
   Yet when the other far doth roam,   30
It leans and harkens after it,
   And grows erect, as that comes home.

Such wilt thou be to me, who must
   Like th' other foot, obliquely run;
Thy firmness makes my circle just,   35
   And makes me end where I begun.

(1633)

A VALEDICTION: FORBIDDING MOURNING. According to Sir Izaak Walton (a contemporary of Donne's), the poem was addressed to Donne's wife and written with great gravity of mind and purpose. 12. *innocent:* Donne refers to the Ptolemaic explanation of slight changes in the positions of the stars, caused in fact by the wobbling of the earth on its axis. Unlike earthquakes ("Moving of th' earth"), which were thought to be evil omens, such "trepidation" (shuddering) was held to be "innocent" (harmless). 13. *sublunary:* beneath the moon, and therefore mundane (of the earth). 35. *circle:* The closed or complete ("just") circle—such as is made with a compass—is a symbol of unity and wholeness.

Sonnet 97

William Shakespeare

How like a winter hath my absence been
From thee, the pleasure of the fleeting year!
What freezings have I felt, what dark days seen!
What old December's bareness everywhere!
And yet this time removed was summer's time,   5
The teeming autumn big with rich increase,
Bearing the wanton burthen of the prime,
Like widowed wombs after their lords' decease;
Yet this abundant issue seemed to me
But hope of orphans and unfathered fruit;   10
For summer and his pleasures wait on thee,
And, thou away, the very birds are mute;
Or, if they sing, 'tis with so dull a cheer
That leaves look pale, dreading the winter's near.

(1609)

SONNET 97.   7. *prime:* spring, which has fathered the progeny that autumn
bears.

from **As You Like It**

William Shakespeare

All the world's a stage
And all the men and women merely players: 140
They have their exits and their entrances;
And one man in his time plays many parts,
His acts being seven ages. At first the infant,
Mewling and puking in the nurse's arms.
Then the whining school-boy, with his satchel   145
And shining morning face, creeping like snail
Unwillingly to school. And then the lover,
Sighing like furnace, with a woeful ballad
Made to his mistress' eyebrow. Then a soldier,
Full of strange oaths, and bearded like the pard,   150
Jealous in honor, sudden and quick in quarrel,
Seeking the bubble reputation
Even in the cannon's mouth. And then the justice,

In fair round belly with good capon lined,
With eyes severe and beard of formal cut,   155
Full of wise saws and modern instances;
And so he plays his part. The sixth age shifts
Into the lean and slipper'd pantaloon,
With spectacles on nose and pouch on side,
His youthful hose, well saved, a world too wide   160
For his shrunk shank; and his big manly voice,
Turning again toward childish treble, pipes
And whistles in his sound. Last scene of all,
That ends this strange eventful history,
Is second childishness and mere oblivion,   165
Sans teeth, sans eyes, sans taste, sans every thing.

(*c. 1599*)

from AS YOU LIKE IT. The speech is from act 2, scene 7.   165. *mere:* entire,
complete. 166. *sans:* without.

The Blessed Virgin Compared
to the Air We Breathe

G. M. Hopkins

Wild air, world-mothering air,
Nestling me everywhere,
That each eyelash or hair
Girdles; goes home betwixt
The fleeciest, frailest-flixed   5
Snowflake; that's fairly mixed
With, riddles, and is rife
In every least thing's life;
This needful, never spent,
And nursing element;   10
My more than meat and drink,
My meal at every wink;
This air, which, by life's law,
My lung must draw and draw
Now but to breathe its praise,   15
Minds me in many ways
Of her who not only
Gave God's infinity
Dwindled to infancy

Welcome in womb and breast,   20
Birth, milk, and all the rest
But mothers each new grace
That does now reach our race—
Mary Immaculate,
Merely a woman, yet   25
Whose presence, power is
Great as no goddess's
Was deemèd, dreamèd; who
This one work has to do—
Let all God's glory through,   30
God's glory which would go
Through her and from her flow
Off, and no way but so.
   I say that we are wound
With mercy round and round   35
As if with air: the same
Is Mary, more by name.
She, wild web, wondrous robe,
Mantles the guilty globe,
Since God has let dispense   40
Her prayers his providence:
Nay, more than almoner,
The sweet alms' self is her
And men are meant to share
Her life as life does air.   45
   If I have understood,
She holds high motherhood
Towards all our ghostly good
And plays in grace her part
About man's beating heart,   50
Laying, like air's fine flood,
The deathdance in his blood;
Yet no part but what will
Be Christ our Saviour still.
Of her flesh he took flesh: 55
He does take fresh and fresh,
Though much the mystery how,
Not flesh but spirit now
And makes, O marvellous!
New Nazareths in us,   60
Where she shall yet conceive
Him, morning, noon, and eve;
New Bethlems, and he born

There, evening, noon, and morn—
Bethlem or Nazareth, 65
Men here may draw like breath
More Christ and baffle death;
Who, born so, comes to be
New self and nobler me
In each one and each one 70
More makes, when all is done,
Both God's and Mary's Son.
    Again, look overhead
How air is azurèd;
O how! Nay do but stand 75
Where you can lift your hand
Skywards: rich, rich it laps
Round the four fingergaps.
Yet such a sapphire-shot,
Charged, steepèd sky will not 80
Stain light. Yea, mark you this:
It does no prejudice.
The glass-blue days are those
When every colour glows,
Each shape and shadow shows. 85
Blue be it: this blue heaven
The seven or seven times seven
Hued sunbeam will transmit
Perfect, not alter it.
Or if there does some soft, 90
On things aloof, aloft,
Bloom breathe, that one breath more
Earth is the fairer for.
Whereas did air not make
This bath of blue and slake 95
His fire, the sun would shake,
A blear and blinding ball
With blackness bound, and all
The thick stars round him roll
Flashing like flecks of coal, 100
Quartz-fret, or sparks of salt,
In grimy vasty vault.
    So God was god of old:
A mother came to mould
Those limbs like ours which are 105
What must make our daystar
Much dearer to mankind;

Whose glory bare would blind
Or less would win man's mind.
Through her we may see him   110
Made sweeter, not made dim,
And her hand leaves his light
Sifted to suit our sight.
    Be thou then, O thou dear
Mother, my atmosphere;   115
My happier world, wherein
To wend and meet no sin;
Above me, round me lie
Fronting my froward eye
With sweet and scarless sky;   120
Stir in my ears, speak there
Of God's love, O live air,
Of patience, penance, prayer:
Worldmothering air, air wild,
Wound with thee, in thee isled,   125
Fold home, fast fold thy child.

(c. 1883)

THE BLESSED VIRGIN COMPARED TO THE AIR WE BREATHE. 5. *-flixed:* -furred ("flix" is the fur on the breast of a rabbit). 42. *almoner:* one who distributes alms. 54. *Christ our Saviour still:* The grace all comes from Christ, not from Mary herself. 56. *fresh and fresh:* over and over—Christ is born anew in each person when accepted through Mary. 74. *azurèd:* blue, Mary's color. 103. *god of old:* The God of the Old Testament was one of wrath and vengeance. It was the advent of Christ through Mary that made meekness and love religious virtues. 119. *froward:* stubbornly contrary and disobedient.

Chapter Five

The Divine Image

William Blake

To Mercy, Pity, Peace, and Love,
All pray in their distress:
And to these virtues of delight
Return their thankfulness.

For Mercy, Pity, Peace, and Love,   5
Is God, our father dear:
And Mercy, Pity, Peace, and Love,
Is Man, his child and care.

For Mercy has a human heart,
Pity, a human face: 10
And Love, the human form divine,
And Peace, the human dress.

Then every man of every clime,
That prays in his distress,
Prays to the human form divine,   15
Love, Mercy, Pity, Peace.

And all must love the human form,
In heathen, Turk, or Jew.
Where Mercy, Love, & Pity dwell,
There God is dwelling too.   20

(1789)

The Human Abstract

William Blake

Pity would be no more,
If we did not make somebody Poor;
And Mercy no more could be,
If all were as happy as we;

And mutual fear brings peace,   5
Till the selfish loves increase;
Then Cruelty knits a snare,
And spreads his baits with care.

He sits down with holy fears,
And waters the ground with tears;   10
Then Humility takes its root
Underneath his foot.

Soon spreads the dismal shade
Of Mystery over his head;
And the Catterpiller and Fly   15
Feed on the Mystery.

And it bears the fruit of Deceit,
Ruddy and sweet to eat;
And the Raven his nest has made
In its thickest shade.   20

The Gods of the earth and sea,
Sought thro' Nature to find this Tree,
But their search was all in vain:
There grows one in the Human Brain.

(1794)

On the Move

Thom Gunn

"Man, you gotta Go."

The blue jay scuffling in the bushes follows
Some hidden purpose, and the gust of birds
That spurts across the field, the wheeling swallows,
Have nested in the trees and undergrowth.
Seeking their instinct, or their poise, or both,   5
One moves with an uncertain violence
Under the dust thrown by a baffled sense
Or the dull thunder of approximate words.

On motorcycles, up the road, they come:
Small, black, as flies hanging in heat, the Boys,   10
Until the distance throws them forth, their hum
Bulges to thunder held by calf and thigh.
In goggles, donned impersonality,
In gleaming jackets trophied with the dust,
They strap in doubt—by hiding it, robust—   15
And almost hear a meaning in their noise.

Exact conclusion of their hardiness
Has no shape yet, but from known whereabouts
They ride, direction where the tires press.
They scare a flight of birds across the field: 20
Much that is natural, to the will must yield.
Men manufacture both machine and soul,
And use what they imperfectly control
To dare a future from the taken routes.

It is a part solution, after all.   25
One is not necessarily discord
On earth; or damned because, half animal,
One lacks direct instinct, because one wakes
Afloat on movement that divides and breaks.
One joins the movement in a valueless world,   30
Choosing it, till, both hurler and the hurled,
One moves as well, always toward, toward.

A minute holds them, who have come to go:
The self-defined, astride the created will
They burst away; the towns they travel through   35
Are home for neither bird nor holiness,
For birds and saints complete their purposes.
At worst, one is in motion; and at best,
Reaching no absolute, in which to rest,
One is always nearer by not keeping still.   40

(1957)

Ideal Landscape

Adrienne Rich

We had to take the world as it was given:
The nursemaid sitting passive in the park
Was rarely by a changeling prince accosted.
The mornings happened similar and stark
In rooms of selfhood where we woke and lay   5
Watching today unfold like yesterday.

Our friends were not unearthly beautiful.
Nor spoke with tongues of gold; our lovers blundered
Now and again when most we sought perfection,
Or hid in cupboards when the heavens thundered.   10
The human rose to haunt us everywhere,
Raw, flawed, and asking more than we could bear.

And always time was rushing like a tram
Through streets of a foreign city, streets we saw
Opening into great and sunny squares   15
We could not find again, no map could show—
Never those fountains tossed in that same light,
Those gilded trees, those statues green and white.

(1955)

These Trees Stand . . .

W. D. Snodgrass

These trees stand very tall under the heavens.
While *they* stand, if I walk, all stars traverse
This steep celestial gulf their branches chart.
Though lovers stand at sixes and at sevens°   *at odds*
While civilizations come down with the curse,   5
Snodgrass is walking through the universe.

I can't make any world go around *your* house.
But note this moon. Recall how the night nurse
Goes ward-rounds, by the mild, reflective art
Of focusing her flashlight on her blouse.   10
Your name's safe conduct into love or verse;
Snodgrass is walking through the universe.

Your name's absurd, miraculous as sperm
And as decisive. If you can't coerce
One thing outside yourself, why you're the poet!   15
What irrefrangible atoms whirl, affirm
Their destiny and form Lucinda's skirts!
She can't make up your mind. Soon as you know it,
Your firmament grows touchable and firm.
If all this world runs battlefield or worse,   20
Come, let us wipe our glasses on our shirts:
Snodgrass is walking through the universe.

(1959)

THESE TREES STAND ... 5. *the curse:* menstruation, bloodshed. 16. *irrefrang-
ible:* that which cannot be deflected. 17. *Lucinda:* a reference in part, per-
haps, to Lucina, Roman goddess of childbirth.

The Destruction of Sennacherib

George Gordon, Lord Byron

1

The Assyrian came down like the wolf on the fold,
And his cohorts were gleaming in purple and gold;
And the sheen of their spears was like stars on the sea,
When the blue wave rolls nightly on deep Galilee.

2

Like the leaves of the forest when summer is green,   5
That host with their banners at sunset were seen:
Like the leaves of the forest when autumn hath blown,
That host on the morrow lay withered and strown.

3

For the Angel of Death spread his wings on the blast,
And breathed in the face of the foe as he passed;   10
And the eyes of the sleepers waxed deadly and chill,
And their hearts but once heaved, and forever grew still!

4

And there lay the steed with his nostril all wide,
But through it there rolled not the breath of his pride;
And the foam of his gasping lay white on the turf,   15
And cold as the spray of the rock-beating surf.

5

And there lay the rider distorted and pale,
With the dew on his brow, and the rust on his mail:
And the tents were all silent, the banners alone,
The lances unlifted, the trumpet unblown.   20

6

And the widows of Ashur are loud in their wail,
And the idols are broke in the temple of Baal;
And the might of the Gentile, unsmote by the sword,
Hath melted like snow in the glance of the Lord!

(1815)

THE DESTRUCTION OF SENNACHERIB. *Sennacherib:* an Assyrian king whose armies, while besieging Jerusalem (701 B.C.), were overcome by a plague, which the Hebrews attributed to the wrath of the Lord (see II Kings 19:35). 21. *Ashur:* Assyria. 22. *Baal:* deity of the Assyrians. 23. *Gentile:* Sennacherib and his non-Hebrew cohorts.

Neither Out Far Nor in Deep

Robert Frost

The people along the sand
All turn and look one way.
They turn their back on the land.
They look at the sea all day.

As long as it takes to pass   5
A ship keeps raising its hull;
The wetter ground like glass
Reflects a standing gull.

The land may vary more;
But wherever the truth may be—   10
The water comes ashore,
And the people look at the sea.

They cannot look out far.
They cannot look in deep.
But when was that ever a bar   15
To any watch they keep?

(1936)

from A Dialogue of Self and Soul

W. B. Yeats

Part 2

MY SELF. A living man is blind and drinks his drop.
  What matter if the ditches are impure?
  What matter if I live it all once more?
  Endure that toil of growing up;
  The ignominy of boyhood; the distress   45
  Of boyhood changing into man;
  The unfinished man and his pain
  Brought face to face with his own clumsiness;

  The finished man among his enemies?—
  How in the name of Heaven can he escape   50
  That defiling and disfigured shape
  The mirror of malicious eyes
  Casts upon his eyes until at last
  He thinks that shape must be his shape?
  And what's the good of an escape   55
  If honor find him in the wintry blast?

  I am content to live it all again
  And yet again, if it be life to pitch
  Into the frog-spawn of a blind man's ditch,
  A blind man battering blind men;   60
  Or into that most fecund ditch of all,
  The folly that man does
  Or must suffer, if he woos
  A proud woman not kindred of his soul.

  I am content to follow to its source   65
  Every event in action or in thought;
  Measure the lot; forgive myself the lot!
  When such as I cast out remorse
  So great a sweetness flows into the breast
  We must laugh and we must sing,   70
  We are blest by everything,
  Everything we look upon is blest.

(1929)

To a Friend Whose Work
Has Come to Nothing

W. B. Yeats

Now all the truth is out,
Be secret and take defeat
From any brazen throat,
For how can you compete,
Being honor bred, with one   5
Who, were it proved he lies,
Were neither shamed in his own
Nor in his neighbours' eyes?
Bred to a harder thing
Than Triumph, turn away   10
And like a laughing string
Whereon mad fingers play
Amid a place of stone,
Be secret and exult,
Because of all things known   15
That is most difficult.

(1914)

TO A FRIEND WHOSE WORK HAS COME TO NOTHING. *Friend:* Yeats refers to
his friend Lady Gregory, who had failed in her effort to secure an art
museum for Dublin.

Fear No More
the Heat o' the Sun

William Shakespeare

Fear no more the heat o' the sun,
    Nor the furious winter's rages;
Thou thy worldly task hast done,
    Home art gone, and ta'en thy wages:
Golden lads and girls all must,   5
As chimney-sweepers, come to dust.

Fear no more the frown o' the great;
    Thou art past the tyrant's stroke;

Care no more to clothe and eat;
　　To thee the reed is as the oak: 10
The scepter, learning, physic, must
All follow this, and come to dust.

Fear no more the lightning flash,
　　Nor the all-dreaded thunder stone;
Fear not slander, censure rash; 15
　　Thou hast finished joy and moan:
All lovers young, all lovers must
Consign to thee, and come to dust.

No exorciser harm thee!
Nor no witchcraft charm thee! 20
Ghost unlaid forbear thee!
Nothing ill come near thee!
Quiet consummation have;
And renownèd by thy grave!

(c. 1610)

FEAR NO MORE THE HEAT O' THE SUN.　from *Cymbeline*. 10. *oak:* In ancient Rome, a crown of oak leaves signified civic merit. 14. *thunder stone:* Thunder was thought to be the sound of meteorites falling through the atmosphere. 19. *exorciser:* one who drives off the spirits of the dead.

The Passionate Man's Pilgrimage

Sir Walter Raleigh

Give me my scallop-shell of quiet,
My staff of faith to walk upon,
My scrip of joy, immortal diet,
My bottle of salvation,
My gown of glory, hope's true gage,° 　　　pledge　5
And thus I'll take my pilgrimage.

Blood must be my body's balmer,
No other balm will there be given,
Whilst my soul like a white palmer
Travels to the land of heaven, 10
Over the silver mountains,

Where spring the nectar fountains;
And there I'll kiss
The bowl of bliss,
And drink my eternal fill   15
On every milken hill.
My soul will be a-dry before,
But after it will ne'er thirst more;
And by the happy blissful way
More peaceful pilgrims I shall see   20
That have shook off their gowns of clay
And go appareled fresh like me.
I'll bring them first
To slake their thirst,
And then to taste those nectar suckets,°   *confections*   25
At the clear wells
Where sweetness dwells,
Drawn up by saints in crystal buckets.

And when our bottles and all we
Are filled with immortality,   30
Then the holy paths we'll travel,
Strewed with rubies thick as gravel,
Ceilings of diamonds, sapphire floors,
High walls of coral, and pearl bowers,
From thence to heaven's bribeless hall   35
Where no corrupted voices brawl,
No conscience molten into gold,
Nor forged accusers bought and sold,
No cause deferred, nor vain-spent journey,
For there Christ is the king's attorney,   40
Who pleads for all, without degrees,
And he hath angels, but no fees.
When the grand twelve million jury
Of our sins and sinful fury,
'Gainst our souls black verdicts give,   45
Christ pleads his death, and then we live.
Be thou my speaker, taintless pleader,
Unblotted lawyer, true proceeder;
Thou movest salvation even for alms,
Not with a bribed lawyer's palms.   50
And this is my eternal plea
To him that made heaven, earth, and sea,
Seeing my flesh must die so soon,
And want a head to dine next noon,

Just at the stroke when my veins start and spread,   55
Set on my soul an everlasting head.
Then am I ready, like a palmer fit,
To tread those blest paths which before I writ.

(1604)

THE PASSIONATE MAN'S PILGRIMAGE.   Raleigh wrote this poem while in the
Tower waiting to be beheaded. He was reprieved, but was beheaded after
all in 1618. 1. *scallop-shell:* a sign of a pilgrim. 3. *scrip:* pilgrim's knapsack.
9. *palmer:* a pilgrim, especially to the Holy Land. 42. *angels:* a reference
(by way of pun) to the gold coin of the same name. 49. *alms:* I.e., Christ
moves that salvation be granted if for no other reason than for the alms
given during life by those he pleads for.

The Splendor Falls

Alfred, Lord Tennyson

The splendor falls on castle walls
  And snowy summits old in story;
The long light shakes across the lakes,
  And the wild cataract leaps in glory.
Blow, bugle, blow, set the wild echoes flying,   5
Blow, bugle; answer echoes, dying, dying, dying.

O, hark, O, hear! how thin and clear,
  And thinner, clearer, farther going!
O, sweet and far from cliff and scar
  The horns of Elfland faintly blowing!   10
Blow, let us hear the purple glens replying,
Blow, bugle; answer, echoes, dying, dying, dying.

O love, they die in yon rich sky,
  They faint on hill or field or river;
Our echoes roll from soul to soul,   15
  And grow for ever and for ever.
Blow, bugle, blow, set the wild echoes flying,
And answer, echoes, answer, dying, dying, dying.

(1850)

THE SPLENDOR FALLS.   9. *scar:* mountainside, slope.

To a Mouse

Robert Burns

On turning her up in her nest with the plough,
November, 1785

Wee, sleekit,° cow'rin, tim'rous beastie,	*sleek*
O, what a panic's in thy breastie!	
Thou need na start awa sae hasty,	
Wi' bickering° brattle!°	*hurried	scamper*
I wad be laith to rin an' chase thee,	5
Wi' murd'ring pattle!°	*plowstaff ("paddle")*
I'm truly sorry man's dominion	
Has broken Nature's social union,	
An' justifies that ill opinion	
Which makes thee startle	10
At me, thy poor earth-born companion,	
An' fellow-mortal!	
I doubt na, whiles,° but thou may thieve;	*sometimes*
What then? poor beastie, thou maun° live!	*must*
A daimen° icker° in a thrave°	*random	corn-ear	shock*
'S a sma' request:	
I'll get a blessin wi' the lave,°	*rest*
And never miss't!	
Thy wee bit housie, too, in ruin!	
Its silly° wa's the win's are strewin!	*frail* 20
An' naething, now, to big° a new ane,	*build*
O' foggage° green!	*mosses*
An' bleak December's winds ensuin,	
Baith snell° an' keen!	*bitter*
Thou saw the fields laid bare and waste,	25
An' weary winter comin fast,	
An' cozie here, beneath the blast,	
Thou thought to dwell,	
Till crash! the cruel coulter° past	*plowshare*
Out thro' thy cell.	30
That wee bit heap o' leaves an' stibble°	*stubble*
Has cost thee mony a weary nibble!	

Now thou's turned out, for a' thy trouble,
        But° house or hald,°   *without | home ("hold")*
To thole° the winter's sleety dribble,   *endure*   35
        An' cranreuch° cauld!   *hoarfrost*

But, Mousie, thou art no thy lane,°   *not alone*
In proving foresight may be vain:
The best laid schemes o' mice an' men
        Gang° aft a-gley.°   *go | astray*   40
An' lea'e us nought but grief an' pain
        For promised joy.

Still thou art blest, compared wi' me!
The present only toucheth thee:
But och! I backward cast my e'e   45
        On prospects drear!
An' forward, tho' I canna see,
        I guess an' fear!

      (1786)

The Shield of Achilles

W. H. Auden

She looked over his shoulder
  For vines and olive trees,
Marble well-governed cities
  And ships upon untamed seas,
But there on the shining metal   5
  His hands had put instead
An artificial wilderness
  And a sky like lead.

A plain without a feature, bare and brown,
  No blade of grass, no sign of neighborhood,   10
Nothing to eat and nowhere to sit down,
  Yet, congregated on its blankness, stood
  An unintelligible multitude,
A million eyes, a million boots in line,
Without expression, waiting for a sign.   15

Out of the air a voice without a face
  Proved by statistics that some cause was just
In tones as dry and level as the place:
  No one was cheered and nothing was discussed;
  Column by column in a cloud of dust   20
They marched away enduring a belief
Whose logic brought them, somewhere else, to grief.

      She looked over his shoulder
        For ritual pieties,
      White flower-garlanded heifers,   25
        Libation and sacrifice,
      But there on the shining metal
        Where the altar should have been,
      She saw by his flickering forge-light
        Quite another scene.   30

Barbed wire enclosed an arbitrary spot
  Where bored officials lounged (one cracked a joke)
And sentries sweated for the day was hot:
  A crowd of ordinary decent folk
  Watched from without and neither moved nor spoke   35
As three pale figures were led forth and bound
To three posts driven upright in the ground.

The mass and majesty of this world, all
  That carries weight and always weighs the same
Lay in the hands of others; they were small   40
  And could not hope for help and no help came:
  What their foes liked to do was done, their shame
Was all the worst could wish; they lost their pride
And died as men before their bodies died.

      She looked over his shoulder   45
        For athletes at their games,
      Men and women in a dance
        Moving their sweet limbs
      Quick, quick, to music,
        But there on the shining shield   50
      His hands had set no dancing-floor
        But a weed-choked field.

A ragged urchin, aimless and alone,
  Loitered about that vacancy, a bird

Flew up to safety from his well-aimed stone: 55
    That girls are raped, that two boys knife a third,
    Were axioms to him, who'd never heard
Of any world where promises were kept,
Or one could weep because another wept.

    The thin-lipped armorer,   60
        Hephaestos hobbled away,
    Thetis of the shining breasts
        Cried out in dismay
    At what the god had wrought
        To please her son, the strong   65
    Iron-hearted man-slaying Achilles
        Who would not live long.

                                    (1955)

THE SHIELD OF ACHILLES. *Shield:* Made by the god Hephaestos at the behest of Thetis, Achilles' mother (the "She" of the poem), this shield depicted on it scenes representing the lives of men and universal law. As described by Homer in the *Iliad* (Book 18, lines 478–608), it depicted the earth, the heavens, the sea, and the planets; a city in peace and a city at war; scenes from country life, e.g., a harvest feast and grape-gathering; and scenes from animal creation and the joyful life of young men and women. Around all of these scenes was a border of ocean. Shortly after receiving the shield, Achilles died (because of his faulty heel).

The Lake Isle of Innisfree

W. B. Yeats

I will arise and go now, and go to Innisfree,
And a small cabin build there, of clay and wattles made:
Nine bean-rows will I have there, a hive for the honeybee,
And live alone in the bee-loud glade.

And I shall have some peace there, for peace comes dropping slow, 5
Dropping from the veils of the morning to where the cricket sings;
There midnight's all a glimmer, and noon a purple glow,
And evening full of the linnet's wings.

I will arise and go now, for always night and day
I hear lake water lapping with low sounds by the shore;   10

While I stand on the roadway, or on the pavements gray,
I hear it in the deep heart's core.

(1892)

THE LAKE ISLE OF INNISFREE. *Innisfree:* an island in Lake Gill, County
Sligo, Ireland, where Yeats went as a boy. 2. *wattles:* stakes interwoven with
sticks and branches.

Blank Verse

from Henry VIII

William Shakespeare

[Wolsey, raised to eminence by Henry VIII but now fallen
from grace, speaks to Cromwell, who was to rise and fall in
his turn.]

WOLSEY. Cromwell, I did not think to shed a tear
In all my miseries; but thou hast forced me,
Out of thy honest truth, to play the woman.   430
Let's dry our eyes; and thus far hear me, Cromwell;
And when I am forgotten, as I shall be,
And sleep in dull cold marble, where no mention
Of me more must be heard of, say I taught thee,
Say, Wolsey, that once trod the ways of glory,   435
And sounded all the depths and shoals of honour,
Found thee a way, out of his wreck, to rise in—
A sure and safe one, though thy master missed it.
Mark but my fall and that that ruined me.
Cromwell, I charge thee, fling away ambition: 440
By that sin fell the angels; how can man then,
The image of his Maker, hope to win by it?
Love thyself last; cherish those hearts that hate thee;
Corruption wins not more than honesty.
Still in thy right hand carry gentle peace   445
To silence envious tongues. Be just, and fear not;
Let all the ends thou aim'st at be thy country's,
Thy God's, and truth's; then if thou fall'st, O Cromwell,

Thou fall'st a blessed martyr. Serve the king;
And,—prithee, lead me in: 450
There take an inventory of all I have
To the last penny; 'tis the king's. My robe,
And my integrity to heaven, is all
I dare now call mine own. O Cromwell, Cromwell,
Had I but served my God with half the zeal   455
I served my king, he would not in mine age
Have left me naked to mine enemies.

(c. 1613)

from HENRY VIII. The speech is from act 3, scene 2.

from **Paradise Lost**

John Milton

from Book I
[General Invocation]

Of man's first disobedience, and the fruit
Of that forbidden tree whose mortal taste
Brought death into the world, and all our woe,
With loss of *Eden,* till one greater Man
Restore us, and regain the blissful seat,   5
Sing, Heavenly Muse, that, on the secret top
Of Oreb, or of Sinai, didst inspire
That shepherd who first taught the chosen seed
In the beginning how the Heavens and Earth
Rose out of Chaos: or, if Sion hill   10
Delight thee more, and Siloa's brook that flowed
Fast° by the oracle of God, I thence   *close*
Invoke thy aid to my adventurous song,
That with no middle flight intends to soar
Above th' Aonian mount, while it pursues   15
Things unattempted yet in prose or rhyme.
And chiefly thou, O Spirit, that dost prefer
Before all temples th' upright heart and pure,
Instruct me, for thou know'st; thou from the first
Wast present, and, with mighty wings outspread,   20
Dovelike sat'st brooding on the vast abyss,
And mad'st it pregnant: what in me is dark

Illumine; what is low, raise and support;
That, to the height of this great argument,°   *theme*
I may assert Eternal Providence,   25
And justify the ways of God to men.

(*1667*)

from PARADISE LOST, BOOK I.   1. *fruit:* the apple and all of its consequences.
2. *mortal:* deadly; also, the taste that initiated our mortality. 4. *greater Man:*
Christ, the second Adam. 6. *Muse:* Milton's Muse is a composite of Urania,
traditional muse of epic poetry, and the Holy Spirit, suggested by the refer-
ences in the next line to Oreb and Sinai, where Moses was inspired to write
Genesis. 10. and 11. *Sion hill* and *Siola's brook:* features of the landscape
around Jerusalem. 15. *Aonian mount:* Helicon, home of the classical muses.
17. *Spirit:* the Holy Spirit. 21. *brooding:* The Holy Spirit is traditionally
imaged as a dove.

from The Prelude

William Wordsworth

from Book XII

There are in our existence spots of time,
That with distinct pre-eminence retain
A renovating virtue, whence—depressed   210
By false opinion and contentious thought,
Or aught of heavier or more deadly weight,
In trivial occupations, and the round
Of ordinary intercourse—our minds
Are nourished and invisibly repaired;   215
A virtue, by which pleasure is enhanced,
That penetrates, enables us to mount,
When high, more high, and lifts us up when fallen.
This efficacious spirit chiefly lurks
Among those passages of life that give   220
Profoundest knowledge to what point, and how,
The mind is lord and master—outward sense
The obedient servant of her will. Such moments
Are scattered everywhere, taking their date
From our first childhood. I remember well,   225
That once, while yet my inexperienced hand
Could scarcely hold a bridle, with proud hopes
I mounted, and we journeyed towards the hills:

An ancient servant of my father's house
Was with me, my encourager and guide;   230
We had not traveled long, ere some mischance
Disjoined me from my comrade; and, through fear
Dismounting, down the rough and stony moor
I led my horse, and, stumbling on, at length
Came to a bottom, where in former times   235
A murderer had been hung in iron chains.
The gibbet-mast had moldered down, the bones
and iron case were gone; but on the turf,
Hard by, soon after that fell deed was wrought,
Some unknown hand had carved the murderer's name.   240
The monumental letters were inscribed
In times long past; but still, from year to year
By superstition of the neighborhood,
The grass is cleared away, and to this hour
The characters are fresh and visible: 245
A casual glance had shown them, and I fled,
Faltering and faint, and ignorant of the road;
Then, reascending the bare common, saw
A naked pool that lay beneath the hills,
The beacon on the summit, and more near,   250
A girl, who bore a pitcher on her head,
And seemed with difficult steps to force her way
Against the blowing wind. It was, in truth,
An ordinary sight; but I should need
Colors and words that are unknown to man,   255
To paint the visionary dreariness
Which, while I looked all round for my lost guide,
Invested moorland waste and naked pool,
The beacon crowning the lone eminence,
The female and her garments vexed and tossed   260
By the strong wind. When, in the blessed hours
Of early love, the loved one at my side,
I roamed, in daily presence of this scene,
Upon the naked pool and dreary crags,
And on the melancholy beacon, fell   265
A spirit of pleasure and youth's golden gleam;
And think ye not with radiance more sublime
For these remembrances, and for the power
They had left behind? So feeling comes in aid
Of feeling, and diversity of strength   270
Attends us, if but once we have been strong.
Oh! mystery of man, from what a depth

Proceed thy honors. I am lost, but see
In simple childhood something of the base
On which thy greatness stands; but this I feel,   275
That from thyself it comes, that thou must give,
Else never canst receive. The days gone by
Return upon me almost from the dawn
Of life: the hiding places of man's power
Open; I would approach them, but they close.   280
I see by glimpses now; when age comes on,
May scarcely see at all; and I would give,
While yet we may, as far as words can give,
Substance and life to what I feel, enshrining.
Such is my hope, the spirit of the Past   285
For future restoration.

                                                     (1850)

from THE PRELUDE, BOOK XII. Compare the treatment of blank verse here
with that of "The Ruined Cottage" (page 344).

Ulysses

Alfred, Lord Tennyson

  It little profits that an idle king,
By this still hearth, among these barren crags,
Matched with an aged wife, I mete and dole
Unequal laws unto a savage race,
That hoard, and sleep, and feed, and know not me.   5

  I cannot rest from travel; I will drink
Life to the lees. All times I have enjoyed
Greatly, have suffered greatly, both with those
That loved me, and alone; on shore, and when
Through scudding drifts the rainy Hyades   10
Vexed the dim sea. I am become a name
For always roaming with a hungry heart;
Much have I seen and known—cities of men
And manners, climates, councils, governments,
Myself not least, but honored of them all—   15
And drunk delight of battle with my peers,
Far on the ringing plains of windy Troy.

I am a part of all that I have met;
Yet all experience is an arch wherethrough
Gleams that untraveled world whose margin fades   20
Forever and forever when I move.
How dull it is to pause, to make an end,
To rust unburnished, not to shine in use!
As though to breathe were life! Life piled on life
Were all too little, and of one to me   25
Little remains; but every hour is saved
From that eternal silence, something more,
A bringer of new things; and vile it were
For some three suns to store and hoard myself,
And this gray spirit yearning in desire   30
To follow knowledge like a sinking star,
Beyond the utmost bound of human thought.

This is my son, mine own Telemachus,
To whom I leave the scepter and the isle—
Well-loved of me, discerning to fulfill   35
This labor, by slow prudence to make mild
A rugged people, and through soft degrees
Subdue them to the useful and the good.
Most blameless is he, centered in the sphere
Of common duties, decent not to fail   40
In offices of tenderness, and pay
Meet adoration to my household gods,
When I am gone. He works his work, I mine.

There lies the port; the vessel puffs her sail;
There gloom the dark, broad seas. My mariners,   45
Souls that have toiled, and wrought, and thought with me—
That ever with a frolic welcome took
The thunder and the sunshine, and opposed
Free hearts, free foreheads—you and I are old;
Old age hath yet his honor and his toil.   50
Death closes all; but something ere the end,
Some work of noble note, may yet be done,
Not unbecoming men that strove with Gods.
The lights begin to twinkle from the rocks;
The long day wanes; the slow moon climbs; the deep   55
Moans round with many voices. Come, my friends,
'Tis not too late to seek a newer world.
Push off, and sitting well in order smite
The sounding furrows; for my purpose holds

To sail beyond the sunset, and the baths   60
Of all the western stars, until I die.
It may be that the gulfs will wash us down;
It may be we shall touch the Happy Isles,
And see the great Achilles, whom we knew.
Though much is taken, much abides; and though   65
We are not now that strength which in old days
Moved earth and heaven, that which we are, we are—
One equal temper of heroic hearts,
Made weak by time and fate, but strong in will
To strive, to seek, to find, and not to yield.   70

(1842)

ULYSSES.   Tennyson's Ulysses is based on Dante's as portrayed in the *Divine
Comedy*. Having returned to Ithaca, Dante's Ulysses became restless and
set out again on a last voyage. 3. *mete and dole:* measure out punishments
and rewards. 10. *scudding drifts:* driving spray and showers. *Hyades:* a
group of stars whose rising was believed to foretell the coming of rain.
61. *western stars:* the outer ocean, which the Greeks thought encircled the
flat earth, and into which the stars descended. 63. *Happy Isles:* Elysium,
thought to be located in the outer ocean and supposed to be the abode
after death of such heroes as Achilles.

The Good Life

Robert Francis

The river plunges to the spillway floor
Then slides into a pool, and here the bathers
Plunge from the rocks and climb back on the rocks—
A hundred, more than a hundred sons of Adam
From smooth small boys a sculptor might have done   5
In a few strokes, to slowly hammered men
From buff to bronze. They have been here before.

Factories face both banks, but the river is wide
And factory windows might as well be blind.
No one comes down the river for the falls.   10
No one comes up the river for the rocks.
Here is a space the city cannot get,
Reserved for do-as-you-please and plenty-of-room
And plenty-of-time. In short, for the good life.

Seven daredevils are climbing up the falls   15
Like high-relief half in, half out of water.
They reach a certain point but not above;
The spillway curves too steep. They pause, they poise,
They cling to the rushing curtain, then climb down.
Off by himself a fat man sleeps in the sun,   20
Hands over belly, a newspaper over face.

Five youths sit on a flat slab playing cards.
If one game ends and another game begins,
If someone loses and if someone wins,
Somebody else will have to say. A boy   25
Stands by the pool edge with a fishing pole.
I watch awhile, but if he gets a fish
Or gets a bite, somebody else must tell.

Nobody hurries, nobody hesitates.
Nobody interferes, nobody stares.   30
Nobody gives commands or calls Come home,
Or if they do nobody seems to hear.
Nobody misses her, nobody cares.
No clock in sight except the tolerant sun.
And there is sun enough and sun to spare.   35

Neighbors are those who share one piece of soap
Like those two lathering each other's back.
Before they plunge to rinse, they cross themselves.
Why do they cross themselves? Where is the evil
Here where the river pours upon the rocks   40
And sun pours on the rocks and on the river?
Here is no Eve. Here is no little snake.

                                                          (*1944*)

The Ruined Cottage

William Wordsworth

First Part

'Twas Summer and the sun was mounted high.
Along the south the uplands feebly glared
Through a pale steam, and all the northern downs,

In clear air ascending, shewed far off
Their surfaces with shadows dappled o'er   5
Of deep embattled clouds. Far as the sight
Could reach those many shadows lay in spots
Determined and unmoved, with steady beams
Of clear and pleasant sunshine interposed—
Pleasant to him who on the soft cool grass   10
Extends his careless limbs beside the root
Of some huge oak whose aged branches make
A twilight of their own, a dewy shade
Where the wren warbles while the dreaming man,
Half conscious of that soothing melody,   15
With sidelong eye looks out upon the scene,
By those impending branches made more soft,
More soft and distant.

              Other lot was mine.
Across a bare wide Common I had toiled
With languid feet which by the slipp'ry ground   20
Were baffled still, and when I stretched myself
On the brown earth my limbs from very heat
Could find no rest, nor my weak arm disperse
The insect host which gathered round my face
And joined their murmurs to the tedious noise   25
Of seeds of bursting gorse that crackled round.
I rose and turned towards a group of trees
Which midway in that level stood alone;
And thither come at length, beneath a shade
Of clustering elms that sprang from the same root   30
I found a ruined house, four naked walls
That stared upon each other. I looked round
And near the door I saw an aged Man,
Alone and stretched upon the cottage bench,
An iron-pointed staff lay at his side.   35
With instantaneous joy I recognized
That pride of nature and of lowly life,
The venerable Armytage, a friend
As dear to me as is the setting sun.

                     Two days before   40
We had been fellow travelers. I knew
That he was in this neighborhood, and now
Delighted found him here in the cool shade.
He lay, his pack of rustic merchandise

Pillowing his head. I guess he had no thought   45
Of his way-wandering life. His eyes were shut,
The shadows of the breezy elms above
Dappled his face. With thirsty heat oppressed
At length I hailed him, glad to see his hat
Bedewed with waterdrops, as if the brim   50
Had newly scooped a running stream. He rose
And pointing to a sunflower, bade me climb
The [   ] wall where that same gaudy flower
Looked out upon the road.

                It was a plot
Of garden ground now wild, its matted weeds   55
Marked with the steps of those whom as they passed,
The gooseberry trees that shot in long lank slips,
Or currants hanging from their leafless stems
In scanty strings, had tempted to o'erleap
The broken wall. Within that cheerless spot,   60
Where two tall hedgerows of thick alder boughs
Joined in a damp cold nook, I found a well
Half covered up with willow flowers and grass.
I slaked my thirst and to the shady bench
Returned, and while I stood unbonneted   65
To catch the motion of the cooler air,
The old Man said, "I see around me here
Things which you cannot see. We die, my Friend,
Nor we alone, but that which each man loved
And prized in his peculiar nook of earth   70
Dies with him, or is changed, and very soon
Even of the good is no memorial left.
The Poets, in their elegies and songs
Lamenting the departed, call the groves,
They call upon the hills and streams to mourn,   75
And senseless rocks—nor idly, for they speak
In these their invocations with a voice
Obedient to the strong creative power
Of human passion. Sympathies there are
More tranquil, yet perhaps of kindred birth,   80
That steal upon the meditative mind
And grow with thought. Beside yon spring I stood,
And eyed its waters till we seemed to feel
One sadness, they and I. For them a bond
Of brotherhood is broken; time has been   85
When every day the touch of human hand

Disturbed their stillness, and they ministered
To human comfort. When I stooped to drink
A spider's web hung to the water's edge,
And on the wet and slimy footstone lay   90
The useless fragment of a wooden bowl.
It moved my very heart.

               The day has been
When I could never pass this road but she
Who lived within these walls, when I appeared,
A daughter's welcome gave me, and I loved her   95
As my own child. Oh Sir, the good die first,
And they whose hearts are dry as summer dust
Burn to the socket. Many a passenger
Has blessed poor Margaret for her gentle looks
When she upheld the cool refreshment drawn   100
From that forsaken spring, and no one came
But he was welcome, no one went away
But that it seemed she loved him. She is dead,
The worm is on her cheek, and this poor hut,
Stripped of its outward garb of household flowers,   105
Of rose and sweetbriar, offers to the wind
A cold bare wall whose earthy top is tricked
With weeds and the rank spear grass. She is dead,
And nettles rot and adders sun themselves
Where we have sate together while she nursed   110
Her infant at her breast. The unshod colt,
The wandring heifer and the Potter's ass,
Find shelter now within the chimney wall
Where I have seen her evening hearthstone blaze
And through the window spread upon the road   115
Its cheerful light. You will forgive me, sir,
But often on this cottage do I muse
As on a picture, till my wiser mind
Sinks, yielding to the foolishness of grief.

She had a husband, an industrious man,   120
Sober and steady. I have heard her say
That he was up and busy at his loom
In summer ere the mower's scythe had swept
The dewy grass, and in the early spring
Ere the last star had vanished. They who passed   125
At evening, from behind the garden fence
Might hear his busy spade, which he would ply

After his daily work till the daylight
Was gone, and every leaf and flower were lost
In the dark hedges. So they passed their days   130
In peace and comfort, and two pretty babes
Were their best hope next to the God in Heaven.

You may remember, now some ten years gone,
Two blighting seasons when the fields were left
With half a harvest. It pleased heaven to add   135
A worse affliction in the plague of war,
A happy land was stricken to the heart,
'Twas a sad time of sorrow and distress.
A wanderer among the cottages,
I with my pack of winter raiment saw   140
The hardships of that season. Many rich
Sunk down as in a dream among the poor,
And of the poor did many cease to be,
And their place knew them not. Meanwhile, abridged
Of daily comforts, gladly reconciled   145
To numerous self-denials, Margaret
Went struggling on through those calamitous years
With cheerful hope. But ere the second autumn
A fever seized her husband. In disease
He lingered long, and when his strength returned   150
He found the little he had stored to meet
The hour of accident, or crippling age,
Was all consumed. As I have said, 'twas now
A time of trouble: shoals of artisans
Were from their daily labor turned away   155
To hang for bread on parish charity,
They and their wives and children, happier far
Could they have lived as do the little birds
That peck along the hedges, or the kite
That makes her dwelling in the mountain rocks.   160

Ill fared it now with Robert, he who dwelt
In this poor cottage. At his door he stood
And whistled many a snatch of merry tunes
That had no mirth in them, or with his knife
Carved uncouth figures on the heads of sticks,   165
Then idly sought about through every nook
Of house or garden any casual task
Of use or ornament, and with a strange
Amusing but uneasy novelty

He blended where he might the various tasks   170
Of summer, autumn, winter, and of spring.
But this endured not, his good humor soon
Became a weight in which no pleasure was,
And poverty brought on a petted mood
And a sore temper. Day by day he drooped,   175
And he would leave his home, and to the town
Without an errand would he turn his steps,
Or wander here and there among the fields.
One while he would speak lightly of his babes
And with a cruel tongue, at other times   180
He played with them wild freaks of merriment,
And 'twas a piteous thing to see the looks
Of the poor innocent children. 'Every smile,'
Said Margaret to me here beneath these trees,
'Made my heart bleed.' "

                At this the old Man paused,   185
And looking up to those enormous elms
He said, " 'Tis now the hour of deepest noon.
At this still season of repose and peace,
This hour when all things which are not at rest
Are cheerful, while this multitude of flies   190
Fills all the air with happy melody,
Why should a tear be in an old man's eye?
Why should we thus with an untoward mind,
And in the weakness of humanity,
From natural wisdom turn our hearts away,   195
To natural comfort shut our eyes and ears,
And, feeding on disquiet, thus disturb
The calm of Nature with our restless thoughts?"

End of the First Part

Second Part

He spake with somewhat of a solemn tone,
But when he ended there was in his face   200
Such easy cheerfulness, a look so mild,
That for a little time it stole away
All recollection, and that simple tale
Passed from my mind like a forgotten sound.
A while on trivial things we held discourse,   205
To me soon tasteless. In my own despite
I thought of that poor woman as of one

Whom I had known and loved. He had rehearsed
Her homely tale with such familiar power,
With such an active countenance, an eye   210
So busy, that the things of which he spake
Seemed present, and, attention now relaxed,
There was a heartfelt chillness in my veins.
I rose, and turning from that breezy shade
Went out into the open air, and stood   215
To drink the comfort of the warmer sun.
Long time I had not stayed ere, looking round
Upon that tranquil ruin, I returned
And begged of the old man that for my sake
He would resume his story.

                    He replied,   220
"It were a wantonness, and would demand
Severe reproof, if we were men whose hearts
Could hold vain dalliance with the misery
Even of the dead, contented thence to draw
A momentary pleasure, never marked   225
By reason, barren of all future good.
But we have known that there is often found
In mournful thoughts, and always might be found,
A power to virtue friendly; were't not so
I am a dreamer among men, indeed   230
An idle dreamer. 'Tis a common tale
By moving accidents uncharactered,
A tale of silent suffering, hardly clothed
In bodily form, and to the grosser sense
But ill adapted, scarcely palpable   235
To him who does not think. But at your bidding
I will proceed.

            While thus it fared with them
To whom this cottage till that hapless year
Had been a blessed home, it was my chance
To travel in a country far remote;   240
And glad I was when, halting by yon gate
That leads from the green lane, again I saw
These lofty elm trees. Long I did not rest:
With many pleasant thoughts I cheered my way
O'er the flat common. At the door arrived,   245
I knocked, and when I entered, with the hope

Of usual greeting, Margaret looked at me
A little while, then turned her head away
Speechless, and sitting down upon a chair
Wept bitterly. I wist not what to do,   250
Or how to speak to her. Poor wretch, at last
She rose from off her seat, and then, oh Sir,
I cannot tell how she pronounced my name.
With fervent love, and with a face of grief
Unutterably helpless, and a look   255
That seemed to cling upon me, she enquired
If I had seen her husband. As she spake
A strange surprise and fear came to my heart,
Nor had I power to answer ere she told
That he had disappeared—just two months gone.   260
He left his house: two wretched days had passed,
And on the third by the first break of light,
Within her casement full in view she saw
A purse of gold. 'I trembled at the sight,'
Said Margaret, 'for I knew it was his hand   265
That placed it there. And on that very day
By one, a stranger, from my husband sent,
The tidings came that he had joined a troop
Of soldiers going to a distant land.
He left me thus. Poor Man, he had not heart   270
To take farewell of me, and he feared
That I should follow with my babes, and sink
Beneath the misery of a soldier's life.'

This tale did Margaret tell with many tears,
And when she ended I had little power   275
To give her comfort, and was glad to take
Such words of hope from her own mouth as served
To cheer us both. But long we had not talked
Ere we built up a pile of better thoughts,
And with a brighter eye she looked around,   280
As if she had been shedding tears of joy.
We parted. It was then the early spring:
I left her busy with her garden tools,
And well remember, o'er that fence she looked,
And, while I paced along the footway path,   285
Called out and sent a blessing after me,
With tender cheerfulness. and with a voice
That seemed the very sound of happy thoughts.

I roved o'er many a hill and many a dale
With this my weary load, in heat and cold,   290
Through many a wood and many an open ground,
In sunshine or in shade, in wet or fair,
Now blithe, now drooping, as it might befall;
My best companions now the driving winds
And now the 'trotting brooks' and whispering trees,   295
And now the music of my own sad steps,
With many a short-lived thought that passed between
And disappeared.

         I came this way again
Towards the wane of summer, when the wheat
Was yellow, and the soft and bladed grass   300
Sprang up afresh and o'er the hay field spread
Its tender green. When I had reached the door
I found that she was absent. In the shade,
Where we now sit, I waited her return.
Her cottage in its outward look appeared   305
As cheerful as before, in any shew
Of neatness little changed, but that I thought
The honeysuckle crowded round the door,
And from the wall hung down in heavier tufts,
And knots of worthless stonecrop started out   310
Along the window's edge, and grew like weeds
Against the lower panes. I turned aside
And strolled into her garden. It was changed.
The unprofitable bindweed spread his bells
From side to side, and with unwieldy wreaths   315
Had dragged the rose from its sustaining wall
And bent it down to earth. The border tufts,
Daisy, and thrift, and lowly camomile,
And thyme, had straggled out into the paths
Which they were used to deck.

                  Ere this an hour   320
Was wasted. Back I turned my restless steps,
And as I walked before the door it chanced
A stranger passed, and guessing whom I sought,
He said that she was used to ramble far.
The sun was sinking in the west, and now   325
I sate with sad impatience. From within
Her solitary infant cried aloud.
The spot though fair seemed very desolate,

The longer I remained more desolate;
And looking round I saw the cornerstones, 330
Till then unmarked, on either side the door
With dull red stains discolored, and stuck o'er
With tufts and hairs of wool, as if the sheep
That feed upon the commons thither came
Familiarly, and found a couching place 335
Even at her threshold.

        The house clock struck eight:
I turned and saw her distant a few steps.
Her face was pale and thin, her figure too
Was changed. As she unlocked the door she said,
'It grieves me you have waited here so long, 340
But in good truth I've wandered much of late,
And sometimes, to my shame I speak, have need
Of my best prayers to bring me back again.'
While on the board she spread our evening meal,
She told me she had lost her elder child, 345
That he for months had been a serving boy,
Apprenticed by the parish. 'I perceive
You look at me, and you have cause. Today
I have been traveling far, and many days
About the fields I wander, knowing this 350
Only, that what I seek I cannot find.
And so I waste my time: for I am changed,
And to myself,' she said, 'have done much wrong,
And to this helpless infant. I have slept
Weeping, and weeping I have waked. My tears 355
Have flowed as if my body were not such
As others are, and I could never die.
But I am now in mind and in my heart
More easy, and I hope,' she said, 'that heaven
Will give me patience to endure the things 360
Which I behold at home.'

             It would have grieved
Your very soul to see her. Sir, I feel
The story linger in my heart. I fear
'Tis long and tedious, but my spirit clings
To that poor woman. So familiarly 365
Do I perceive her manner and her look
And presence, and so deeply do I feel
Her goodness, that not seldom in my walks

A momentary trance comes over me,
And to myself I seem to muse on one   370
By sorrow laid asleep or borne away,
A human being destined to awake
To human life, or something very near
To human life, when he shall come again
For whom she suffered. Sir, it would have grieved   375
Your very soul to see her: evermore
Her eyelids drooped, her eyes were downward cast,
And when she at her table gave me food
She did not look at me. Her voice was low,
Her body was subdued. In every act   380
Pertaining to her house affairs appeared
The careless stillness which a thinking mind
Gives to an idle matter. Still she sighed,
But yet no motion of the breast was seen,
No heaving of the heart. While by the fire   385
We sate together, sighs came on my ear,
I knew not how, and hardly whence they came.
I took my staff, and when I kissed her babe
The tears stood in her eyes. I left her then
With the best hope and comfort I could give: 390
She thanked me for my will, but for my hope
It seemed she did not thank me.

                          I returned
And took my rounds along this road again
Ere on its sunny bank the primrose flower
Had chronicled the earliest day of spring.   395
I found her sad and drooping. She had learned
No tidings of her husband; if he lived,
She knew not that he lived; if he were dead,
She knew not he was dead. She seemed the same
In person or appearance, but her house   400
Bespoke a sleepy hand of negligence.
The floor was neither dry nor neat, the hearth
Was comfortless,
The windows too were dim, and her few books,
Which one upon the other heretofore   405
Had been piled up against the corner panes
In seemly order, now with straggling leaves
Lay scattered here and there, open or shut,
As they had chanced to fall. Her infant babe
Had from its mother caught the trick of grief,   410

And sighed among its playthings. Once again
I turned towards the garden gate, and saw
More plainly still that poverty and grief
Were now come nearer to her. The earth was hard,
With weeds defaced and knots of withered grass;   415
No ridges there appeared of clear black mould,
No winter greenness. Of her herbs and flowers
It seemed the better part were gnawed away
Or trampled on the earth. A chain of straw,
Which had been twisted round the tender stem   420
Of a young apple tree, lay at its root;
The bark was nibbled round by truant sheep.
Margaret stood near, her infant in her arms,
And, seeing that my eye was on the tree,
She said, 'I fear it will be dead and gone   425
Ere Robert come again.'

               Towards the house
Together we returned, and she inquired
If I had any hope. But for her Babe,
And for her little friendless Boy, she said,
She had no wish to live—that she must die   430
Of sorrow. Yet I saw the idle loom
Still in its place. His Sunday garments hung
Upon the selfsame nail, his very staff
Stood undisturbed behind the door. And when
I passed this way beaten by Autumn winds,   435
She told me that her little babe was dead,
And she was left alone. That very time,
I yet remember, through the miry lane
She walked with me a mile, when the bare trees
Trickled with foggy damps, and in such sort   440
That any heart had ached to hear her, begged
That wheresoe'r I went I still would ask
For him whom she had lost. We parted then,
Our final parting; for from that time forth
Did many seasons pass ere I returned   445
Into this tract again.

               Five tedious years
She lingered in unquiet widowhood,
A wife and widow. Needs must it have been
A sore heart-wasting. I have heard, my friend,
That in that broken arbor she would sit   450

The idle length of half a sabbath day;
There, where you see the toadstool's lazy head;
And when a dog passed by she still would quit
The shade and look abroad. On this old Bench
For hours she sate, and evermore her eye   455
Was busy in the distance, shaping things
Which made her heart beat quick. Seest thou that path?—
The green sward now has broken its gray line—
There to and fro she paced through many a day
Of the warm summer, from a belt of flax   460
That girt her waist, spinning the long-drawn thread
With backward steps. Yet ever as there passed
A man whose garments shewed the Soldier's red,
Or crippled Mendicant in Sailor's garb,
The little child who sate to turn the wheel   465
Ceased from his toil, and she, with faltering voice,
Expecting still to hear her husband's fate,
Made many a fond inquiry; and when they
Whose presence gave no comfort, were gone by,
Her heart was still more sad. And by yon gate,   470
Which bars the traveler's road, she often stood,
And when a stranger horseman came, the latch
Would lift, and in his face look wistfully,
Most happy if from aught discovered there
Of tender feelings she might dare repeat   475
The same sad question.

                    Meanwhile her poor hut
Sunk to decay; for he was gone, whose hand
At the first nippings of October frost
Closed up each chink, and with fresh bands of straw
Chequered the green-grown thatch. And so she lived   480
Through the long winter, reckless and alone,
Till this reft house, by frost, and thaw, and rain,
Was sapped; and when she slept, the nightly damps
Did chill her breast, and in the stormy day
Her tattered clothes were ruffled by the wind   485
Even at the side of her own fire. Yet still
She loved this wretched spot, nor would for worlds
Have parted hence; and still that length of road,
And this rude bench, one torturing hope endeared,
Fast rooted at her heart. And here, my friend,   490
In sickness she remained; and here she died,
Last human tenant of these ruined walls."

The old Man ceased: he saw that I was moved.
From that low bench rising instinctively,
I turned aside in weakness, nor had power   495
To thank him for the tale which he had told.
I stood, and leaning o'er the garden gate
Reviewed that Woman's sufferings; and it seemed
To comfort me while with a brother's love
I blessed her in the impotence of grief.   500
At length towards the cottage I returned
Fondly, and traced with milder interest,
That secret spirit of humanity
Which, 'mid the calm oblivious tendencies
Of nature, 'mid her plants, her weeds and flowers,   505
And silent overgrowings, still survived.
The old man seeing this resumed, and said,
"My friend, enough to sorrow have you given,
The purposes of Wisdom ask no more:
Be wise and cheerful, and no longer read   510
The forms of things with an unworthy eye.
She sleeps in the calm earth, and peace is here.
I well remember that those very plumes,
Those weeds, and the high spear grass on that wall,
By mist and silent raindrops silvered o'er,   515
As once I passed, did to my mind convey
So still an image of tranquillity,
So calm and still, and looked so beautiful
Amid the uneasy thoughts which filled my mind,
That what we feel of sorrow and despair   520
From ruin and from change, and all the grief
The passing shews of being leave behind,
Appeared an idle dream that could not live
Where meditation was. I turned away,
And walked along my road in happiness."   525

  He ceased. By this the sun declining shot
A slant and mellow radiance, which began
To fall upon us where beneath the trees
We sate on that low bench. And now we felt,
Admonished thus, the sweet hour coming on: 530
A linnet warbled from those lofty elms,
A thrush sang loud, and other melodies
At distance heard, peopled the milder air.
The old man rose and hoisted up his load.
Together casting then a farewell look   535

Upon those silent walls, we left the shade;
And, ere the stars were visible, attained
A rustic inn, our evening resting place.

The End

(c. 1799)

THE RUINED COTTAGE. 19–26. Compare the mood and attitude toward the realities of nature here with the mere idyllic fantasy of the first verse paragraph and the calm acceptance of the last. The shift from fantasy and alienation to a realistic outlook springing from relatedness is accomplished by the head-on facing of human suffering that the story of Margaret brings the speaker to. 53. [   ]: manuscript unintelligible at this point. 264. *purse of gold:* the bounty that Robert had been paid for enlisting in the militia. 311. *grew like weeds:* From this point on, follow the slow, silent growth of the weeds round the cottage. That growth is a central image in the latter part of the poem. 508. *enough to sorrow have you given:* The radical reversal of mood here suggests what it is to master grief and see human suffering against the broader background of natural process (un-mythologized).

Chapter Six

All My Pretty Ones

Anne Sexton

> All my pretty ones?
> Did you say all? O hell-kite! All?
> What! all my pretty chickens and their dam
> At one fell swoop? . . .
> I cannot but remember such things were,
> That were most precious to me.
>
> *Macbeth*

Father, this year's jinx rides us apart
where you followed our mother to her cold slumber,
a second shock boiling its stone to your heart,
leaving me here to shuffle and disencumber
you from the residence you could not afford: 5
a gold key, your half of a woollen mill,
twenty suits from Dunne's, an English Ford,
the love and legal verbiage of another will,
boxes of pictures of people I do not know.
I touch their cardboard faces. They must go.   10

But the eyes, as thick as wood in this album,
hold me. I stop here, where a small boy
waits in a ruffled dress for someone to come . . .
for this soldier who holds his bugle like a toy
or for this velvet lady who cannot smile.   15
Is this your father's father, this commodore
in a mailman suit? My father, time meanwhile
has made it unimportant who you are looking for.
I'll never know what these faces are all about.
I lock them into their book and throw them out.   20

This is the yellow scrapbook that you began
the year I was born; as crackling now and wrinkly
as tobacco leaves: clippings where Hoover outran
the Democrats, wiggling his dry finger at me

and Prohibition; news where the *Hindenburg* went   25
down and recent years where you went flush
on war. This year, solvent but sick, you meant
to marry that pretty widow in a one-month rush.
But before you had that second chance, I cried
on your fat shoulder. Three days later you died.   30

These are the snapshots of marriage, stopped in places.
Side by side at the rail toward Nassau now;
here, with the winner's cup at the speedboat races,
here, in tails at the Cotillion, you take a bow,
here, by our kennel of dogs with their pink eyes,   35
running like show-bred pigs in their chain-link pen;
here, at the horseshow where my sister wins a prize;
and here, standing like a duke among groups of men.
Now I fold you down, my drunkard, my navigator,
my first lost keeper, to love or look at later.   40

I hold a five-year diary that my mother kept
for three years, telling all she does not say
of your alcoholic tendency. You overslept,
she writes. My God, father, each Christmas Day
with your blood, will I drink down your glass   45
of wine? The diary of your hurly-burly years
goes to my shelf to wait for my age to pass.
Only in this hoarded span will love persevere.
Whether you are pretty or not, I outlive you,
bend down my strange face to yours and forgive you.   50

(1962)

ALL MY PRETTY ONES.   *Macbeth:* Macduff's lament on learning that Macbeth
has had his wife and children murdered. 24. *Democrats:* in the presidential
election of 1928. 25. *Hindenburg:* The German zeppelin exploded at Lake-
ville, N.J., in 1936. 32. *Nassau:* in the Bahamas.

Legend

Frederick Morgan

Lonesome on the cliffside
lonesome on the prairie
twilight to twilight the
ageless American rides

long prick tucked into   5
sweat-shiny britches
between his thighs the on-
ward undulations of the horse

past the flat-top mesa
where a last saurian lurks   10
past the claptrap vistas
of dead movie sets

to where an ancient judgment
waits in the salt canyon
unlinked from all the past   15
which somehow passed him by

(1977)

LEGEND.   10. *saurian:* a kind of lizard.

Pitcher

Robert Francis

His art is eccentricity, his aim
How not to hit the mark he seems to aim at,

His passion how to avoid the obvious,
His technique how to vary the avoidance.

The others throw to be comprehended. He   5
Throws to be a moment misunderstood.

Yet not too much. Not errant, arrant, wild,
But every seeming aberration willed.

Not to, yet still, still to communicate
Making the batter understand too late.   10

(1960)

in Just-

e. e. cummings

in Just-
spring   when the world is mud-
luscious the little
lame balloonman

whistles   far   and wee   5

and eddieandbill come
running from marbles and
piracies and it's
spring

when the world is puddle-wonderful   10

the queer
old balloonman whistles
far   and   wee
and bettyandisbel come dancing

from hop-scotch and jump-rope and   15

it's
spring
and
      the

            goat-footed   20
balloonMan   whistles
far
and
wee

                                        (1923)

To a Poor Old Woman

W. C. Williams

munching a plum on
the street a paper bag
of them in her hand

They taste good to her
They taste good   5
to her. They taste
good to her

You can see it by
the way she gives herself
to the one half   10
sucked out in her hand

Comforted
a solace of ripe plums
seeming to fill the air
They taste good to her   15

(1935)

Composed upon
Westminster Bridge,
September 3, 1802

William Wordsworth

Earth has not anything to show more fair:
Dull would he be of soul who could pass by
A sight so touching in its majesty;
This City now doth, like a garment, wear
The beauty of the morning; silent, bare,   5
Ships, towers, domes, theaters, and temples lie
Open unto the fields, and to the sky;
All bright and glittering in the smokeless air.
Never did sun more beautifully steep
In his first splendor, valley, rock, or hill;   10
Ne'er saw I, never felt, a calm so deep!
The river glideth at his own sweet will:
Dear God! the very houses seem asleep;
And all that mighty heart is lying still!

(1807)

from **The Lotos-Eaters**

Alfred, Lord Tennyson

"Courage!" he said, and pointed toward the land,
"This mounting wave will roll us shoreward soon."
In the afternoon they came unto a land
In which it seemèd always afternoon.
All round the coast the languid air did swoon,   5
Breathing like one that hath a weary dream.
Full-faced above the valley stood the moon;
And, like a downward smoke, the slender stream
Along the cliff to fall and pause and fall did seem.

A land of streams! some, like a downward smoke,   10
Slow-dropping veils of thinnest lawn, did go;
And some through wavering lights and shadows broke,
Rolling a slumbrous sheet of foam below.
They saw the gleaming river seaward flow
From the inner land; far off, three mountaintops,   15
Three silent pinnacles of aged snow,
Stood sunset-flushed; and, dewed with showery drops,
Up-clomb the shadowy pine above the woven copse.

The charmèd sunset lingered low adown
In the red West; through mountain clefts the dale   20
Was seen far inland, and the yellow down
Bordered with palm, and many a winding vale
And meadow, set with slender galingale;
A land where all things always seemed the same!
And round about the keel with faces pale,   25
Dark faces pale against that rosy flame,
The mild-eyed melancholy Lotos-eaters came.

Branches they bore of that enchanted stem,
Laden with flower and fruit, whereof they gave
To each, but whoso did receive of them   30
And taste, to him the gushing of the wave
Far far away did seem to mourn and rave
On alien shores; and if his fellow spake,
His voice was thin, as voices from the grave;

And deep-asleep he seemed, yet all awake,   35
And music in his ears his beating heart did make.
They sat them down upon the yellow sand,
Between the sun and moon upon the shore;
And sweet it was to dream of Fatherland,
Of child, and wife, and slave; but evermore   40
Most weary seemed the sea, weary the oar,
Weary the wandering fields of barren foam.
Then some one said, "We will return no more";
And all at once they sang, "Our island home
Is far beyond the wave; we will no longer roam."   45

(1832)

from THE LOTOS-EATERS. The poem is based on an episode in the *Odyssey*
(Book IX, 82–97): "On the tenth day we set foot on the land of the lotos-
eaters.... I [Ulysses] sent forth certain of my company... [who]mixed with
the men of the lotos-eaters, who... gave them of the lotos to taste. Now
whoever of them did eat of the honey-sweet fruit of the lotos had no more
wish to... come back, but there he chose to abide... forgetful of his home-
ward way." 1. *he:* Ulysses. 3. *land:* The repetition of "land" is deliberate.
Tennyson said that this "no rhyme" is "lazier" in its effect. The same
reasoning applies to "adown/down" (lines 19, 21). 11. *lawn:* a sheer cotton
fabric. 21 *down:* an open plain. 23. *galingale:* a reed-like plant. 44. *island
home:* Ithaca, to return to which required struggle and travail.

Kubla Khan

Samuel Taylor Coleridge

In Xanadu did Kubla Khan
A stately pleasure dome decree:
Where Alph, the sacred river, ran
Through caverns measureless to man
    Down to a sunless sea.   5
So twice five miles of fertile ground
With walls and towers were girdled round:
And there were gardens bright with sinuous rills,
Where blossomed many an incense-bearing tree;
And here were forests ancient as the hills,   10
Enfolding sunny spots of greenery.

But oh! that deep romantic chasm which slanted
Down the green hill athwart a cedarn cover!
A savage place! as holy and enchanted
As e'er beneath a waning moon was haunted   15
By woman wailing for her demon lover!
And from this chasm, with ceaseless turmoil seething,
As if this earth in fast thick pants were breathing,
A mighty fountain momently was forced:
Amid whose swift half-intermitted burst   20
Huge fragments vaulted like rebounding hail,
Or chaffy grain beneath the thresher's flail:
And 'mid these dancing rocks at once and ever
It flung up momently the sacred river.
Five miles meandering with a mazy motion   25
Through wood and dale the sacred river ran,
Then reached the caverns measureless to man,
And sank in tumult to a lifeless ocean:
And 'mid this tumult Kubla heard from far
Ancestral voices prophesying war!   30
   The shadow of the dome of pleasure
   Floated midway on the waves;
   Where was heard the mingled measure
   From the fountain and the caves.
It was a miracle of rare device,   35
A sunny pleasure dome with caves of ice!

   A damsel with a dulcimer
   In a vision once I saw:
   It was an Abyssinian maid,
   And on her dulcimer she played,   40
   Singing of Mount Abora.
   Could I revive within me
   Her symphony and song,
   To such a deep delight 'twould win me,
That with music loud and long,   45
I would build that dome in air,
That sunny dome! those caves of ice!
And all who heard should see them there,
And all should cry, Beware! Beware!
His flashing eyes, his floating hair!   50
Weave a circle round him thrice,

And close your eyes with holy dread,
For he on honey-dew hath fed,
And drunk the milk of Paradise.

(c. 1797–98)

KUBLA KHAN.   The first ruler of the Mongol dynasty in 13th-century China.
But the poem's incidents, topography, and place-names are all fictitious, as
its subtitle suggests: "A Vision in a Dream." 37. *dulcimer:* a harplike in-
strument. 51. *Weave a circle round him thrice:* a ritual to guard the inspired
poet from intrusion. 54. *Paradise:* Lines 50ff. ring of Plato's description of
inspired poets (*Ion*): "like Bacchic maidens who draw milk and honey from
the rivers when they are under the influence of Dionysus but not when
they are in their right minds."

Break, Break, Break

Alfred, Lord Tennyson

Break, break, break,
 On thy cold gray stones, O Sea!
And I would that my tongue could utter
 The thoughts that arise in me.

O, well for the fisherman's boy,   5
 That he shouts with his sister at play!
O, well for the sailor lad,
 That he sings in his boat on the bay!

And the stately ships go on
 To their haven under the hill;   10
But O for the touch of a vanished hand,
 And the sound of a voice that is still!

Break, break, break,
 At the foot of thy crags, O Sea!
But the tender grace of a day that is dead   15
 Will never come back to me.

(1842)

Mariana

Alfred, Lord Tennyson

"Mariana in the moated grange."
Measure for Measure

With blackest moss the flower plots
  Were thickly crusted, one and all;
The rusted nails fell from the knots
  That held the pear to the gable wall.
The broken sheds looked sad and strange: 5
  Unlifted was the clinking latch;
  Weeded and worn the ancient thatch
Upon the lonely moated grange.
    She only said, "My life is dreary,
      He cometh not," she said;   10
    She said, "I am aweary, aweary,
      I would that I were dead!"

Her tears fell with the dews at even;
  Her tears fell ere the dews were dried;
She could not look on the sweet heaven,   15
  Either at morn or eventide.
After the flitting of the bats,
  When thickest dark did trance the sky,
  She drew her casement curtain by,
And glanced athwart the glooming flats.   20
    She only said, "The night is dreary,
      He cometh not," she said;
    She said, "I am aweary, aweary,
      I would that I were dead!"

Upon the middle of the night,   25
  Waking she heard the nightfowl crow;
The cock sung out an hour ere light;
  From the dark fen the oxen's low
Came to her; without hope of change,
  In sleep she seemed to walk forlorn,   30
  Till cold winds woke the gray-eyed morn
About the lonely moated grange.
    She only said, "The day is dreary,
      He cometh not," she said;
    She said, "I am aweary, aweary,   35
      I would that I were dead!"

About a stonecast from the wall
    A sluice with blackened waters slept,
And o'er it many, round and small,
    The clustered marish-mosses crept.   40
Hard by a poplar shook alway,
    All silver-green with gnarled bark:
    For leagues no other tree did mark
The level waste, the rounding gray.
      She only said, "My life is dreary,   45
        He cometh not," she said;
      She said, "I am aweary, aweary,
        I would that I were dead!"

And ever when the moon was low,
    And the shrill winds were up and away,   50
In the white curtain, to and fro,
    She saw the gusty shadow sway.
But when the moon was very low,
    And wild winds bound within their cell,
    The shadow of the poplar fell   55
Upon her bed, across her brow.
      She only said, "The night is dreary,
        He cometh not," she said;
      She said, "I am aweary, aweary,
        I would that I were dead!"   60

All day within the dreamy house,
    The doors upon their hinges creaked;
The blue fly sung in the pane; the mouse
    Behind the moldering wainscot shrieked,
Or from the crevice peered about.   65
    Old faces glimmered through the doors,
    Old footsteps trod the upper floors,
Old voices called her from without.
      She only said, "My life is dreary,
        He cometh not," she said;   70
      She said, "I am aweary, aweary,
        I would that I were dead!"

The sparrow's chirrup on the roof,
    The slow clock ticking, and the sound
Which to the wooing wind aloof   75
    The poplar made, did all confound

Her sense; but most she loathed the hour
When the thick-moted sunbeam lay
Athwart the chambers, and the day
Was sloping toward his western bower.   80
Then, said she, "I am very dreary,
He will not come," she said;
She wept, "I am aweary, aweary,
Oh God, that I were dead!"

(1830)

MARIANA. *Mariana:* In Shakespeare's *Measure for Measure,* Mariana, who
has been deserted by her lover, waits for him in a grange (an outlying
farmhouse). 18. *trance:* enrapture, traverse. 40. *marish-mosses:* "The little
marsh-moss lumps that float on the surface of the water"—Tennyson's
note. 54. *cell:* In Virgil's *Aeneid* (I, lines 50–59), Aeolus, god of the winds,
keeps the winds imprisoned in a cave.

from **The Leaden Echo
and the Golden Echo**

G. M. Hopkins

The Leaden Echo

How to kéep—is there ány any, is there none such, nowhere known
    some, bow or brooch or braid or brace, láce, latch or catch or key
    to keep
Back beauty, keep it, beauty, beauty, beauty, . . . from vanishing
    away?
Ó is there no frowning of these wrinkles, rankèd wrinkles deep,
Dówn? no waving off of these most mournful messengers, still mes-
    sengers, sad and stealing messengers of grey?—
No there's none, there's none, O no there's none,   5
Nor can you long be, what you now are, called fair,
Do what you may do, what, do what you may,
And wisdom is early to despair:
Be beginning; since, no, nothing can be done
To keep at bay   10
Age and age's evils, hoar hair,
Ruck and wrinkle, drooping, dying, death's worst, winding sheets,
    tombs and worms and tumbling to decay;
So be beginning, be beginning to despair.

O there's none; no no no there's none:
Be beginning to despair, to despair,   15
Despair, despair, despair, despair.

(c. 1882)

from THE LEADEN ECHO AND THE GOLDEN ECHO.   4. *Dówn:* i.e., "frowning . . . /
Dówn."

The Flaw in Paganism

Dorothy Parker

Drink and dance and laugh and lie,
   Love, the reeling midnight through,
For tomorrow we shall die!
   (But, alas, we never do.)

(1933)

Unfortunate Coincidence

Dorothy Parker

By the time you swear you're his,
   Shivering and sighing,
And he vows his passion is
   Infinite, undying—
Lady, make a note of this: 5
   One of you is lying.

(1926)

The Lover's Song

W. B. Yeats

Bird sighs for the air,
Thought for I know not where,
For the womb the seed sighs.
Now sinks the same rest
On mind, on nest,   5
On straining thighs.

(1936)

Song

John Donne

Go and catch a falling star,
   Get with child a mandrake root,
Tell me where all past years are,
   Or who cleft the Devil's foot,
Teach me to hear mermaids singing,   5
Or to keep off envy's stinging,
       And find
       What wind
Serves to advance an honest mind.

If thou beest born to strange sights,   10
   Things invisible to see,
Ride ten thousand days and nights,
   Till age snow white hairs on thee.
Thou, when thou return'st, wilt tell me
All strange wonders that befell thee,   15
       And swear
       Nowhere
Lives a woman true, and fair.

If thou find'st one, let me know,
   Such a pilgrimage were sweet;   20
Yet do not, I would not go,
   Though at next door we might meet;
Though she were true when you met her,
And last till you write your letter,
       Yet she   25
       Will be
False, ere I come, to two, or three.

                         (1633)

SONG. 2. *mandrake root:* a large, forked root, which, because it resembles the human body, was reputed (in folk legend) to possess human attributes and to be an aphrodisiac. Donne invokes the legend only to deny it: to get with child by a mandrake root or to get one with child would be as impossible as to catch a falling star. 5. *mermaids singing:* possibly an allusion to the sirens, whose song only Odysseus heard and survived.

A Lullaby

Randall Jarrell

For wars his life and half a world away
The soldier sells his family and days.
He learns to fight for freedom and the State;
He sleeps with seven men within six feet.

He picks up matches and he cleans out plates;   5
Is lied to like a child, cursed like a beast.
They crop his head, his dog tags ring like sheep
As his stiff limbs shift wearily to sleep.

Recalled in dreams or letters, else forgot,
His life is smothered like a grave, with dirt;   10
And his dull torment mottles like a fly's
The lying amber of the histories.

(1945)

The Mermaid

W. B. Yeats

A mermaid found a swimming lad,
Picked him for her own,
Pressed his body to her body,
Laughed; and plunging down
Forgot in cruel happiness   5
That even lovers drown.

(1928)

The Garden of Love

William Blake

I went to the Garden of Love,
And saw what I never had seen:
A Chapel was built in the midst,
Where I used to play on the green.

And the gates of this Chapel were shut,   5
And "Thou shalt not" writ over the door;
So I turn'd to the Garden of Love,
That so many sweet flowers bore,

And I saw it was filled with graves,
And tomb-stones where flowers should be: 10
And Priests in black gowns were walking their rounds,
And binding with briars my joys & desires.

(1794)

Chapter Seven

Sir Patrick Spens

Anonymous

The king sits in Dumferline town,
    Drinking the blude-reid° wine: *blood-red*
"O whar will I get a guid sailor
    To sail this ship of mine?"

Up and spak an eldern° knicht,   *ancient*   5
    Sat at the king's richt knee:
"Sir Patrick Spens is the best sailor
    That sails upon the sea."

The king has written a braid° letter   *broad*
    And signed it wi' his hand,   10
And sent it to Sir Patrick Spens,
    Was walking on the sand.

The first line that Sir Patrick read,
    A loud lauch° lauched he;   *laugh*
The next line that Sir Patrick read,   15
    The tear blinded his ee.°   *eye*

"O wha° is this has done this deed,   *who*
    This ill deed done to me,
To send me out this time o' the year,
    To sail upon the sea?   20

"Make haste, make haste, my mirry men all,
    Our guid ship sails the morn."
"O say na° sae,° my master dear,   *not / so*
    For I fear a deadly storm.

"Late late yestre'en I saw the new moon   25
    Wi' the auld° moon in her arm,   *old*
And I fear, I fear, my dear master,
    That we will come to harm."

O our Scots nobles were richt laith° *loath*
 To weet° their cork-heeled shoon,° *wet / shoes* 30
But lang owre° a' the play were played *ere*
 Their hats they swam aboon.° *above*

O lang, lang may their ladies sit,
 Wi' their fans into their hand,
Or e're they see Sir Patrick Spens 35
 Come sailing to the land.

O lang, lang may the ladies stand,
 Wi' their gold kembs° in their hair, *combs*
Waiting for their ain° dear lords, *own*
 For they'll see thame na mair.° *more* 40

Half o'er, half o'er to Aberdour
 It's fifty fadom° deep, *fathoms*
And there lies guid Sir Patrick Spens,
 Wi' the Scots lords at his feet.

         (15th cen.)

SIR PATRICK SPENS. 41. *half o'er:* halfway over.

from **An Essay on Criticism**

Alexander Pope

Part II

 Of all the causes which conspire to blind
Man's erring judgment, and misguide the mind,
What the weak head with strongest bias rules,
Is pride, the never-failing vice of fools.
Whatever Nature has in worth denied, 205
She gives in large recruits of needful pride;
For as in bodies, thus in souls, we find
What wants in blood and spirits swelled with wind:
Pride, where wit fails, steps in to our defense,
And fills up all the mighty void of sense. 210
If once right reason drives that cloud away,
Truth breaks upon us with resistless day.
Trust not yourself: but your defects to know,

Make use of every friend—and every foe.
   A little learning is a dangerous thing;   215
Drink deep, or taste not the Pierian spring.
There shallow draughts intoxicate the brain,
And drinking largely sobers us again.
Fired at first sight with what the Muse imparts,
In fearless youth we tempt the heights of arts,   220
While from the bounded level of our mind
Short views we take, nor see the lengths behind;
But more advanced, behold with strange surprise
New distant scenes of endless science rise!
So pleased at first the towering Alps we try,   225
Mount o'er the vales, and seem to tread the sky,
The eternal snows appear already past,
And the first clouds and mountains seem the last;
But, those attained, we tremble to survey
The growing labors of the lengthened way,   230
The increasing prospect tires our wandering eyes,
Hills peep o'er hills, and Alps on Alps arise!

   A perfect judge will read each work of wit
With the same spirit that its author writ:
Survey the whole, nor seek slight faults to find   235
Where Nature moves, and rapture warms the mind;
Nor lose, for that malignant dull delight,
The generous pleasure to be charmed with wit.
But in such lays as neither ebb nor flow,
Correctly cold, and regularly low,   240
That, shunning faults, one quiet tenor keep,
We cannot blame indeed—but we may sleep.
In wit, as nature, what affects our hearts
Is not the exactness of peculiar parts;
'Tis not a lip, or eye, we beauty call,   245
But the joint force and full result of all.
Thus when we view some well-proportioned dome
(The world's just wonder, and even thine, O Rome!),
No single parts unequally surprise,
All comes united to the admiring eyes: 250
No monstrous height, or breadth, or length appear;
The whole at once is bold and regular.
    . . .
   True wit is Nature to advantage dressed,
What oft was thought, but ne'er so well expressed;
Something whose truth convinced at sight we find,

That gives us back the image of our mind.   300
As shades more sweetly recommend the light,
So modest plainness sets off sprightly wit;
For works may have more wit than does them good,
As bodies perish through excess of blood.
　　Others for language all their care express,   305
And value books, as women men, for dress.
Their praise is still—the style is excellent;
The sense they humbly take upon contént.
Words are like leaves; and where they most abound,
Much fruit of sense beneath is rarely found.   310
False eloquence, like the prismatic glass,
Its gaudy colors spreads on every place;
The face of Nature we no more survey,
All glares alike, without distinction gay.
But true expression, like the unchanging sun,   ⎱   315
Clears and improves whate'er it shines upon;   ⎬
It gilds all objects, but it alters none.   ⎰
Expression is the dress of thought, and still
Appears more decent as more suitable.
A vile conceit in pompous words expressed   320
Is like a clown in regal purple dressed:
For different styles with different subjects sort,
As several garbs with country, town, and court.
Some by old words to fame have made pretense,
Ancients in phrase, mere moderns in their sense.   325
Such labored nothings, in so strange a style,
Amaze the unlearn'd, and make the learned smile;
Unlucky as Fungoso in the play,   ⎱
These sparks with awkward vanity display   ⎬
What the fine gentleman wore yesterday;   ⎰   330
And but so mimic ancient wits at best,
As apes our grandsires in their doublets dressed.
In words as fashions the same rule will hold,
Alike fantastic if too new or old:
Be not the first by whom the new are tried,   335
Nor yet the last to lay the old aside.
　　But most by numbers judge a poet's song,
And smooth or rough with them is right or wrong.
In the bright Muse though thousand charms conspire,
Her voice is all these tuneful fools admire,   340
Who haunt Parnassus but to please their ear,   ⎱
Not mend their minds; as some to church repair, ⎬
Not for the doctrine, but the music there.   ⎰

These equal syllables alone require,
Though oft the ear the open vowels tire, 345
While expletives their feeble aid do join,
And ten low words oft creep in one dull line:
While they ring round the same unvaried chimes,
With sure returns of still expected rhymes;
Where'er you find "the cooling western breeze," 350
In the next line, it "whispers through the trees";
If crystal streams "with pleasing murmurs creep,"
The reader's threatened (not in vain) with "sleep";
Then, at the last and only couplet fraught
With some unmeaning thing they call a thought, 355
A needless Alexandrine ends the song
That, like a wounded snake, drags its slow length along.
Leave such to tune their own dull rhymes, and know
What's roundly smooth or languishingly slow;
And praise the easy vigor of a line 360
Where Denham's strength and Waller's sweetness join.
True ease in writing comes from art, not chance,
As those move easiest who have learned to dance.
'Tis not enough no harshness gives offense,
The sound must seem an echo to the sense. 365
Soft is the strain when Zephyr gently blows,
And the smooth stream in smoother numbers flows;
But when loud surges lash the sounding shore,
The hoarse, rough verse should like the torrent roar.
When Ajax strives some rock's vast weight to throw, 370
The line too labors, and the words move slow;
Not so when swift Camilla scours the plain,
Flies o'er the unbending corn, and skims along the main.
Hear how Timotheus' varied lays surprise,
And bid alternate passions fall and rise! 375
While at each change the son of Libyan Jove
Now burns with glory, and then melts with love;
Now his fierce eyes with sparkling fury glow,
Now sighs steal out, and tears begin to flow:
Persians and Greeks like turns of nature found 380
And the world's victor stood subdued by sound!
The power of music all our hearts allow,
And what Timotheus was is Dryden now.
    Avoid extremes; and shun the fault of such
Who still are pleased too little or too much. 385
At every trifle scorn to take offense:
That always shows great pride, or little sense.

Those heads, as stomachs, are not sure the best,
Which nauseate all, and nothing can digest.
Yet let not each gay turn thy rapture move; 390
For fools admire, but men of sense approve:
As things seem large which we through mists descry,
Dullness is ever apt to magnify.

(1711)

from AN ESSAY ON CRITICISM, Part II. In this poem Pope lays down the
standards of critical judgment of the period, standards rather different from
our own (e.g., see line 213). 205. *Nature:* To Pope, "Nature" meant more
or less what we mean by "human nature," the peculiar characteristic of
which (to the 18th-century mind) being reason, viewed as a kind of univer-
sal common sense. 206. *recruits:* supplies—but catch the military overtone
(i.e., the troops of Pride are legion). 216. *Pierian spring:* a spring sacred to
the Muses in Pieria on Mt. Olympus. 220. *tempt:* attempt, as one attempts
(to scale) a mountain—e.g., Mt. Parnassus, home of the Muses. 248. *Rome:*
the dome of St. Peter's, designed by Michelangelo. 304. *excess of blood:*
according to medical theory of the day. Thus leeching (the application of
leeches) was often the prescribed treatment for illness. 308. *contént:* un-
thinking acquiescence. 312. *colors . . . place:* a reference to Newton's *Optics,*
which deals with the prism and its breaking of white light into its compo-
nent colors. 321. *clown:* country bumpkin, boor. 328. *Fungoso:* an unlucky
character in Ben Jonson's comedy *Every Man out of His Humor* (1599).
337. *numbers:* metrics, versification (so "most" people judge). 345. *open
vowels tire:* Notice how throughout this passage Pope makes his own met-
rics and diction illustrate the very faults that he's naming. 346. *expletives:*
i.e., words used merely for the sake of filling out the given metrical pattern.
356. *Alexandrine:* a line of verse containing six iambic feet (see the next
line for an example). 361. *Denham* and *Waller:* Sir John Denham (1615–69)
and Edmund Waller (1606–87), poets whom John Dryden (1631–1700) held
to have been the prime shapers of the heroic couplet. Pope here alludes to
Dryden's praise of the two, Dryden himself having been one of the great
practitioners of the form. 374. *Timotheus:* Pope refers to the poet-musician
in Dryden's poem "Alexander's Feast," the story of which Pope summarizes
in the following lines. Timotheus here stands also for Dryden himself. 376.
son of Libyan Jove: Alexander the Great. 380. *turns of nature:* successive
changes of emotion. 391. *admire:* i.e., "Fools" overpraise.

Ode to the West Wind

Percy Bysshe Shelley

1

O wild West Wind, thou breath of Autumn's being,
Thou, from whose unseen presence the leaves dead
Are driven, like ghosts from an enchanter fleeing,

Yellow, and black, and pale, and hectic red,   5
Pestilence-stricken multitudes: O thou,
Who chariotest to their dark wintry bed

The wingèd seeds, where they lie cold and low,
Each like a corpse within its grave, until
Thine azure sister of the Spring shall blow

Her clarion o'er the dreaming earth, and fill   10
(Driving sweet buds like flocks to feed in air)
With living hues and odors plain and hill:

Wild Spirit, which art moving everywhere;
Destroyer and preserver; hear, oh, hear!

2

Thou on whose stream, mid the steep sky's commotion,   15
Loose clouds like earth's decaying leaves are shed,
Shook from the tangled boughs of Heaven and Ocean,

Angels of rain and lightning: there are spread
On the blue surface of thine aëry surge,
Like the bright hair uplifted from the head   20

Of some fierce Maenad, even from the dim verge
Of the horizon to the zenith's height,
The locks of the approaching storm. Thou dirge

Of the dying year, to which this closing night
Will be the dome of a vast sepulcher,   25
Vaulted with all thy congregated might

Of vapors, from whose solid atmosphere
Black rain, and fire, and hail will burst: oh, hear!

3

Thou who didst waken from his summer dreams
The blue Mediterranean, where he lay,   30
Lulled by the coil of his crystalline streams,

Beside a pumice isle in Baiae's bay,
And saw in sleep old palaces and towers
Quivering within the wave's intenser day,

All overgrown with azure moss and flowers   35
So sweet, the sense faints picturing them! Thou
For whose path the Atlantic's level powers

Cleave themselves into chasms, while far below
The sea-blooms and the oozy woods which wear
The sapless foliage of the ocean, know   40

Thy voice, and suddenly grow gray with fear,
And tremble and despoil themselves: oh, hear!

4

If I were a dead leaf thou mightest bear;
If I were a swift cloud to fly with thee;
A wave to pant beneath thy power, and share   45

The impulse of thy strength, only less free
Than thou, O uncontrollable! If even
I were as in my boyhood, and could be

The comrade of thy wanderings over Heaven,
As then, when to outstrip thy skyey speed   50
Scarce seem a vision; I would ne'er have striven

As thus with thee in prayer in my sore need.
Oh, lift me as a wave, a leaf, a cloud!
I fall upon the thorns of life! I bleed!

A heavy weight of hours has chained and bowed   55
One too like thee: tameless, and swift, and proud.

5

Make me thy lyre, even as the forest is:
What if my leaves are falling like its own!
The tumult of thy mighty harmonies

Will take from both a deep, autumnal tone,   60
Sweet though in sadness. Be thou, Spirit fierce,
My spirit! Be thou me, impetuous one!

Drive my dead thoughts over the universe
Like withered leaves to quicken a new birth!
And, by the incantation of this verse,   65

Scatter, as from an unextinguished hearth
Ashes and sparks, my words among mankind!
Be through my lips to unawakened earth

The trumpet of a prophecy! O Wind,
If Winter comes, can Spring be far behind?   70

(1820)

ODE TO THE WEST WIND. *Wind:* As in many romantic poems, the wind here serves to inspire (which means, etymologically, "to breathe into") the poet and to rouse him from apathy to spiritual excitement. 10. *clarion:* trumpet call. 18. *Angels:* from the Greek meaning "divine messengers." 21. *Maenad:* a frenzied worshiper of Dionysus, a vegetation deity who dies each fall to be resurrected in the spring. 32. *Baiae's bay:* near Naples. Italy. 41–42. "The vegetation at the bottom of the sea . . . sympathizes with that of the land in the change of seasons"—Shelley's note. 57. *lyre:* i.e., Eolian lyre, or wind harp (a musical device fashioned to respond to the wind). 69. *prophecy:* a reference to line 10 and to the trumpet call of the apocalypse.

The Eve of St. Agnes

John Keats

1

St. Agnes' Eve—Ah, bitter chill it was!
The owl, for all his feathers, was a-cold;
The hare limped trembling through the frozen grass,
And silent was the flock in woolly fold:
Numb were the Beadsman's fingers, while he told   5
His rosary, and while his frosted breath,
Like pious incense from a censer old,
Seemed taking flight for heaven, without a death,
Past the sweet Virgin's picture, while his prayer he saith.

2

His prayer he saith, this patient, holy man;   10
Then takes his lamp, and riseth from his knees,
And back returneth, meager, barefoot, wan,
Along the chapel aisle by slow degrees:
The sculptured dead, on each side, seem to freeze,
Imprisoned in black, purgatorial rails: 15
Knights, ladies, praying in dumb orat'ries,
He passeth by; and his weak spirit fails
To think how they may ache in icy hoods and mails.

3

Northward he turneth through a little door,
And scarce three steps, ere Music's golden tongue   20
Flattered to tears this aged man and poor;
But no—already had his deathbell rung:
The joys of all his life were said and sung:
His was harsh penance on St. Agnes' Eve:
Another way he went, and soon among   25
Rough ashes sat he for his soul's reprieve,
And all night kept awake, for sinner's sake to grieve.

4

That ancient Beadsman heard the prelude soft;
And so it chanced, for many a door was wide,
From hurry to and fro. Soon, up aloft,   30
The silver, snarling trumpets 'gan to chide:
The level chambers, ready with their pride,
Were glowing to receive a thousand guests:
The carvèd angels, ever eager-eyed,
Stared, where upon their heads the cornice rests,   35
With hair blown back, and wings put cross-wise on their breasts.

5

At length burst in the argent revelry,
With plume, tiara, and all rich array,
Numerous as shadows haunting fairily
The brain, new stuffed, in youth, with triumphs gay   40
Of old romance. These let us wish away,
And turn, sole-thoughted, to one Lady there,
Whose heart had brooded, all that wintry day,
On love, and winged St. Agnes' saintly care,
As she had heard old dames full many times declare.   45

6

They told her how, upon St. Agnes' Eve,
Young virgins might have visions of delight,
And soft adorings from their loves receive
Upon the honeyed middle of the night,
If ceremonies due they did aright;   50
As, supperless to bed they must retire,
And couch supine their beauties, lily white;
Nor look behind, nor sideways, but require
Of Heaven with upward eyes for all that they desire.

7

Full of this whim was thoughtful Madeline: 55
The music, yearning like a God in pain,
She scarcely heard: her maiden eyes divine,
Fixed on the floor, saw many a sweeping train
Pass by—she heeded not at all: in vain
Came many a tiptoe, amorous cavalier,   60
And back retired; not cooled by high disdain;
But she saw not: her heart was otherwhere:
She sighed for Agnes' dreams, the sweetest of the year.

8

She danced along with vague, regardless eyes,
Anxious her lips, her breathing quick and short: 65
The hallowed hour was near at hand: she sighs
Amid the timbrels, and the thronged resort
Of whisperers in anger, or in sport;
'Mid looks of love, defiance, hate, and scorn,
Hoodwinked with faery fancy; all amort,   70
Save to St. Agnes and her lambs unshorn,
And all the bliss to be before tomorrow morn.

9

So, purposing each moment to retire,
She lingered still. Meantime, across the moors,
Had come young Porphyro, with heart on fire   75
For Madeline. Beside the portal doors,
Buttressed from moonlight, stands he, and implores
All saints to give him sight of Madeline,
But for one moment in the tedious hours,
That he might gaze and worship all unseen;   80
Perchance speak, kneel, touch, kiss—in sooth such things have been.

10

He ventures in: let no buzzed whisper tell:
All eyes be muffled, or a hundred swords
Will storm his heart, Love's fev'rous citadel:
For him, those chambers held barbarian hordes,   85
Hyena foemen, and hot-blooded lords,
Whose very dogs would execrations howl
Against his lineage: not one breast affords
Him any mercy, in that mansion foul,
Save one old beldame, weak in body and in soul.   90

11

Ah, happy chance! the aged creature came,
Shuffling along with ivory-headed wand,
To where he stood, hid from the torch's flame,
Behind a broad hall-pillar, far beyond
The sound of merriment and chorus bland: 95
He startled her; but soon she knew his face,
And grasped his fingers in her palsied hand,
Saying, "Mercy, Porphyro! hie thee from this place;
They are all here tonight, the whole bloodthirsty race!

12

"Get hence! get hence! there's dwarfish Hildebrand;   100
He had a fever late, and in the fit
He cursèd thee and thine, both house and land:
Then there's that old Lord Maurice, not a whit
More tame for his gray hairs—Alas me! flit!
Flit like a ghost away."—"Ah, Gossip dear,   105
We're safe enough; here in this armchair sit,
And tell me how"—"Good Saints! not here, not here;
Follow me, child, or else these stones will be thy bier."

13

He followed through a lowly archèd way,
Brushing the cobwebs with his lofty plume,   110
And as she muttered "Well-a—well-a-day!"
He found him in a little moonlight room,
Pale, latticed, chill, and silent as a tomb.
"Now tell me where is Madeline," said he,
"O tell me, Angela, by the holy loom   115
Which none but secret sisterhood may see,
When they St. Agnes' wool are weaving piously."

14

"St. Agnes! Ah! it is St. Agnes' Eve—
Yet men will murder upon holy days:
Thou must hold water in a witch's sieve,   120
And be liege lord of all the Elves and Fays,
To venture so: it fills me with amaze
To see thee, Porphyro!—St. Agnes' Eve!
God's help! my lady fair the conjuror plays
This very night: good angels her deceive!   125
But let me laugh awhile, I've mickle° time to grieve."   *much*

15

Feebly she laugheth in the languid moon,
While Porphyro upon her face doth look,
Like puzzled urchin on an aged crone
Who keepeth closed a wondrous riddle-book,   130
As spectacled she sits in chimney nook.
But soon his eyes grew brilliant, when she told
His lady's purpose; and he scarce could brook
Tears, at the thought of those enchantments cold,
And Madeline asleep in lap of legends old.   135

16

Sudden a thought came like a full-blown rose,
Flushing his brow, and in his painèd heart
Made purple riot: then doth he propose
A stratagem, that makes the beldame start:
"A cruel man and impious thou art: 140
Sweet lady, let her pray, and sleep, and dream
Alone with her good angels, far apart
From wicked men like thee. Go, go!—I deem
Thou canst not surely be the same that thou didst seem."

17

"I will not harm her, by all saints I swear,"   145
Quoth Porphyro: "O may I ne'er find grace
When my weak voice shall whisper its last prayer,
If one of her soft ringlets I displace,
Or look with ruffian passion in her face:
Good Angela, believe me by these tears;   150
Or I will, even in a moment's space,
Awake, with horrid shout, my foemen's ears,
And beard them, though they be more fanged than wolves and
    bears."

18

"Ah! why wilt thou affright a feeble soul?
A poor, weak, palsy-stricken, churchyard thing,   155
Whose passing bell may ere the midnight toll;
Whose prayers for thee, each morn and evening,
Were never missed."—Thus plaining, doth she bring
A gentler speech from burning Porphyro;
So woeful and of such deep sorrowing,   160
That Angela gives promise she will do
Whatever he shall wish, betide her weal or woe.

19

Which was, to lead him, in close secrecy,
Even to Madeline's chamber, and there hide
Him in a closet, of such privacy   165
That he might see her beauty unespied,
And win perhaps that night a peerless bride,
While legioned faeries paced the coverlet,
And pale enchantment held her sleepy-eyed.
Never on such a night have lovers met,   170
Since Merlin paid his Demon all the monstrous debt.

20

"It shall be as thou wishest," said the Dame:
"All cates and dainties shall be storèd there
Quickly on this feast night: by the tambour frame
Her own lute thou wilt see: no time to spare,   175
For I am slow and feeble, and scarce dare
On such a catering trust my dizzy head.
Wait here, my child, with patience; kneel in prayer
The while: Ah! thou must needs the lady wed,
Or may I never leave my grave among the dead."   180

21

So saying, she hobbled off with busy fear.
The lover's endless minutes slowly passed:
The dame returned, and whispered in his ear
To follow her; with aged eyes aghast
From fright of dim espial. Safe at last,   185
Through many a dusky gallery, they gain
The maiden's chamber, silken, hushed, and chaste;
Where Porphyro took covert, pleased amain.
His poor guide hurried back with agues in her brain.

22

Her falt'ring hand upon the balustrade,   190
Old Angela was feeling for the stair,
When Madeline, St. Agnes' charmèd maid,
Rose, like a missioned spirit, unaware:
With silver taper's light, and pious care,
She turned, and down the aged gossip led   195
To a safe level matting. Now prepare,
Young Porphyro, for gazing on that bed;
She comes, she comes again, like ringdove frayed and fled.

23

Out went the taper as she hurried in;
Its little smoke, in pallid moonshine, died: 200
She closed the door, she panted, all akin
To spirits of the air, and visions wide:
No uttered syllable, or, woe betide!
But to her heart, her heart was voluble,
Paining with eloquence her balmy side;   205
As though a tongueless nightingale should swell
Her throat in vain, and die, heart-stifled, in her dell.

24

A casement high and triple-arched there was,
All garlanded with carven imag'ries
Of fruits, and flowers, and bunches of knot-grass,   210
And diamonded with panes of quaint device,
Innumerable of stains and splendid dyes,
As are the tiger moth's deep-damasked wings;
And in the midst, 'mong thousand heraldries,
And twilight saints, and dim emblazonings,   215
A shielded scutcheon blushed with blood of queens and kings.

25

Full on this casement shone the wintry moon,
And threw warm gules on Madeline's fair breast,
As down she knelt for heaven's grace and boon;
Rose-bloom fell on her hands, together pressed,   220
And on her silver cross soft amethyst,
And on her hair a glory, like a saint:
She seemed a splendid angel, newly dressed,
Save wings, for heaven—Porphyro grew faint:
She knelt, so pure a thing, so free from mortal taint.   225

26

Anon his heart revives: her vespers done,
Of all its wreathèd pearls her hair she frees;
Unclasps her warmèd jewels one by one;
Loosens her fragrant bodice; by degrees
Her rich attire creeps rustling to her knees: 230
Half-hidden, like a mermaid in sea-weed,
Pensive awhile she dreams awake, and sees,
In fancy, fair St. Agnes in her bed,
But dares not look behind, or all the charm is fled.

27

Soon, trembling in her soft and chilly nest,   235
In sort of wakeful swoon, perplexed she lay,
Until the poppied warmth of sleep oppressed
Her soothèd limbs, and soul fatigued away;
Flown, like a thought, until the morrow-day;
Blissfully havened both from joy and pain;   240
Clasped like a missal where swart Paynims pray;
Blinded alike from sunshine and from rain,
As though a rose should shut, and be a bud again.

28

Stol'n to this paradise, and so entranced,
Porphyro gazed upon her empty dress,   245
And listened to her breathing, if it chanced
To wake into a slumberous tenderness;
Which when he heard, that minute did he bless,
And breathed himself: then from the closet crept,
Noiseless as fear in a wide wilderness,   250
And over the hushed carpet, silent, stepped,
And 'tween the curtains peeped, where, lo!—how fast she slept.

29

Then by the bedside, where the faded moon
Made a dim, silver twilight, soft he set
A table, and, half anguished, threw thereon   255
A cloth of woven crimson, gold, and jet—
O for some drowsy Morphean amulet!
The boisterous, midnight, festive clarion,
The kettledrum, and far-heard clarinet,
Affray his ears, though but in dying tone—   260
The hall door shuts again, and all the noise is gone.

30

And still she slept an azure-lidded sleep,
In blanchèd linen, smooth, and lavendered,
While he from forth the closet brought a heap
Of candied apple, quince, and plum, and gourd,   265
With jellies soother than the creamy curd,
And lucent syrups, tinct with cinnamon;
Manna and dates, in argosy transferred
From Fez; and spicèd dainties, every one,
From silken Samarcand to cedared Lebanon.   270

31

These delicates he heaped with glowing hand
On golden dishes and in baskets bright
Of wreathèd silver: sumptuous they stand
In the retired quiet of the night,
Filling the chilly room with perfume light.—   275
"And now, my love, my seraph fair, awake!
Thou art my heaven, and I thine eremite:
Open thine eyes, for meek St. Agnes' sake,
Or I shall drowse beside thee, so my soul doth ache."

32

Thus whispering, his warm, unnervèd arm   280
Sank in her pillow. Shaded was her dream
By the dusk curtains: 'twas a midnight charm
Impossible to melt as icèd stream:
The lustrous salvers in the moonlight gleam;
Broad golden fringe upon the carpet lies: 285
It seemed he never, never could redeem
From such a steadfast spell his lady's eyes;
So mused awhile, entoiled in woofèd fantasies.

33

Awakening up, he took her hollow lute—
Tumultuous—and, in chords that tenderest be,   290
He played an ancient ditty, long since mute,
In Provence called *"La belle dame sans merci"*:
Close to her ear touching the melody;
Wherewith disturbed, she uttered a soft moan:
He ceased—she panted quick—and suddenly   295
Her blue affrayèd eyes wide open shone:
Upon his knees he sank, pale as smooth-sculptured stone.

34

Her eyes were open, but she still beheld,
Now wide awake, the vision of her sleep:
There was a painful change, that nigh expelled   300
The blisses of her dream so pure and deep,
At which fair Madeline began to weep,
And moan forth witless words with many a sigh;
While still her gaze on Porphyro would keep,
Who knelt, with joinèd hands and piteous eye,   305
Fearing to move or speak, she looked so dreamingly.

35

"Ah, Porphyro!" said she, "but even now
Thy voice was at sweet tremble in mine ear,
Made tunable with every sweetest vow;
And those sad eyes were spiritual and clear: 310
How changed thou art! how pallid, chill, and drear!
Give me that voice again, my Porphyro,
Those looks immortal, those complainings dear!
Oh leave me not in this eternal woe,
For if thou diest, my Love, I know not where to go."   315

36

Beyond a mortal man impassioned far
At these voluptuous accents, he arose,
Ethereal, flushed, and like a throbbing star
Seen mid the sapphire heaven's deep repose;
Into her dream he melted, as the rose   320
Blendeth its odor with the violet—
Solution sweet: meantime the frost-wind blows
Like Love's alarum pattering the sharp sleet
Against the windowpanes; St. Agnes' moon hath set.

37

'Tis dark: quick pattereth the flaw-blown sleet: 325
"This is no dream, my bride, my Madeline!"
'Tis dark: the icèd gusts still rave and beat:
"No dream, alas! alas! and woe is mine!
Porphyro will leave me here to fade and pine.—
Cruel! what traitor could thee hither bring?   330
I curse not, for my heart is lost in thine,
Though thou forsakest a deceivèd thing—
A dove forlorn and lost with sick unprunèd wing."

38

"My Madeline! sweet dreamer! lovely bride!
Say, may I be for aye thy vassal blest?   335
Thy beauty's shield, heart-shaped and vermeil dyed?
Ah, silver shrine, here will I take my rest
After so many hours of toil and quest,
A famished pilgrim—saved by miracle.
Though I have found, I will not rob thy nest   340
Saving of thy sweet self; if thou think'st well
To trust, fair Madeline, to no rude infidel.

39

"Hark! 'tis an elfin-storm from faery land,
Of haggard seeming, but a boon indeed:
Arise—arise! the morning is at hand—   345
The bloated wassaillers will never heed—
Let us away, my love, with happy speed;
There are no ears to hear, or eyes to see—
Drowned all in Rhenish and the sleepy mead:
Awake! arise! my love, and fearless be,   350
For o'er the southern moors I have a home for thee."

40

She hurried at his words, beset with fears,
For there were sleeping dragons all around,
At glaring watch, perhaps, with ready spears—
Down the wide stairs a darkling way they found.—   355
In all the house was heard no human sound.
A chain-drooped lamp was flickering by each door;
The arras, rich with horseman, hawk, and hound,
Fluttered in the besieging wind's uproar;
And the long carpets rose along the gusty floor.   360

41

They glide, like phantoms, into the wide hall;
Like phantoms, to the iron porch, they glide;
Where lay the Porter, in uneasy sprawl,
With a huge empty flagon by his side:
The wakeful bloodhound rose, and shook his hide,   365
But his sagacious eye an inmate owns:
By one, and one, the bolts full easy slide:
The chains lie silent on the footworn stones;
The key turns, and the door upon its hinges groans.

42

And they are gone: aye, ages long ago   370
These lovers fled away into the storm.
That night the Baron dreamt of many a woe,
And all his warrior-guests, with shade and form
Of witch, and demon, and large coffin-worm,
Were long be-nightmared. Angela the old   375
Died palsy-twitched, with meager face deform;
The Beadsman, after thousand aves told,
For aye unsought for slept among his ashes cold.

(1820)

THE EVE OF ST. AGNES. *St. Agnes:* the patron saint of virgins. According to legend, a young girl who performs the right rituals will have a dream-vision of her future husband on the eve before St. Agnes' Day (January 21). Keats fused this legend with a Romeo-and-Juliet situation to produce a poem richly expressive of human ambivalence. Note as you read the texture of contrast: between cold and heat, youth and age, revelry and severe penance, life and death, and so forth. 5. *Beadsman:* One paid to pray for his bene-factor. He "tells" (counts) the beads of his rosary. 16. *dumb orat'ries:* silent chapels. 18. *To think:* i.e., when he thinks. 21. *flattered:* charmed, beguiled. 32. *pride:* ostentatious display. 37. *argent revelry:* silver-clad revelers. 67. *timbrels:* small drums. 70. *Hoodwinked with faery fancy:* blinded by the magic of the imagination. *all amort:* as though dead. 71. *lambs unshorn:* It was customary on St. Agnes' Day to offer lambs' wool at the altar. The wool was thereafter made into cloth by nuns. 77. *Buttressed from moonlight:* sheltered from the moonlight by supporting buttresses. 90. *beldame:* in English, an old, homely woman (in French, "beautiful lady"). 92. *wand:* walking staff. 95. *bland:* soft and melodious. 105. *Gossip:* grandmother or old female (archaic). 120. *witch's sieve:* a sieve that holds water by witch-craft. 124. *conjuror plays:* because of her attempt to evoke a vision of her future husband. 125. *deceive:* i.e., with a vision. 133. *brook:* endure, re-strain. 156. *passing bell:* death knell. 158. *plaining:* mournfully complain-ing. 171. *monstrous debt:* In the Arthurian legends, the magician Merlin loses his life when the wily Vivian turns one of his spells against him. 173. *cates:* delicacies (cf. "cater"). 174. *tambour frame:* a drum-shaped embroi-dery frame. 188. *amain:* greatly, mightily. 193. *missioned spirit:* like an angel on a mission. 198. *frayed:* sorely frightened. 216. *blood of queens and kings:* Along with the "heraldries" (genealogical emblems) and "emblazon-ings," the colors of an heraldic shield signified lineage. 218. *gules:* the color red in heraldry. 219. *boon:* gift, blessing. 229. *degrees:* cf. line 13. 236. *per-plexed:* because in that odd state between waking and sleeping. 241. *Clasped:* held tightly, as a Christian prayer book ("missal") would be by a believer in a place of dark-skinned pagans ("swart Paynims"). 257. *drowsy Mor-phean amulet:* sleep-induced charm. 258. *clarion:* high-pitched trumpet. 265. *apple, quince, and plum, and gourd:* According to legend, the virgin is brought in her dream a feast of such delicacies by her dream lover. For a gloss of the next five lines, see page 158. 276. *seraph:* one of the higher orders of angel. 277. *eremite:* a religious hermit. 288. *entoiled in woofèd fantasies:* entangled in a net of fantasies. 292. *La belle dame sans merci:* "The Lovely Lady Without Pity"—a medieval lyric used by Keats elsewhere (see page 196). Cf. line 90. 325. *flaw-blown:* wind-blown. 336. *vermeil:* vermilion (bright red). 344. *haggard:* wildness (originally, a wild hawk). 346. *bloated wassaillers:* drunken partiers. 349. *Rhenish and the sleepy mead:* Rhine wine and the sleep-inducing "mead" (a fermented drink made with honey). 355. *darkling:* in the dark. 366. *an inmate owns:* recognizes a member of the household. 377. *aves:* prayers, i.e., Hail Marys.

from **In Memoriam**

Alfred, Lord Tennyson

55

The wish, that of the living whole
   No life may fail beyond the grave,
   Derives it not from what we have
The likest God within the soul?

Are God and Nature then at strife,   5
   That Nature lends such evil dreams?
   So careful of the type° she seems,   *species*
So careless of the single life,

That I, considering everywhere
   Her secret meaning in her deeds,   10
   And finding that of fifty seeds
She often brings but one to bear,

I falter where I firmly trod,
   And falling with my weight of cares
   Upon the great world's altar-stairs   15
That slope through darkness up to God,

I stretch lame hands of faith, and grope,
   And gather dust and chaff, and call
   To what I feel is Lord of all,
And faintly trust the larger hope.   20

56

"So careful of the type?" but no.
　　From scarpèd cliff and quarried stone
　　She cries, "A thousand types are gone;
I care for nothing, all shall go.

"Thou makest thine appeal to me: 　　　　　　　　　　　5
　　I bring to life, I bring to death;
　　The spirit does but mean the breath:
I know no more." And he, shall he,

Man, her last work, who seemed so fair,
　　Such splendid purpose in his eyes, 　　　　　　　　10
　　Who rolled the psalm to wintry skies,
Who built him fanes° of fruitless prayer, 　　*temples, churches*

Who trusted God was love indeed
　　And love Creation's final law—
　　Though Nature, red in tooth and claw 　　　　　　15
With ravine, shrieked against his creed—

Who loved, who suffered countless ills,
　　Who battled for the True, the Just,
　　Be blown about the desert dust,
Or sealed within the iron hills? 　　　　　　　　　　20

No more? A monster then, a dream,
　　A discord. Dragons of the prime,
　　That tare each other in their slime,
Were mellow music matched with him.

O life as futile, then, as frail! 　　　　　　　　　　25
　　O for thy voice to soothe and bless!
　　What hope of answer, or redress?
Behind the veil, behind the veil.

　　　　　　　　　　　　　　　　　　　(1850)

---

from IN MEMORIAM. 　No. 56./2. *scarpèd:* cut away so that the strata are exposed. 3. *She:* Nature. 23. *tare:* tore (archaic).

from **Astrophel and Stella**

Sir Philip Sidney

No. 1

Loving in truth, and fain in verse my love to show,
That the dear she might take some pleasure of my pain,
Pleasure might cause her read, reading might make her know,
Knowledge might pity win, and pity grace obtain,
I sought fit words to paint the blackest face of woe: 5
Studying inventions fine, her wits to entertain,
Oft turning others' leaves, to see if thence would flow
Some fresh and fruitful showers upon my sunburnt brain.
But words came halting forth, wanting Invention's stay;
Invention, Nature's child, fled stepdame Study's blows;   10
And others' feet still seemed but strangers in my way.
Thus, great with child to speak, and helpless in my throes,
Biting my truant pen, beating myself for spite:
"Fool," said my Muse to me, "look in thy heart, and write!"

(1582)

---

from ASTROPHEL AND STELLA.   1. *fain:* eager, desirous.   9. *halting:* limping.
stay: crutch, support.   11. *feet:* a pun on metrical feet.

Sonnet 29

William Shakespeare

When, in disgrace with fortune and men's eyes,
I all alone beweep my outcast state,
And trouble deaf heaven with my bootless° cries,   *futile*
And look upon myself, and curse my fate,
Wishing me like to one more rich in hope,   5
Featured like him, like him with friends possessed,
Desiring this man's art and that man's scope,
With what I most enjoy contented least;
Yet in these thoughts myself almost despising,
Haply I think on thee—and then my state,   10

Like to the lark at break of day arising
From sullen earth, sings hymns at heaven's gate;
For thy sweet love remembered such wealth brings
That then I scorn to change my state with kings.

(1609)

SONNET 29.   10. *state:* general condition, state of mind.

Sonnet 30

William Shakespeare

When to the sessions of sweet silent thought
I summon up remembrance of things past,
I sigh the lack of many a thing I sought,
And with old woes new wail my dear time's waste:
Then can I drown an eye, unused to flow,   5
For precious friends hid in death's dateless° night,   *endless*
And weep afresh love's long since canceled woe,
And moan the expense° of many a vanished sight: *loss*
Then can I grieve at grievances foregone,
And heavily from woe to woe tell° o'er   *count*   10
The sad account of fore-bemoanèd moan,
Which I new pay as if not paid before.
But if the while I think on thee, dear friend,
All losses are restored and sorrows end.

(1609)

SONNET 30.   1. *sessions:* sittings of a court (the poem's dominant meta-
phor). 4. *new wail:* wail anew. 9. *foregone:* gone by, in the past.

Sonnet 130

William Shakespeare

My mistress' eyes are nothing like the sun,
Coral is far more red than her lips' red;
If snow be white, why then her breasts are dun;
If hairs be wires, black wires grow on her head.
I have seen roses damasked,° red and white,   *variegated*   5

But no such roses see I in her cheeks;
And in some perfumes is there more delight
Than in the breath that from my mistress reeks.
I love to hear her speak, yet well I know
That music hath a far more pleasing sound;   10
I grant I never saw a goddess go;°   *walk*
My mistress, when she walks, treads on the ground.
And yet, by heaven, I think my love as rare
As any she belied with false compare.

(*1609*)

SONNET 130. 1. *nothing like the sun:* The sonnet is anti-traditional: all of the things commonly attributed by poets to their mistresses are here listed and denied.

Sonnet 146

William Shakespeare

Poor soul, the center of my sinful earth,
Lord of these rebel powers that thee array,
Why dost thou pine within and suffer dearth,
Painting thy outward walls so costly gay?
Why so large cost, having so short a lease,   5
Dost thou upon thy fading mansion spend?
Shall worms, inheritors of this excess,
Eat up thy charge? Is this thy body's end?
Then, soul, live thou upon thy servant's loss,
And let that pine to aggravate thy store;   10
Buy terms divine in selling hours of dross;
Within be fed, without be rich no more.
So shalt thou feed on death, that feeds on men,
And death once dead, there's no more dying then.

(*1609*)

SONNET 146. 2. *array:* clothe, adorn with dress. 10. *that:* the body. *pine:* decay. *aggravate:* increase. *thy store:* the riches of the soul. 11. *terms:* periods of time. *dross:* waste matter, refuse.

from **Idea**

Michael Drayton

No. 61

Since there's no help, come let us kiss and part;
Nay, I have done, you get no more of me,
And I am glad, yea glad with all my heart
That thus so cleanly I myself can free;
Shake hands forever, cancel all our vows,   5
And when we meet at any time again,
Be it not seen in either of our brows
That we one jot of former love retain.
Now at the last gasp of love's latest breath,
When, his pulse failing, passion speechless lies,   10
When faith is kneeling by his bed of death,
And innocence is closing up his eyes,
   Now if thou wouldst, when all have given him over,
   From death to life thou mightst him yet recover.

(1619)

from **Holy Sonnets**

John Donne

No. 7

At the round earth's imagined corners, blow
Your trumpets, angels; and arise, arise
From death, you numberless infinities
Of souls, and to your scattered bodies go;
All whom the flood did, and fire shall, o'erthrow,   5
All whom war, dearth, age, agues, tyrannies,
Despair, law, chance hath slain, and you whose eyes
Shall behold God, and never taste death's woe.
But let them sleep, Lord, and me mourn a space;
For, if above all these, my sins abound,   10
'Tis late to ask abundance of Thy grace
When we are there. Here on this lowly ground,
Teach me how to repent; for that's as good
As if Thou hadst sealed my pardon with Thy blood.

(1633)

from HOLY SONNETS, NO. 7.   2. *angels:* "I saw four angels standing on the four corners of the earth, holding the four winds of the earth [Revelation 7:1]." 5. *fire shall:* At the last trumpet call (the end of the world), "the elements shall melt with fervent heat, the earth also and the works that are therein shall be burned up [II Peter 3:10]." 8. *death's woe:* "But I tell you of a truth, there be some standing here, which shall not taste of death, till they see the kingdom of God [Christ's words to his disciples, Luke 9:27]."

from **Holy Sonnets**

John Donne

No. 10

Death, be not proud, though some have callèd thee
Mighty and dreadful, for thou art not so;
For those whom thou think'st thou dost overthrow
Die not, poor Death, nor yet canst thou kill me.
From rest and sleep, which but thy pictures be,   5
Much pleasure; then from thee much more must flow,
And soonest our best men with thee do go,
Rest of their bones, and soul's delivery.
Thou art slave to fate, chance, kings, and desperate men,
And dost with poison, war, and sickness dwell,   10
And poppy or charms can make us sleep as well
And better than thy stroke; why swell'st thou then?
One short sleep past, we wake eternally
And death shall be no more; Death, thou shalt die.

(1633)

from HOLY SONNETS, NO. 10.   8. *soul's delivery:* i.e., our best men go with you to find rest for their bones and freedom ("delivery") for their souls. 12. *swell'st:* puff up with pride.

Ozymandias

Percy Bysshe Shelley

I met a traveler from an antique land
Who said: Two vast and trunkless legs of stone
Stand in the desert . . . Near them, on the sand,

Half sunk, a shattered visage lies, whose frown,
And wrinkled lip, and sneer of cold command, 5
Tell that its sculptor well those passions read
Which yet survive, stamped on these lifeless things,
The hand that mocked them, and the heart that fed:
And on the pedestal these words appear:
"My name is Ozymandias, king of kings: 10
Look on my works, ye Mighty, and despair!"
Nothing beside remains. Round the decay
Of that colossal wreck, boundless and bare
The lone and level sands stretch far away.

(1818)

OZYMANDIAS. *Ozymandias:* Greek name for the Egyptian monarch Ramses
II (13th century B.C.), a builder of such things as are described in the poem.

Felix Randal

G. M. Hopkins

Felix Randal the farrier, O he is dead then? my duty all ended,
Who have watched his mold of man, big-boned and hardy-handsome
Pining, pining, till time when reason rambled in it and some
Fatal four disorders, fleshed there, all contended?

Sickness broke him. Impatient he cursed at first, but mended 5
Being anointed and all; though a heavenlier heart began some
Months earlier, since I had our sweet reprieve and ransom
Tendered to him. Ah, well, God rest him all road ever he offended!

This seeing the sick endears them to us, us too it endears.
My tongue had taught thee comfort, touch had quenched thy tears, 10
Thy tears that touched my heart, child, Felix, poor Felix Randal;

How far from then forethought of, all thy more boisterous years,
When thou at the random grim forge, powerful amidst peers,
Didst fettle for the great gray drayhorse his bright and battering
  sandal!

(c. 1880)

FELIX RANDAL. 1. *farrier:* a blacksmith. 8. *all road ever:* i.e., in what-
ever way. 13. *random:* built with stones of irregular shapes and sizes. 14.
fettle: prepare.

Lucifer in Starlight

George Meredith

On a starred night Prince Lucifer uprose.
Tired of his dark dominion, swung the fiend
Above the rolling ball, in cloud part screened,
Where sinners hugged their specter of repose.
Poor prey to his hot fit of pride were those.   5
And now upon his western wing he leaned,
Now his huge bulk o'er Afric's sands careened,
Now the black planet shadowed Arctic snows.
Soaring through wider zones that pricked his scars
With memory of the old revolt from Awe,   10
He reached a middle height, and at the stars,
Which are the brain of heaven, he looked, and sank.
Around the ancient track marched, rank on rank,
The army of unalterable law.

(1883)

LUCIFER IN STARLIGHT.   9. *pricked his scars:* The vast waste of space, like
the spectacle of natural law witnessed in the movement of the stars, pricks
Satan's pride and reminds him of the indignities he suffered when, his re-
volt having failed, he was hurled by God from heaven.

Design

Robert Frost

I found a dimpled spider, fat and white,
On a white heal-all, holding up a moth
Like a white piece of rigid satin cloth—
Assorted characters of death and blight
Mixed ready to begin the morning right,   5
Like the ingredients of a witches' broth—
A snow-drop spider, a flower like a froth,
And dead wings carried like a paper kite.

What had that flower to do with being white,
The wayside blue and innocent heal-all?   10
What brought the kindred spider to that height,

Then steered the white moth thither in the night?
What but design of darkness to appall?—
If design govern in a thing so small.

(*1936*)

Our Bias

W. H. Auden

The hour-glass whispers to the lion's roar,
The clock-towers tell the gardens day and night
How many errors Time has patience for,
How wrong they are in being always right.

Yet Time, however loud its chimes or deep,   5
However fast its falling torrent flows,
Has never put one lion off his leap
Nor shaken the assurance of a rose.

For they, it seems, care only for success:
While we choose words according to their sound   10
And judge a problem by its awkwardness;

And Time with us was always popular.
When have we not preferred some going round
To going straight to where we are?

(*1940*)

Counting-Out Rhyme

Helen Adam

Seven bonnie sisters on an isle in the west:
The youngest was the fairest, and she was loved the best.

Seven wistful sisters hankering tae wed:
On the beach the mocking waves cast up a sailor dead.

The eldest, as she lugged him from the waves whaur they ran,   5
Said, "A drooned man is better than nae living man.

For a reel i' the munelicht his banes will be braw;
We'll dance hot taegither while his flesh rots awa."

Six sisters racing, till a boat it was sunk:
The waves cast up a boozing man, reeking, roudy drunk.   10

Five sisters hustled back, the sixth chose tae bide.
"A brawl, and a buffet, a black eye for a bride!
But a boozing man is better than nae man at my side."

Five siren sisters vividly aflame:
The surges brought a greedy man, he gobbled as he came;   15

His tusks fast crunching on a muckle fish-tail.
The fifth sister grumbled, "He's as huge as a whale!

He gorges wi' a gusto that is daunting indeed,
But a greedy man is better than nae man tae feed."

Rough waves sprachaling, a man plunging through: 20
He gripped the fourth sister, and beat her black and blue.

The fourth sobbed, "A cruel man clouts me tae my knees,
But a cruel man is better than nae man tae please."

Three hopeful sisters turning towards the foam:
There came a dull man floating in, as if he floated home.   25

The third sighed, "A dull man will haver and prate.
He'll harp and carp and din my ear, early and late.
But a dull man is better than nae man tae hate."

Twa bonnie sisters naked in the night,
The cauld waves breaking, the mune shining bright.   30

The cauld waves breaking, the surf drenching doun:
It rolled in a mucky man on sands like the mune.

He was crusted thick wi' barnacles, tarry from the sea.
He scarted, and he scratched, and he girned in a gree.

"He's mucky as a tousled tyke!" the second sister said.   35
"But a mucky man is better than nae man in my bed."

The youngest and the fairest, she was alone,
The first star flickering, the seagulls flown.

"A dull man, a dirty man, a drunk man," she said,
"A cruel man, a greedy man, or a drooned man in my bed?   40

The sea waves may dunk them deep, for I'd refuse them a'.
I'll live alane, and happily, and love nae man at a'."

The cats o' the kirk-yard drifted tae her side.
The hither and thither cats cam' wi' her tae bide.

Wi' cats hurra-purrying and fish swimming slaw   45
She lived as light-hearted as the sea-breezes blaw.

The waves broke around her wi' a rush and a roar.
They shone in the munelicht but cast nae man ashore.
By sunlicht, and munelicht, they cast nae man ashore.

One sister walking neath a wierd sickle mune: 50
The waves phosphorescent, the night clear as noon.

A long wave lifting, it birreled as it broke.
The spray frae its flying brow went up like altar smoke.

Then cam' the unicorn, brichter than the mune,
Prancing frae the wave wi' his braw crystal croon.   55

Up the crisp and shelly strand he trotted unafraid.
Agin' the lanesome lassie's knee his comely head he laid.

Upon the youngest sister's lap he leaned his royal head.
She stabbed him tae the hert, and Oh! how eagerly he bled!

He died triumphant and content, his horn agin' her knee.   60
The crescent mune fled doun tae meet the phosphorescent sea.

"Seven!" yowled the kirk-yard cats. "Seven!" thrummed the breeze.
"Seven!" sang the fish o' yon seraphic seas.

"Seven doomed sisters on an isle in the west:
The youngest was the fairest, and she was loved the best."   65

(1972)

Chapter Eight

Paired Poems

I

The Cuckoo Song

Anonymous

Sumer is ycomen° in,	*coming*
Loude° sing cuckou!	*loudly*
Groweth seed and bloweth meed,	
And springth the wode° now.	*wood*
Sing cuckou!	5
Ewe bleteth after lamb,	
Loweth after calve cow,	
Bulloc sterteth,° bucke verteth,°	*leaps / break wind*
Merye sing cuckou!	
Cuckou, cuckou,	10
Wel singest thou cuckou:	
Ne swik° thou never now!	*cease*
	(14th cen.)

THE CUCKOO SONG. 3. *meed:* the meadow blossoms. 7. *Loweth after calve
cow:* the cow lows after the calf.

Ancient Music

Ezra Pound

Winter is icummen in,
    Lhude sing Goddamm,
      Raineth drop and staineth slop,
And how the wind doth ramm!
              Sing: Goddamm.   5
Skiddeth bus and sloppeth us,

An ague hath my ham.
Freezeth river, turneth liver,
                Damn you, sing: Goddamm.
Goddamm, Goddamm, 'tis why I am, Goddamm,   10
                So 'gainst the winter's balm.
Sing goddamm, damm, sing Goddamm,
Sing goddamm, sing goddamm, DAMM.

                                   (1915)

II

The Passionate Shepherd
to His Love

Christopher Marlowe

Come live with me and be my love,
And we will all the pleasures prove°   *try*
That valleys, groves, hills, and fields,
Woods, or steepy mountain yields.

And we will sit upon the rocks,   5
Seeing the shepherds feed their flocks,
By shallow rivers to whose falls
Melodious birds sing madrigals.

And I will make thee beds of roses
And a thousand fragrant posies,   10
A cap of flowers, and a kirtle
Embroidered all with leaves of myrtle;

A gown made of the finest wool
Which from our pretty lambs we pull;
Fair lined slippers for the cold,   15
With buckles of the purest gold;

A belt of straw and ivy buds,
With coral clasps and amber studs:
And if these pleasures may thee move,
Come live with me, and be my love.   20

The shepherds' swains shall dance and sing
For thy delight each May morning:

If these delights thy mind may move,
Then live with me and be my love.

(1599)

The Nymph's Reply
to the Shepherd

Sir Walter Raleigh

If all the world and love were young,
And truth in every shepherd's tongue,
These pretty pleasures might me move
To live with thee and be thy love.

Time drives the flocks from field to fold   5
When rivers rage and rocks grow cold,
And Philomel becometh dumb;
The rest complains of cares to come.

The flowers do fade, and wanton fields
To wayward winter reckoning yields;   10
A honey tongue, a heart of gall,
Is fancy's spring, but sorrow's fall.

Thy gowns, thy shoes, thy beds of roses,
Thy cap, thy kirtle, and thy posies
Soon break, soon wither, soon forgotten—   15
In folly ripe, in reason rotten.

Thy belt of straw and ivy buds,
Thy coral clasps and amber studs,
All these in me no means can move
To come to thee and be thy love.   20

But could youth last and love still breed,
Had joys no date nor age no need,
Then these delights my mind might move
To live with thee and be thy love.

(1600)

III

How Soon Hath Time

John Milton

How soon hath Time, the subtle thief of youth,
   Stoln on his wing my three and twentieth year!
   My hasting days fly on with full career,
   But my late spring no bud or blossom show'th.
Perhaps my semblance might deceive the truth,   5
   That I to manhood am arrived so near,
   And inward ripeness doth much less appear,
   That some more timely-happy spirits endu'th.°   *endow*
Yet be it less or more, or soon or slow,
   It shall be still° in strictest measure even   *always* 10
   To that same lot, however mean or high,
Toward which Time leads me, and the will of Heaven;
   All is, if I have grace to use it so,
   As ever in my great Taskmaster's eye.

                         (1631)

HOW SOON HATH TIME. 10. *even:* equal, like the measures of a piece of music. 14. *Taskmaster's eye:* The sonnet concludes with a pledge to fulfill in due course the Gospel command to labor.

When I Consider How My Light Is Spent

John Milton

When I consider how my light is spent
   Ere half my days, in this dark world and wide,
   And that one talent which is death to hide,
   Lodged with me useless, though my soul more bent
To serve therewith my Maker, and present   5
   My true account, lest he returning chide;
   "Doth God exact day-labor, light denied?"
   I fondly° ask; but Patience to prevent°   *foolishly / forestall*

Anthology

That murmur, soon replies, "God doth not need
    Either man's work or his own gifts; who best   10
    Bear his mild yoke, they serve him best. His state
Is kingly. Thousands at his bidding speed
    And post o'er land and ocean without rest:
    They also serve who only stand and wait."

                                    (c. 1652)

WHEN I CONSIDER HOW MY LIGHT IS SPENT. *spent:* Total blindness overtook
Milton in 1651, roughly in the middle of his life. So, his light spent, if not
his talent, he feels keen doubts about his future. Cf. the doubts and resolu-
tion of "How Soon Hath Time." 3. *that one talent which is death to hide:*
See Christ's parable of the talents (measures of money), Matthew 25:14–30.
Milton here associates himself with the servant who hid away the one talent
he had been given, in consequence of which he was rebuked by his master
as "wicked and slothful." Such a servant, Christ bids, should be "cast . . .
into outer darkness."

When I Have Fears

John Keats

When I have fears that I may cease to be
    Before my pen has gleaned my teeming brain,
Before high-pilèd books, in charact'ry,°   *written symbols*
    Hold like rich garners the full-ripened grain;
When I behold, upon the night's starred face,   5
    Huge cloudy symbols of a high romance,
And think that I may never live to trace
    Their shadows, with the magic hand of chance;
And when I feel, fair creature of an hour,
    That I shall never look upon thee more,   10
Never have relish in the faery° power   *magical*
    Of unreflecting love!—then on the shore
Of the wide world I stand alone, and think
Till Love and Fame to nothingness do sink.

                                    (c. 1818)

IV

She Dwelt Among
the Untrodden Ways

William Wordsworth

She dwelt among the untrodden ways
   Beside the springs of Dove.
A Maid whom there were none to praise
   And very few to love;

A violet by a mossy stone   5
   Half hidden from the eye!
—Fair as a star, when only one
   Is shining in the sky.

She loved unknown, and few could know
   When Lucy ceased to be;   10
But she is in her grave, and, oh,
   The difference to me!

(1800)

SHE DWELT AMONG THE UNTRODDEN WAYS. 2. *Dove:* a river in the Lake District of England, where Wordsworth lived.

He Lived Amidst
th' Untrodden Ways

Hartley Coleridge

He lived amidst th' untrodden ways
   To Rydal Lake that lead;
A bard whom there were none to praise,
   And very few to read.

Behind a cloud his mystic sense,   5
   Deep hidden, who can spy?
Bright as the night when not a star
   Is shining in the sky.

Unread his works—his "Milk White Doe"
   With dust is dark and dim;   10
It's still in Longman's shop, and oh!
   The difference to him!

                                          (*1833*)

HE LIVED AMIDST TH' UNTRODDEN WAYS. 2. *Rydal Lake:* in the Lake District.
9. *"Milk White Doe":* a reference to "The White Doe of Rylstone," a long
poem by Wordsworth. 11. *Longman's shop:* the shop of Wordsworth's
publisher.

V

When Lovely Woman
Stoops to Folly

Oliver Goldsmith

When lovely woman stoops to folly,
   And finds too late that men betray,
What charm can soothe her melancholy,
   What art can wash her guilt away?

The only art her guilt to cover,   5
   To hide her shame from every eye,
To give repentance to her lover,
   And wring his bosom—is to die.

                                          (*1766*)

Bonie Doon

Robert Burns

Ye flowery banks o' bonie Doon,
   How can ye blume sae fair?
How can ye chant, ye little birds,
   And I sae fu' o' care?

Thou'll break my heart, thou bonie bird,   5
   That sings upon the bough;
Thou minds me o' the happy days,
   When my fause° luve was true.   *false*

Thou'll break my heart, thou bonie bird,
   That sings beside thy mate;   10
For sae I sat, and sae I sang,
   And wist° na o' my fate.   *knew*

Aft hae I roved by bonie Doon
   To see the wood-bine twine,
And ilka° bird sang o' its luve,   *every* 15
   And sae did I o' mine.

Wi' lightsome heart I pu'd a rose
   Frae aff its thorny tree;
And my fause luver staw° my rose   *stole*
   But left the thorn wi' me.   20

(*1791*)

from **The Waste Land**

T. S. Eliot

The time is now propitious, as he guesses,   235
The meal is ended, she is bored and tired,
Endeavors to engage her in caresses
Which still are unreproved, if undesired.
Flushed and decided, he assaults at once;
Exploring hands encounter no defense;   240
His vanity requires no response,
And makes a welcome of indifference.

     . . .

Bestows one final patronizing kiss,
And gropes his way, finding the stairs unlit . . .

She turns and looks a moment in the glass,
Hardly aware of her departed lover;   250
Her brain allows one half-formed thought to pass;
"Well now that's done: and I'm glad it's over."
When lovely woman stoops to folly and
Paces about her room again, alone,
She smoothes her hair with automatic hand,   255
And puts a record on the gramophone.

(*1922*)

VI

The Retreat

Henry Vaughan

Happy those early days! when I
Shined in my angel infancy.
Before I understood this place
Appointed for my second race,
Or taught my soul to fancy aught   5
But a white, celestial thought;
When yet I had not walked above
A mile or two from my first love,
And looking back, at that short space,
Could see a glimpse of His bright face;   10
When on some gilded cloud or flower
My gazing soul would dwell an hour,
And in those weaker glories spy
Some shadows of eternity;
Before I taught my tongue to wound   15
My conscience with a sinful sound,
Or had the black art to dispense
A several sin to every sense,
But felt through all this fleshly dress
Bright shoots of everlastingness.   20
  O, how I long to travel back,
And tread again that ancient track!
That I might once more reach that plain
Where first I left my glorious train,
From whence th' enlightened spirit sees   25
That shady city of palm trees.
But, ah! my soul with too much stay
Is drunk, and staggers in the way.
Some men a forward motion love;
But I by backward steps would move,   30
And when this dust falls to the urn,
In that state I came, return.

(1650)

THE RETREAT.   4. *second race:* There's a suggestion here of the concept of preexistence, Platonic in its origins. 18. *several:* i.e., different. 26. *city of palm trees:* the New Jerusalem, the city of Heaven. 27. *too much stay:* staying, delay.

Ode
Intimations of Immortality from Recollections of Early Childhood

William Wordsworth

The Child is father of the Man;
And I could wish my days to be
Bound each to each by natural piety.

1

There was a time when meadow, grove, and stream,
The earth, and every common sight,
  To me did seem
  Appareled in celestial light,
The glory and the freshness of a dream.   5
It is not now as it hath been of yore—
  Turn whereso'er I may,
   By night or day,
The things which I have seen I now can see no more.

2

  The Rainbow comes and goes,   10
  And lovely is the Rose,
  The Moon doth with delight
Look round her when the heavens are bare,
  Waters on a starry night
  Are beautiful and fair;   15
 The sunshine is a glorious birth;
 But yet I know, where'er I go,
That there hath passed away a glory from the earth.

3

Now while the birds thus sing a joyous song,
 And while the young lambs bound   20
  As to the tabor's sound,
To me alone there came a thought of grief:
A timely utterance gave that thought relief,
  And I again am strong:
The cataracts blow their trumpets from the steep;   25
No more shall grief of mine the season wrong;
I hear the Echoes through the mountains throng,

The Winds come to me from the fields of sleep,
 And all the earth is gay;
  Land and sea   30
  Give themselves up to jollity,
   And with the heart of May
  Doth every Beast keep holiday—
   Thou Child of Joy,
Shout round me, let me hear thy shouts, thou happy 35
  Shepherd-boy!

4

Ye blessed Creatures, I have heard the call
 Ye to each other make; I see
The heavens laugh with you in your jubilee;
 My heart is at your festival,   40
  My head hath its coronal,
The fullness of your bliss, I feel—I feel it all.
  Oh, evil day! if I were sullen
  While Earth herself is adorning,
   This sweet May morning,   45
  And the Children are culling
   On every side,
  In a thousand valleys far and wide,
  Fresh flowers; while the sun shines warm,
And the Babe leaps up on his Mother's arm— 50
  I hear, I hear, with joy I hear!
  —But there's a Tree, of many, one,
A single Field which I have looked upon,
Both of them speak of something that is gone:
   The Pansy at my feet   55
   Doth the same tale repeat:
Whither is fled the visionary gleam?
Where is it now, the glory and the dream?

5

Our birth is but a sleep and a forgetting:
The Soul that rises with us, our life's Star, 60
  Hath had elsewhere its setting,
   And cometh from afar:
  Not in entire forgetfulness,
  And not in utter nakedness,
But trailing clouds of glory do we come 65
  From God, who is our home:
Heaven lies about us in our infancy!

Shades of the prison-house begin to close
    Upon the growing Boy
        But he   70
Beholds the light, and whence it flows,
    He sees it in his joy;
The Youth, who daily farther from the east
      Must travel, still is Nature's Priest,
      And by the vision splendid   75
      Is on his way attended;
At length the Man perceives it die away,
And fade into the light of common day.

6

Earth fills her lap with pleasures of her own;
Yearnings she hath in her own natural kind,   80
And, even with something of a Mother's mind,
      And no unworthy aim,
      The homely Nurse doth all she can
To make her foster child, her Inmate Man,
      Forget the glories he hath known,   85
And that imperial palace whence he came.

7

Behold the Child among his newborn blisses,
A six-years' Darling of a pygmy size!
See, where 'mid work of his own hand he lies,
Fretted by sallies of his mother's kisses,   90
With light upon him from his father's eyes!
See, at his feet, some little plan or chart,
Some fragment from his dream of human life,
Shaped by himself with newly-learned art;
      A wedding or a festival,   95
      A mourning or a funeral;
        And this hath now his heart,
      And unto this he frames his song;
        Then will he fit his tongue
To dialogues of business, love, or strife;   100
      But it will not be long
      Ere this be thrown aside,
      And with new joy and pride
The little Actor cons another part;
Filling from time to time his "humorous stage"   105
With all the Persons, down to palsied Age,

That Life brings with her in her equipage;
     As if his whole vocation
     Were endless imitation.

     8

Thou, whose exterior semblance doth belie   110
     Thy Soul's immensity;
Thou best Philosopher, who yet dost keep
Thy heritage, thou Eye among the blind,
That, deaf and silent, read'st the eternal deep,
Haunted forever by the eternal mind—   115
     Mighty Prophet! Seer blest!
     On whom those truths do rest,
Which we are toiling all our lives to find,
In darkness lost, the darkness of the grave;
Thou, over whom thy Immortality   120
Broods like the Day, a Master o'er a Slave,
A Presence which is not to be put by;
Thou little Child, yet glorious in the might
Of heaven-born freedom on thy being's height,
Why with such earnest pains dost thou provoke   125
The years to bring the inevitable yoke,
Thus blindly with thy blessedness at strife?
Full soon thy Soul shall have her earthly freight,
And custom lie upon thee with a weight,
Heavy as frost, and deep almost as life!   130

     9

     O joy! that in our embers
     Is something that doth live,
     That nature yet remembers
     What was so fugitive!
The thought of our past years in me doth breed   135
Perpetual benediction: not indeed
For that which is most worthy to be blest;
Delight and liberty, the simple creed
Of Childhood, whether busy or at rest,
With new-fledged hope still fluttering in his breast—   140
     Not for these I raise
     The song of thanks and praise;
     But for those obstinate questionings
     Of sense and outward things,
     Fallings from us, vanishings;   145
     Bland misgivings of a Creature

Moving about in worlds not realized,
High instincts before which our mortal Nature
Did tremble like a guilty Thing surprised;
    But for those first affections, 150
    Those shadowy recollections,
   Which, be they what they may,
Are yet the fountain light of all our day,
Are yet a master light of all our seeing;
    Uphold us, cherish, and have power to make 155
Our noisy years seem moments in the being
Of the eternal Silence: truths that wake,
     To perish never;
Which neither listlessness, nor mad endeavor,
    Nor Man nor Boy, 160
Nor all that is at enmity with joy,
Can utterly abolish or destroy!
    Hence in a season of calm weather
    Though inland far we be,
Our Souls have sight of that immortal sea 165
    Which brought us hither,
   Can in a moment travel thither,
And see the Children sport upon the shore,
And hear the mighty waters rolling evermore.

10

Then sing, ye Birds, sing, sing a joyous song! 170
    And let the young Lambs bound
    As to the tabor's sound!
We in thought will join your throng,
    Ye that pipe and ye that play,
    Ye that through your hearts today 175
    Feel the gladness of the May!
What though the radiance which was once so bright
Be now forever taken from my sight,
    Though nothing can bring back the hour
Of splendor in the grass, of glory in the flower; 180
    We will grieve not, rather find
    Strength in what remains behind;
    In the primal sympathy
    Which having been must ever be;
    In the soothing thoughts that spring 185
    Out of human suffering;
    In the faith that looks through death,
In years that bring the philosophic mind.

11

And O, ye Fountains, Meadows, Hills, and Groves,
Forebode not any severing of our loves!   190
Yet in my heart of hearts I feel your might;
I only have relinquished one delight
To live beneath your more habitual sway.
I love the Brooks which down their channels fret,
Even more than when I tripped lightly as they;   195
The innocent brightness of a newborn Day
      Is lovely yet;
The clouds that gather round the setting sun
Do take a sober coloring from an eye
That hath kept watch o'er man's mortality;   200
Another race hath been, and other palms are won,
Thanks to the human heart by which we live,
Thanks to its tenderness, its joys, and fears,
To me the meanest flower that blows can give
Thoughts that do often lie too deep for tears.   205

                                                 (1807)

ODE: INTIMATIONS OF IMMORTALITY. *The Child is father of the Man . . . :*
the last three lines of Wordsworth's "My Heart Leaps Up." 21. tabor:
a small drum used to beat time for dancing. 23. *timely utterance:* per-
haps "My Heart Leaps Up"—see epigraph. 28. *Winds:* Wordsworth often
associated wind and inspiration (which means etymologically, "to breathe
into"). 41. *coronal:* wreath of flowers such as would be worn at a May
Day festival. 59. *forgetting:* The concept of preexistence is here suggested,
but Wordsworth's use of the concept is metaphorical, not literal. 60.
Star: the sun. 83. *homely:* simple and friendly (an older sense. 90. *Fretted:*
checkered over (an older sense). 105. *"humorous stage":* From a sonnet by
the Elizabethan poet Samuel Daniel. In the Renaissance, "humorous" re-
ferred to the various types of temperament ("humors") and personality. It
also meant "capricious." 147. *not realized:* not seeming real. 201. *palms are
won:* In ancient Greece, the winners of foot races won a branch or wreath
of palm leaves. With the figure, Wordsworth suggests that one stage of life
is over and has yielded to another stage in the process of growth, with yet
other palms still to be won. Also, cf. Vaughan's "The Retreat," line 4.

VII

Reread Marvell's "To His Coy Mistress," page 49. Then read the next
two poems with the Marvell poem in mind.

You, Andrew Marvell

Archibald MacLeish

And here face down beneath the sun
And here upon earth's noonward height
To feel the always coming on
The always rising of the night

To feel creep up the curving east   5
The earthy chill of dusk and slow
Upon those under lands the vast
And ever climbing shadow grow

And strange at Ecbatan the trees
Take leaf by leaf the evening strange   10
The flooding dark about their knees
The mountains over Persia change

And now at Kermanshah the gate
Dark empty and the withered grass
And through the twilight now the late   15
Few travelers in the westward pass

And Baghdad darken and the bridge
Across the silent river gone
And through Arabia the edge
Of evening widen and steal on   20

And deepen on Palmyra's street
The wheel rut in the ruined stone
And Lebanon fade out and Crete
High through the clouds and overblown

And over Sicily the air   25
Still flashing with the landward gulls
And loom and slowly disappear
The sails above the shadowy hulls

And Spain go under and the shore
Of Africa the gilded sand   30
And evening vanish and no more
The low pale light across that land

Nor now the long light on the sea
And here face downward in the sun
To feel how swift how secretly   35
The shadow of the night comes on. . . .

(1930)

YOU, ANDREW MARVELL. 9. *Ecbatan:* Following the westward course of the
sun, the speaker's thoughts move through time and space from Ecbatan,
the capital of ancient Persia, to Kermanshah, Baghdad, and so on.

The Love Song
of J. Alfred Prufrock

T. S. Eliot

S'io credesse che mia risposta fosse
A persona che mai tornasse al mondo,
Questa fiamma staria senza piu scosse.
Ma perciocche giammai di questo fondo
Non torno vivo alcun, s'i'odo il vero,
Senza tema d'infamia ti rispondo.

Let us go then, you and I,
When the evening is spread out against the sky
Like a patient etherized upon a table;
Let us go, through certain half-deserted streets,
The muttering retreats   5
Of restless nights in one-night cheap hotels
And sawdust restaurants with oyster-shells:
Streets that follow like a tedious argument
Of insidious intent
To lead you to an overwhelming question. . . .   10
Oh, do not ask, "What is it?"
Let us go and make our visit.

In the room the women come and go
Talking of Michelangelo.

The yellow fog that rubs its back upon the window-panes   15
The yellow smoke that rubs its muzzle on the window-panes
Licked its tongue into the corners of the evening,
Lingered upon the pools that stand in drains,

Let fall upon its back the soot that falls from chimneys,
Slipped by the terrace, made a sudden leap,   20
And seeing that it was a soft October night,
Curled once about the house, and fell asleep.

And indeed there will be time
For the yellow smoke that slides along the street,
Rubbing its back upon the window-panes;   25
There will be time, there will be time
To prepare a face to meet the faces that you meet;
There will be time to murder and create,
And time for all the works and days of hands
That lift and drop a question on your plate;   30
Time for you and time for me,
And time yet for a hundred indecisions,
And for a hundred visions and revisions,
Before the taking of a toast and tea.

In the room the women come and go   35
Talking of Michelangelo.

And indeed there will be time
To wonder, "Do I dare?" and, "Do I dare?"
Time to turn back and descend the stair,
With a bald spot in the middle of my hair—   40
[They will say: "How his hair is growing thin!"]
My morning coat, my collar mounting firmly to the chin,
My necktie rich and modest, but asserted by a simple pin—
[They will say: "But how his arms and legs are thin!"]
Do I dare   45
Disturb the universe?
In a minute there is time
For decisions and revisions which a minute will reverse.

For I have known them all already, known them all:
Have known the evenings, mornings, afternoons,   50
I have measured out my life with coffee spoons;
I know the voices dying with a dying fall
Beneath the music from a farther room.
   So how should I presume?

And I have known the eyes already, known them all—   55
The eyes that fix you in a formulated phrase,
And when I am formulated, sprawling on a pin,

When I am pinned and wriggling on the wall,
Then how should I begin
To spit out all the butt-ends of my days and ways?   60
    And how should I presume?

And I have known the arms already, known them all—
Arms that are braceleted and white and bare
[But in the lamplight, downed with light brown hair!]
Is it perfume from a dress   65
That makes me so digress?
Arms that lie along a table, or wrap about a shawl.
    And should I then presume?
    And how should I begin?
                    . . .
Shall I say, I have gone at dusk through narrow streets   70
And watched the smoke that rises from the pipes
Of lonely men in shirt-sleeves, leaning out of windows? . . .

I should have been a pair of ragged claws
Scuttling across the floors of silent seas.
                    . . .
And the afternoon, the evening, sleeps so peacefully!   75
Smoothed by long fingers,
Asleep . . . tired . . . or it malingers,
Stretched on the floor, here beside you and me.
Should I, after tea and cakes and ices,
Have the strength to force the moment to its crisis?   80
But though I have wept and fasted, wept and prayed,
Though I have seen my head [grown slightly bald] brought in
        upon a platter,
I am no prophet—and here's no great matter;
I have seen the moment of my greatness flicker,
And I have seen the eternal Footman hold my coat, and snicker,   85
And in short, I was afraid.

And would it have been worth it, after all,
After the cups, the marmalade, the tea,
Among the porcelain, among some talk of you and me,
Would it have been worth while,   90
To have bitten off the matter with a smile,
To have squeezed the universe into a ball
To roll it toward some overwhelming question,
To say: "I am Lazarus, come from the dead,
Come back to tell you all, I shall tell you all"—   95

If one, settling a pillow by her head,
   Should say: "That is not what I meant at all.
   That is not it, at all."

And would it have been worth it, after all,
Would it have been worth while,   100
After the sunsets and the dooryards and the sprinkled streets,
After the novels, after the teacups, after the skirts that trail
    along the floor—
And this, and so much more?—
It is impossible to say just what I mean!
But as if a magic lantern threw the nerves in patterns on a
    screen: 105
Would it have been worth while
If one, settling a pillow or throwing off a shawl,
And turning toward the window, should say:
   "That is not it at all,
   That is not what I meant, at all."   110
          . . .

No! I am not Prince Hamlet, nor was meant to be;
Am an attendant lord, one that will do
To swell a progress, start a scene or two,
Advise the prince; no doubt, an easy tool,
Deferential, glad to be of use,   115
Politic, cautious, and meticulous;
Full of high sentence,° but a bit obtuse;   *sententiousness*
At times, indeed, almost ridiculous—
Almost, at times, the Fool.

I grow old . . . I grow old . . .   120
I shall wear the bottoms of my trousers rolled.

Shall I part my hair behind? Do I dare to eat a peach?
I shall wear white flannel trousers, and walk upon the beach.
I have heard the mermaids singing, each to each.

I do not think that they will sing to me.   125

I have seen them riding seaward on the waves
Combing the white hair of the waves blown back
When the wind blows the water white and black.
We have lingered in the chambers of the sea

By sea-girls wreathed with seaweed red and brown   130
Till human voices wake us, and we drown.

(1917)

THE LOVE SONG OF J. ALFRED PRUFROCK. *epigraph:* Dante, *Inferno* XXVII:
61–66. These are the words of Guido da Montefeltro, whom Dante encoun-
ters in the Eighth Circle, that of False Counselors, each a spirit within a
flame. Dante asks for Guido's story, and Guido answers: "If I thought that
my reply would be to one who would ever return to the world, I would not
speak; but since none has ever returned alive from this depth, if what
I hear is true, I answer you without fear of infamy." Guido proceeds to tell
his story, that of a deceiver. 23. *time:* cf. "To His Coy Mistress," line 1.
29. *works and days: Works and Days* is the title of a poem about farming
by the Greek poet Hesiod (8th Century B.C.). The contrast is ironic. 73.
pair of ragged claws: a crab, perhaps, whose motion is sideways. 82. *platter:*
an allusion to the martyrdom of John the Baptist (Matthew 14:1–12),
whose head was presented to Salome by Herod. 92. *ball:* cf. "To His Coy
Mistress," line 42. 94. *Lazarus:* whom Christ brought back from the dead
(see Luke 16:19–31). 113. *progress:* in the Elizabethan sense: a journey
made by a royal personage and his followers. 121. *trousers rolled:* cuffed—
a new fashion of the day. 124. *mermaids singing:* Cf. line 5 of Donne's
"Song" (page 372).

VIII

from **Paradise Lost**

John Milton

from Book VII

[*Invocation*]

Descend from Heaven, Urania, by that name
If rightly thou art called, whose voice divine
Following, above th' Olympian hill I soar,
Above the flight of Pegasean wing!
The meaning, not the name I call: for thou   5
Nor of the Muses nine, nor on the top
Of old Olympus dwell'st, but heavenly born,
Before the hills appeared, or fountain flowed,
Thou with eternal Wisdom didst converse,
Wisdom thy sister, and with her didst play   10
In presence of th' Almighty Father, pleased

With thy celestial song. Up led by thee
Into the Heaven of Heavens I have presumed,
An earthly guest, and drawn empyreal air,
Thy tempering; with like safety guided down,   15
Return me to my native element:
Lest from this flying steed unreined (as once
Bellerophon, though from a lower clime),
Dismounted, on th' *Aleian* Field I fall
Erroneous there to wander and forlorn.   20
Half yet remains unsung, but narrower bound
Within the visible diurnal sphere;
Standing on Earth, not rapt above the pole,
More safe I sing with mortal voice, unchanged
To hoarse or mute, though fall'n on evil days,   25
On evil days though fall'n, and evil tongues;
In darkness, and with dangers compassed round,
And solitude; yet not alone, while thou
Visit'st my slumbers nightly, or when morn
Purples the east: still govern thou my song,   30
Urania, and fit audience find, though few.
But drive far off the barbarous dissonance
Of Bacchus and his revelers, the race
Of that wild rout that tore the Thracian bard
In Rhodope, where woods and rocks had ears   35
To rapture, till the savage clamor drowned
Both harp and voice; nor could the Muse defend
Her son. So fail not thou, who thee implores:
For thou art heavenly, she an empty dream.

(1667)

---

from PARADISE LOST, BOOK VII. 1. *Urania:* classical muse of epic poetry, Milton's only in part; for with his Christian theme, Milton means to outstrip anything done by pagan poets ("above th' Olympian hill I soar"). In this regard, see the "General Invocation" (page 338). 4. *Pegasean wing:* The flying horse Pegasus was the classical symbol of poetic inspiration. 11. *Almighty Father:* In Proverbs 7:30, Wisdom speaks of "playing always befor God" even before the Creation. 15. *Thy tempering:* i.e., tempered by thee. 18. *Bellerophon:* Bellerophon tried to ride Pegasus to the stars, but fell onto the Aleian plain, where he wandered about and died. 27. *with dangers compassed round:* Blind, Milton was now also a political outcast. 30. *east:* Milton wrote mainly at night or in the early morning. 34. *Thracian bard:* The mythic singer Orpheus, who charmed even the rocks and trees with his song, was torn to pieces in Rhodope by the Thracian Bacchanites, female worshipers of Bacchus, god of wine and nature's energy.

from **Prospectus to *The Recluse***

William Wordsworth

On Man, on Nature, and on Human Life,
Musing in solitude, I oft perceive
Fair trains of imagery before me rise,
Accompanied by feelings of delight
Pure, or with no unpleasing sadness mixed;   5
And I am conscious of affecting thoughts
And dear remembrances, whose presence soothes
Or elevates the Mind, intent to weigh
The good and evil of our mortal state.
—To these emotions, whencesoe'er they come,   10
Whether from breath of outward circumstance,
Or from the Soul—an impulse to herself—
I would give utterance in numerous verse.
Of Truth, of Grandeur, Beauty, Love, and **Hope**,
And melancholy Fear subdued by Faith;   15
Of blessed consolations in distress;
Of moral strength and intellectual Power;
Of joy in widest commonalty spread;
Of the individual Mind that keeps her own
Inviolate retirement, subject there   20
To Conscience only, and the law supreme
Of that Intelligence which governs all,
I sing—"fit audience let me find though few!"
    So prayed, more gaining than he asked, the Bard—
In holiest mood. Urania, I shall need   25
Thy guidance, or a greater Muse, if such
Descend to earth or dwell in highest heaven!
For I must tread on shadowy ground, must sink
Deep—and, aloft ascending, breathe in worlds
To which the heaven of heavens is but a veil.   30
All strength—all terror, single or in bands,
That ever was put forth in personal form—
Jehovah—with his thunder, and the choir
Of shouting Angels, and the empyreal thrones—
I pass them unalarmed. Not Chaos, not   35
The darkest pit of lowest Erebus,
Nor aught of blinder vacancy, scooped out
By help of dreams—can breed such fear and awe
As fall upon us often when we look
Into our Minds, into the Mind of Man—   40

My haunt, and the main region of my song.
—Beauty—a living Presence of the earth,
Surpassing the most fair ideal Forms
Which craft of delicate Spirits hath composed
From earth's materials—waits upon my steps;   45
Pitches her tents before me as I move,
An hourly neighbor. Paradise, and groves
Elysian, Fortunate Fields—like those of old
Sought in the Atlantic Main—why should they be
A history only of departed things,   50
Or a mere fiction of what never was?
For the discerning intellect of Man,
When wedded to this goodly universe
In love and holy passion, shall find these
A simple produce of the common day.   55
—I, long before the blissful hour arrives,
Would chant, in lonely peace, the spousal verse
Of this great consummation—and, by words
Which speak of nothing more than what we are,
Would I arouse the sensual from their sleep   60
Of Death, and win the vacant and the vain
To noble raptures; while my voice proclaims
How exquisitely the individual Mind
(And the progressive powers perhaps no less
Of the whole species) to the external World   65
Is fitted—and how exquisitely, too—
Theme this but little heard of among men—
The external World is fitted to the Mind;
And the creation (by no lower name
Can it be called) which they with blended might   70
Accomplish—this is our high argument.

                                                         (*1814*)

---

from PROSPECTUS TO THE RECLUSE. *The Recluse:* Wordsworth's unfinished
masterwork, of which *The Prelude* forms the first part. 13. *numerous verse:*
i.e., verse that is harmonious. 23. *though few:* See the "Invocation" to Book
VII of *Paradise Lost,* line 31. 25. *Urania:* The Muse Milton invokes in
Book VII of *Paradise Lost,* lines 1–39. Compare the passage that follows
with Milton's "Invocation" to Book VII. 30. *heaven of heavens:* In *Paradise
Lost* the sphere of God, beyond the visible heavens. 36. *Erebus:* a dark re-
gion of the underworld in classical mythology. 48. *Elysian:* in classical
myth, the abode of the blessed, thought to be far out in the Atlantic Main
(ocean). 57. *spousal:* marital—Wordsworth would join mind and nature. 71.
argument: theme, as in *Paradise Lost,* Book I, line 24 (see page 339).

Sunday Morning

Wallace Stevens

1

Complacencies of the peignoir, and late
Coffee and oranges in a sunny chair,
And the green freedom of a cockatoo
Upon a rug mingle to dissipate
The holy hush of ancient sacrifice.   5
She dreams a little, and she feels the dark
Encroachment of that old catastrophe,
As a calm darkens among water-lights.
The pungent oranges and bright, green wings
Seem things in some procession of the dead,   10
Winding across wide water, without sound.
The day is like wide water, without sound,
Stilled for the passing of her dreaming feet
Over the seas, to silent Palestine,
Dominion of the blood and sepulchre.   15

2

Why should she give her bounty to the dead?
What is divinity if it can come
Only in silent shadows and in dreams?
Shall she not find in comforts of the sun,
In pungent fruit and bright, green wings, or else   20
In any balm or beauty of the earth,
Things to be cherished like the thought of heaven?
Divinity must live within herself:
Passions of rain, or moods in falling snow;
Grievings in loneliness, or unsubdued   25
Elations when the forest blooms; gusty
Emotions on wet roads on autumn nights;
All pleasures and all pains, remembering
The bough of summer and the winter branch.
These are the measures destined for her soul.   30

3

Jove in the clouds had his inhuman birth.
No mother suckled him, no sweet land gave
Large-mannered motions to his mythy mind
He moved among us, as a muttering king,
Magnificent, would move among his hinds,°   *shepherds*   35

Until our blood, commingling, virginal,
With heaven, brought such requital to desire
The very hinds discerned it, in a star.
Shall our blood fail? Or shall it come to be
The blood of paradise? And shall the earth   40
Seem all of paradise that we shall know?
The sky will be much friendlier then than now,
A part of labor and a part of pain,
And next in glory to enduring love,
Not this dividing and indifferent blue.   45

4

She says, "I am content when wakened birds,
Before they fly, test the reality
Of misty fields, by their sweet questionings;
But when the birds are gone, and their warm fields
Return no more, where, then, is paradise?"   50
There is not any haunt of prophecy,
Nor any old chimera of the grave,
Neither the golden underground, nor isle
Melodious, where spirits gat them home,
Nor visionary south, nor cloudy palm   55
Remote on heaven's hill, that has endured
As April's green endures; or will endure
Like her remembrance of awakened birds,
Or her desire for June and evening, tipped
By the consummation of the swallow's wings.   60

5

She says, "But in contentment I still feel
The need of some imperishable bliss."
Death is the mother of beauty, hence from her,
Alone, shall come fulfilment to our dreams
And our desires. Although she strews the leaves   65
Of sure obliteration on our paths,
The path sick sorrow took, the many paths
Where triumph rang its brassy phrase, or love
Whispered a little out of tenderness,
She makes the willow shiver in the sun   70
For maidens who were wont to sit and gaze
Upon the grass, relinquished to their feet.
She causes boys to pile new plums and pears
On disregarded plate. The maidens taste
And stray impassioned in the littering leaves.   75

6

Is there no change of death in paradise?
Does ripe fruit never fall? Or do the boughs
Hang always heavy in that perfect sky,
Unchanging, yet so like our perishing earth,
With rivers like our own that seek for seas   80
They never find, the same receding shores
That never touch with inarticulate pang?
Why set the pear upon those river-banks
Or spice the shores with odors of the plum?
Alas, that they should wear our colors there,   85
The silken weavings of our afternoons,
And pick the strings of our insipid lutes!
Death is the mother of beauty, mystical,
Within whose burning bosom we devise
Our earthly mothers waiting, sleeplessly.   90

7

Supple and turbulent, a ring of men
Shall chant in orgy on a summer morn
Their boisterous devotion to the sun,
Not as a god, but as a god might be,
Naked among them, like a savage source.   95
Their chant shall be a chant of paradise,
Out of their blood, returning to the sky;
And in their chant shall enter, voice by voice,
The windy lake wherein their lord delights,
The trees, like serafin,° and echoing hills,   *celestial beings*
That choir among themselves long afterward.
They shall know well the heavenly fellowship
Of men that perish and of summer morn.
And whence they came and whither they shall go
The dew upon their feet shall manifest.   105

8

She hears, upon that water without sound,
A voice that cries, "The tomb in Palestine
Is not the porch of spirits lingering.
It is the grave of Jesus, where he lay."
We live in an old chaos of the sun,   110
Or old dependency of day and night,
Or island solitude, unsponsored, free,
Of that wide water, inescapable.

Deer walk upon our mountains, and the quail
Whistle about us their spontaneous cries;   115
Sweet berries ripen in the wilderness;
And, in the isolation of the sky,
At evening, casual flocks of pigeons make
Ambiguous undulations as they sink,
Downward to darkness, on extended wings.   120

(1923)

SUNDAY MORNING.   1. *peignoir:* a woman's loose-fitting dressing gown. 7. *old catastrophe:* the Crucifixion. 38. *star:* Star of Bethlehem. 52. *chimera:* an imaginary monster or fanciful fear. Stanza 4 (46–60): Compare this passage and Wordsworth's "Prospectus," lines 47–51. 63. *mother of beauty:* for death is the author of change, which marks all that we feel to be beautiful. 74. *disregarded plate:* "Plate is used in the sense of . . . family plate. Disregarded refers to the disuse into which things fall that have been possessed for a long time. I mean, therefore, that death releases and renews [Stevens, *Letters*]." 91. *ring of men:* Compare with Milton's "Invocation" to Book VII of *Paradise Lost,* lines 32–37. 112. *unsponsored:* without godparents.

Of Modern Poetry

Wallace Stevens

The poem of the mind in the act of finding
What will suffice. It has not always had
To find: the scene was set; it repeated what
Was in the script.
        Then the theatre was changed
To something else. Its past was a souvenir.   5
It has to be living, to learn the speech of the place.
It has to face the men of the time and to meet
The women of the time. It has to think about war
And it has to find what will suffice. It has
To construct a new stage. It has to be on that stage   10
And, like an insatiable actor, slowly and
With meditation, speak words that in the ear,
In the delicatest ear of the mind, repeat,
Exactly, that which it wants to hear, at the sound

Of which, an invisible audience listens,   15
Not to the play, but to itself, expressed
In an emotion as of two people, as of two
Emotions becoming one. The actor is
A metaphysician in the dark, twanging
An instrument, twanging a wiry string that gives   20
Sounds passing through sudden rightnesses, wholly
Containing the mind, below which it cannot descend,
Beyond which it has no will to rise.
                                        It must
Be the finding of a satisfaction, and may
Be of a man skating, a woman dancing, a woman   25
Combing. The poem of the act of the mind.

(*1942*)

The City Limits

A. R. Ammons

When you consider the radiance, that it does not withhold
itself but pours its abundance without selection into every
nook and cranny not overhung or hidden; when you consider

that birds' bones make no awful noise against the light but
lie low in the light as in a high testimony; when you consider   5
the radiance, that it will look into the guiltiest

swervings of the weaving heart and bear itself upon them,
not flinching into disguise or darkening; when you consider
the abundance of such resource as illuminates the glow-blue

bodies and gold-skeined wings of flies swarming the dumped   10
guts of a natural slaughter or the coil of shit and in no
way winces from its storms of generosity; when you consider

that air or vacuum, snow or shale, squid or wolf, rose or lichen,
each is accepted into as much light as it will take, then
the heart moves roomier, the man stands and looks about, the   15

leaf does not increase itself above the grass, and the dark
work of the deepest cells is of a tune with May bushes
and fear lit by the breadth of such calmly turns to praise.

(*1971*)

Lapis Lazuli

W. B. Yeats

I have heard that hysterical women say
They are sick of the palette and fiddle-bow,
Of poets that are always gay,
For everybody knows or else should know
That if nothing drastic is done   5
Aeroplane and Zeppelin will come out,
Pitch like King Billy bomb-balls in
Until the town lie beaten flat.

All perform their tragic play,
There struts Hamlet, there is Lear,   10
That's Ophelia, that Cordelia;
Yet they, should the last scene be there,
The great stage curtain about to drop,
If worthy their prominent part in the play,
Do not break up their lines to weep.   15
They know that Hamlet and Lear are gay;
Gaiety transfiguring all that dread.
All men have aimed at, found and lost;
Black out; Heaven blazing into the head:
Tragedy wrought to its uttermost.   20
Though Hamlet rambles and Lear rages,
And all the drop-scenes drop at once
Upon a hundred thousand stages,
It cannot grow by an inch or an ounce.

On their own feet they came, or on shipboard,   25
Camelback, horseback, ass-back, mule-back,
Old civilizations put to the sword.
Then they and their wisdom went to rack:
No handiwork of Callimachus,
Who handled marble as if it were bronze,   30
Made draperies that seemed to rise
When sea-wind swept the corner, stands;
His long lamp-chimney shaped like the stem
Of a slender palm, stood but a day;
All things fall and are built again,   35
And those that build them again are gay.

Two Chinamen, behind them a third,
Are carved in lapis lazuli,

Over them flies a long-legged bird,
A symbol of longevity;   40
The third, doubtless a serving-man,
Carries a musical instrument.

Every discoloration of the stone,
Every accidental crack or dent,
Seems a water-course or an avalanche,   45
Or lofty slope where it still snows
Though doubtless plum or cherry-branch
Sweetens the little half-way house
Those Chinamen climb towards, and I
Delight to imagine them seated there;   50
There, on the mountain and the sky,
On all the tragic scene they stare.
One asks for mournful melodies;
Accomplished fingers begin to play.
Their eyes mid many wrinkles, their eyes,   55
Their ancient, glittering eyes, are gay.

(1938)

LAPIS LAZULI.   Yeats wrote to his friend Dorothy Wellesley: "I notice that
you have much lapis lazuli [a beautiful dark blue stone]; someone has sent
me a present of a great piece carved by some Chinese sculptor into the
semblance of a mountain with temple, trees, paths, and an ascetic and
pupil about to climb the mountain. Ascetic, pupil, hard stone, eternal
theme of the sensual east. The heroic cry in the midst of despair. But no,
I am wrong, the east has its solutions always and therefore knows nothing
of tragedy. It is we, not the east, that must raise the heroic cry." 6. *Aero-
plane:* The poem was written on the eve of World War II. 7. *King Billy:*
The reference is to William III, who defeated the army of King James II
at the Battle of the Boyne in 1690. 29. *Callimachus:* a famous Greek sculp-
tor, whose work survives only in descriptions of contemporaries.

Glossary

abstraction   any word that denotes some general quality or concept or feeling without stimulating in the mind a particular sensation. For example, *refraction* as opposed to *green, red, blue*. Compare *concretion*.

accentual-syllabic meter   a meter characterized by a set number of stressed syllables alternating with a set number of slack (unstressed) syllables per line. Stressed and slack syllables form a pattern of pulses called "beats" or "feet." For example:

What oft/was thought/but ne'er/so well/expressed.

This meter is typical of English verse. See *meter*.

accentuation   the emphasis placed on one syllable as opposed to another in pronunciation. See *stress*.

alexandrine   a line composed of six iambic beats. For example, the last line of the Spenserian stanza.

alliteration   the repetition of a consonantal sound (placed conspicuously at the beginning of a word or of an internal stressed syllable) in a sequence of nearby words. For example, "When to the *s*essions of *s*weet *s*ilent thought."

allusion   an indirect reference to something assumed to be known by listener or reader. Poetic allusion, which usually involves the reference in one poem to some other poem, compresses and enriches a poem.

anapest/anapestic   a rhythmic unit or beat consisting of two unstressed syllables followed by a stressed syllable. For example:

In the heat/of the night.

assonance   the repetition of similar vowel sounds in a sequence of nearby words. For example, "Thou still unravished br*i*de of qu*i*etness,/Thou foster ch*i*ld of s*i*lence and slow t*i*me."

ballad   a short narrative poem (one that tells a story) that proceeds by incremental repetition (that is, with each repetition of line, stanza, or whatever, there is enough new information to advance the plot step by step). There are two types of ballad: the folk balland and the literary ballad. Folk ballads are song lyrics composed and transmitted orally. Literary ballads are narrative poems written in imitation of the folk ballad.

ballad stanza   a quatrain (four-line unit), the second and fourth lines of which rhyme (*abcb*). The stanza derives its name from the folk ballad, such ballads often composed of stanzas in this form.

beat   the basic rhythmic unit (also called a "foot") of which a metrical line is composed. The common beats of English verse are: iamb ($\smile$/), trochee (/$\smile$), anapest ($\smile\smile$/), dactyl (/$\smile\smile$). Every beat consists of a stressed syllable—the beat itself—and one or two unstressed or slack syllables. If a given beat recurs a set number of times per line, then we have a meter. We can describe meters by the kind of beat and the number of recurrences (or pulses) of that beat per line. See, for example, *iambic pentameter*.

blank verse   lines in iambic pentameter that are unrhymed (*blank* means "unrhymed"). See *iambic pentameter*.

caesura   any marked pause *within* a line. For example, "That time of year thou mayest in me behold/When yellow leaves,$_\wedge$or none,$_\wedge$or few,$_\wedge$do hang."

closed couplet   two rhymed lines that form a self-contained (closed) grammatical unit and express a complete thought. For example, "Had we but world enough and time,/This coyness, lady, were no crime." Compare *open couplet*.

conceit   a metaphor whose comparison is felt to be particulary unexpected, even shocking. For example, "Death is a housewife." Because the so-called Metaphysical poets (Donne, Herbert, Marvell) were especially fond of this kind of metaphor, it is often called a "metaphysical conceit."

concretion   generally, any aspect of a text that has immediate sensory effect (a poem's division into lines, or the way it sounds when read aloud); specifically, any word that denotes something (an object, an action, a quality) perceptible to the senses and that to some extent stimulates in the mind the sensation(s) associated with whatever it is the word denotes. For example, "*Stretching* for a *tangy red apple*." Compare *abstraction*.

connotation   the emotional overtones that words carry beyond their straight (denotative) dictionary definitions. For example, the word *home* connotes warmth, intimacy, safety, whereas it denotes "one's dwelling place or abode." Compare *denotation*.

consonance   the repetition of a sequence of consonants in nearby words with a change in the intervening vowels. For example, "tick/tock," "life/loaf," "breed/bread."

context   the whole passage or work in which a given element is found and from which it gains its meaning.

couplet two contiguous lines that rhyme. See *closed couplet, heroic couplet, open couplet.*

dactyl/dactylic a rhythmic unit or beat consisting of a stressed syllable followed by two unstressed syllables. For example:

family, elephant

dead metaphor any metaphorical phrase that seems literal because of constant use. For example, "head of state."

decorum the aptness of diction, metaphor, style to the subject at hand.

denotation the straight dictionary definitions of words as distinguished from whatever emotional overtones they carry. For example, the denotation of home is "one's dwelling place or abode." Compare *connotation.*

diction the selection of words, or the kind of words selected, in a given passage or utterance. Possible kinds of words are: abstract or concrete, denotative or connotative, formal or colloquial, technical or common. These are some of the qualities that words possess, qualities that contribute to a statement's effect, whether it is written or spoken.

dissonance sounds that seem harsh or grating. Dissonance is often produced in poetry by consonance, off-rhyme, and the use of such hard consonants as *k* or *x.*

dramatic monologue a poem clearly spoken by a character (not by the poet or some unidentified persona). The object of the dramatic monologue is to reveal character.

end rhyme the rhymes that occur at the ends of lines in rhymed poems.

end-stopped a line of poetry that comes to a marked pause at its end. For example, "A thing of beauty is a joy forever: /Its loveliness increases . . .". Compare *enjambed.*

enjambed a line of poetry that does not come to a marked pause at its end, but forces the reader (because of grammar or syntax) to read on without a break into the next line. For example, "Its loveliness increases; it will never/Pass into nothingness . . ." Compare *end-stopped.*

epic a long poem in which the major concerns and preoccupations of a culture are brought into focus.

epigram/epigrammatic a short, concise statement that makes a single point. Epigrams are usually witty.

etymology the study of the origins and historical development of words, or the origin and development of a specific word.

explicit metaphor a metaphor in which the tenor (subject) and vehicle (defining word) are both expressed. For example, "*Deserts* [vehicle] of vast *eternity* [tenor]." Compare *implicit metaphor.*

falling meter   any meter with trochees or dactyls as dominant beats. For these beats begin with the stress and then, as to the movement of the voice, fall off. For example:

Fálling, fálling, dównward tŏ dárkness.

Compare *rising meter*.

figurative language   any use of words not meant to be taken literally. Any phrase involving metaphor or hyperbole is figurative. For example, "He's an ox"; "It's time to get hopping"; "I won the race by a mile." Compare *literal language*.

figure of speech   any phrase that is figurative as opposed to literal. Common figures of speech are: personification, hyperbole, understatement, synesthesia, metonymy, synecdoche, and metaphor.

fixed form   a stanza or poem written in accordance with some traditional rhyme scheme and/or metrical pattern. See *Spenserian stanza* and *sonnet*.

foot   the basic rhythmic unit (also called a "beat") of which a metrical line is composed. See *beat*.

free verse   any piece of writing divided into lines (unlike prose), but not conforming to a regular metrical pattern. Most poems in free verse have highly irregular line lengths and do not rhyme.

genre   the category into which a literary work falls as determined by its style, form, and purpose. Tragedy and comedy are distinct genres, as are epic and lyric poetry.

haiku   a Japanese poetic form composed of three lines of five, seven, and five syllables exactly. Haikus usually convey the poet's impression of a natural object or scene.

heroic couplet   two self-contained (closed) rhymed lines in iambic pentameter. Heroic couplets always belong to longer poems composed all of such units. Compare *closed couplet* and *open couplet*.

hexameter   a meter that consists of six beats per line. (*Hex-* means "six.")

hyperbole   a deliberate exaggeration not meant to be taken literally. For example, "He won the race by a mile." Compare *understatement*.

iamb/iambic   a rhythmic unit or beat consisting of an unstressed syllable followed by a stressed syllable. For example:

ĕnóugh, ălthóugh, tŏdáy

iambic pentameter   a line composed of five iambs ($\smile\prime$) or ten syllables alternating between unstressed and stressed. For example:

Thĕ wórld ĭs tóo múch wĭth ús; lăte ănd sóon.

This is the meter of blank verse specifically, and the fundamental meter of English verse generally.

imagery (images)   verbal concretions (words that call up sensations—visual, olfactory, auditory, gustatory, tactile, kinesthetic) used to convey states of mind or feeling through sense impression.

implicit metaphor   a metaphor in which the vehicle or tenor or both are not expressed, but somehow immediately implied. For example, "biting words" implies that the words (tenor) are teeth (implicit vehicle). Compare *explicit metaphor*.

incremental repetition   repetition with variation, which introduces enough new information to advance a plot step by step. This style is associated especially with the ballad.

inflection   the degree of stress (emphasis) thrown on a syllable or word in pronunciation. See *stress*.

In-Memoriam stanza   a quatrain (four-line unit) used as a stanzaic form that rhymes *abba*. It is also called the "envelope" stanza.

internal rhyme   any rhyme that occurs within (as opposed to at the end of) a line of poetry.

inversion (syntactical)   some change in normal word order. For example, "My money, I earn" is an inversion of "I earn my money." See *syntax*.

inverted foot   a metrically deviant foot (or beat), the opposite of the dominant foot. In an iambic context, a trochee would be an inverted foot.

irony   any use of language in which there is a sharp discrepancy between literal and implied meanings. For example, "You're a pretty sight," when it means, "You look awful"; or, "He's a real bad man," when it is a compliment. Particularly derisive verbal irony is called "sarcasm." There are other types of irony as well. Whenever we perceive a discrepancy between cause and effect, or between intention and outcome, or between what we judge should be as opposed to what we see is, then we are dealing with irony.

juxtaposition   the placement of two or more elements (images, words, scenes) next to each other so as to produce a specific meaning or effect (say, irony).

levels of diction   the choice of words according to audience and occasion. A funeral oration, for example, requires a formal level; a chat with a friend usually calls for an informal level.

lexical stress   the stress (emphasis) normally placed on syllables in polysyllabic words as indicated by the dictionary.

limerick a fixed form that rhymes *aabba* and is usually anapestic. The first, second, and fifth lines are anapestic trimeters (or some variant), and the third and fourth lines are anapestic dimeters (that is, consisting of two anapestic beats each).

literal language any use of words meant to be taken strictly, or to communicate exactly what they mean. For example, "It's time to get to work" as opposed to "It's time to get hopping." Compare *figurative language*.

lyric/lyrical the term *lyric* originally meant a poem sung to the accompaniment of the lyre. Now, however, it refers to any short poem that gives voice to the mental and emotional state of a speaker. Closer to its etymological root, *lyrical* refers to any aspect of a poem that is songlike.

metaphor any figurative construction that entails an analogy—whether explicit or implicit—between two terms (called *tenor* and *vehicle*). The object of metaphor, or making of metaphors, is definition: definition of one term (the tenor) in terms of another (the vehicle). For example, "He [tenor] is an ox [vehicle]." See *tenor, vehicle, explicit metaphor, implicit metaphor*.

metaphorical extension the sustaining of a prime metaphor over a passage of some duration. Metaphors are extended either by a writer's staying with one vehicle or by drawing all subsequent vehicles from the same general area. For example, "You *light* up my life. You are a *candle* in the darkness, the *rays* of my hope, the *sun* of all my days." See *vehicle*.

metaphysical conceit see *conceit*.

meter the regular recurrence of some rhythmic configuration or pulse. The meter characteristic of verse in English is called "accentual-syllabic," for our sense of recurrence derives from our perception of a set number of syllables per line and a set pattern of accentuation (that is, a set pattern of stressed and unstressed syllables). Such a pattern is normally analyzed by the pulse that recurs and the number of pulses (called "beats" or "feet") per line. The basic beats of English verse are: the iamb, the trochee, the anapest, and the dactyl; the usual number of recurrences is three (trimeter), four (tetrameter), five (pentameter), or six (hexameter). Thus, a metrical composition (a piece of writing that exhibits rhythmic recurrence) containing five iambs per line would be said to be in "iambic pentameter"; a piece containing three trochees per line would be in "trochaic trimeter."

metonymy a figure of speech in which one thing is called by the name of something else with which it is closely associated. For example, a *jock* for a male athlete; *Tex* for someone from Texas. Compare *synecdoche*.

metrical deviation   any beat in a metered poem that does not conform to the metrical norm.

metrical stress   the stress (emphasis) or pattern of stress established in verse by the metrical norm. See *meter*.

mixed metaphor   metaphors that in extension or combination do not work. For example, "We must, therefore, take a firm stand in the public eye."

monosyllable/monosyllabic   a word of one syllable only. For example, *a, word, of, one.* Compare *polysyllable*.

octave   the first eight lines of the Petrarchan sonnet specifically, which rhyme *abbaabba* and form an integral thematic unit.

off-rhyme   a term used to describe words that are close in sound (like rhymes), but that do not rhyme. For example, "down/noon," "crawl/cool."

onomatopoeia/onomatopoetic   specifically, words whose sounds imitate the sounds of what they name (*buzz, splash, moo*). Generally, language that sounds like what it means.

open couplet   two rhymed lines that do not form a self-contained grammatical unit. For example, "Now therefore, while the youthful hue/Sits on thy skin like morning dew,//And while thy willing soul transpires/At every pore with instant fires,//Now . . . ." Compare *closed couplet* and *heroic couplet*.

ottava rima   an eight-line stanza that rhymes *abababcc*.

oxymoron   a phrase consisting of two terms that in ordinary usage are contraries. For example, "a heavy lightness," "a frugal plenty," "the living dead."

pace   the rapidity or slowness of an utterance.

paradox   any statement that seems to be self-contradictory, yet that upon analysis turns out to be valid. For example, "And death once dead, there's no more dying then."

paraphrase   a restatement of the gist of a passage or work in other (simpler) words, or the act of so restating.

pastoral   a poem laid in an idyllic landscape and that concerns nostalgia for the beauty and peace of nature.

pause   the points in an utterance at which the voice rests. Poetic analysis entails a distinction between two types of pause: (1) caesural pause, any marked pause *within* a line; (2) end-line pause, a pause at the end of a line that results from the line's being end-stopped.

pentameter   a meter that consists of five beats per line. (*Pent-* means "five.")

persona   the speaker of a poem as distinguished from its author. Some-
times the distinction is moot; but often it is essential, as, for example,
in a dramatic monologue or in a poem by a male author clearly spoken
by a female, or by a female author clearly spoken by a male.

personification   a figure of speech in which some human quality, or
motive, or potential is attributed to an abstraction, an inanimate ob-
ject, an animal, or whatever. For example, "Justice will *decide*"; "the
fury of the gale"; "the birds *hope* for spring."

Petrarchan sonnet   a type of sonnet that rhymes *abbaabba/cdecde*. (There
are many Petrarchan sonnets, however, in which the rhyme scheme of
the last six lines is varied). Because of its rhyme scheme, the Petrarchan
sonnet divides itself into an octave (an eight-line unit) and a sestet (a
six-line unit); and, further, into two quatrains (four-line units) and two
tercets (three-line units). Usually, there is some sort of shift (called a
"volta") between octave and sestet.

pitch   the property of a tone determined by the frequency of its sound
waves. Some tones—of vowels and of voice—are high-pitched, some
low-pitched, and some in-between. For example, *e* as in *beet* versus *oo*
as in *boot*.

polysyllable/polysyllabic   a word of two or more syllables. For example,
syl·la·ble. Compare *monosyllable*.

polysyllabic rhyme   rhymes of two or more syllables in succession. For
example, "bending/ending," "anticipate/dissipate."

pyrrhic   a deviant (nonrecurring) metrical foot consisting of two un-
stressed syllables. For example:

$$\breve{in} \ \breve{the}/\text{bĕgín}/\text{nĭng God}.$$

quatrain   any four-line stanzaic unit: for example, the stanza character-
istic of the ballad (*abcb*) or the *In-Memoriam* stanza (*abba*). The four-
line units that compose the octave of the Petrarchan sonnet and the
first twelve lines of the Shakespearean sonnet are also called quatrains.

rhetorical stress   the stress (emphasis) thrown by the voice for the pur-
pose of delineation.

rhyme scheme   the pattern of end-rhymes that characterizes a fixed form,
whether stanza or poem. Rhyme schemes are signified with letters: like
letters indicate what lines, by virtue of the words with which they end,
rhyme with what other lines. For example, *abab* indicates that the
first and third lines rhyme and the second and fourth; *abab/cdcd/efef*
indicates a likeness in the *pattern* of rhyme, though the particular rhyme
sounds change between stanzas (if they remained the same, the notation
would be: *abab/abab/abab*). Capital letters are used to signify the repe-
tition of an entire line.

rhythm the way words move (*rhythm* comes from a Greek word meaning "to flow") as determined by the variables of the five basic qualities of English speech: accentuation, inflection, volume, pace, and pause. In that these qualities affect how a statement is interpreted, rhythm is a prime determinant of meaning.

rising meter any meter the dominant beats of which are iambs or anapests. For these beats begin with unstressed syllables and then, as to the movement of the voice, rise to stressed syllables. For example:

$$\text{Ă}\acute{\text{rise}} \text{ ă}\text{nd sh}\acute{\text{ine}}, \text{ fŏr tŏd}\acute{\text{ay}} \text{ ĭs th}\acute{\text{ine}}.$$

Compare *falling meter*.

scansion metrical analysis or notation. We scan a metrical composition by dividing its lines into syllables and then indicating which syllables are stressed and which are not. The purpose of scansion is to determine what kind of beat recurs in a given passage, how many beats there are to a line, and, thus, what the basic meter of the piece is. For example:

$$\text{Whă}t \acute{\text{oft}}/\text{wăs th}\acute{\text{ought}}/\text{bŭt ne'er}/\text{sŏ we}\acute{\text{ll}}/\text{exprĕ}\acute{\text{ssed}}"$$

(iambic pentameter)

See *meter*.

sestet the last six lines of the Petrarchan sonnet specifically, which rhyme *cdecde* (or some variant thereof).

Shakespearean sonnet a type of sonnet that rhymes *abab/cdcd/efef/gg*. By virtue of its rhyme scheme, the Shakespearean sonnet divides itself into three quatrains (four-line units) and a concluding couplet. This is the norm, though some Shakespearean sonnets seem divided also (like the Petrarchan sonnet) into an octave (eight-line unit) and a sestet (six-line unit).

simile an explicit metaphor made logical by the introduction of *as* or *like* or sometimes the suffix *-y*. For example:

My love is like a red, red rose.

See *explicit metaphor*.

sonnet normally a fourteen-line poem in iambic pentameter that conforms to one or another traditional rhyme scheme. The dominant types of sonnet written in English are: (1) Shakespearean: *abab/cdcd/efef/gg* and (2) Petrarchan: *abbaabba/cdecde*. See *Shakespearean sonnet* and *Petrarchan sonnet*.

speaker in that every poem should be heard as spoken, every poem has a speaker. Sometimes the speaker can be thought of as the poet speaking in his or her own voice; more often, the speaker should be thought of as a persona or a full-blown character.

Spenserian stanza a nine-line stanza that rhymes *ababbcbcc,* with the first eight lines in iambic pentameter and the ninth, iambic hexameter. (Such a line is called an "alexandrine.")

spondee/spondaic a deviant (non-recurring) metrical foot consisting of two stressed syllables. For example:

The lóng/*líght shákes*/acróss/thĕ lákes.

stanza a grouping of lines usually demarked by spacing, a recurrent rhyme scheme, and a repeating pattern of lines as per number and length. Many unrhymed poems are also divided into stanzas (demarked by spacing), in which case what recurs is a set number of lines per stanzaic unit. Poems divided into stanzas are called "stanzaic."

stress the emphasis placed on one syllable as opposed to another in pronunciation. For example, the word *pronunciation* has the following pattern of stress, or accentuation: pro·nun′ci·a″tion. The first, third, and fifth syllables are unstressed; the second and fourth are stressed, the fourth being more heavily stressed (inflected) than the second.

strong ending said of a line of poetry that ends with a stressed syllable. For example, each of the following lines has a strong ending:

Hád wĕ bŭt wórld ĕnóugh ănd *tíme,*/Thĭs cóynĕss, lády, wére no críme.

Compare *weak ending.*

surreal/surrealistic adjectives used in connection with any work of art that is dreamlike or that seems to tap the workings of the unconscious.

symbol any concretion that, because of the literary and/or cultural context, suggests something (usually an abstraction) over and above what it (the concretion) literally is or brings to mind by virtue of its inherent characteristics alone. For example, the rose has long been a symbol of romantic love; and Marilyn Monroe became a symbol of femininity to a whole generation in the 1950s. We might think of the symbol, therefore, as being either (1) a complex synecdoche or metonymy in which a concrete agent comes to stand for the more general and inclusive class of which it is a part or with which it is associated, or (2) as a vehicle of a metaphor whose tenor is not immediately implied. Whatever the model, symbols figure larger realms of abstraction and yield their meanings by being considered in connection with the larger literary and/or cultural context.

synecdoche a figure of speech in which a part or an attribute of something gives its name to the whole. For example, "hands" for laborers; a "bow-wow" for a dog; "wheels" for a car. Compare *metonymy.*

synesthesia a figure of speech that involves speaking of one sensation in terms of another, or speaking of something in terms of a sensory mode not actually appropriate to it. For example, "a cool green," "a loud tie," "a dry martini."

syntax the position of words in a sentence. In English, our understanding of the relationships between the words that compose a sentence and thus its meaning is determined primarily by position.

tenor the subject of a metaphor, or the term being defined by way of the transference (from vehicle to tenor) that metaphor entails. In the metaphor "Deserts of vast eternity," "eternity" is the tenor, which "Deserts" defines. Compare *vehicle*.

tercet any three-line unit, such as the terza rima stanza or the tercets that compose the sestet of the Petrarchan sonnet.

terza rima a stanzaic form composed of tercets (three-line units) marked by interlinking rhymes: *aba/bcb/cdc/ded* and so on.

tetrameter a meter that consists of four beats per line. (*Tetr-* means "four.")

tone the way something is said ("tone of voice") as that way reveals the feelings of a speaker about the subject and/or the audience.

trimeter a meter that consists of three beats per line. (*Tri-* means "three.")

triolet a fixed form consisting of two quatrains (four-line units) on two rhymes. The first line is repeated as the fourth and seventh lines, and the second line is repeated as the last line (*ABaAabAB*).

trochee/trochaic a rhythmic unit or beat consisting of a stressed syllable followed by an unstressed syllable. For example:

$$\text{mó}\breve{\text{ther}}, \text{fá}\breve{\text{ther}}, \text{tró}\breve{\text{chee}}$$

understatement a figurative statement in which emphasis is gained by a deliberate underplaying of the magnitude or effect of what is being described. For example, "Last week I saw a woman flayed, and you will hardly believe how much it altered her person for the worse." Compare *hyperbole*.

vehicle the figurative word in a metaphor, or the term used to define a tenor by way of the transference (from vehicle to tenor) that metaphor entails. In the metaphor "Deserts of vast eternity," "Deserts" is the vehicle—the term that defines the abstraction "eternity" (the tenor). Compare *tenor*.

verse any composition that is deliberately divided into lines or the lines themselves. (The word *verse* comes from the Latin meaning "to turn," which suggests a crucial difference between prose and poetry. In prose, line breaks are arbitrary; in poetry, line breaks are deliberate.) However, in contemporary usage, *verse* normally signifies "metrical writing" and is equivalent to *meter,* denoting that a given piece of writing (said to be "in verse") exhibits rhythmic recurrence.

verse paragraph   the unit of division in nonstanzaic poems. The formal divisions of poems in blank verse and heroic couplets are called "verse paragraphs."

villanelle   a fixed form consisting of five tercets (three-line units) and a quatrain (four-line unit) on two rhymes. The first line is repeated as the sixth, twelfth, and eighteenth lines, and the third line is repeated as the ninth, fifteenth, and nineteenth lines (*AbA′/abA/abA′/abA/ abA′/abAA′*).

voice   refers to all aspects of a poem that give it the quality or flavor of a spoken utterance.

volume   the degree of loudness or softness of an utterance.

vowel gradation   the step-by-step shifting of vowels from high-pitched to low or low to high. For example, "*I hate to see that evenin' sun go down.*" There is here a clearly gradated movement from high-pitched to low-pitched vowel sounds.

vowel length   the length of time it takes to say a vowel, some vowels being short and some long. (Also called vowel "quantity.") For example, *e* as in bet versus *ee* as in beet.

weak ending   said of a line of poetry that ends with an unstressed syllable. Each of the following lines has a weak ending:

> A thing of beauty is a joy forever:/Its loveliness increases; it will never/Pass. . . .

Compare *strong ending.*

ACKNOWLEDGMENTS

HELEN ADAM "Counting-Out Rhyme" from *Selected Poems and Ballads*. Copyright 1974 by Helikon Press. Reprinted by permission of Helikon Press.

LEONIE ADAMS "Song from a Country Fair" from *Poems: A Selection* by Leonie Adams. Copyright 1954 by Funk and Wagnalls, Inc.

LEWIS ALLAN "Strange Fruit" © Copyright: Edward B. Marks Music Corporation. Used by permission.

A. R. AMMONS "Chaos Staggered Up the Hill," "Corson's Inlet," "So I Said I Am Ezra," and "The City Limits" are reprinted from *Collected Poems, 1951–1971*, by A. R. Ammons, with the permission of W. W. Norton & Company, Inc. Copyright © 1972 by A. R. Ammons.

W. H. AUDEN "The Unknown Citizen," "Our Bias," "As I Walked Out One Evening," and extract from "Musée des Beaux Arts" copyright 1940 and renewed 1968 by W. H. Auden. Reprinted from *Collected Paems*, by W. H. Auden, edited by Edward Mendelson, by permission of Random House, Inc., and Faber and Faber Ltd. "The Shield of Achilles" copyright 1952 by W. H. Auden. Reprinted from *Collected Poems*, by W. H. Auden, edited by Edward Mendelson, by permission of Random House, Inc.

HILAIRE BELLOC "On His Books" from *Complete Verse*, by Hilaire Belloc. Reprinted by permission of A. D. Peters & Co. Ltd.

JOHN BERRYMAN Dream Songs 1 and 14 reprinted with the permission of Farrar, Straus & Giroux, Inc. from 77 *Dream Songs* by John Berryman. Copyright © 1959, 1962, 1963, 1964 by John Berryman.

GWENDOLYN BROOKS "We Real Cool: The Pool Players. Seven at the Golden Shovel" (p. 275) from *The World of Gwendolyn Brooks* by Gwendolyn Brooks. Copyright © 1959 by Gwendolyn Brooks. Reprinted by permission of Harper & Row, Publishers, Inc.

OLGA BROUMAS "Cinderella" is reprinted by permission of Yale University Press from *Beginning With O* by Olga Broumas. Copyright © 1977 by Olga Broumas.

JOHN CIARDI "Thoughts on Looking into a Thicket" from *As If* by John Ciardi. © 1955 by Rutgers, the State University. Reprinted by permission of the author.

JOHN CLARE "Badger" from *The Poems of John Clare*, ed. by Tibble. Reprinted by permission of J. M. Dent & Sons Ltd., Publishers.

E. E. CUMMINGS Poem I from "Chansons Innocentes" is reprinted from *Tulips & Chimneys* by E. E. Cummings, with the permission of Liveright Publishing Corporation. Copyright © 1923, 1925, and renewed 1951, 1953, by E. E. Cummings. Copyright © 1973, 1976 by Nancy T. Andrews. Copyright © 1973, 1976 by George Firmage. Copyright © 1976 by Richard S. Kennedy.

EMILY DICKINSON Poems #214 ("I taste a liquor never brewed"), #258 ("There's a certain slant of light"), #341 ("After great pain, a formal feeling comes"), #465 ("I heard a Fly buzz—when I died"), #585 ("I like to see it lap the Miles"), #632 ("The Brain—is wider than the sky"), and #986 ("A narrow fellow in the grass") reprinted by permission of the publishers and the Trustees of Amherst College from *The Poems of Emily Dickinson*, edited by Thomas H. Johnson, Cambridge, Mass.: The Belknap Press of Harvard University Press, Copyright © 1951, 1955 by the President and Fellows of Harvard College. Poem #341 ("After great pain") from *The Complete Poems of Emily Dickinson*, edited by Thomas H. Johnson. Copyright 1929 by Martha Dickinson Bianchi. Copyright © 1957 by Mary L. Hampson. Reprinted by permission of Little, Brown and Co.

RICHARD EBERHART "United 555" from *Collected Poems 1930–1976*, by Richard Eberhart. Copyright © Richard Eberhart 1976. Reprinted by permission of Oxford University Press, Inc., and Chatto and Windus Ltd.

T. S. ELIOT All selections from *Collected Poems 1909–1962*, by T. S. Eliot. Copyright © 1936, by Harcourt Brace Jovanovich, Inc.; copyright 1963, 1964, by T. S. Eliot. Reprinted by permission of Harcourt Brace Jovanovich, Inc., and Faber and Faber Ltd.

JOHN FANDEL Two poems from *Out of our Blue*, by John Fandel. Copyright 1977. Reprinted by permission of Sparrow Press. "About My Students" from *Testament and Other Poems*, by John Fandel. Copyright © 1959 by Sheed and Ward. Reprinted by permission of Sheed and Ward, Inc.

ROBERT FRANCIS "As Near to Eden" and "The Good Life" copyright c 1944, 1972 by Robert Francis, reprinted from *Robert Francis: Collected Poems, 1936–1976* (University of Massachusetts Press, 1976). "Pitcher" Copyright © 1953 by Robert Francis. Reprinted from *The Orb Weaver* by permission of Wesleyan University Press.

ROBERT FROST All selections from *The Poetry of Robert Frost*, edited by Edward Connery Lathem. Copyright 1916, 1923, 1928, 1930, 1939, © 1969 by Holt, Rinehart and Winston. Copyright 1936, 1942, 1944, 1951, © 1956, 1958 by Robert Frost. Copyright © 1964, 1967, 1970 by Lesley Frost Ballantine. Reprinted by permission of Holt, Rinehart and Winston, Publishers.

ROBERT GRAVES "The Cool Web," "Down, Wanton, Down!" and "The Face in the Mirror" from *Collected Poems* by Robert Graves. Reprinted by permission of Curtis Brown, Ltd. Copyright © 1958, 1961 by CO-Productions Roturman S.A.

THOM GUNN "On the Move" reprinted by permission of Faber and Faber Ltd. from *The Sense of Movement* by Thom Gunn.

ARLO GUTHRIE Excerpt in Chapter 3 from "The Motorcycle Song" © Copyright 1967, 1969 by Appleseed Music Inc. All Rights Reserved. Used by permission.

A. D. HOPE "The Brides" from *Collected Poems: 1930–1965*, by A. D. Hope. Copyright © 1960, 1962 by A. D. Hope. Copyright 1963, 1966 in all countries of the International Copyright Union by A. D. Hope. Reprinted by permission of The Viking Press.

GERARD MANLEY HOPKINS All selections from *Poems of Gerard Manley Hopkins*, Fourth Edition, ed. by W. H. Gardner and N. H. MacKenzie. Copyright © The Society of Jesus 1967. Reprinted by permission of Oxford University Press, Inc.

LANGSTON HUGHES "Dream Deferred" ("Harlem") copyright 1951 by Langston Hughes. Reprinted from *The Panther and the Lash: Poems of our Times,* by Langston Hughes, by permission of Alfred A. Knopf, Inc. "Theme for English B" from *Montage of a Dream Deferred* by Langston Hughes. Reprinted by permission of Harold Ober Associates Incorporated. Copyright 1951 by Langston Hughes.

RANDALL JARRELL "A Lullaby" and "The Death of the Ball Turret Gunner" reprinted with the permission of Farrar, Straus & Giroux, Inc. from *The Complete Poems* by Randall Jarrell. Copyright 1944, 1945. Copyright renewed © 1972, 1973 by Mrs. Randall Jarrell.

ROBINSON JEFFERS "The Purse-Seine" from *Selected Poems of Robinson Jeffers.* Copyright 1937 and renewed 1965 by Donnan Jeffers and Garth Jeffers. Reprinted by permission of Random House, Inc.

ERICA JONG "Penis Envy" from *Loveroot* by Erica Jong. Copyright © 1968, 1969, 1973, 1974, 1975 by Erica Mann Jong. Reprinted by permission of Holt, Rinehart and Winston, Publishers.

LINCOLN KIRSTEIN "Fall In" from *Rhymes and More Rhymes of a PFC* by Lincoln Kirstein. Copyright © 1964, 1966 by Lincoln Kirstein. Reprinted by permission of the author.

PHILIP LARKIN "Wants" by Philip Larkin is reprinted from *The Less Deceived* by permission of The Marvell Press, England. "High Windows" from *High Windows* by Philip Larkin. Copyright © 1974 by Philip Larkin. Reprinted with the permission of Farrar, Straus & Giroux, Inc. and Faber and Faber Ltd.

D. H. LAWRENCE "Bavarian Gentians" and "Cherry Robbers" from *The Complete Poems of D. H. Lawrence,* edited by Vivian deSola Pinto & F. Warren Roberts. Copyright © 1964, 1971 by Angelo Ravagli & C. M. Weekley, Executors of the Estate of Frieda Lawrence Ravagli. Reprinted by permission of The Viking Press. The prose excerpt in Chapter 2 is from *Sons and Lovers* by D. H. Lawrence. Copyright 1913 by Thomas Seltzer, Inc. All Rights Reserved. Reprinted by permission of The Viking Press.

ROBERT LOWELL A selection from "Commander Lowell" and "For Sale" from *Life Studies* by Robert Lowell, copyright © 1956, 1959 by Robert Lowell. Reprinted with the permission of Farrar, Straus & Giroux, Inc.

ARCHIBALD MACLEISH "Ars Poetica" and "You, Andrew Marvell" from *New and Collected Poems 1917–1976* by Archibald MacLeish. Copyright © 1976 by Archibald MacLeish. Reprinted by permission of Houghton Mifflin Company.

CHARLOTTE MEW "The Farmer's Bride" from *Collected Poems of Charlotte Mew.* Reprinted by permission of Duckworth and Company Ltd.

JOSEPHINE MILES "Reason" from *Poems 1930–1960* by Josephine Miles. Copyright © 1960 by Indiana University Press. Reprinted by permission of the publisher.

MARIANNE MOORE "No Swan So Fine" reprinted with permission of Macmillan Publishing Co., Inc. from *Collected Poems* by Marianne Moore. Copyright 1935 by Marianne Moore, renewed 1963 by Marianne Moore and T. S. Eliot.

FREDERICK MORGAN "Legend" from *Poems of the Two Worlds* by Frederick Morgan. Reprinted by permission of The University of Illinois Press.

EDWIN MUIR "The Animals" from *Collected Poems* by Edwin Muir. Copyright © 1960 by Willa Muir. Reprinted by permission of Oxford University Press, Inc., and Faber and Faber Ltd.

OGDEN NASH "Portrait of the Artist as a Prematurely Old Man" and "Very Like a Whale" from *Verses from 1929 On* by Ogden Nash. Copyright 1934 by Ogden Nash. Reprinted by permission of Little, Brown and Co.

FRANK O'HARA "Why I Am Not a Painter." Copyright © 1958 by Maureen Granville-Smith, Administratrix of the Estate of Frank O'Hara. Reprinted from *The Collected Poems of Frank O'Hara* by permission of Alfred A. Knopf, Inc.

WILFRED OWEN "Arms and the Boy" from Wilfred Owen, *Collected Poems.* Copyright © Chatto & Windus, Ltd. 1946, 1963. Reprinted by permission of New Directions, The Owen Estate, and Chatto & Windus Ltd.

DOROTHY PARKER "One Perfect Rose," "The Flaw in Paganism," and "Unfortunate Coincidence" from *The Portable Dorothy Parker.* Copyright 1926, 1954 by Dorothy Parker. Reprinted by permission of The Viking Press.

EZRA POUND "Alba," "Ancient Music," and "The Jewel Stairs' Grievance" from Ezra Pound, *Personae.* Copyright 1926 by Ezra Pound. Reprinted by permission of New Directions.

EDWARD PROFFITT "Our Decor" copyright 1975 by Commonweal Publishing Co., Inc.; "New Uses for Old Utensils" copyright 1976 by Commonweal Publishing Co., Inc. Reprinted by permission. "Terrible Dactyl, Son of Rodan" copyright 1977 by The New York State English Council, reprinted by permission of *The English Record.* Thanks also to *The Humanist* and *The Manhattan Quarterly.*

JOHN CROWE RANSOM "Bells for John Whiteside's Daughter" Copyright 1924 by Alfred A. Knopf, Inc. and renewed 1952 by John Crowe Ransom. "Dead Boy" Copyright 1927 by Alfred A. Knopf, Inc. and renewed 1955 by John Crowe Ransom. Reprinted from *Selected Poems,* Third Edition, Revised and Enlarged, by John Crowe Ransom, by permission of Alfred A. Knopf, Inc.

HENRY REED "Naming of Parts" from *A Map of Verona* by Henry Reed. Reprinted by permission of Jonathan Cape Ltd.

ADRIENNE RICH "A Valediction Forbidding Mourning" and "Ideal Landscape" are reprinted from *Poems, Selected and New, 1950–1974,* by Adrienne Rich, with the permission of W. W. Norton & Company, Inc. Copyright © 1975, 1973, 1971, 1969, 1966 by W. W. Norton & Company, Inc. Copyright © 1967, 1963, 1962, 1961, 1960, 1959, 1958, 1957, 1956, 1955, 1954, 1953, 1952, 1951 by Adrienne Rich.

E. A. ROBINSON E. A. Robinson's "Reuben Bright" from *The Children of the Night* and "How Annandale Went Out" from *The Town Down the River* are reprinted with the permission of Charles Scribner's Sons, copyright 1910 Charles Scribner's Sons.

THEODORE ROETHKE "Dolor," "Root Cellar" copyright 1943 by Modern Poetry Association, Inc.; "My Papa's Walltz," copyright 1942 by Hearst Magazines, Inc.; and "Long Live the Weeds," copyright

Acknowledgments

1936 by Theodore Roethke, all from the book *The Collected Poems of Theodore Roethke.* Reprinted by permission of Doubleday & Company, Inc.

MURIEL RUKEYSER "Effort at speech between two people" from *Theory of Flight / Waterlilly Fire* by Muriel Rukeyser. Reprinted by permission of Monica McCall, International Creative Management. Copyright © 1935, 1962 by Muriel Rukeyser.

CARL SANDBURG "Clean Curtains" from *Smoke and Steel* by Carl Sandburg, copyright, 1920, by Harcourt Brace Jovanovich, Inc.; copyright, 1950, by Carl Sandburg. Reprinted by permission of the publisher.

ANNE SEXTON "All My Pretty Ones" and "To a Friend Whose Work Has Come to Triumph" from *All My Pretty Ones* by Anne Sexton. Copyright © 1961, 1962 by Anne Sexton. Reprinted by permission of Houghton Mifflin Company.

KARL SHAPIRO "The Fly." Copyright 1942 and renewed 1970 by Karl Shapiro. Reprinted from *Collected Poems 1940–1978,* by Karl Shapiro, by permission of Random House, Inc.

W. D. SNODGRASS "These Trees Stand" from *Heart's Needle,* by W. D. Snodgrass, copyright © 1956 by W. D. Snodgrass. Reprinted by permission of Alfred A. Knopf, Inc.

GARY SNYDER "Marin-An" from Gary Snyder, *The Back Country.* Copyright © 1968 by Gary Snyder. Reprinted by permission of New Directions.

WALLACE STEVENS "Six Significant Landscapes," "Le Monocle de Mon Oncle," "Disillusionment of Ten O'Clock," "Domination of Black," "Sunday Morning," "The Emperor of Ice-Cream," "Thirteen Ways of Looking at a Blackbird" and "On the Manner of Addressing Clouds," copyright 1923 and renewed 1951 by Wallace Stevens; "Of Modern Poetry" copyright 1942 by Wallace Stevens and renewed 1970 by Holly Stevens; "The Pleasures of Merely Circulating" copyright 1936 and renewed 1964 by Holly Stevens Stephenson.

MAY SWENSON "The Centaur" by May Swenson is reprinted by permission of the author from *A Cage of Spines,* copyright © 1958 by May Swenson.

DYLAN THOMAS "Do Not Go Gentle into that Good Night" from *The Poems of Dylan Thomas.* Copyright 1952 by Dylan Thomas. Reprinted by permission of New Directions, J. M. Dent & Sons Ltd. Publishers, and the Trustees for the Copyrights of the late Dylan Thomas. Prose excerpt in Chapter 8 from *Selected Letters of Dylan Thomas* ed. Constantine FitzGibbon. Copyright © 1965, 1966 by the Trustees for the Copyrights of Dylan Thomas. Reprinted by permission of New Directions and J. M. Dent & Sons Ltd. Publishers.

ROBERT PENN WARREN "Red-Tail Hawk and Pyre of Youth" copyright © 1977 by Robert Penn Warren. Reprinted from *Now and Then: Poems 1976–1978,* by Robert Penn Warren, by permission of Random House, Inc. Originally appeared in *The New Yorker.* Prose excerpt in Chapter 8 from "Poetry in a Time of Crack Up" by Robert Penn Warren. Reprinted by permission of William Morris Agency, Inc. on behalf of the Author. Copyright © 1971 by Nyrev, Inc.

RICHARD WILBUR "The Death of a Toad" and "The Pardon by Richard Wilbur" From *Ceremony and Other Poems,* copyright, 1948, 1949, 1950, by Richard Wilbur. Reprinted by permission of Harcourt Brace Jovanovich, Inc. "Playboy" by Richard Wilbur" © 1968 by Richard Wilbur. Reprinted from his volume *Walking to Sleep: New Poems and Translations* by permission of Harcourt Brace Jovanovich, Inc.

WILLIAM CARLOS WILLIAMS "Danse Russe," "To a Poor Old Woman," and "Portrait of a Lady," William Carlos Williams, *Collected Earlier Poems.* Copyright 1938 by New Directions Publishing Corporation. Reprinted by permission of New Directions. "The Dance" and "A Sort of a Song" William Carlos Williams, *Collected Later Poems.* Copyright 1944, 1948 by William Carlos Williams. Reprinted by permission of New Directions. Excerpts from "Asphodel, That Greeny Flower," William Carlos Williams, *Pictures from Brueghel and Other Poems.* Copyright 1954 by William Carlos Williams. Reprinted by permission of New Directions.

YVOR WINTERS "Sir Gawaine and the Green Knight" Yvor Winters, *Collected Poems.* Copyright 1943 by New Directions Publishing Corporation. Reprinted by permission of New Directions.

W. B. YEATS The 1912 version of "The Sorrow of Love," reprinted with permission of Macmillan Publishing Co., Inc., M. B. Yeats, Miss Anne Yeats, and the Macmillan Co. of London & Basingstoke, from *The Variorum Edition of the Poems of W. B. Yeats,* editors: Peter Allt and Russell K. Alspach. "The Lover's Song" and "Lapis Lazuli" reprinted with permission of Macmillan Publishing Co., Inc., M. B. Yeats, Miss Anne Yeats, and the Macmillan Co. of London & Basingstoke from *Collected Poems of W. B. Yeats* by W. B. Yeats. Copyright 1940 by Georgie Yeats, renewed 1968 by Bertha Georgie Yeats, Michael Butler Yeats and Anne Yeats. "Crazy Jane Talks with the Bishop," 32 lines from "A Dialogue of Self and Soul," and "Parting" reprinted with permission of Macmillan Publishing Co., Inc., M. B. Yeats, Miss Anne Yeats, and the Macmillan Co. of London & Basingstoke from *Collected Poems of W. B. Yeats,* by W. B. Yeats. Copyright 1933 by Macmillan Publishing Co., Inc., renewed 1961 by Bertha Georgie Yeats. "The Mermaid," "Among School Children," and "Leda and the Swan" reprinted with permission of Macmillan Publishing Co., Inc., M. B. Yeats, Miss Anne Yeats, and the Macmillan Co. of London & Basingstoke from *Collected Poems of W. B. Yeats* by W. B. Yeats. Copyright 1928 by Macmillan Publishing Co., Inc., renewed 1956 by Georgie Yeats. "The Dolls" and "To a Friend whose Work Has Come to Nothing" reprinted with permission of Macmillan Publishing Co., Inc., M. B. Yeats, Miss Anne Yeats, and the Macmillan Co. of London & Basingstoke from *Collected Poems of W. B. Yeats* by W. B. Yeats. Copyright 1916 by Macmillan Publishing Co., Inc., Renewed 1944 by Bertha Georgie Yeats. "That the Night Come" reprinted with permission of Macmillan Publishing Co., Inc., M. B. Yeats, Miss Anne Yeats, and the Macmillan Co. of London & Basingstoke from *Collected Poems of W. B. Yeats* by W. B. Yeats. Copyright 1912 by Macmillan Publishing Co., Inc., renewed 1940 by Bertha Georgie Yeats. "The Sorrow of Love," "The Lake Isle of Innisfree," and "The Lover Mourns for the Loss of Love" reprinted with permission of Macmillan Publishing Co., Inc., M. B. Yeats, Miss Anne Yeats, and the Macmillan Co. of London & Basingstoke from *Collected Poems of W. B. Yeats* by W. B. Yeats. Copyright 1906 by Macmillan Publishing Co., Inc., renewed 1934 by W. B. Yeats. "Adam's Curse" reprinted with permission of M. B. Yeats, Miss Anne Yeats, and the Macmillan Co. of London & Basingstoke from *Collected Poems of W. B. Yeats* by W. B. Yeats.

Index of First Lines

Included are the first lines of all longer excerpts.

Index of Poets and Poems